CliffsNotes®
Praxis® Core

CliffsNotes®

Praxis® Core

by
BTPS Testing

Contributing Authors:

Joy Mondragon-Gilmore, Ph.D.

Kyle Marion, M.A.

Jean Eggenschwiler, M.A.

Jerry Bobrow, Ph.D.

Consultants:

Ida Donaghho, M.A.

Ron Podrasky, M.S.

Paula Moseley, Ph.D.

Carol Nicholson, Ph.D.

Ed Kohn, M.S.

Houghton Mifflin Harcourt
Boston • New York

About the Author

BTPS Testing is a national authority in the field of test preparation. BTPS Testing has offered test-preparation workshops at the California State Universities for over 35 years. The faculty at BTPS Testing has authored more than 30 test-preparation books sold nationwide, including *CliffsNotes* preparation guides for the GRE, CSET, GMAT, CBEST, Praxis, RICA, and ACT. Each year the authors of this study guide conduct lectures for thousands of students preparing for graduate, college, and teacher credentialing exams.

Acknowledgments

The authors would like to thank Christina Stambaugh for her attention to detail in editing the manuscript and for her patience and support during the production process.

Editorial

Executive Editor: Greg Tubach

Senior Editor: Christina Stambaugh

Production Editor: Erika West

Copy Editor: Lynn Northrup

Technical Editors: Barbara Swovelin, Mary Jane Sterling, and Tom Page

Proofreader: Elizabeth Kuball

Table of Contents

Preface . . . . **xi**
How This Book Is Organized xi
Getting Started: Five Steps to Success on the Praxis Core xii

Introduction to the Praxis Core Academic Skills for Educators Test **1**
Test Format 1
Questions Commonly Asked about the Praxis Core 2
Taking the Praxis Core: Two Successful Overall Approaches 4
    The "Plus-Minus" Approach 4
    The Elimination Strategy 6
Taking the Computer-Delivered Praxis Core 6
    Computer Tutorial 6
    Computer Screen Icons 6
    Question Types 7
        Select One Answer Question Type 7
        Select All That Apply Question Type 8
        Numeric Entry Question Type 8

Chapter 1: The Core Reading Test (5712) **9**
Overview of the Reading Test 9
Skills and Concepts Tested 9
Content Categories 10
    Key Ideas and Details 10
    Craft, Structure, and Language Skills 11
    Integration of Knowledge and Ideas 11
Format of Passages and Questions 12
    Passages 12
    Question Types 13
    Directions 13
    Sample #1: Reading Comprehension Passage and Question 14
    Sample #2: Reading Comprehension Select Sentences In Passage 15
    Sample #3: Reading Comprehension Statement with Graph and Question 16
Reading Comprehension: A Three-Step Approach 16
    Step One: Read the Passage Actively 17
    Step Two: Read Then Re-Read the Question 17
    Step Three: Respond to the Question 18
General Strategies 18
Suggested Strategies with Sample Passages 19
    Strategy 1: Look for the Main Idea of the Passage 19
    Strategy 2: Look for Supporting Details 20
    Strategy 3: Make Inferences 20
    Strategy 4: Identify the Author's Attitude 21
    Strategy 5: Watch for Important Evidence That Might Support a Conclusion 21
    Strategy 6: Summarize the Main or Supporting Ideas of the Passage 22
    Strategy 7: Identify the Significance or Meaning of a Word or Phrase
    in the Context of the Passage 23
    Strategy 8: Identify Logical Assumptions 23
    Strategy 9: Evaluate Strengths and Weaknesses 24
    Strategy 10: Analyze Graphs to Locate Information .25
Practice Questions 26
Answers and Explanations 34

Chapter 2: The Core Writing Test (5722): Essay Writing. 39

Overview of the Essay Writing Section 39
Skills and Concepts Tested 40
Directions 40
Computer Word Processor. 40
Scoring 40
   Scoring Guidelines 41
   Scoring Rubric 42
General Strategies 45
Specific Strategies 45
The Three-Step Writing Process 46
   Step 1: Pre-Writing 47
      Brainstorming 47
      Using Graphic Organizers 47
      Outlining 49
   Step 2: Writing the Essay 49
      Five-Paragraph Model. 50
      Four-Paragraph Model 51
   Step 3: Proofreading. 51
Sample Argumentative Essay 52
   Sample Topic: Argumentative Essay. 52
      Step 1: Pre-Writing. 52
      Step 2: Writing 53
      Step 3: Proofreading 53
      Essay 1: Well-Written Response – Score 5. 54
      Essay 2: Average to Below-Average Response – Score 3. 55
Sample Informative/Explanatory (Source-Based) Essay 56
   Sample Topic: Informative/Explanatory Essay. 56
      Step 1: Pre-Writing. 57
      Step 2: Writing 57
      Step 3: Proofreading 58
      Essay 1: Well-Written Response – Score 5. 59
      Essay 2: Average to Below-Average Response – Score 3. 60
Evaluating Your Essays 61

Chapter 3: The Core Writing Test (5722): Selected Response Questions 63

Overview of the Selected Response Writing Section 63
Skills and Concepts Tested. 64
Question Types 64
   Usage Questions 64
      Directions 64
   Sentence Correction Questions. 64
      Directions 65
   Research Skills Questions 65
      Directions 65
   Revision-in-Context Questions 66
      Directions 66
General Strategies 67
Parts of Speech 67
Common Language Skills Errors 68
Language Skills Review. 69
   Grammatical Relationships 69
      Agreement Errors. 69
      Verb Tense Errors 74
      Adjective/Adverb Errors 75

Structural Relationships 77
   Parallel Structure Errors 77
   Misplaced or Dangling Modifiers 78
   Sentence Fragments 78
   Run-on Sentences 79
   Comparative Errors 79
   Coordination and Subordination Errors 80
Word Choice (Diction) 81
   Lie/Lay 82
   Redundancy Errors 82
   Idiomatic Expression Errors 83
Mechanics 84
   Punctuation Errors 84
   Capitalization Errors 87
Research Skills 87
Revision-in-Context 89

Chapter 4: The Core Mathematics Test (5732) 93

Overview of the Core Mathematics Test 93
Skills and Concepts Tested 94
Calculator Use 94
   Use the Calculator for Time-Consuming Problems 95
   Transfer Display 95
   Practice Before the Exam Date 95
Question Types 95
   Selected Response (Select One Answer Choice) Questions 96
      Directions 96
   Selected Response (Select One or More Answer Choices) Questions 96
      Directions 97
   Numeric Entry (Fill in the Blank) Questions 97
      Directions 97
General Strategies 98
Suggested Strategies with Example Questions 99
   Focus on Reasoning 99
   Write Down Key Words to Pull Out Information 100
   Avoid Unnecessary Calculations .100
   Substitute Simple Numbers 101
   Work Backward from the Answer Choices 101
   Approximate 102
   Look for Relationships Among the Answer Choices 102
   Make Comparisons 103
   Draw a Simple Diagram 104
   Try "Possibilities" in Probability Problems 105
   Determine the Most Efficient Method to Solve the Problem 105
   Accurately Interpret Data—Graphs, Charts, Tables, and Diagrams 106

Chapter 5: Arithmetic Review (Numbers and Quantity) 111

Arithmetic Diagnostic Test 112
   Scoring the Diagnostic Test 113
      Answer Key 113
   Charting and Analyzing Your Diagnostic Test Results 114
Arithmetic Review 115
   The Real Number System 115
      Sets of Numbers 115
      Integers 117
      Math Operation Symbols 118

Number Grouping Symbols 118
Order of Operations 119
Math Properties and Operations 119
Multiplication Notation 120
Math Operations and Number Rules 121
Fractions 124
Decimals 133
Ratios and Proportional Relationships 136
Ratio 136
Proportion 137
Percents 138
Changing Decimals to Percents 138
Changing Fractions to Percents 139
Fraction-Decimal-Percent Equivalents 139
Solving Percentage Problems 140
Solving Percentage Problems Using Proportion Methods 140
Percent Change: Finding Percent Increase or Percent Decrease 141
Quantitative Reasoning (Quantities) 142
Steps to Solving Quantitative Reasoning Questions 142
Quantitative Word Problems 142
Units of Measurement Problems 143
Graph Interpretation Problems 145
Arithmetic Practice Questions 148
Answers and Explanations 151

Chapter 6: Algebra and Functions Review 153
Algebra Diagnostic Test 154
Scoring the Diagnostic Test 155
Answer Key 155
Charting and Analyzing Your Diagnostic Test Results 157
Algebra and Functions Review 158
Basic Rules 159
Exponents 159
Scientific Notation 159
Square Roots 160
Seeing the Structure in Algebraic Expressions 161
Variables 161
Algebraic Multiplication 162
Order of Operations and Algebraic Expressions 162
Algebraic Word Problems 163
Polynomials: Monomials, Binomials, and Trinomials 166
Reasoning with Equations and Inequalities 167
Solving Linear Equations 167
Solving Linear Inequalities 169
Analyzing Linear Relationships: Coordinate Graphs 170
Simultaneous Linear Equations 173
Functions 175
Algebra Practice Questions 176
Answers and Explanations 178

Chapter 7: Geometry Review 183
Geometry Diagnostic Test 184
Scoring the Diagnostic Test 185
Answer Key 185
Charting and Analyzing Your Diagnostic Test Results 186
Geometry Review 186
Basic Geometric Formulas 186

Geometry Terms. 188
  Types and Measurements of Angles .189
Congruence and Similarity. 191
  Congruence. 192
  Symmetry and Transformation 192
  Similarity. 194
Polygons 195
  Special Polygons 195
  Triangles 195
  Pythagorean Theorem 200
  Quadrilaterals 203
  Circles 205
Geometric Measurement and Dimension 206
  Perimeter 206
  Surface Area 208
  Volume 208
Modeling with Geometry 209
Geometry Practice Questions 210
  Answers and Explanations 212

Chapter 8: Statistics and Probability Review **215**
Statistics and Probability Diagnostic Test. 216
  Scoring the Diagnostic Test. 216
    Answer Key 216
  Charting and Analyzing Your Diagnostic Test Results 217
Basic Statistics Review. 217
  Frequency Distribution 217
  Measures of Central Tendency. 218
    Mean 218
    Median 219
    Mode 220
  Statistical Variability. 220
  Interpreting Categorical and Quantitative Data 221
    Bivariate Data 221
Probability Review 222
  Making Inferences and Justifying Conclusions 222
    Random Sampling 222
    Chance 222
    Probability and Methods for Counting 223
  Measuring Probability 223
Statistics and Probability Practice Questions 226
  Answers and Explanations 228

Chapter 9: Practice Test 1 . . . .**231**
Reading Test 231
Writing Test: Selected Response 244
Writing Test: Essay 252
  Essay 1: Argumentative Essay. 252
  Essay 2: Informative/Explanatory Essay. 253
Mathematics Test. 255
Scoring the Practice Test. 266
  Answer Key 266
    Reading Test 266
    Writing Test: Selected Response. .267
    Mathematics Test 267
Charting and Analyzing Your Test Results .268

Answers and Explanations 268
    Reading Test 268
    Writing Test: Selected Response 273
    Writing Test: Essay 276
        Essay 1: Argumentative Essay 276
        Essay 2: Informative/Explanatory Essay 277
    Mathematics Test. 279

Chapter 10: Practice Test 2 . . . . **293**
    Reading Test 293
    Writing Test: Selected Response 305
    Writing Test: Essay 312
        Essay 1: Argumentative Essay. 312
        Essay 2: Informative/Explanatory Essay. 313
    Mathematics Test. 315
    Scoring the Practice Test. 326
        Answer Key 326
        Reading Test. 326
        Writing Test: Selected Response. 327
        Mathematics Test 327
    Charting and Analyzing Your Test Results 328
    Answers and Explanations 328
        Reading Test 328
        Writing Test: Selected Response 333
        Writing Test: Essay. 337
        Essay 1: Argumentative Essay 337
        Essay 2: Informative/Explanatory Essay 338
        Mathematics Test. 339

Preface

CliffsNotes Praxis Core is a comprehensive and easy to follow study guide that will assist you in preparing for the Praxis Core Academic Skills for Educators Test. This book is not meant to be a substitute for formal classroom instruction, but it will give you important learning tools to improve your reading, writing, and mathematical reasoning skills. The skills and concepts presented in this study guide will not only help you pass the Praxis Core, but also provide you with essential instructional material aligned with the Common Core State Standards (CCSS).

Exam-oriented approaches and practice material help you evaluate your strengths, while providing you with instructional tools to overcome your weaknesses. There are many pathways to learning that make use of different learning styles. This is why we have included hundreds of sample or practice problems with step-by-step explanations that are designed to enhance your learning style. If you follow the lessons and strategies in this book and study regularly, you will deepen your understanding of Praxis Core critical-thinking concepts, which will strengthen your performance on the exam.

In keeping with the fine tradition of *CliffsNotes,* leading educators in the field of test and college entrance preparation developed this guide. For more than 35 years, the authors of this text have been successfully teaching thousands of credential candidates to prepare for and perform well on standardized teacher examinations. The materials, strategies, and techniques presented in this guide have been researched, tested, and evaluated in teacher-preparation classes at leading California universities and school districts.

How This Book Is Organized

As you work through this book, follow the recommended sequence of topics and take detailed notes on the pages of the book to highlight important facts and concepts. Most people find it useful to start by learning general principles and skills that are widely applicable to many problems and progressing to memorizing important facts and concepts. For example, you should start your *general* math review with basic arithmetic (fractions, percents, decimals, and so on), and then move to a *specific* plan to tackle certain types of basic arithmetic problems (mixed fractions, converting percents to decimals, and so on). Remember to start with general information and then move to more specific problems and concepts.

Each chapter presents subject matter in a structured format to enhance your learning.

- **Introduction to the Praxis Core Academic Skills for Educators Test**   The Introduction is a general description of the Praxis Core exam, covering test format, content areas, question types, scoring, frequently asked questions, general strategies, and general tips.
- **Chapter 1: The Core Reading Test (5712)**   Chapter 1 reviews the types of reading comprehension passages, question types, basic skills and concepts tested, directions, and suggested strategies with samples.
- **Chapter 2: The Core Writing Test (5722): Essay Writing**   Chapter 2 focuses on the constructed-response essays portion of the Writing Test. It contains important strategies to improve your writing skills and will assist you in planning and writing two well-organized essays on two assigned topics: an argumentative essay and an informative/explanatory essay.
- **Chapter 3: The Core Writing Test (5722): Selected Response Questions**   Chapter 3 focuses on the selected response questions on the Writing Test. It contains a review of basic grammar, sentence structure, punctuation, revision, and research that will help you detect and correct errors in English and in research documentation.
- **Chapter 4: The Core Mathematics Test (5732)**   Chapter 4 is an introduction to the Math Test and contains the test format, question types, skills and concepts tested, general strategies, and specific math strategies. Specific review of math content is covered in chapters 5–8.
- **Chapters 5–8: Mathematic Review chapters**   Chapters 5–8 offer diagnostic tests, illustrated sample problems, and practice exercises on each math topic. Take the diagnostic test at the beginning of each chapter to evaluate your skills and provide you with a baseline starting point in each math category.

- Chapter 5: Arithmetic Review (Numbers and Quantity)
- Chapter 6: Algebra and Functions Review
- Chapter 7: Geometry Review
- Chapter 8: Statistics and Probability Review

- **Chapters 9–10: Two Full-Length Practice Tests**   The practice tests include answers and in-depth explanations. They are followed by analysis worksheets to assist you in evaluating your progress.

Getting Started: Five Steps to Success on the Praxis Core

1. **Awareness:** Become familiar with the test format, test directions, test material, and scoring by visiting *The Praxis Series* website at www.ets.org/praxis.

2. **Basic Skills:** Review the basic abilities required for success on the Core Reading, Writing, and Mathematics tests in each review chapter. You'll find this information in the "Skills and Concepts Tested" section. Know what to expect on the exam. This will help you to determine your strengths and weakness so that you can develop a study plan unique to your individual needs.

3. **Question Types:** Become familiar with the types of questions in each area of the Praxis Core, as detailed in chapters 1–4.

4. **Strategies and Techniques:** Practice using the strategies outlined in the introduction of this book to determine which ones work best for you. Remember that if it takes you longer to recall a strategy than to solve the problem, it's probably not a good strategy for you to adopt. The purpose of offering strategies is to enable you to work easily, quickly, and efficiently.

5. **Practice:** In addition to the sample practice problems in each review chapter, this book offers you two full-length practice tests. You can also take an online simulated practice test available at www.ets.org/praxis. Remember, practice, practice, practice is the key to your success on the Praxis Core.

Introduction to the Praxis Core Academic Skills for Educators Test

The Praxis Core Academic Skills for Educators Test (Praxis Core) is a computer-delivered test for prospective teachers. It measures knowledge and reasoning abilities in reading, writing, and mathematics. The Praxis Core is required by most university teacher education programs to evaluate admission and by many state departments of education before teacher licensure and certification are issued. The criteria for successfully passing the Praxis Core varies from state to state. Contact your state's Department of Education to learn more about required standards.

The Praxis Core is aligned with the Common Core State Standards (CCSS) and focuses on practical applications for solving everyday problems through analysis, reasoning, and critical thinking. Questions on the Praxis Core reflect the interwoven relationship between common core skills and your knowledge of reading, writing, and math when applied to real-world scenarios. For example, questions on the Praxis Core may require you to reason, deconstruct, and translate math word problems into numeric equations. These skills are fundamental to all educators.

Test Format

There are a total of 152 questions on the Praxis Core, plus two constructed response essays. The entire test is 4½ hours (270 minutes). The chart below summarizes the format of the three Praxis Core tests. The Praxis Core may contain some experimental questions, which will not count toward your score. Essay scores are combined with the Writing selected response score for a combined scaled score. Format and scoring are subject to change.

Format of the Tests

Test	Content	Minutes	Question Types	Approx. # of Questions	Score Range (Average Passing Score*)
Reading (5712)	I. Key Ideas and Details II. Craft, Structure, and Language Skills III. Integration of Knowledge and Ideas	85 minutes	• Select one answer. • Select **all** that apply (one or multiple answers). • Select the answer by clicking on it in the passage.	17–22 14–19 17–22 **56 total questions**	100–200 (Average: 156)
Writing (5722)	I. Text Types, Purposes, and Production II. Language and Research Skills for Writing	40 minutes	• Select one answer. • Select the answer by clicking on a word or phrase in a sentence.	6–12 28–34 **40 total questions**	100–200 (Average: 162)

Verify the average passing score with your state licensing agency.

continued

Test	Content	Minutes	Question Types	Approx. # of Questions	Score Range (Average Passing Score*)
	III. Essays Writing Arguments Writing Informative/ Explanatory Texts	**60 minutes** 30 minutes 30 minutes	• Written constructed response	**2 essays** 1 essay 1 essay	1–6 (Average: 4) 1–6 (Average: 4)
Mathematics (5732)	I. Numbers and Quantity II. Algebra and Functions III. Geometry IV. Statistics and Probability	**85 minutes**	• Select one answer. • Select all that apply (one or multiple answers). • Type a numeric answer in an answer box (fill in the blank).	17 17 11 11 **56 total questions**	100–200 (Average: 150)

Verify the average passing score with your state licensing agency.

The Praxis Core is composed of three selected response tests (also called "multiple choice") and two essays:

- **The Reading Test.** This test evaluates your ability to read, comprehend, and analyze passages or statements and answer selected response questions based upon the content of those passages. The reading passages are taken from a wide range of topics in humanities, social science, science, and visual and performing arts. No prior knowledge of these topics is necessary to answer the questions. All questions are based upon the content of the passage provided.

- **The Writing Test.** This test is divided into two sections. One part is a selected response section and contains questions related to English usage, sentence correction, revising text, and research skills. Most of the questions in this section assess your ability to detect and correct errors in English and your knowledge of research skills. The second part of this test is constructed response essay writing, which evaluates your ability to plan and write two well-organized essays on assigned topics: an argumentative essay and an informative/explanatory essay.

- **The Mathematics Test.** This test consists primarily of selected response questions, along with some numeric entry questions. It requires a cumulative understanding of basic math skills and mathematical reasoning in arithmetic, algebra, geometry, statistics, and probability. Knowledge should include basic middle school math through at least one year of high school and possibly one year of college. An on-screen calculator is available to assist you in selecting the correct response.

Questions Commonly Asked about the Praxis Core

Q. Who administers the Praxis Core?

A. Educational Testing Service (ETS)® prepares and scores the Praxis Core. For further information regarding test administration, contact *The Praxis Series,* Educational Testing Service, Box 6051, Princeton, NJ 08541-6051, (609) 771-7395, email: praxis@ets.org, URL: www.ets.org/praxis.

Q. How do I register for the Praxis Core?

A. Registration is available for one, two, or all three computer-delivered tests:

- Reading (5712)
- Writing (5722)
- Mathematics (5732)
- Combined Tests (5751)

Contact ETS® to set up an online *My Praxis* account, register for the test, change your test center, change your test date, add a test, or cancel a test. *Note:* Cancellation service fees may apply. All changes must be made no later than 4 days prior to your test date.

The computer-delivered administration of the Praxis Core is made by appointment online at www.ets.org/praxis/register or by phone at (800) 772-9476 (additional fees apply for telephone registration).

Q. Where is the Praxis Core administered?

A. Computer-delivered tests are administered throughout the United States and U.S. territories at *Prometric®* Testing Centers. To locate a test center near you, visit http://etsis4.ets.org/tcenter/tcenter.jsp.

Q. Is the Praxis Core part of *The Praxis Series*?

A. Yes. ETS® has grouped a number of its beginning teacher tests under the title *The Praxis Series*. Praxis Core tests measure reading, writing, and math aligned with the Common Core State Standards (CCSS). Praxis I includes the PPST tests of reading, writing, and mathematics skills that some universities require for their teacher education programs or for state licensure. Praxis II includes "content knowledge" examinations on the specific subjects prospective teachers will actually teach.

Q. Who needs to pass the Praxis Core?

A. Most states require the Praxis Core for the initial issuance of a teacher's credential. It may also be required for issuance of a permit, certificate, authorization, administrative credential, or renewal of an emergency credential. Some states require the Praxis I, while other states administer their own versions of the Praxis Core. Use this link to check with your state's department of education to see which test you are required to take: www.ets.org/praxis/states.

Q. How long is the Praxis Core?

A. If you take all three tests in one day, the computer-delivered Praxis Core is 4½ hours long. However, you should allow at least 5½ hours for the test, since there are computer tutorials and a verification process that collects your background information.

Q. How is the Praxis Core scored?

A. The Praxis Core tests are scored on a scale ranging from 100 to 200. Separate scores are reported for each test. The Reading Test (5712) and the Mathematics Test (5732) are scored solely on the number of items answered correctly. The Writing Test (5722) score is a composite score, adjusted to give approximately equal weight to the number correct on the selected response and essay sections. Since each state determines passing standards, it is important to check the passing score required for certification in your state.

Q. How is the Praxis Core score used?

A. The Praxis Core may be used for selection, admission, evaluation, and certification in conjunction with other relevant information. Because each institution or agency may set its own minimum standards and requirements, you should contact the appropriate institution, district, department, or agency to find out if you must take the test and to learn the required standards.

Q. **How long does it take to receive my score?**

A. Unofficial score results for the selected response section of the computer-delivered test are available immediately on the day of your test. The official test report, including the written essay portion of the Praxis Core, will be sent to you by mail approximately 2 to 3 weeks after your test date. Official score reports are available through your online ETS® account.

Q. **Are there any special arrangements for taking the Praxis Core?**

A. Special arrangements are available for those who meet the disability requirements. For more information, download a special supplement at www.ets.org/praxis/register/disabilities. Additional information about special arrangements is at www.ets.org/disabilities.

Q. **What materials should I bring to the Praxis Core?**

A. Bring an original photo-bearing identification (valid government-issued driver's license or passport) and a watch. You may *not* bring cell phones, smart watches, scratch paper, calculators (including watch calculators), books, compasses, rulers, papers of any kind, or recording or photographic devices.

Q. **Should I guess on the Praxis Core?**

A. Yes. There is no penalty for wrong answers. Your score is based on the number of questions you answer correctly. If possible, use the process of elimination (see page 6) to increase your chances of guessing the correct answer. Don't leave any questions unanswered.

Taking the Praxis Core: Two Successful Overall Approaches

This section presents overall test-taking approaches to help you prepare for success. Although you will be taking the test by computer, take advantage of the scratch paper (or a writing board) provided by the proctor to take notes and work out your answers. Keep in mind that there is no right or wrong way to answer questions, but there are general strategies that can help you to get your best possible score.

The "Plus-Minus" Approach

Many people who take the Praxis Core do not get their best possible score because they spend too much time on difficult questions, leaving insufficient time to answer easier questions. While it is important to take time to answer the most difficult questions on the test correctly, be aware that losing valuable test time won't get you the score you deserve. Most important, remember to answer every question, even if you answer with an educated guess. There is no penalty for wrong answers, so it is to your advantage to answer all questions.

The plus-minus approach will help you categorize problems so that you can focus your attention on problems that you are able to answer quickly. Since every question is worth the same point value, using this approach will help you to quickly identify problems that are *easy* or *solvable* (+) and those that are *difficult* (–) and to move quickly through the test.

You'll start by drawing two columns on the scratch paper (or writing board) provided at the test center. Label the top of the first column with a plus sign (+) and the top of the second column with a minus sign (–). Follow the instructions in the following table:

Guidelines to Identifying Problems

Symbol	Type of Problem	Strategy	Description
	Easy	Answer easy questions immediately.	This type of question is answered with little or no difficulty and requires little or minimal thought. Solve all of the easy questions first.
+	Solvable	Use the "+" column to write down the question number (and possible answer choices) for any problem that is possibly *solvable* but seems to be too time-consuming.	Some questions require additional time. For example, long reading passages and math word problems are designed to take longer. You will recognize this type of question because it appears to be solvable but is overly time-consuming. This type of question leaves you thinking, "I can answer this question, but I need more time." A time-consuming question is a question that you estimate will take you more than 1½ minutes to answer, so you decide to answer it later. When you face this type of question, write down the problem number (with possible answer choices and any other notes), click on the "review" icon at the bottom of the screen, make an educated guess, and then quickly move on to the next question. When you review the list of incomplete or flagged questions (using the navigator button), you can easily refer to your notes to know which question has been eliminated. Go back to flagged solvable problems after you have solved all of the easy problems. Remember that you can only work on one test at a time, but you should take advantage of moving around within a test. Do not proceed to the next test without answering all possible questions. ***Remember:*** You are not penalized for wrong answers, so guess before moving on to the next test; never leave a question blank. If you run out of time, at least you will have recorded an answer.
–	Difficult	Use the minus "–" column to write down the question number (and possible answer choices) for any problem that seems too difficult to solve.	A difficult question appears "impossible to solve." When you come to a question that seems impossible to answer, write down the question number, with any notes, on your scratch paper. Don't bother with difficult questions until after you have checked all of your work and have answered all of the "easy" and "solvable" ones. Your time may be better spent reviewing your work to be sure you didn't make any careless mistakes on the questions you thought were easier to answer. ***Remember:*** There is no penalty for wrong answers, and, statistically, your chances are better if you pick one position and use it on all unanswered questions.

Your scratch paper might look like this, using the letters A, B, C, D, and E to help you remember the position of each answer choice:

+	–
3. B or E 11. A, not B 15. C? 17. not D	6. not D or E 14. A?

The Elimination Strategy

The Praxis Series recommends that you try to eliminate as many of the answer choices as possible and then make an educated guess. On the computer-delivered exam, you may find it helpful to quickly write the positions (using letters) of the answer choices you wish to eliminate on your scratch paper, so you don't keep reconsidering them. Your scratch paper should resemble the example on page 5.

Taking the Computer-Delivered Praxis Core

All of the material covered in this book—subject matter reviews, the practice test questions and explanations, and the essay practice problems—will help to prepare you for the computer-delivered test. Because the Praxis Core is computer-delivered, once you have reviewed the material presented in this book, it is important that you practice questions in a computer-generated format. An online simulated practice test is available at www.ets.org/praxis.

Advantages of the computer-delivered Praxis Core format include the following:

- Numerous test dates are available because appointments can be scheduled throughout the year. Be sure to call early to make your appointment because time slots fill up quickly.
- You are allowed time on the computer-delivered exam to review a computer tutorial program.
- Computer-friendly functions help you to navigate freely on the test. The computer will allow you to "mark a question" for later review and will allow you to view a list of incomplete, complete, or unseen questions.
- The on-screen calculator will help you perform calculations for math problems. Calculators can be viewed in a "standard" or "scientific" format. When you review the problems in this study guide, practice using a similar calculator. *A word of caution:* Only use the on-screen calculator for time-consuming problems (square roots, long division, etc.); if you use the calculator for every problem, you will lose valuable test time.
- Writing tools for the written essay assignment include cut, paste, undo, redo, copy, and a word counter.
- Your unofficial scores are available immediately after the test (selected response sections only).
- Your answers are recorded electronically, which can often reduce the chance of human error in posting your written responses.

Computer Tutorial

Immediately before taking the computer-delivered test, you will be led through a tutorial in order to show you how to read and answer the questions for each test on the Praxis Core. You do not need advanced computer skills to take the computer-delivered exam. Basic computer skills are sufficient to operate the mouse, keyboard, and word processor. The same types of questions given on the test are used in the tutorial. Remember that you are allowed time to work through a tutorial, so take advantage of this excellent opportunity to learn more about what you will encounter on the test.

Computer Screen Icons

The following is list of icons you will see on the computer screen:

- **Timer.** You should regularly check the time remaining to help pace yourself. If you prefer not to see the timer, click **Hide Timer.** The clock will not appear again until the last 5 minutes of your test.
- **Review.** The review icon instantly pulls up a list of all questions (answered and unanswered). Click on the "review" icon to remind yourself to answer an unanswered question later. Take advantage of this feature during the last few minutes of your exam so that you can go back and answer all questions.

- **Help.** The help screen provides you with information, directions, and format. Note that the clock will continue to run while you view the **Help** file.
- **Previous** and **Next.** After entering your answer, click **Next.** This process saves your answer and allows a new question to appear on the screen. You can go back to a previous question and change your answer by clicking on the **Previous** icon.

Question Types

Questions on the Praxis Core computer-delivered test are presented and organized within specific question types that require you to "click on" or "fill in" your answer. Question types may vary slightly by test. Specific instructions about question types are detailed in Chapters 1, 3, and 4: Reading, Writing Selected Response, and Math. Read the directions carefully before you answer each question.

Types of Selected Response Questions

Question Type	Answer Choice Symbol	Description
Select One Answer	⬭	Read the question and click on the "oval" that is the best response from among five answer choices. This is the most common type of question.
Select One or Multiple Answers	☐	Read the question and click on the "square" that is the best response from among three to five answer choices (select <u>all</u> that apply).
Select In Passage	Highlight the answer	Read the passage and question, then "click on" (highlight) the word(s), phrase, or sentence within the passage to answer the question.
Numeric Entry	☐	Read the question and use the keyboard to type your answer in the answer box provided (fill in the blank). *Note:* When using the on-screen calculator, you can use the "transfer display" feature to move your answer to the box provided.
	☐ / ☐	Read the question and use the keyboard to type your "fraction" in the numerator and denominator answer boxes provided (fill in the blank).

Select One Answer Question Type

Core Academic Skills for Educators – Writing (5722)

Answer the question below by clicking on the correct response.

After receiving the estimate from the insurance company, the car was delivered to McConnell's Auto Body Shop to be repaired.

- ⬭ After receiving the estimate from the insurance company, the car was delivered
- ⬭ After I received the estimate from the insurance company, I delivered the car
- ⬭ The car was delivered, after I received the estimate from the insurance company,
- ⬭ After having received the estimate from the insurance company, the car was delivered
- ⬭ The car was to be delivered, after having received the estimate from the insurance company,

◀━ **Previous**   **Question 23 of 40**   **Next** ━▶

Select All That Apply Question Type

Question 25 refers to the following.

Answer the question below by clicking on the correct response.

Below is a table of the ten largest U.S. cities, sorted by population. The land area for each city is also listed in square miles.

Which of the following cities fall into the top half of the list in population and the bottom half in area?

Select **all** that apply.

10 Largest U.S. Cities by Population			
City	State	Area (sq. miles)	Population (2015)
New York	New York	302.6	8,405,837
Los Angeles	California	468.7	3,884,307
Chicago	Illinois	227.6	2,718,782
Houston	Texas	599.6	2,195,914
Philadelphia	Pennsylvania	134.1	1,553,165
Phoenix	Arizona	516.7	1,513,367
San Antonio	Texas	460.9	1,409,019
San Diego	California	325.2	1,355,896
Dallas	Texas	340.5	1,257,676
San Jose	California	176.5	998,537

☐ Chicago

☐ New York

☐ San Jose

← **Previous**   **Question 25 of 56**   **Next** ➡

Numeric Entry Question Type

Click on each box and type in a number. Backspace to erase.

If you flip a fair coin four times, what is the probability of getting at least two heads?

☐
☐

← **Previous**   **Question 19 of 56**   **Next** ➡

8

Chapter 1

The Core Reading Test (5712)

The Core Reading Test (5712) evaluates your ability to comprehend, interpret, and analyze multiple written passages aligned to the Common Core State Standards (CCSS) in reading. In this chapter, you will review a variety of reading passages, answer questions, and learn how to apply specific strategies to respond to sample problems.

Several sample exercises will provide you with plenty of practice to help you solidify your skills. Take your time to learn the reading strategies presented, observe your mistakes, and practice your reading skills regularly before you take the exam. As you work through this chapter, you should notice an improvement in your *consistent* ability to answer questions with proficiency. After you review this chapter, you can sharpen your skills and practice what you have learned by taking two full-length practice tests provided at the end of this study guide.

Overview of the Reading Test

85 minutes • 56 selected response questions

Studying for the Core Reading Test may be the most important part of your preparation for the Praxis Core Academic Skills Test series. Developing good reading skills will help you effectively navigate through all of the problems on the test—even the Praxis Core Mathematics Test.

Successful readers use a variety of strategies. The ability to visualize, note details, make predictions, draw conclusions, identify the main idea, and summarize reading passages will assist you in performing well on the test. The reading framework developed in this chapter will focus your attention on understanding the written material as you analyze the passages and questions.

If you do not read regularly, it is essential to learn some of these reading strategies. Be patient with yourself as you work through the information presented, and keep in mind that reading competency naturally improves with time and practice.

Skills and Concepts Tested

You will not be expected to understand every detail presented in the passages, but you must be able to evaluate passages that are taken from a wide variety of topics in:

- **Social Studies:** History, government, politics, psychology, sociology
- **Humanities:** Literature (nonfiction), language
- **Natural Sciences:** Biology, environmental science, astronomy
- **Arts:** Fine arts, music, theater

Each passage will be followed by questions based on its content, structure, or style. You are not expected to be familiar with the subject matter of the passage or with its specific content, and you will not be expected to have any prior knowledge of the subject. *Everything you need to know will be provided in the passage.*

Content Categories

Let's begin by discussing the content categories that you will be expected to know.

The test examines your understanding of the content in each passage. You will be asked to identify content that is *directly* and *indirectly* stated in each passage. Examples of what you will need to identify in each passage include the author's main idea; supporting ideas; specific details; the author's purpose, attitude, or tone; the strengths and weaknesses of the author's argument; and supporting evidence to draw conclusions.

Although the reading passages are from a broad spectrum of general-interest print and digital topics (i.e., journals, newspapers, magazines, nonfiction books, novels, and graphic representations), no outside knowledge of the topic is necessary to answer the questions.

Content Categories	Types of Questions	Approximate Number of Questions	Approximate Percentage
I. Key Ideas and Details	• Identify the main idea of the passage • Identify reasons or details that support the main idea • Make inferences from information explicitly stated • Summarize or paraphrase the main or supporting ideas	17–22	35%
II. Craft, Structure, and Language Skills	• Identify the author's attitude, opinion, or tone • Determine the meaning of a word or phrase • Analyze the structure and organization of the passage	14–19	30%
III. Integration of Knowledge and Ideas	• Analyze graphs to locate information • Make logical assumptions or predictions • Draw conclusions • Evaluate strengths and weaknesses • Compare and contrast information	17–22	35%

Key Ideas and Details

Number of questions: 17–22

These are straightforward questions used to determine if you comprehend the passage and its direct meaning. These types of questions ask you to make logical inferences based on what is *directly stated* in the passage.

The three types of key ideas and details questions will assess your ability to identify the following:

- The main idea or primary purpose of the passage, and the summary or paraphrasing of the main and supporting ideas of the passage
- The supporting details or central themes that inform the author's point of view
- The inferences and implications that can be reasonably drawn from material that is directly stated in the passage

Sample Questions

Main Idea	Supporting Details	Inferences
• What is the primary purpose of the passage? • Which of the following identifies the main idea of the passage? • What is the author most concerned with? • What best summarizes the passage as a whole? • Which of the following best describes the main point of the passage?	• What [specific fact] supports the author's point of view? • In the second sentence, the author mentions _____ in order to… • Which of the following, if true, provides evidence for the author's argument? • The author uses the word _____ in line _____ to mean…	• The author would most likely agree that… • What can be inferred [implied] by…? • The author suggests… • Which of the following best describes the relationship between…? • Which of the following, if true, would suggest…?

Craft, Structure, and Language Skills

Number of questions: 14–19

These are questions that require you to identify the author's point of view, so that you can analyze specific words and phrases in the context of the passage. Look for information that is *stated directly* in the passage, and remember that you can always find the answer somewhere in the passage. Look for subtle differences in specific words, phrases, or facts that are contained in the passage, and work actively back and forth between the passage and the question.

Craft, structure, and language skills questions will assess your ability to evaluate the following:

- The author's underlying attitude, opinion, or tone
- The meaning of a word or phrase in the context of the passage
- The organization and structure of the passage
- The author's use of figurative language
- The information presented from fact or opinion

Sample Questions

Author's Attitude or Tone	Structure and Meaning
• The author's attitude can be described as… • Which of the following best describes the tone of the passage? • The author would most likely feel that the characters are… • The overall mood of the passage is… • The author uses the word _____ to create the feeling of…	• Which of the following best describes the organization of the passage? • The use of an exclamation point suggests… • The author mentions ___ in order to… • In [line 5], the author refers to the phrase _____ in order to… • Which of the following best characterizes the meaning of…? • The reference to _____ most nearly means…

Integration of Knowledge and Ideas

Number of questions: 17–22

These *indirect* questions require you to read "beneath the surface" and understand deeper meanings that can be concluded from the passage. Indirect questions can be slightly more difficult than direct questions. Indirect questions require you to understand the relationship between ideas and find a flow of logic to solve the problem as you draw reasonable conclusions from the passage. As you search for the answer in the passage, look for supporting proof and evidence within the author's words. Do not over-think this type of question. The answer is never vague and is always based on evidence from the passage. Once you understand what the author is communicating in the passage, your idea should be logical and make sense.

Integration of knowledge and ideas questions will assess your ability to evaluate the following:

- The logical assumptions drawn from the passage
- The conclusions that can be drawn from the passage
- The argument's strengths or weaknesses
- The differences and similarities (compare and contrast) in the information presented
- The interpretation of a brief statement and a graphic illustration

Sample Questions

Analyze Statements	Analyze Graphs
<u>**Look for Logical Assumptions**</u> • The author would most likely recommend… • Which of the following provides the most likely explanation…? • The author would most likely agree that… • Details in the passage suggest… • The passage suggests ____ for which of the following reasons? <u>**Draw Conclusions**</u> • Which of the following statements best summarizes…? • Based on the passage, the author would conclude… • Which of the following conclusions about ____ is best supported by the passage…? • What conclusion can be drawn by…? <u>**Determine Strengths and Weaknesses**</u> • Which of the following would strengthen the argument…? • Which of the following, if true, would most weaken the author's argument? <u>**Compare and Contrast**</u> • According to the passage, one way to distinguish between ____ and ____ is to… • Determine if the author would agree or disagree • Identify similarities and differences • The author makes which of the following comparisons?	• Which conclusion is best supported by the data presented? • According to the graph, which of the following identifies the highest…? • Which of the following best explains the differences in the graph? • Which of the following is best supported by the information provided?

Format of Passages and Questions

Now that we have covered the content categories, it's time to learn the setup of the reading passages and question types. It is not important to memorize each passage and question type. Just be familiar with them so you won't be surprised when you see the different types on the exam.

Passages

You can anticipate reading about 25 passages: approximately 4 to 5 long passages, 4 to 5 short passages, 1 paired passage, 15 brief statements, and 1 brief statement with a graphic illustration. Passages appear in five different categories:

- **Long passages:** 200 words with 4–7 questions for each passage
- **Short passages:** 100 words with 2–3 questions for each passage
- **Paired passages:** 200 words with 4–7 questions for both passages combined
- **Brief statements:** 2–3 sentences with 1 question per statement
- **Statement and graphic illustration:** 2–3 sentences and 1 graph with 2–3 questions

Question Types

Each passage or statement may contain any one of the three types of selected response questions:

- **Select one answer:** Read the passage and select ONE given choice that best answers the question. This type of question is followed by five OVAL answer choices.
- **Select one or more answers:** Read the passage and select one or more answers that best answer the question. Your task is to select ALL of the choices that accurately answer the question. Partial credit is NOT given for partial answers. This type of question is followed by three SQUARE answer choices.
- **Select sentences in-passage answer:** Read the passage and "click" on the sentence (or sentences) to highlight your answer. When you click on the sentence, your answer will appear highlighted on the screen.

Tip: Changing your answer on the computer-delivered test is simple:

- **Select one answer: Click a different answer choice, and your answer automatically updates.**
- **Select one or more answers: Click on a selected answer choice to unselect it. Then click on a different answer choice, and your answer automatically updates.**
- **Select sentences in-passage answer: Click on a different sentence, and your answer automatically updates.**

Directions

Each reading passage or statement is followed by one or more questions based on the passage's content. After reading the statement or passage, use the given directions to answer the question by choosing the *best* answer from among the choices given. Using only the *stated* or *implied* information given in the statement or passage, try to answer all of the questions.

Mark your answer to the question by selecting the corresponding oval or square(s) on the screen. You may refer to the passage as often as necessary when answering the question. Remember that you are not expected to have any previous knowledge of the topics in the passages or statements.

Sample #1: Reading Comprehension Passage and Question

The diagram below illustrates the most common type of passages and questions on the Core Reading Test. Long, short, and paired passages will appear with line numbers every five lines on the left side of the computer screen, and the question with five answer choices will appear on the right. Questions will appear on the computer screen one at a time; you will be able to see the corresponding passage related to the question on the split screen.

Tip: Always follow the directions provided on the computer screen. If a question has answer choices with ovals, the correct response consists of ONE answer choice. But if a question has answer choices with squares, the correct response consists of ONE or MORE answer choices.

Core Academic Skills for Educators – Reading (5712)

Questions 13–16 refer to the following passage.

Answer the question below by clicking on the correct response.

Line
(5)
(10)
(15)
(20)
(25)

If you sharply increase the light falling upon a normal eye, you observe an immediate adjustment of the iris to reduce the size of the pupil. As this is an instinctive, unlearned response, it is called an unconditioned response, and the increased light is called an unconditioned stimulus. Now, if you make numerous trials taking care to sound a buzzer whenever the light is increased, the iris can be taught to reduce the pupil at the sound of the buzzer alone. This learned response is called a conditioned response, and the sound of the buzzer, a conditioned stimulus.

Symbols are our most important conditioned stimuli, and successful communication depends upon complementary conditioning, or complementary experience. When we find ourselves irrationally shouting at listeners who do not speak our language, we wrongly assume that those with whom we attempt to communicate are equipped with complementary sets of conditioned responses to our own common stock of symbols. While it is easy to see why one should not expect a non-English speaker to converse in English, it is more difficult to realize that a non-English speaker may not have been conditioned to operate with the same set of responses to symbols.

The primary purpose of the passage is to

○ emphasize the importance of symbols in modern, everyday life.

○ reconcile differing theories on intercultural communication.

○ provide guidance on how to communicate with those who speak foreign languages.

○ define and describe the importance of conditioned responses.

○ explain a possible source of the perceived arrogance of English speakers.

Line numbers are provided on the left side of the passage for long, short, and paired passages.

◀━━ Previous   Question 13 of 56   Next ━━▶

Sample #2: Reading Comprehension Select Sentences In Passage

The diagram below illustrates how to select a sentence in a passage. By clicking on a sentence (or sentences) within a passage, your answer will be highlighted on the screen. Remember to reread the sentence(s) to be sure that you have clicked on the correct part of the passage before moving to the next question.

The example below is for informational purposes only. On the actual exam, select sentences in-passage problems may have questions that require a one-sentence answer or may have questions that require an answer with more than one sentence.

Core Academic Skills for Educators – Reading (5712)	
Questions 3–6 refer to the following passage.	**Answer the question below by clicking on the correct sentence in the passage.**
Line *(5)* *(10)* *(15)* People who Googled anything the first day of spring this year were met with a particularly charming version of the search engine's logo. *The Very Hungry Caterpillar,* a beloved children's book character created by Eric Carle in 1969, crawled across the page, eating holes in letters brilliantly colored in characteristic collage style. The only other children's literature icon the Internet giant has deemed recognizable enough to grace its opening search page is Dr. Seuss. No wonder *The Very Hungry Caterpillar,* celebrating almost 50 years in print, the same year its creator celebrates his 86th year, has sold 29 million copies in 45 languages. Among the 70 or so books Carle has written and illustrated, it holds a special place. Every 30 seconds, somewhere in the world, a copy of the book is sold, and its publisher crows.	Which sentence in the passage strengthens the writer's opinion that Carle is a prominent author?
⬅ **Previous**　　　　　　**Question 5 of 56**　　　　　　**Next** ➡	

Sample #3: Reading Comprehension Statement with Graph and Question

The diagram below illustrates the basic structure of a passage in the form of a graph with a brief statement. A graphic display and brief statement will appear on the left side of the computer screen, and the question with three to five answer choices will appear on the right.

The example below is for informational purposes only. On the actual exam, graphic illustration problems may have questions that require one answer choice or may have questions with one or more answer choices.

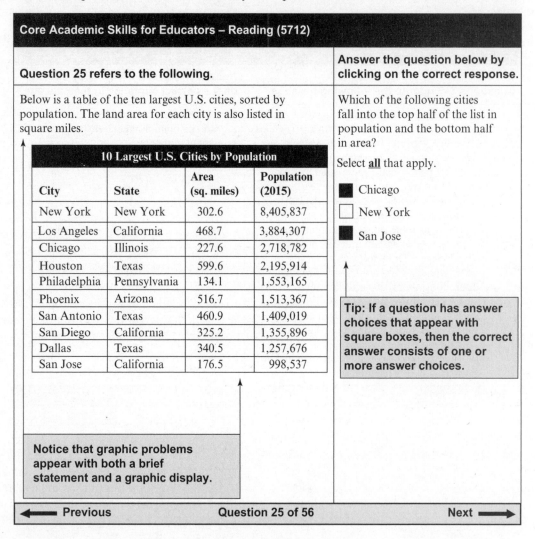

Core Academic Skills for Educators – Reading (5712)

Question 25 refers to the following.

Answer the question below by clicking on the correct response.

Below is a table of the ten largest U.S. cities, sorted by population. The land area for each city is also listed in square miles.

Which of the following cities fall into the top half of the list in population and the bottom half in area?

Select **all** that apply.

■ Chicago

☐ New York

■ San Jose

| 10 Largest U.S. Cities by Population |||
City	State	Area (sq. miles)	Population (2015)
New York	New York	302.6	8,405,837
Los Angeles	California	468.7	3,884,307
Chicago	Illinois	227.6	2,718,782
Houston	Texas	599.6	2,195,914
Philadelphia	Pennsylvania	134.1	1,553,165
Phoenix	Arizona	516.7	1,513,367
San Antonio	Texas	460.9	1,409,019
San Diego	California	325.2	1,355,896
Dallas	Texas	340.5	1,257,676
San Jose	California	176.5	998,537

Tip: If a question has answer choices that appear with square boxes, then the correct answer consists of one or more answer choices.

Notice that graphic problems appear with both a brief statement and a graphic display.

← **Previous**   **Question 25 of 56**   **Next** ➡

Reading Comprehension: A Three-Step Approach

Good reading skills require that you understand what you are reading so that you can derive meaning from written passages and then use this knowledge to answer specific questions related to the passages. Improving reading comprehension skills is not about moving your eyes across a page more quickly. It is about forming a mental framework to shape your thoughts.

This type of reading is called *active reading* because it requires you to search, locate, and extract information in its given context, style, and tone. Active reading enables you to accurately respond to the questions.

Repeated and consistent practice is the key to your reading comprehension success. Work through the practice examples and practice tests in this study guide, paying careful attention to the answer explanations. The explanations provide you with clues about the thinking patterns on the test that help you understand how to determine the correct answer choice.

Now, let's walk through a specific step-by-step approach to improve your reading skills.

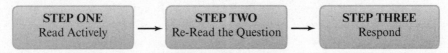

Step One: Read the Passage Actively

The technique of active reading involves steady concentration while reading the passage. You must read the passage while thinking purposefully, not casually, to keep your mind actively engaged in the reading process. Like an investigator, gather clues from the passage to help you answer the questions.

Briefly write down key words or phrases along with the line numbers (if available) on the scratch paper (or writing board) provided. This will help trigger your memory for subsequent questions. As you become mindful of the passage's content, you will be directing your attention to clues and will be able to respond with a greater sense of awareness. Use the techniques of paraphrasing, clarifying, and predicting to support your answer.

- **Paraphrase:** Restating written material in your own words will help you concentrate as you read to analyze difficult passages. Always look for the main point of the passage and try to restate or summarize the content of the passage in your own words. When working through practice questions in this study guide, gather information to paraphrase by writing down key words and phrases. Use these key words and phrases to assist you in summarizing and restating the passage in your own words. Try to use your restatement to answer the questions, and keep in mind that selecting the best answer choice is your goal.

  You can also practice reading actively by jotting down authors' main ideas in whatever articles you happen to read (magazines, newspapers, scholarly journals, etc.). Read the article, turn it over, and then write down what you remember about the author's main point of view. Compare your written notes to the article itself. As you practice this technique and hone your skills, you will find that you will become more proficient at paraphrasing.

- **Clarify:** Some passages are difficult to understand, but the answer to every question is always stated directly within the selection or can be reasonably inferred from the information stated in the passage. Pay attention to the written material. If you find a word, phrase, or concept that you don't understand, write a quick note to yourself and seek further clarification.

  Documenting material that requires clarification will help you complete the task at hand; often, the answers to your questions may appear later in the passage. This strategy helps you to form visual representations of the written material. Your written notes from the passage will often trigger your memory and enable you to make mental associations to remember content from the passages. All test-takers have different learning styles, but this technique helps you center on the passage's main ideas and avoid distractions during the exam. You may be surprised at the information you can recall when writing down just a few trigger words to clarify information as you link mental word associations to the context of the reading passage.

- **Predict:** Make predictions so that your mind is continuously guessing at, or anticipating, what is going to come next. For example, in a passage that introduces "complex carbohydrates" in the first sentence, you might immediately predict that the passage will be a nutrition-based science topic.

Step Two: Read Then Re-Read the Question

Read the question, then re-read when necessary to clarify what you should focus on in the passage. Write down important key words to trigger your memory and give you clues about what to look for in the passage. To save time, remember to abbreviate words when possible. This can be especially helpful with unfamiliar reading material. For example, if a question asks you to locate specific facts presented in the passage, write down key words and phrases from the question. If asked to make an inference or to draw a conclusion, write down an abbreviated word for *inference* or *conclusion* to remind you what to look for as you read the passage. Make mental notes of the main points and key words in the question so that you can find the answer in the passage.

Step Three: Respond to the Question

After you have read actively through the passage and read and re-read the question, it's time to answer the question. Be sure that you understand exactly what you are being asked. Reading the questions too quickly can result in choosing the wrong answer(s)—a common mistake made by test-takers.

Always make sure that the answer you choose agrees with the information contained in the passage and that it answers the specific question asked. Use the incorrect answer choices to help guide you toward the correct answer. Often, you can arrive at the right answer by eliminating answer choices that are not supported by the passage. If you get stuck on any one question, make an educated guess by eliminating as many of the choices as you can and proceed to the next question. *Remember:* You can mark questions for review and go back to them later if there's time.

General Strategies

The following general strategies apply to all reading questions. Review these before you study the suggested strategies and sample questions following the next section.

- **Use only the information that is directly provided in the passage.** Answer all questions about the passage on the basis of what is *stated* or *implied* in that passage. Do not consider outside information, even if it seems more accurate than the given information.

- **Develop good reading habits.** Good reading habits develop through time and practice. Spend about 15 to 20 minutes per day, at least six to eight weeks before your exam, reading faster than your normal reading speed. As you read, pay special attention to key words, transitional words, and negative words. This process will help strengthen your cognitive reading development. Developing good reading habits is similar to going to the gym to build and strengthen your muscles. You must practice reading skills frequently and consistently to build and strengthen your "brain muscles." You can read newspaper editorials, Internet news, magazine articles, or book excerpts. Don't get hooked into reading only interesting, thought-provoking articles. Try to read material that you might not normally read because you have no interest in the topic. Most likely, the passages on the Core Reading Test will be ones that you may not normally choose to read.

- **Manage your time wisely.** At first glance you might calculate that you have about 1½ minutes to read and answer each reading question, but this does not include the time it takes you to read the passage. To allow time to read the passages, never spend more than 1 minute on any one question. Reading questions are time-consuming, so do not let the long passages slow your pace. Test-takers sometimes believe that the shorter passages are easier to read, but this is not necessarily true. All passages require careful consideration and focus.

- **Focus on the main point.** Do not try to memorize the passage. Instead, think of each paragraph as a "thought unit," and try to move your eyes rapidly down the passage while taking notes. Write down main points, key words (names, definitions, places, and numbers), or any other items you feel are important.

- **Refer to the line numbers in the passages.** Most passages contain line numbers for easy reference. In questions that mention specific line numbers, you will have the advantage of being able to quickly spot where the information is located. After you spot the location, be sure to read the line(s) just before and after the line(s) mentioned in the question. The information that comes before and after the line(s) in the question can be helpful in putting the information in the proper context.

- **Eliminate incorrect answer choices.** If you don't know the answer, try to eliminate some of the obvious incorrect choices as soon as you recognize them. Use the elimination strategy discussed on page 6. If you get stuck on any one question, take an educated guess by eliminating as many of the other choices as you can and proceed to the next question. Try to answer every question because there is no penalty for incorrect answers. *Remember:* You can mark questions for review and go back to them later if there's time.

- **Be on alert for the "attractive distracter" answer choice.** Watch out for attractive distracters—answer choices that look good but are not the *best* answer choice. Just because an answer choice is a true statement does not mean that it is the best choice. The facts and concepts presented on the exam are often written with subtle variations of selected answer choices that make it difficult for test-takers to narrow down the correct answer. Attractive distracters are carefully written to be close to the *best* answer. When you narrow your answer down to two choices, one is probably the attractive distracter. If this happens, read the question again and select the answer that does not have any ambiguous words or phrases. The correct answer always fits the *meaning* of the question more exactly. Remember that the answer does not have to be perfect, just the *best* among the five answer choices.
- **Use computer tools.** The complete passage may not fit on the screen, so make sure you are comfortable with the method of scrolling up and down on the screen.

Suggested Strategies with Sample Passages

Questions 1–5 are based on the following passage.

The idea of America as a "melting pot" has changed over time because the demographics of the country have changed. In many communities, immigrant populations are transforming American society rather than being transformed by it. Some sociologists argue that assimilation isn't always a positive experience—for either society or the immigrants themselves. According to some commentators, assimilation sometimes
(5)   means "Anglo conformity." Ruben G. Rumbaut, a sociology professor at Michigan State University, says, "If assimilation is a learning process, it involves learning good things and bad things." In a development referred to as "segmented" assimilation, immigrants follow different paths into American society. At one end, many follow the classic American ideal of blending into the middle class, while at the other end some become part of an adversarial underclass. In the middle are those who form "immigrant enclaves"—living together and
(10)   maintaining their ethnic heritage while also adopting many aspects of mainstream American culture.

Strategy 1: Look for the Main Idea of the Passage

Always look for the main point of the passage. Looking for the author's main point will always provide you with a holistic view of the passage and give you insights into its content. After you read and take notes from the passage, try to synthesize the ideas, and ask yourself, "What is the author really saying?" or "What point is the author trying to make?"

Example:

---

1. The author's main purpose in writing this passage is to

    A. argue that immigration has a negative impact on immigrants.

    B. describe how American demographics have changed over time.

    C. describe modern relationships between immigrants and society.

    D. present a professor's theory on the cultural assimilation of immigrants.

    E. explain why conformity is sometimes beneficial to immigrants.

Choice A is an overstatement of the author's position, and choice E contradicts the passage. Choices B and D are secondary points; each is mentioned in only one sentence. Choice C describes both the introductory sentences and the specific theories presented by the author, making it the best summary of the main idea of the passage as a whole. The correct answer is C.

Strategy 2: Look for Supporting Details

Your answer must be supported by information either stated or implied in the passage. This type of question often requires that you know the difference between ideas stated clearly in the passage and ideas that are implied by the author.

These questions require you to break the passage down and examine its smaller components and identify reasons, details, or facts that support the author's main point. To develop this skill, practice identifying supporting ideas on a regular basis with newspaper articles, Internet news articles, magazine articles, or excerpts from books. In the following example, eliminate choices that the passage does not support.

Example:

> **2.** Which of the following does the author imply about the history of American immigrant communities?
>
> **A.** They have tended to be segregated across religious lines.
> **B.** Their members have generally belonged to the lower class of society.
> **C.** They have caused the "melting pot" idea of America to become irrelevant.
> **D.** They have traditionally adapted themselves to American culture, rather than vice versa.
> **E.** They have recently grown susceptible to "Anglo conformity."

Choice A can immediately be identified as incorrect, as the passage does not mention religion. Choice B is also not implied by the passage; while it does mention that *some* immigrants become part of an *underclass,* it also notes that *many* blend into the middle class. Choice C is incorrect because the author suggests that the idea has *changed over time,* rather than become irrelevant, and the word *recently* mentioned in choice E is never implied. The correct answer is D; the first sentence of the passage discusses a change in American cultural dynamics over time, while the second sentence describes how many immigrant communities are now transforming society, *rather than being transformed by it.* This statement infers that immigrant communities have traditionally adapted themselves to American society, rather than vice versa.

Strategy 3: Make Inferences

Some information is not stated directly in the passage but can be gleaned by "reading between the lines." Look for confirming *proof* and *evidence* among the author's words and tone from the information stated in the passage. "Read between the lines" and write down key words as you gather evidence to support your conclusion. Ask yourself, "What is not stated directly by the author?" For example, you can infer from the statement, *Only a minority of children under the age of six have visited a dentist,* that a majority of children under the age of six have not visited a dentist. Once you understand what the author is communicating in the passage, your inference should be logical and make perfect sense. Review the following five answer choices to determine which answer is most plausible *based on the evidence* that you have gathered from the passage.

Example:

> **3.** It can be inferred that proponents of the theory of segmented assimilation would most likely agree with which of the following statements?
>
> **A.** Distinct trends appear when immigration patterns are segmented across time periods.
> **B.** Immigrants must choose whether to adopt American customs or to remain true to their roots.
> **C.** Immigrant enclaves are formed by immigrants who reject the idea of assimilation.
> **D.** A significant portion of immigrants maintain their cultural traditions after assimilating into American society.
> **E.** An adversarial underclass is necessary for the preservation of unique cultural identities.

The author defines *segmented assimilation* in the sixth sentence (lines 6–7). Examples of the different segments are then provided. Choice A is not mentioned in the passage, and choices B and C conflict with the author's description of *cultural enclaves.* Choice E is not implied by the discussion of the adversarial underclass; rather, the author explains how the middle segment of immigrants is able to both maintain their heritage and adopt new customs, as stated in choice D. The correct answer is D.

Strategy 4: Identify the Author's Attitude

Identify the attitude or "mood" of the passage by looking for and identifying the author's *mood*. The overall tone of the passage is communicated through the author's choice of language and words that help the reader feel a sense of connection with the written material. The words that the author uses to describe events, people, or places will provide clues about how or what the author wants you to feel or think.

Questions can be as simple as identifying positive or negative words that set the entire mood of the passage. Pay careful attention to the *types* of words the author uses. For example, if you read the word *tentative,* you may feel a sense of something *unsure, cautious,* or *hesitant.* Also, look for words that stir up a subtle feeling or emotion. Remember that punctuation marks and/or italicized words or phrases can convey the author's tone as well.

Understand the meaning and possible reason for using certain words or phrases in the passage above and answer the question below. Remember to take advantage of the line numbers given.

Example:

---

4. As used in line 9, *adversarial* is used to describe the

    A.   hostility held by poor immigrants against their more successful peers.
    B.   resistance to assimilation of one immigrant segment.
    C.   violent nature of the immigrant underclass.
    D.   rivalry between different cultural groups of immigrants.
    E.   competitive culture among immigrants in cultural enclaves.

The word *adversarial* is used to describe the underclass of immigrants at the opposite end of the spectrum from those who attempt to blend fully into middle-class American society; thus, those immigrants who are most resistant (or *adversarial*) to assimilation, as put forth by choice B. Choices A, C, D, and E describe claims about immigrant culture that are not mentioned or implied by the passage, and would not fit in the context of the point being made by the author. The correct answer is B.

Strategy 5: Watch for Important Evidence That Might Support a Conclusion

If you are asked to draw a conclusion, watch for evidence that might support a conclusion. There must be a relationship between the evidence and the answer choices. Your answer must be supported by evidence from the material in the passage. When in doubt, one of the best strategies for answering this type of question is to plug in each answer choice to see which one best fits the evidence provided. Several answer choices in the following question may be logically feasible. You are asked to choose the one option that is not only possible, but must also logically follow from a line of reasoning and conditions presented in the passage.

Remember, a conclusion can be logical, but it may not be true unless a valid statement precedes it.

Example:

> **5.** Which of the following conclusions is best supported by Ruben G. Rumbaut's statement about immigration in lines 5–6?
>
>   A.   Some aspects of American culture should not be adopted by immigrants.
>   B.   Much of America's modern culture has been shaped by immigrants.
>   C.   Some immigrants learn positive things from assimilation, while others pick up bad habits.
>   D.   It is a learning process that benefits both the immigrant and society.
>   E.   It provides the opportunity for workers to learn professional skills they would not otherwise have.

The correct answer must be directly supported by Rumbaut's statement, "If assimilation is a learning process, it involves learning good things and bad things." Choices B and E are unrelated to the statement and can be eliminated. Choice D is also incorrect, as the claim does not reference any benefit to society. Choice C mischaracterizes Rumbaut's claim by describing a separation between immigrants who learn good things and others who learn bad things. Choice A is directly supported by Rumbaut's claim that immigration involves learning "bad things." The correct answer is A.

Questions 6 and 7 are based on the following passage.

The emphasis on children's health and fitness has even reached the White House; in a campaign to end childhood obesity in the United States, the first lady launched an initiative called "Let's Move" to encourage healthy lifestyles among kids. The Centers for Disease Control and Prevention (CDC) recommend that children participate in one hour or more of physical activity per day to improve cardiovascular health, muscle (5)   strength, and bone strength. Studies suggest that a comprehensive physical education program is the most significant factor in the development of cardio-respiratory endurance, which includes the ability of the heart, blood vessels, and respiratory system to sustain work by delivering oxygen and nutrients to the tissues of the body over a period of time. The most important education we can give our children is one that gives them the tools to maintain a healthy heart.

Strategy 6: Summarize the Main or Supporting Ideas of the Passage

The best method of isolating the main point or supporting ideas of the passage is to *paraphrase* the passage by summarizing and distilling the author's ideas into your own words. Practicing main point questions will not only help you master this question type, but it will also serve to develop a foundation of the analytic skills needed to tackle the slightly more challenging inference questions.

Example:

> **6.** Which of the following best characterizes the author's opinion on the importance of physical education?
>
>   A.   It should be considered equally important as traditional academic fields in a well-rounded education.
>   B.   It has become even more important since the implementation of the "Let's Move" initiative.
>   C.   It should be the top priority in a child's schooling.
>   D.   It should be included in a student's core curriculum when possible.
>   E.   It is the solution to childhood obesity in the United States.

The author claims that physical education is *the most important education we can give to our children,* as paraphrased by choice C. Choices A and D understate the author's opinion of the importance of physical education, while choices B and E are not implied. The correct answer is C.

Strategy 7: Identify the Significance or Meaning of a Word or Phrase in the Context of the Passage

Pay close attention to the word or phrase in the *context* of the whole sentence, paragraph, or passage. Use the context to figure out the meaning, even if you're unfamiliar with the words. Look for logic and context clues to understand the author's intent to persuade the readers. Identify the author's reasoning and structure of the passage, including specific words, phrases, or context that the author develops and presents.

Sometimes you will need to read the sentence just before and after where the word is presented to understand the word's association to the surrounding text. In cases where several answer choices might fit, select the one that fits the *meaning* of the author's intent most exactly.

In the following example, look for the answer choice that fits the meaning of the passage. Remember that there may be more than one answer choice that appears to be correct, but there is never more than one correct answer. If you feel stuck, consider all of your options and literally plug in each answer choice to see which one makes the most sense (or sounds the best).

Example:

---

7. The author's reference to the White House (line 1) serves to

  A. give authority to an otherwise subjective claim.
  B. illustrate how rapidly a trend can spread to the highest levels.
  C. show an example of a successful grassroots fitness movement.
  D. emphasize how serious a problem the neglect of physical education has become.
  E. provide additional validity to her argument.

The author makes reference to the White House's campaign to provide support to her argument that children's physical education is of the utmost importance, as suggested by choice E. Choice A incorrectly characterizes the argument as *otherwise subjective,* as the author presents supporting evidence from the CDC in the next sentence. Choices B and C incorrectly describe the primary purpose of the reference. Choice D is incorrect because the author does not claim that the *neglect* of physical education has become a serious problem. The correct answer is E.

Question 8 is based on the following passage.

   Surpluses in hydroelectric power are not always advantageous. For example, during years with heavy precipitation in the winter and spring seasons, the Pacific Northwest often experiences a power surplus from its hydroelectric dams. This surplus has allowed the region to lessen its dependency on more dangerous, environmentally damaging power sources such as coal and nuclear energy. However, the surplus also comes
(5)   with potentially negative consequences: The leading power provider in the region could be forced to shut down many of its wind farms—a major blow to the burgeoning wind power industry—and inconsistent river surges could result in unstable employment conditions at coal and nuclear power plants in the region.

Strategy 8: Identify Logical Assumptions

To make accurate assumptions, consider the author's overall attitude about the argument and notice the author's language and choice of words. Look for the relationship among the ideas presented by the author.

When you identify this type of question, ask yourself, "What is the foundation from which the author based the argument?" or "What is assumed by the author to be true (but is not directly stated by the author) that will provide evidence to support the conclusion?" In other words, look for clues about the author's underlying opinion and do not over-think the answer.

Example:

> **8.** Which of the following best addresses the author's concerns about hydroelectric power surpluses?
>
>   **A.**   Excess power can be sold to other energy providers in regions of need.
>   **B.**   Employees of coal and nuclear power plants in the region are hard, reliable workers.
>   **C.**   Viable alternatives to hydroelectric power as safe, clean power sources exist.
>   **D.**   During years without heavy rain, hydroelectric dams do not produce significant energy.
>   **E.**   Riverside communities in the Pacific Northwest are well equipped to handle flooding.

The specific concerns raised by the author about hydroelectric power relate to 1) unstable employment caused by inconsistent hydroelectric power production and 2) the shutdown of wind power plants. Choice A helps alleviate these concerns by providing a way to eliminate this surplus energy in a beneficial manner. Choice B does not address the *unstable conditions* for employment, while choice C does not address the hydroelectric-specific concern mentioned in the question. Choice D addresses only low-output years rather than surplus years, and choice E is irrelevant to the author's concerns. The correct answer is A.

Strategy 9: Evaluate Strengths and Weaknesses

Look for information that "supports" or "disproves" the argument's conclusion.

Use the following steps to help you break down the answer choices:

1. Read the passage and write down key words or phrases that will help you understand the main point.
2. Analyze the statements in the answer choices and look for information that strengthens or weakens the argument's conclusion by finding information in the answer choices that is not available in the passage.
3. If an answer choice provides a *different* assumption, immediately eliminate that answer as a possible choice.
4. Once you have narrowed down your answer choices, read the remaining choices to check for relevance. Eliminate any answer choice that is irrelevant to the author's topic.

Example:

> Ethologists, people who study animal behavior, have traditionally divided an organism's actions into two categories: learned behavior (based on experience) and instinctive behavior (based on genotype). Contemporary scholars reject this distinction, claiming that all behavior is a predictable interaction of genetic and environmental factors.

> **9.** Which of the following statements, if true, would most weaken the claim of the contemporary scholars?
>
>   **A.**   All organisms with identical genotypes and identical experience always respond identically in different situations.
>   **B.**   All organisms with identical genotypes and different experience always respond identically in identical situations.
>   **C.**   All organisms with similar genotypes and similar experience sometimes respond differently in identical situations.
>   **D.**   All organisms with identical genotypes and different experience always respond differently in identical situations.
>   **E.**   All organisms with different genotypes and identical experience always respond differently in identical situations.

The question expects you to find a statement that weakens the claim of the contemporary scholars—that behavior derived is from an interaction of both experience and genotype. Choice A is incorrect because it is too vague; it could support either the traditional view or the claim of the contemporary scholars. Choice C is incorrect because the words *similar* and *sometimes* are undefined and too vague to be of any use in this context. Choices D and E are incorrect because they support the contemporary view that behaviors are not products of solely genotype or experience. Choice B, on the other hand, contradicts this view by suggesting that genotype is the only factor influencing behavior. The correct answer is B.

Strategy 10: Analyze Graphs to Locate Information

Draw upon your knowledge of interpretation to analyze statements and graphic illustrations (tables, charts, or graphs). In order to answer this type of question, you will need to combine your reading comprehension skills and critical thinking skills. Use only the information that is directly provided to analyze the data in the graphic illustration from general to specific. This means that you should briefly examine the statement and whole display to see how it is organized before you answer the specific questions.

Look for obvious high points or low points and look at the headings that clarify the data (legends, units of measurement, or tabs). Remember to scan the graphic display. Do not try to memorize the data; just get a general sense of the overall picture.

Example:

Allison tutors six different seventh-grade students. The following chart tracks the scores of each student across three major tests.

Student Scores on Class Tests

Last Name	Test 1	Test 2	Test 3
Smith	72	80	76
Johnson	90	80	70
Alexander	86	82	84
Jones	70	90	82
Carroll	74	84	80
Ellison	82	90	86

10. Which of the following students scored in the top two on at least two tests?

Select **all** that apply:

A. Johnson
B. Alexander
C. Jones
D. Carroll
E. Ellison

The top scorers on Test 1 were Johnson and Alexander; on Test 2, Jones and Ellison; and on Test 3, Ellison and Alexander. Ellison and Alexander are the only two names that appear twice; therefore, the correct answers are choices B and E.

Reminder: "Select one or more answer" questions will have squares around the answer choice letters rather than ovals, and you must select ALL correct answers to receive credit.

Practice Questions

Now let's practice the approaches and strategies you have learned. Read the following passages and answer the questions that follow. Question types are intermingled and are not arranged by level of difficulty. Answers and explanations are provided at the end of the section.

Directions: Each passage is followed by one or more questions based on the passage's content. After reading a passage, read the question and choose the best answer among three to five choices to answer the question. Answer all questions about the passage on the basis of what is *stated* or *implied* in that passage.

Question 1 is based on the following passage.

Like many birds, the monarch butterfly is migratory. Once per year, more than 100 million of the insects fly from their summer homes in the north to areas in the south. Unlike migratory animals that learn their routes from their parents or other members of the species, the life span of the monarch is 90 days or less; an older generation cannot instruct a younger one.

1. Based on the information provided, all of the following could potentially explain how butterflies find their way when they migrate EXCEPT

A. the direction of the prevailing winds in the area.

B. knowledge gained from a previous migration.

C. the position of the sun relative to the earth.

D. force lines of the earth's magnetic field.

E. the changing length of days and nights.

Question 2 is based on the following passage.

Contrary to traditional belief, contemporary research shows that a child's measure of intelligence is multidimensional and is primarily influenced by a combination of hereditary and learned
(5)   environmental influences. For many years, studies have shown that children's IQ scores can improve when environmental factors are enriched. Further studies show that cognition can be influenced as early as infancy. Recent research indicates that
(10) children who were breastfed for at least six months during infancy score higher on tests later in life.

2. The passage is primarily concerned with

A. the impact of nonhereditary influences on a child's intelligence.

B. recent research in the field of psychology.

C. the ways in which intelligence can be genetically inherited.

D. socioeconomic factors that can lead to developmental advantages.

E. presenting examples of both the hereditary and learned factors in IQ testing.

Question 3 is based on the following passage.

Since the writings of Aristotle, the doctrine of association has been the basis for explaining how one idea leads to another. In other words, when you experience two items contiguously—in the same place, at the same time, or both—they become linked in your mind. In psychology, word association tests are based on contiguity, the idea being that your response to a particular word is based on your personal history.

3. Which of the following examples most strengthens the main point of the passage?

   A. Some people are able to experience more than two items contiguously.

   B. Unexpected pain instinctively provokes fear in most people.

   C. Aristotle's writing is full of unexplained associations.

   D. People who make unusual associations are often mentally disturbed, whereas people who make overly predictable associations often lack creativity.

   E. Many Afghan refugees who endured bombings are still frightened by loud noises.

Questions 4 and 5 are based on the following passage.

German goldsmith Johannes Gutenberg is credited with inventing the first printing press in 1451. This made it possible to use interchangeable metal type in different combinations to print (5) books. The printing press was one of the most revolutionary inventions known in human history. It had a profound and immediate impact on the political, economic, and social structure of Europe and ushered an information revolution (10) in the "period of modernity." Literacy among lay people accelerated, scientific critical scholarship became more reliable, and the diffusion of knowledge produced economic growth.

4. The passage is primarily concerned with

   A. emphasizing why the printing press was the crowning achievement of German inventor Johannes Gutenberg.

   B. providing background for the intellectual renaissance in European society in the 15th century.

   C. placing the invention of the printing press within its proper context in human history.

   D. explaining the mechanisms by which the first printing press operated.

   E. describing the effect of the printing press on the class structure of Europe.

5. According to the passage, the invention of the printing press produced improvements in all of the following EXCEPT the

   A. ability of lower-class workers to read.

   B. political oppression in Europe.

   C. widespread availability of information and wisdom.

   D. consistency and trustworthiness of claimed scientific advances.

   E. production and output of European economies.

Questions 6 and 7 are based on the following passage.

The term *meteorology* has been around since the 17th century, but meteorology as we know it today didn't actually exist until instruments that could accurately measure temperatures were (5) developed. This wasn't an easy task; an accurate reading depended on putting a very even bore in a glass tube. Daniel Gabriel Fahrenheit solved the problem and produced an accurate thermometer in 1717, but for some unknown reason, he (10) calibrated it so that freezing was put at 32 degrees and the boiling point at 212 degrees. This seemed odd to many people, among them astronomer Anders Celsius, who in 1748 came up with a competing scale that he felt made more sense: Zero (15) would be the boiling point and 100 the freezing point. However, that certainly wasn't the end of the story. Celsius's scale was soon reversed, and zero became freezing and 100 the boiling point. Both the Fahrenheit and Celsius scales are used (20) today, confusing many people who simply want to know how cold or warm the weather is going to be.

6. The author's main purpose in the passage is to

   A. describe the history and early origins of meteorology.

   B. demonstrate how scientists and inventors do not always agree.

   C. summarize the origins of the Fahrenheit and Celsius temperature scales.

   D. explain the technical difficulties in producing an accurate thermometer.

   E. compare and contrast the merits and drawbacks of the Fahrenheit and Celsius temperature scales.

7. The author of the passage would most likely agree with which of the following statements?

A. The Celsius temperature scale is more logical than, and therefore superior to, the Fahrenheit scale.

B. It would be ideal if only one of the systems were still used today.

C. Anders Celsius questioned the measurement methods of Daniel Gabriel Fahrenheit.

D. The widespread use of two different temperature scales can lead to serious problems and should cease.

E. Fahrenheit's thermometer, though accurate, was inefficient.

Questions 8–11 are based on the following paired passages.

Passage 1

The poet Emily Dickinson was an eccentric, almost reclusive, woman who never married. In the town of Amherst, Massachusetts, where she lived, people knew she could write verse, but of
(5) what real use was that, except for writing a condolence note or a compliment to accompany a gift? During her lifetime, her writing was treated as not very significant. Of course, there wasn't much of it, at least that people knew
(10) about; she only chose to publish a few of her many poems while she was alive. Now, in our own time, she is one of America's most celebrated poets. In some ways, Emily Dickinson's legacy is a variation on the Cinderella story. She was
(15) transformed from a rather drab spinster to a fascinating woman—not by a fairy godmother, but by the poetry she wrote.

Passage 2

The ideas in Emily Dickinson's poems are provocative, and she is skillful with metaphors,
(20) rhythm, and euphony. But it is Dickinson's attention to the individual word that distinguishes her style. From extant manuscripts, it is obvious that she weighed each word of her poems and was meticulous in choosing the right one. In
(25) some manuscripts, she would write down nine or ten different words for the same idea so that she could study which one would best suit her purpose in a poem. One of the main reasons her poems are so economical is that she respected the
(30) importance of every word she chose.

8. The author of Passage 1 focuses most on which of the following about Emily Dickinson?

A. The contrast between her ordinary life and her talent

B. Her inability to achieve recognition as a talented writer

C. The lack of appreciation of her local community for her work

D. Her modern-day reputation as a classic American poet

E. The underlying psychological motivations for her poetry

9. In Passage 1, the author's reference to Cinderella's transformation (lines 13–17) is made to

A. draw a parallel to another rags-to-riches literary icon.

B. romanticize an otherwise sad story about an unappreciated author.

C. illustrate how the success of Dickinson's poetry changed her formerly mundane life.

D. show a similar example of a woman succeeding outside of her place in the social hierarchy.

E. create an analogy to Dickinson's rise to fame after death.

10. The author of Passage 2 is most impressed by Emily Dickinson's

A. provocative ideas and skill with various literary devices.

B. innate sense of how to conjure up vivid imagery.

C. ability to get the most out of a small number of words.

D. diligence in revising her work.

E. knack for choosing perfect descriptive words.

11. Which of the following best describes the relationship between the two passages in their discussion of Emily Dickinson?

  A. Passage 2 provides specific examples of why the early criticisms of her work presented in Passage 1 are invalid.

  B. Passage 2 provides a counterargument to an argument made in Passage 1.

  C. Passage 2 portrays her as brilliant, while Passage 1 portrays her as reclusive and simple.

  D. Passage 2 describes the mechanisms of her greatness, while Passage 1 provides context.

  E. Passage 2 focuses on her place in history, while Passage 1 focuses on her creative process.

Question 12 is based on the following passage.

Many species of male birds perform elaborate dances to attract a mate. Female birds that witness these performances tend to be drawn to these males because the dance demonstrates (5) strength, agility, and other desirable genetic attributes. In one species of bird, the presence of a younger male assistant in the dance significantly raises the likelihood that the lead male's courtship will be successful. However, the assistant is not (10) mature enough to mate and is usually not related to the lead male, so his participation in the performance seems paradoxical.

12. Which of the following statements provides the most logical explanation for the apparent paradox above?

  A. Once he matures, a young male assistant is more likely to find an assistant of his own than is a young male who never assisted.

  B. In some cases, a female onlooker challenges the female who is being courted for the right to mate with the lead male.

  C. A young male who assists is more likely to die of hunger before maturity than one who does not assist.

  D. Young males who later participate as assistants can be shown, early on, to be stronger and more agile than males who do not.

  E. Offspring of birds who mate as a result of a mating dance are more likely to survive to maturity than offspring of birds who do not.

Questions 13–16 are based on the following passage.

If you sharply increase the light falling upon a normal eye, you observe an immediate adjustment of the iris to reduce the size of the pupil. As this is an instinctive, unlearned response, it is called (5) an unconditioned response, and the increased light is called an unconditioned stimulus. Now, if you make numerous trials taking care to sound a buzzer whenever the light is increased, the iris can be taught to reduce the pupil at the sound of (10) the buzzer alone. This learned response is called a conditioned response, and the sound of the buzzer, a conditioned stimulus.

Symbols are our most important conditioned stimuli, and successful communication depends (15) upon complementary conditioning, or complementary experience. When we find ourselves irrationally shouting at listeners who do not speak our language, we wrongly assume that those with whom we attempt to communicate are equipped (20) with complementary sets of conditioned responses to our own common stock of symbols. While it is easy to see why one should not expect a non-English speaker to converse in English, it is more difficult to realize that a non-English speaker may (25) not have been conditioned to operate with the same set of responses to symbols.

13. The primary purpose of the passage is to

  A. emphasize the importance of symbols in modern, everyday life.

  B. reconcile differing theories on intercultural communication.

  C. provide guidance on how to communicate with those who speak foreign languages.

  D. define and describe the importance of conditioned responses.

  E. explain a possible source of the perceived arrogance of English speakers.

14. According to the author of the passage, which of the following examples best illustrates an unconditioned response?

  A. A businessman reaches for his pocket when he feels a vibration where he usually keeps his cell phone.

  B. Factory workers immediately stop working when a whistle blows at five o'clock every weekday.

  C. A child starts to cry after receiving a poor grade in school.

  D. A cigarette smoker recoils when she accidentally burns her finger on the end of her lit cigarette.

  E. A tired college student immediately presses the snooze button on her alarm when it goes off in the morning.

15. Based on the information in the passage, a child who begins feeling hungry as the school lunch bell rings each day may be responding to

    A. a developing internal clock.
    B. a conditioned stimulus.
    C. a conditioned response.
    D. an unconditioned stimulus.
    E. an unconditioned response.

16. The passage suggests that those who speak English when attempting to communicate with those who do not speak English are

    A. bound to fail completely.
    B. still dependent upon complementary responses to common symbols.
    C. likely to be more successful if they raise their voices, since listeners are conditioned to respond to louder voices with greater attentiveness.
    D. likely to be able to communicate fully when using words common to both speakers' vocabularies.
    E. inevitably subject to the limitations of third-party translators or translation software.

Questions 17–19 are based on the following passage.

The realization that bacteria are capable of chemical communication first came from investigations of marine bacteria able to glow in the dark. In 1970, Kenneth H. Nealson and John
(5) Woodland Hastings of Harvard University observed that luminous bacteria glow at variable intensities and emit no light at all until the population reaches high density.

Nealson and Hastings knew the glow resulted
(10) from chemical reactions catalyzed by the enzyme luciferase inside each bacterial cell. They hypothesized that this enzyme was ultimately controlled not by some mechanism within each cell, but by a molecular messenger that traveled
(15) between cells. Once reaching target cells, the messenger, called an autoinducer, induced expression of the genes for luciferase and other proteins involved in light production. That is, the autoinducer stimulated synthesis of the encoded
(20) proteins, causing the bacteria to glow.

This theory was initially met with skepticism, but it has since been confirmed and even hailed as a landmark achievement in bacterial science research. Growing sentiment in the scientific
(25) community since that time has focused more

energy and resources on research based on the autoinducer theory, especially as the control of glowing bacteria has valuable potential applications in medicine and bioengineering.

17. According to the passage, the most important finding of Nealson and Hastings' research was that

    A. bacteria communicate through molecular messengers that travel between cells.
    B. luminous bacteria glow not at a constant density but at variable densities.
    C. bacteria are genetically coded by the autoinducer.
    D. the molecular messenger luciferase causes bacteria to glow at high densities.
    E. the autoinducer, not the enzyme luciferase, produces the luminosity of certain marine bacteria.

18. Which of the following characteristics describes the autoinducer's role in light production?

    A. It catalyzes chemical reactions inside bacterial cells.
    B. It stimulates synthesis of light-emitting proteins.
    C. It communicates messages between the brain and bacterial cells.
    D. It encodes genes within bacterial cells.
    E. It produces light when its genes are expressed by luciferase and other proteins.

19. The primary purpose of the third paragraph of the passage is to provide

    A. insight into the difficult scientific climate faced by the scientists at the time of their discovery.
    B. supporting evidence for the theory presented by the scientists.
    C. specific examples that show the validity of the author's argument.
    D. context that underscores the importance of what was previously discussed.
    E. information about new breakthroughs in the fields of medicine and bioengineering.

Questions 20–24 are based on the following passage.

Woodrow Wilson's meteoric career trajectory took off in 1910, when he was elected to his first office as governor of New Jersey. At the time, Wilson was a conservative Democrat. Thus,
(5) when the Democratic machine first proposed Wilson's nomination in 1912, the young New Jersey progressives were not interested. They decided to work for his election only after Wilson assured them he would champion the progressive
(10) cause. Between 1911 and 1913, he enacted many progressive reforms as governor.

In the election of 1912, Wilson secured the Democratic nomination. In the campaign, he emerged as a moderate candidate between the
(15) conservative Republican, William H. Taft, and the more radical Progressive, Theodore Roosevelt. Wilson called his pro-business program the New Freedom, which called for the restoration of free market competition, as it had existed before the
(20) rise of the trusts. In contrast, Roosevelt advocated New Nationalism, which called for major federal interventions in the economy. Wilson believed the trusts should be destroyed, but he distinguished between monopoly-seeking trusts and legitimately
(25) successful big business. Roosevelt, on the other hand, accepted the trusts as inevitable but believed the government should establish a new regulatory agency to provide oversight and make them accountable.

20. The author's main purpose in writing this passage is to

A. argue that Wilson is one of the great U.S. presidents.

B. survey the differences between Wilson, Taft, and Roosevelt.

C. explain Wilson's concept of the New Freedom.

D. trace major developments in Wilson's political career.

E. point out the importance of gubernatorial experience for presidential candidates.

21. The author implies which of the following about the New Jersey progressives?

A. They did not support Wilson after he was governor.

B. They were not conservative Democrats.

C. They were more interested in political expediency than in political causes or reforms.

D. They did not support Wilson in his bid for election.

E. They particularly admired Wilson's experience as president of Princeton University.

22. The passage supports which of the following conclusions about the progress of Wilson's political career?

A. His rapid progression to higher office was enabled by a willingness to change his core political principles.

B. Failures late in his career caused him to be regarded as a president who regressed instead of progressed.

C. He encountered little opposition once he decided to seek the presidency.

D. The League of Nations marked the end of his reputation as a strong leader.

E. His political allies were Roosevelt and Taft.

23. The *major federal interventions* mentioned in lines 21–22 of the passage refer to which of the following?

A. Roosevelt's proposal to regulate trusts by establishing a new government agency

B. Roosevelt's proposal to weaken trusts by subsidizing legitimately successful businesses to encourage competition

C. Wilson's proposal to destroy the trusts to restore free competition as it had existed before

D. Wilson's call for the government to take a more active stance in the economic life of the nation

E. Wilson's New Freedom plan, which opposed monopolies and championed business enterprise

24. According to the passage, which of the following was probably true about the presidential campaign of 1912?

   A. Woodrow Wilson won the election by an overwhelming majority.

   B. The inexperience of Theodore Roosevelt accounted for his radical position.

   C. Wilson was unable to attract two-thirds of the votes but won anyway.

   D. There were three prominent candidates for the presidency.

   E. Wilson's New Freedom did not represent Democratic interests.

Question 25 is based on the following table.

Below is a table of the ten largest U.S. cities, sorted by population. The land area for each city is also listed in square miles.

10 Largest U.S. Cities by Population

City	State	Area (sq. miles)	Population (2015)
New York	New York	302.6	8,405,837
Los Angeles	California	468.7	3,884,307
Chicago	Illinois	227.6	2,718,782
Houston	Texas	599.6	2,195,914
Philadelphia	Pennsylvania	134.1	1,553,165
Phoenix	Arizona	516.7	1,513,367
San Antonio	Texas	460.9	1,409,019
San Diego	California	325.2	1,355,896
Dallas	Texas	340.5	1,257,676
San Jose	California	176.5	998,537

25. Which of the following cities fall into the top half of the list in population and the bottom half in area?

Select **all** that apply.

   A. Chicago

   B. New York

   C. San Jose

Question 26 is based on the following passage.

Cinco de Mayo (the 5th of May) is observed in many states with celebrations of Mexican culture, food, music, and customs. Cinco de Mayo is popularly misunderstood as Mexican Independen-
(5) dence Day. Contrary to popular belief, Cinco de Mayo actually commemorates the victory of the poorly equipped Mexican militia over the occupying French army in 1862. Mexico had incurred a large debt to France and other European
(10) nations following the Mexican-American War (1846–1848). France used the debt crisis in an attempt to expand its empire and invade Mexico.

26. Which of the following best describes the organization of the passage?

   A. A description of a period of Mexican war history is preceded by an introduction.

   B. A faulty argument is presented and then corrected by the author.

   C. A misconception of a commemoration is corrected and then background about it is provided.

   D. A rundown of events commemorated by a modern holiday is given, followed by a more detailed explanation of why the events occurred.

   E. An ongoing controversy is presented and then the history behind the controversy is explained.

Questions 27 and 28 are based on the following passage:

The author Bill Bryson attempts to explain Einstein's famous equation ($E = mc^2$) by saying that mass and energy have equivalence, or, that "energy is liberated matter, and matter is energy (5) waiting to happen." C^2 refers to the speed of light squared—a "truly huge number." This means that there is an enormous amount of energy in every material thing.

Among other things, Einstein's theory (10) explains how a star could burn for billions of years and not use up its fuel. It also explains how radiation works; a small lump of uranium can throw out streams of energy "without melting away like an ice cube." The most energetic thing (15) we have produced so far is a uranium bomb, and it releases 1% of the energy it would if we could successfully "liberate" it.

27. The main purpose of the passage is to

A. explain the science behind and destructive potential of the uranium bomb.

B. provide the reader with a basic understanding of Einstein's famous equation.

C. emphasize Einstein's pivotal role in the history of physics.

D. present the background for one possible explanation of how stars can burn for billions of years.

E. discuss the mysteries of the relationship of mass and energy.

28. According to the passage, the c^2 in Einstein's equation represents the

A. speed of energy squared.

B. relationship between energy and radiation.

C. necessary amount of energy for the production of radiation.

D. speed at which matter is converted into energy.

E. amount of energy per unit of mass in all material things.

Question 29 is based on the following passage.

Locomotor skills are basic movement skills that are performed in different directions and at different speeds. They are dynamic movements that propel the body upward, forward, or (5) backward. These movements are the foundation of gross motor coordination, involving large and small muscle movements. There are many different combinations of movement patterns that can describe the type of locomotor skills.

29. The author suggests that which of the following would require the use of locomotor skills?

Select **all** that apply:

A. A Frisbee player jumping to catch an overthrown pass

B. A farmer slapping a fly off of his arm

C. A teacher slowly walking down a hallway while reading a paper

Questions 30–32 are based on the following passage.

The evolution of the various forms of life from a given biochemical mass must not be considered a linear progression. Rather, the fossil record (5) suggests an analogy between evolution and a bush whose branches go every which way. Like branches, some evolutionary lines simply end, while others branch again. Many biologists believe the pattern of evolution had the following course: Bacteria (10) emerged first and from them branched viruses, red algae, blue-green algae, and green flagellates. From the latter branched green algae, from which higher plants evolved, as well as colorless rhizoflagellates, from which diatoms, molds, sponges, and protozoa (15) evolved. From ciliated protozoa (ciliophora) evolved multinucleate (syncytial) flatworms. These branched into five lines, one of which leads to the echinoderms and chordates. The remaining lines (20) lead to most of the other phyla of the animal kingdom.

30. The reference to a bush serves to

A. show how microscopic bacteria can eventually evolve into something entirely different.

B. create an analogy between its branches and the constantly improving nature of evolution.

C. provide a visual representation of the linear evolutionary paths of a particular species.

D. illustrate the unpredictability and finiteness of many evolutionary lines.

E. preface a discussion of botanical evolution with the current form of the species.

31. According to the passage, it can be inferred that which of the following life forms have branched off first in the evolutionary process?

A. Green algae
B. Blue-green algae
C. Molds
D. Flatworms
E. Ciliated protozoa

32. According to the passage, the evolutionary line of sponges in its proper order is

A. bacteria → viruses → green algae → sponges

B. bacteria → viruses → rhizoflagellates → sponges

C. bacteria → red algae → blue-green algae → rhizoflagellates → sponges

D. bacteria → blue-green algae → green flagellates → rhizoflagellates → sponges

E. bacteria → green flagellates → rhizoflagellates → sponges

Answers and Explanations

1. **B.** The paragraph mentions that monarchs only migrate once per year and do not live longer than 90 days. Therefore, each monarch is alive only for a maximum of one migration. Choice B is correct. All other choices are consistent with information in the passage.

2. **A.** The majority of the passage discusses environmental and nonhereditary influences on the development of intelligence, and while the first sentence (*Contrary to…*) does discuss the multidimensionality of intelligence, its phrasing emphasizes the nonhereditary side. Choice A is correct. Choices B and C are secondary points, and choice D is not mentioned. Choice E is incorrect because no examples of hereditary factors in intelligence are presented.

3. **E.** The main point of the paragraph is expressed in the second sentence: …*when you experience two items contiguously in the same place or at the same time or both, they become linked in your mind.* This idea is strengthened by the example of refugees still carrying with them the association of loud noises to bombings, choice E. Choices A, C, and D are irrelevant to the author's point, while choice B points to an instinctive reaction, rather than an example, of a specific association with something that once occurred.

4. **C.** Choice C is correct; the passage describes the invention of the first printing press and explains why it was one of the *most revolutionary inventions known in human history*. Choice A incorrectly frames the passage within the context of Johannes Gutenberg's achievements, while choices B, D, and E describe secondary purposes of the passage.

5. **B.** To answer this question, you must identify the answer that is not presented as having *improved* by the invention of the printing press. Choices A, D, and E are all presented as improvements in the final sentence of the passage, as is choice C, albeit more subtly (the *diffusion of knowledge*). Choice B is the correct answer; the passage only claims the invention had a *profound and immediate impact on the political…structure of Europe,* but it does not assert a positive change in the amount of political oppression.

6. **C.** Choices A, B, D, and E might seem like possible answers, but not enough detail and focus is given to any of them in the passage to make any of them a main point. The history and early origins of meteorology are only secondary discussion points (choice A); there is no discussion of general discord between scientists and inventors (choice B); the mechanics of thermometers are discussed only in one sentence (choice D); and the passage spends too much time on the origins of the two temperature scales for its primary purpose to merely compare and contrast the two (choice E). Choice C is the correct answer, as the entire passage serves to educate the reader on the origins of the two competing temperature scales.

7. **B.** The author notes that *both the Fahrenheit and Celsius scales are used today, confusing many people who simply want to know how cold or warm the weather is going to be*. This claim, combined with the lack of arguments presented in favor of maintaining two systems, makes choice B the best answer. Choice A is incorrect because the author makes no judgment, despite mentioning that others have questioned Fahrenheit's designations. There is no evidence in the passage that Celsius questioned Fahrenheit's measurement methods, as in choice C, even though he chose a different freezing point. Choice D is incorrect because the author does not claim that the use of the two methods can cause *serious* problems or should be eliminated, merely that it can be confusing. Choice E is not addressed in the passage.

8. **A.** The author seems to focus equally on the contrast between Dickinson's ordinary life and her talent (as put forth by choice A), and the lack of widespread acclaim for her work until after her death. Choice B may seem like a viable answer, but it is phrased in a way that contradicts the author's assertion that *people knew she could write verse;* in addition, the word *inability* ignores the fact that she did not attempt to publish many of her poems. Choices C and D are minor secondary points, and choice E is not addressed. Choice A is the best answer.

9. **E.** The reference is made to create an analogy between Cinderella's transformation into a princess and Dickinson's transformation into a cultural icon after her death, which makes choice E the correct answer. Choice A is incorrect, as Dickinson never experienced riches in her lifetime. Choice B is incorrect in that it characterizes the passage in an overly negative fashion. Choice C is incorrect because Dickinson's poetry did not change her life. Choice D is incorrect because the author does not focus on women succeeding outside of the social hierarchy.

10. **C.** The author focuses on the economy of Emily Dickinson's poems, and the painstaking processes she underwent to ensure that she got the most out of every word; choice C best fits this characterization. Choice A reiterates the skills mentioned by the author before Dickinson's most impressive trait is introduced. Choice B is not mentioned in the passage. Choice D provides the method by which Dickinson achieves her greatest quality, but it is not merely her work ethic that impresses the author. Choice E may appear to be viable, but it ignores the economy of Dickinson's prose and erroneously focuses only on descriptive words.

11. **D.** The first passage discusses the historical context of Emily Dickinson and her work; while the second gives insight into the processes by which she produced her great works, as posited by choice D, the correct answer. Choice A is incorrect, because the first passage does not present criticisms. Choice B is an inaccurate description of the arguments in both passages and how they relate to each other. Choice C incorrectly characterizes the presentation of Dickinson in Passage 1 as *simple* (while also ignoring the complementary portions), and choice E gets the order backward.

12. A. To resolve the paradox, look for an incentive for a young male bird to assist in the mating dance. Being the lead bird in a mating dance significantly increases the likelihood that the courtship will lead to mating. Therefore, an incentive could be that assisting in the dance increases a young male bird's likelihood of finding his own assistant when the time comes, choice A. Rule out choice B, as the presence of a second female would be irrelevant to the presence of a second, younger male and would not help resolve the paradox. Choice C is incorrect because being more likely to die of hunger would be a disincentive to being an assistant rather than an incentive. Choice D is incorrect because the greater strength and agility of a bird before becoming an assistant would not help to explain why it becomes an assistant. Eliminate choice E because the health and livelihood of the dancing bird's future offspring provides no incentive for the unrelated, younger bird to participate.

13. D. The first half of the passage is devoted to defining the concept of the conditioned response, while the second half emphasizes the importance of these responses in communication and everyday life. Therefore, choice D is correct. The discussion of communication with non-English speakers is merely an example to underscore this main point, which makes answer choices B, C, and E incorrect. The discussion of symbols in everyday life is prominent in the second paragraph but completely absent from the first paragraph, which makes choice A incorrect. The primary purpose of the passage should be discussed in most, if not all, of the paragraphs in the passage.

14. D. An unconditioned response is not learned and is unaffected by previous knowledge, experiences, or expectations. Recoiling from unexpected pain is an example. Thus, the correct answer is choice D. The other behaviors are conditioned responses. The businessman (choice A) has been conditioned to reach for his cell phone upon feeling a vibration; the workers (choice B) have been conditioned to stop work when the whistle blows; the child (choice C) has been conditioned through negative reinforcement to react negatively to poor grades; and the college student (choice E) has been conditioned to press a button to stop an unwanted noise.

15. B. The bell elicits the child's response, just as the buzzer elicits the eye's response in the example in the passage. That is, after many days of associating the bell with lunch, the child has been "conditioned" to feel hungry when the bell rings. Therefore, the child is responding to a conditioned stimulus. Thus, choice B is correct. Choices C and E are incorrect because one cannot respond to a response. Choice D is incorrect because the stimulus is conditioned, not unconditioned. Choice A is not mentioned in the passage and contradicts the passage's logic.

16. B. The passage suggests that complementary responses to common symbols are crucial in communication, even when there is no common language. Thus, choice B is correct. It does not imply that communication is hopeless, as choice A suggests, and if anything, it implies the opposite of choice C (calling a raised voice irrational). Choice D is incorrect because the passage implies that differences in complementary responses to symbols may prevent complete communication, even with shared vocabulary. Choice E is not mentioned in the passage.

17. A. Although the research focused on marine bacteria that glow, its broader significance is that it shows the chemical communication between bacteria. Thus, the correct answer is choice A. Choice B is the observation that led to the breakthrough theory, but it is not the most important finding of their research. Choice C is inaccurate; an autoinducer does not code genes; it induces their expression. The molecular messenger that causes bacteria to glow is not the enzyme luciferase, so choice D is incorrect. Choice E is incorrect because while the autoinducer allows the expression of the light-producing enzymes such as luciferase, it does not produce light itself.

18. B. Notice that you must search for specific details in the passage to find the correct answer. Choice A is incorrect because the enzyme luciferase, not the autoinducer, catalyzes the reactions that cause light (lines 9–11). Choice C is incorrect because, while the autoinducer acts as a messenger between bacteria cells (lines 14–15), it does not communicate messages between the brain and bacteria. Choice D is incorrect because the autoinducer stimulates the expression of genes but does not encode them. Choice E is incorrect because the autoinducer itself does not glow. Choice B is the correct answer and is supported by the following section of the passage (lines 15–20): … *the messenger, called an autoinducer, induced expression of the genes for luciferase and other proteins involved in light production. That is, the autoinducer stimulated synthesis of the encoded proteins, causing the bacteria to glow.*

19. D. The first two paragraphs describe the details of a scientific breakthrough, and the third paragraph places this breakthrough in a historical context that shows its growing acceptance and importance in modern society, as summarized by choice D, the correct answer. Choices A and E describe secondary purposes of the third paragraph but are not the best answers when considered within the context of the entire passage. Choice B incorrectly characterizes the paragraph as supporting evidence for the theory rather than information on its implementation and reception over time. Choice C is incorrect because the author is describing a theory and breakthrough rather than making an argument.

20. D. Choice A is not implied in the passage, and choices B, C, and E identify supporting details rather than the main purpose, which is expressed in the opening phrase of the passage and implied in choice D. Thus, the importance of gubernatorial experience for prospective presidents (choice E), Wilson's New Freedom plan (choice C), and the differences among the candidates (choice B) may be individual factors in Wilson's career; however, tracing major developments of his career (choice D) most clearly clarifies the passage's main purpose.

21. B. In the first paragraph, Wilson's decision to champion the progressive cause after 1912 is contrasted with his earlier career, when he seemed to be a conservative Democrat. Thus, you may conclude that the progressives, whom Wilson finally joined, were not conservative Democrats as Wilson was earlier in his career. Choices A and D contradict information in the paragraph, while choices C and E are not suggested by any information given in the passage.

22. A. The first sentence describes Wilson's ascension as *meteoric,* which supports the first portion of choice A. The author also describes how Wilson's 1913 Democratic nomination was made possible by changing from conservative to progressive over the span of several years, which supports the second portion of choice A. Choice B is incorrect because late-career failures are not discussed in the passage. Choice C is never implied and contradicts the opposition from New Jersey progressives described in the first paragraph. Choice D is incorrect because the League of Nations is never discussed. Choice E is incorrect because Roosevelt and Taft are described as Wilson's competition for the presidency.

23. A. Major federal interventions were a feature of Roosevelt's New Nationalism, but according to the passage, Roosevelt accepted trusts rather than sought to weaken them and was not pro-business; this eliminates answer choice B. Choices C, D, and E are incorrect because they instead refer to features of Wilson's New Freedom plan, which did not call for major federal interventions.

24. D. Choices A, B, and C contain information that the passage does not address. You may eliminate them as irrelevant. Choice E contradicts the fact that Wilson was a Democratic candidate. The discussion of Taft and Roosevelt as the candidates who finally ran against Wilson for the presidency supports choice D. The passage states that Wilson *emerged as a middle-of-the-road candidate between [Taft and Roosevelt],* which implies that they were the three primary candidates in the election.

25. A and B. The list is already organized by population, so San Jose, choice C, can be eliminated. Chicago has the third-smallest area on the list, so choice A is correct. New York has the fourth-smallest area on the list, which still puts it in the bottom half of the cities, so choice B is also correct.

26. C. The author describes a misconception about the meaning of Cinco de Mayo, and then provides the true background for the holiday, as put forth by the correct answer, choice C. Choice A erroneously ignores Cinco de Mayo, while choice B is incorrect because no argument is presented. Choice D is incorrect because it ignores the correction of the misconception. Choice E is incorrect in its reference to an *ongoing controversy.*

27. B. The first sentence of the passage provides a statement of its purpose; the rest of the first paragraph defines the equation, while the second paragraph provides examples of its application, which shows that the passage gives the reader a basic understanding of Einstein's famous equation. Therefore, choice B is the correct answer. Choices A, C, and D are secondary points. Choice E is incorrect due to its use of the word *mysteries,* as the passage focuses on what is already known about the relationship between mass and energy.

28. E. According to the explanation of the equation, c^2 represents the amount of energy contained in each unit of mass in any matter, as put forth by choice E. Choice A confuses the *speed of energy* with the *speed of light,* while choices B, C, and D are not suggested by the passage.

29. A and C. The author describes locomotor skills as *dynamic movements that propel the body upward, forward, or backward.* Choice A is correct, as the player propels upward to catch an overthrown pass. Choice C is also correct; the qualifier *at different speeds* in the passage indicates that walking slowly still requires the use of locomotor skills. Choice B, however, is incorrect, as slapping one's arm does not fit the criteria described for locomotor skills.

30. D. The author makes the bush analogy to represent how evolutionary lines *go every which way* and sometimes *simply end,* rather than continue in a linear progression; the correct choice is D. Choices A and E mistakenly connect the analogy to the later discussion of early evolutionary patterns, while choice B misses the point of the analogy. Choice C's reference to the *linear* nature of evolution contradicts the main point of the passage and analogy.

31. B. Of the answer choices, blue-green algae are the earliest step on the evolutionary ladder, as we can see from the following section of the passage: *Bacteria emerged first and from them branched viruses, red algae, blue-green algae* (choice B), *and green flagellates. From the latter branched green algae* (choice A), *from which higher plants evolved, and colorless rhizoflagellates, from which diatoms, molds* (choice C), *sponges, and protozoa evolved. From ciliated protozoa (ciliophora)*—choice E—*evolved multinucleate (syncytial) flatworms* (choice D).

32. E. The passage presents sponges as evolving from rhizoflagellates, which came from green flagellates, which came from bacteria. Thus, choice E is correct. Choices A, B, C, and D all show a different evolutionary pattern and, therefore, are incorrect.

The Core Writing Test examines your ability to apply the rules of standard written English as you write clear, coherent essays and answer selected response questions. This chapter will walk you through the fundamental concepts and strategies that are important to advance your essay writing skills. Chapter 3 will identify selected response question types and present strategies and practice exercises that will assist you in reading; evaluating, identifying, and revising errors in grammar and sentence structure; and research skills.

Overview of the Essay Writing Section

The essay writing section (also called "text production") of the Core Writing Test evaluates your ability to compose two original essays on assigned topics. One essay is described as "argumentative" and the other as "informative/explanatory" (or "source-based"). Some organizational ideas apply to both types of essays, but some composition strategies may be different for each essay type. The argumentative task asks you to take a stand on a topic and provide support for your opinion. The informative/explanatory task asks you to analyze two passages and write your response by incorporating facts, quotes, and citations from the two sources. Our study guide will lead you through the process of developing your ideas to produce effective essays and will help you learn skills that will improve your score for each type of essay. If you feel a little uneasy about this section, remember that you have already written many essays, reports, assignments, and research papers for your college classes. Reviewing and practicing the writing guidelines presented in this chapter will give you an additional edge on the test.

The following table presents an overview of the Writing Test.

Content Category	Approximate Percent of the Writing Test Score	Approximate Number of Questions	Time	Question Type
Text Types, Purposes, and Production	60% (includes score for revision-in-context questions)	1 essay 1 essay	30 minutes 30 minutes	Chapter 2 Writing Argumentative Essays Writing Informative/ Explanatory Texts
		6–12 selected response questions	40 minutes (includes test time for revision-in-context questions)	Chapter 3 Revision-in-Context
Language and Research Skills for Writing	40%	28–34 selected response questions		Chapter 3 Language Skills 　Usage 　Sentence Correction Research Skills
Total Questions and Testing Time		2 essays 40 selected response questions	100 minutes (1 hr. 40 min.)	

Skills and Concepts Tested

The essay portion of the Writing Test consists of two tasks: writing an argumentative essay and writing an informative/explanatory essay.

To achieve a top score, your response should

- present a clear thesis statement on the topic and stay focused on the main topic throughout the essay.
- be organized and develop your topic into a logical sequence of ideas.
- use smooth transitions that flow from idea to idea and from one paragraph to another paragraph.
- provide supporting examples and relevant evidence, details, and reasons.
- respond to *all parts* of the essay question.
- use the correct mechanics of writing—including spelling, sentence structure, punctuation, and word choice.
- use a variety of sentence types.

In addition, the informative/explanatory (source-based) essay response should

- identify and explain the issues related to both sources.
- provide supporting connections between both sources.
- cite both sources appropriately when using quotes or paraphrasing.

Directions

Each essay is intended to give you an opportunity to demonstrate your writing skills. Be sure to express your ideas on each topic clearly and effectively. The quality of your writing is much more important than the quantity, but to cover the topic adequately, plan to write three to five paragraphs for each essay. Be specific and provide relevant examples that are related to the topic.

Each essay topic will be presented in a short paragraph at the top of your computer screen. The on-screen clock prompt will inform you how much time you have remaining on the test. You have 30 minutes to read, plan, and write on each assigned topic. *Do not write on another topic* because an essay on another topic will not be considered. If your essay is not written in English, it will not be scored.

Computer Word Processor

The essay prompt will appear in a box at the top of the screen and remain there as you prepare, compose, and edit your essay in a separate box below. Although you can take notes to plan your essay, you must type your essay response on a computer keyboard that is connected to a very simple word processing software program. The word processor includes basic functions: cut, copy, paste, undo, and redo. You can use either a computer mouse or a keyboard to perform these functions. Remember that this basic word processor does *not* include a spell-check or grammar tool, but minor errors will not affect your score.

Scoring

Each section of the Writing Test will be scored individually and combined: (1) essays, (2) selected response, and (3) a total score for these two combined sections.

Two constructed response essays combined with revision-in-context selected response questions count for 60 percent of your overall Writing Test score (essays are approximately 50 percent, and revision-in-context questions are approximately 10 percent). Since the essays count for approximately 50 percent of your Writing Test score, it is important that you take time to review this chapter to get your best possible score. Each essay is scored independently by two different education professionals or a computerized e-reader using a scale of 1 (lowest score) to 6 (highest score).

Due to the limited time that is allotted for you to write your essays (30 minutes each), readers take into consideration that even the highest-scoring essay may contain minor errors of grammar or word mechanics. Essays are expected to be superior in content, organization, and development, but they are scored *holistically*. This means that the readers consider the overall quality of the work. Readers keep in mind that your essays are technically considered a "first draft" and will probably not be errorless, even with a score of 6.

Scoring Guidelines

In general, readers use the following questions as guidelines for computing each essay writing score:

- ❏ **Does the essay stay focused on the assigned topic?** The main topic is the foundation for your essay. Because time management is critical, the hurried test-taker will frequently read the topic and merely scan the assignment. However, answering each part of the assignment is crucial to receiving a high score. Too often test-takers neglect to complete all parts of the assignment, and their scores are adversely affected as a result. To help you stay focused, write down key words and phrases as you develop your ideas. Refer to your list of key words as often as necessary.

- ❏ **Is the essay organized and does it demonstrate a logical flow of ideas?** Essays written under time constraints may contain minor errors, but your essay must be organized. Start with a strong *opening paragraph* (use the generalize-focus-preview strategy described on page 50), a well-developed *body* that includes specific examples, and an effective *conclusion* that completes your response. Remember that you must demonstrate a logical sequence of events from one idea to another in order to receive credit in this category. Transitions from one thought, phrase, or sentence should be smooth and easy to read.

- ❏ **Does the essay contain supporting examples?** Your thesis topic or position must be supported by examples, reasons, evidence, and specific details. Each general statement must be backed up with supporting details and information. In addition, when writing an *informative/explanatory* essay, you must incorporate well-developed examples taken from *both* passages. Remember to cite quotes and paraphrasing from each passage.

- ❏ **Does the essay contain ideas that are well developed?** Your ideas in each paragraph must connect to the main thesis topic and your main position. Some test-takers lose credit because they scatter short, fragmented ideas throughout their essay. When you prepare to write, use the pre-writing strategies described on pages 47–49 to help you develop your ideas. Using the techniques of *brainstorming, graphic organizers,* and *outlining* will help you to break down the main topic into subtopics. You can then individually develop your ideas about a few subtopics while remembering to relate your ideas back to your main thesis topic.

- ❏ **Is the essay coherent?** Essays should be clear, concise, and consistent. Inconsistent writing will receive a lower score.

- ❏ **Does the essay demonstrate the correct use of English mechanics and language?** Essays must follow the rules of standard written English and show a proficiency in the use of language skills. Even though minor errors are allowed, frequent technical mistakes will lower your score. It is important to use appropriate vocabulary, punctuation, and grammar.

Scoring Rubric

The following chart contains the scoring rubrics used by the readers for argumentative and informative/explanatory essays. The scoring criteria may appear similar, but there are differences in the two types of essays. The differences are delineated by an asterisk (*).

	Argumentative Essay	Informative/Explanatory Essay (Source-Based)
SCORE 6	**Score 6 is a well-organized analysis with few errors, and** *Presents a clear thesis statement that responds directly to the task. *Clearly explains key points and ideas. *Provides exemplary evidence, reasons, examples, and specific details to support the position. Develops ideas in a logical and organized sequence. Uses well-chosen transitions to connect ideas. Uses well-chosen and varied vocabulary for an audience of educated adults. Uses sentence variety. Demonstrates a command of the correct usage of the conventions of standard written English.	**Score 6 shows a high degree of competence with few errors, and** *Identifies effective and insightful aspects of the task. *Synthesizes important aspects of the two sources with well-chosen reasons, examples, and specific details to support analysis. *Uses both sources and cites appropriately when paraphrasing or quoting. Develops multiple ideas logically and coherently. Uses well-chosen and varied vocabulary for an audience of educated adults. Uses variety in sentence openings, lengths, and structure. Demonstrates a command of the correct usage of the conventions of standard written English.
SCORE 5	**Score 5 is thoughtful and fairly well organized with minor errors, and** *Presents a clear thesis statement that responds directly to the task. *Explains aspects of the key points and ideas. *Provides evidence, reasons, examples, and specific details to support the position. Presents organized ideas and connects them with clear transitions. Uses appropriate and varied vocabulary for an audience of educated adults. Uses some variety of sentence openings, lengths, and structure. Demonstrates general knowledge of the correct usage of the conventions of standard written English.	**Score 5 is thoughtful and well developed with occasional minor errors, and** *Identifies all aspects of the task. *Links adequate features of both sources with appropriate supporting reasons, examples, and specific details to support analysis. *Uses both sources and cites appropriately when paraphrasing or quoting. Organizes ideas logically and coherently. Uses appropriate and varied vocabulary for an audience of educated adults. Uses a variety of sentence openings, lengths, and structure. Demonstrates general knowledge of the correct usage of the conventions of standard written English.

continued

	Argumentative Essay	Informative/Explanatory Essay (Source-Based)
SCORE 4	**Score 4 shows adequate competency with occasional errors, and** *States or implies a reasonably developed thesis statement that shows the context of the writer's position. *Responds to most key points and ideas. *Provides satisfactory evidence, reasons, examples, and details to support the position. Presents adequate sequencing and organization, although connecting ideas may be simple. Uses adequate language and sufficient sentence variety for an audience of educated adults. Demonstrates general control of the correct usage of the conventions of standard written English, but has occasional errors in grammar, spelling, and sentence structure.	**Score 4 demonstrates adequate competency with occasional errors, and** *Identifies some relevant aspects of the task, but may address some unrelated points. *Provides some connections between both sources with adequate supporting reasons, examples, and specific details to support analysis. *Uses both sources and cites sources when paraphrasing or quoting. Demonstrates adequate organization and a logical flow of ideas. Uses adequate word choices and some sentence variety for an audience of educated adults. Demonstrates general control of the correct usage of the conventions of standard written English, but has occasional errors in grammar, spelling, and sentence structure.
SCORE 3	**Score 3 expresses some competency, but has frequent errors, and** *Provides limited development of a thesis statement in the context of the writer's position. *Provides limited references to the main key points and ideas. *Provides insufficient evidence, reasons, examples, and details to support the position. Presents limited organization, development, and connecting ideas. Demonstrates errors in language usage, word choice, grammar, spelling, and sentence structure. Demonstrates minimal control of the correct usage of the conventions of standard written English.	**Score 3 expresses some competency, but has frequent errors, and** *Provides marginal knowledge of the task and addresses unrelated points. *Identifies only one source, or provides weak supporting evidence when analyzing the two sources. *Cites some sources when paraphrasing or quoting. Demonstrates inadequate organization and connecting ideas. Demonstrates errors in language usage, word choice, grammar, spelling, and sentence structure. Demonstrates minimal control of the correct usage of the conventions of standard written English.

continued

	Argumentative Essay	Informative/Explanatory Essay (Source-Based)
SCORE 2	**Score 2 demonstrates weaknesses in argumentative writing, and** *Fails to identify a clear thesis statement or position. *Provides little or no references to the main key points. *Provides inadequate evidence, reasons, examples, and details to support the position. Organizes ideas illogically. Demonstrates serious errors in language usage, word choice, grammar, spelling, and sentence structure. Demonstrates no control of the correct usage of the conventions of standard written English.	**Score 2 demonstrates inadequate competency in source-based writing, and** *Fails to identify aspects of the assigned task, or may instead provide the writer's own opinion regarding an unrelated topic. *Provides weak links between the two sources, and few or no supporting analysis, reasons, examples, and details. *Neglects to cite sources when paraphrasing or quoting. Presents illogical organization and connecting idea development. Demonstrates serious errors in language usage, word choice, grammar, spelling, and sentence structure. Demonstrates no control of the correct usage of the conventions of standard written English.
SCORE 1	**Score 1 reveals fundamental deficiencies in argumentative writing, and** *Shows no understanding of the argument. Provides short or disorganized ideas. *Provides incoherent or off-topic supporting evidence. Contains language that is incoherent or difficult to understand. Makes serious, frequent errors in word choice, grammar, spelling, and sentence structure.	**Score 1 demonstrates fundamental writing deficiencies in source-based writing, and** *Demonstrates little or no understanding of the assigned task. *Provides short or disorganized links between both sources. *Fails to cite sources when paraphrasing or quoting. Contains unintelligible language that is difficult to understand. Makes serious, frequent errors in the conventions of standard written English.

Now that we have covered the scoring for both types of essays, review the general strategies for both types of essays: argumentative or informative/explanatory.

General Strategies

- **Write notes on the scratch paper provided.** You have 30 minutes to plan and write an essay on one assigned topic. Use the scratch paper or writing board provided for writing notes to help you organize your thoughts. (These notes will not be read or scored by the people scoring your essay.)

- **Paraphrase the topic.** Some assignments can be confusing. It is helpful to put the topic in your own words. (Write this down on your scratch paper or writing board.)

- **Use your time wisely.** Take about 5 minutes to pre-write and organize your thoughts. Take about 20 minutes to write your essay and about 5 minutes to proofread your essay. *Note:* For the informative/explanatory essay (source-based), take 10 minutes to read the two sources and organize your thoughts. Five minutes is not enough time to digest, paraphrase, cite, and respond to the important aspects of the task. Then take about 15 minutes to write your essay and about 5 minutes to proofread your essay.

- **Write three to five paragraphs.** The general instructions include the sentence that suggests that "you may want to write more than one paragraph." This remark is a polite way of saying that if you expect to score well, you *had better* write more than one paragraph. Very short essays usually receive very low scores. Aim for a minimum of three paragraphs.

- **Be specific.** Your readers are looking for specific details—concrete evidence of some kind to support your points.

Specific Strategies

Now let's examine specific approaches to help you organize a timed essay. The following three-step writing process is an effective method to plan and compose a well-written essay:

1. Pre-writing: brainstorming, using graphic organizers, using outlines
2. Writing: using the five-paragraph model or four-paragraph model
3. Proofreading: reviewing your work

While both argumentative and informative/explanatory essays follow similar organizational steps outlined in the three-step writing process on page 46, some of the composition strategies may be different for each essay. For both essays, readers are looking at your ability to express ideas clearly and use the conventions of standard written English, but you are also expected to respond to specific directions for each task. One of the biggest mistakes a test-taker can make is beginning to write an essay without following the directions related to each specific task. To avoid this mistake, refer to the flowchart on page 46 for strategic guidelines before you review the three-step writing process.

A Strategic Plan of Attack

Read the topic TWICE and note the directions, topic prompt, and passage (sources).

ARGUMENTATIVE ESSAY

Argumentative writing is *biased*. The essay synthesizes your position and sound reasoning related to the topic. When planning an argumentative essay, think about *your opinion* related to the topic prompt.

INFORMATIVE/EXPLANATORY ESSAY

Informative/explanatory writing is *unbiased*. The essay draws from evidence that is extracted from the two sources. When planning an informative/explanatory essay, think about *evaluating and citing specific facts* related to the two sources.

PRE-WRITE. Use a "cluster" graphic organizer (pages 47–48) to structure your ideas after you formulate a position on the topic (i.e., do you agree or disagree with the author of the passage?).

PRE-WRITE. Organize your ideas using a Venn diagram (pages 48–49) to compare and contrast elements from the two sources.

WRITE THE ESSAY. Follow the five-paragraph model (pages 50–51).

Stay on topic and create a logical flow. Support your position with specific examples, reasons, and evidence. Draw from your personal observations, readings, or experiences.

WRITE THE ESSAY. Follow the four-paragraph model (page 51).

Stay on topic, support your analysis, and create a logical flow. Remember to cite quotes and paraphrase from *both* sources. Draw from reasons, examples, facts, and details. Link information from both sources in the concluding paragraph.

PROOFREAD AND EDIT. Leave yourself some time to correct errors and make minor changes.

The Three-Step Writing Process

For any timed writing task, you should take three steps leading to the finished product: *pre-writing, writing,* and *proofreading*. If you are able to practice the stages of the writing process, you will gain control over any writing assignment. Envision these three steps leading to the finished product.

STEP 1	STEP 2	STEP 3
Pre-writing	Writing	Proofreading
Time: 5 minutes	Time: 20 minutes	Time: 5 minutes

Note: For the informative/explanatory essay (source-based), take 10 minutes to read the two sources and organize your thoughts. Five minutes is not enough time to digest, paraphrase, cite, and respond to the important aspects of the task.

Step 1: Pre-Writing

Many students believe that good writers just sit down and miraculously produce an essay. On the contrary, most experienced writers know that effective writing requires *pre-writing,* an organization and planning process. The pre-writing process helps you gather information and ideas as you prepare to write your essay.

Before you begin pre-writing, read the topic and the assignment very carefully. On scratch paper or the writing board, write down key words to help you focus on the assigned task. Reread the assignment. If there are several tasks given, number them and write them down. Let the nature of the assignment determine the structure of your essay.

Developing and organizing information on short notice can be difficult unless you are prepared with an effective technique. Organize your thoughts before writing your essay by using one of the following basic pre-writing techniques: brainstorming, using graphic organizers, or outlining.

Brainstorming

The technique of creating and accumulating ideas and examples is called *brainstorming.* Brainstorming is an exploration process that allows you to imagine and generate ideas about your topic. Your "imaginings" will help you to compile words and phrases about the essay topic by simply jotting down as many thoughts, ideas, and possibilities as you can remember, invent, or otherwise bring to mind to address the topic. It is important to remember that *all ideas are acceptable* during the brainstorming process and that neatness, order, and spelling do not matter at this stage.

After generating as many ideas or examples as you can within a couple of minutes, evaluate and organize your notes by looking for patterns or themes so you can group your ideas into categories. Remember that development relies on specific facts and/or examples. Decide which examples best support your main points. Cross out those you do not wish to use and number those remaining in the order in which you will want to address them in your essay. Add any notes regarding more specific details or new thoughts that come to mind. However, do not worry about developing everything because you will be the only one using these notes. Your time will be better spent developing these points in the actual writing of your essay and not in your notes.

Remember, too, that you can change the order of your main points later. In the brainstorming stage, it is important to just consider each idea and how it might support the central purpose of your essay.

Using Graphic Organizers

Using graphic organizers is a technique well suited to the timed essay. After reading the topic prompt, use this technique as a way of organizing visual representations of your thoughts, ideas, and words before you write.

Tip: For your argumentative essay, use clustering. For your informative/explanatory essay, use a Venn diagram.

Clustering

One type of graphic organization is called *clustering.* Clustering can help you visualize subtopics related to your main thesis topic. It begins with a key word related to the topic. Ideas are then clustered around the key word and numbered in the order you will present them in your essay. The connecting ideas in the new clusters are thoughts that will be written in supporting sentences. They will reveal an important relationship with the original core idea. You do not have to use all the ideas in each cluster; simply cross out any you decide not to use.

For a few moments, think of all the elements of that side of the issue and connect them to the central topic cluster. You can then number the parts of the cluster to give an order to your thoughts. You don't have to use all the elements of your graphic organizer.

Example:

After you choose a topic, write it down on your scratch paper or writing board and draw a circle around it. The example below focuses on an argumentative essay.

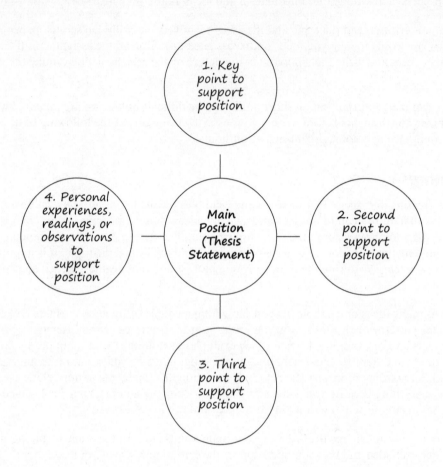

Venn Diagram

Another type of graphic organizer is called a *Venn diagram*. Venn diagrams are useful when you are presented with a task that requires you to distinguish between two viewpoints and their commonalities of the issues presented in the two passages. Creating a Venn diagram will help you clearly see the differences and similarities as they relate to the supporting facts, reasons, and examples in each passage.

Begin by drawing two overlapping circles. Write down key themes, phrases, or concepts related to Source 1 in the left circle. (*Note:* Remember to put quotation marks around any direct quotes to remind you to cite them in your essay.) Next, write down key themes, phrases, or concepts related to Source 2 in the right circle. If there are any interconnected considerations, write them down in the center space. When you are done, you may want to number these ideas in the order of importance.

The example below focuses on the informative/explanatory essay.

Example:

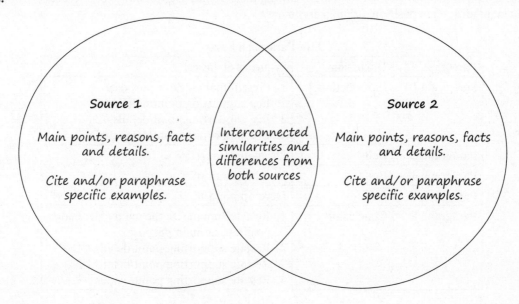

Source 1

Main points, reasons, facts and details.

Cite and/or paraphrase specific examples.

Interconnected similarities and differences from both sources

Source 2

Main points, reasons, facts and details.

Cite and/or paraphrase specific examples.

Outlining

Outlining is a traditional form of pre-writing. Some people are familiar with this type of organization and find the strategy useful. Your outline is meant to help you organize your thoughts in a pattern and can clearly arrange your main point and connect supporting points. Most test-takers do not have time to write an extensive outline, but it is provided here as an example of organizing your ideas. If you use the outline, keep it simple so you can save time to write your essay.

Example:

I.   Introduction
II. Body (discussion of first point)
III. Body (discussion of second point)
IV. Body (discussion of third point)
V.   Conclusion (summary)

Notice that this outline is informal, but the basic parts—*introduction, body*, and *conclusion*—help you to focus and organize your response. *Remember:* Spend about 5 minutes pre-writing and organizing your ideas before you start writing.

> **Reminder:** For the informative/explanatory essay (source-based), take 10 minutes to read the two sources and organize your thoughts. Five minutes is not enough time to digest, paraphrase, cite, and respond to the important aspects of the task.

Step 2: Writing the Essay

The actual writing step of the essay should take approximately 20 minutes of the total 30 minutes allowed. There are two writing models for the essays: the five-paragraph model and the four-paragraph model.

> **Reminder:** For your argumentative essay, use the five-paragraph model. For your informative/explanatory essay, use the four-paragraph model.

Five-Paragraph Model

The five-paragraph model format looks like the following table. Remember to always connect supporting points back to the main idea, main position, or main argument.

Five-Paragraph Essay

Paragraph	Discussion	Sequence of Ideas
Paragraph 1	Introduction	1. Present main idea or purpose. 2. List supporting point/details #1. 3. List supporting point/details #2. 4. List supporting point/details #3.
Paragraph 2	Body	Develop point #1.
Paragraph 3	Body	Develop point #2.
Paragraph 4	Body	Develop point #3.
Paragraph 5	Conclusion	1. Restate/summarize the main idea, main position, or main purpose. 2. Restate supporting point/details #1. 3. Restate supporting point/details #2. 4. Restate supporting point/details #3.

Paragraph 1: Introduction

The introduction invites the reader to read on. A strong opening paragraph tells the reader what to expect in the body of your essay. Try to avoid a long introduction; you'll want to keep it about the same length as your conclusion.

Organize your brainstorming ideas from general to specific. One easy-to-master, yet extremely effective, type of introduction is a GENERALIZE-FOCUS-PREVIEW structure. In this three- to four-sentence paragraph, the first sentence *generalizes* about the given topic, the second sentence *focuses* on what you have chosen to discuss, and the last one or two sentences *preview* the particulars you intend to present.

- **Generalize**—The first sentence provides a general overview of the assigned topic or question, establishing its importance.
- **Focus**—The second sentence focuses more specifically on the subject you have chosen to discuss and states your position.
- **Preview**—The last one or two sentences provide the specific points you will discuss and develop in your essay (in order).

Paragraphs 2, 3, and 4: Body

Next, the supporting examples or reasons (three are usually sufficient) should provide evidence for your point. Be realistic about how much time you have to write. The body should consist of three short paragraphs. Make sure that each paragraph consists of at least three sentences. Very short paragraphs may make your response appear insubstantial and scattered.

Writing the body of the response involves presenting specific details and examples that relate to the aspects you introduced in the first paragraph. You should spend more time on the body than on your introduction and conclusion, but keep the writing concise and to the point.

Each paragraph should begin with a unifying sentence and provide supporting evidence. Each paragraph elaborates and provides examples (or details) of the main points briefly mentioned in paragraph one.

Note: For your *argumentative* essay, provide specific examples from your readings, experiences, or observations. For your *informative/explanatory* essay, provide sources, facts, citations, and details from both sources to support your analysis.

Transitional Words

Another aspect of organizing the body is to provide transitions that guide the reader through your essay. Words and phrases like *first, initial,* and *a primary consideration* indicate the beginning of a chain of logic. Words and phrases like *another, also,* and *in addition* let the reader know you are continuing with the development of your reasoning. To show another point of view (for example, in a concession), words and phrases such as *although* and *however* help provide contrast.

Paragraph 5: Conclusion

While these short essays do not require an extensive conclusion, the words *finally* or *lastly* may be used to let the reader know that you are drawing your essay to a close. Having a lengthy conclusion is unnecessary, but a good conclusion will add a sense of continuity and structural integrity to your writing. You should refer to the ideas in your thesis sentence. Your conclusion should be about the same length as your introduction. As you prepare to write the conclusion, you should pay special attention to time. The conclusion can serve to

- summarize the main points from your introduction (in the same order).
- complete your response to the assigned question.
- clarify any points presented that may need further illumination.
- point toward the future.

Some Praxis essay readers comment that an essay can "start out strong but end up weak." Don't let this happen to you. Be sure to emphasize the importance of the topic in your final paragraph.

Four-Paragraph Model

The four-paragraph essay is an acceptable alternative to the five-paragraph essay and is particularly useful when responding to the informative/explanatory task that asks you to address an issue by comparing important concerns from two different sources ("compare and contrast," "cause and effect," or "pro and con").

Follow the format below when writing a four-paragraph essay for informative/explanatory essays. Notice that you will write about divergent ideas in paragraphs two and three.

Paragraph 1: introduction

Paragraph 2: body (source 1 position on topic/issue)

Paragraph 3: body (source 2 position on topic/issue)

Paragraph 4: conclusion (link both sources)

Remember that you must allow enough time to prepare and write your conclusion and that you should leave at least 3 to 5 minutes at the end to proofread your essay.

Step 3: Proofreading

Always allow a few minutes to proofread your essay for errors in grammar, usage, and spelling. If you detect an error, carefully replace or insert the correction. Pay special attention to words you have left out. Watch the clock on the computer screen! Once the 30 minutes is up, you will be unable to make any more changes.

Sample Argumentative Essay

Now let's try out the strategies and tips given in this chapter. This section will cover a sample argumentative essay. The next section will cover a sample informative/explanatory essay.

Your task is to clearly define your position based on readings, experiences, and observations and then provide examples to explain your viewpoint. There is no "right" or "wrong" viewpoint. The readers are looking for how well you address the main points in the passage and how well you support your response with examples.

Sample Topic: Argumentative Essay

Directions: You will have 30 minutes to plan and write an argumentative essay on the topic specified. You will probably find it best to spend time considering the topic and organizing your thoughts before you begin writing. Do not write on a topic other than the one specified. The essay should be based on your readings, experiences, or observations. You must write on the specified topic. An essay on another topic will not be accepted.

The essay is intended to give you an opportunity to demonstrate your writing skills. Be sure to express your ideas clearly and effectively. The quality of your writing is much more important than the quantity, but to cover the topic adequately, you will likely want to write more than one paragraph. Be specific and provide relevant examples that are related to the topic.

Read the opinion stated below.

"The U.S. Department of Agriculture has issued new proposals to ban high-calorie, high-salt drinks and snack foods available in the nation's school vending machines and cafeterias. Providing nutritious, healthy options with less fat and sugar throughout school cafeterias and vending machines will benefit our kids."

Assignment: Discuss the extent to which you agree or disagree with this point of view. Support your position with specific reasons and examples from your own experiences, observations, or readings.

Step 1: Pre-Writing

After you choose a topic, pre-write by taking a few minutes to write simple notes or draw a cluster diagram.

Brainstorming Example:

Writing Simple Notes

Making a Simple Chart

	Agree	Disagree
Healthy junk food		
Enhance learning	Improved thinking	Freedom to choose
Attention span	Attention span	Cost to schools
Creates habits	Creates habits	Dosen't mean will create a habit
Decreases obesity	Prevents obesity	Can't influence parents
Prevents illnesses	Prevents illnesses	

Clustering Example:

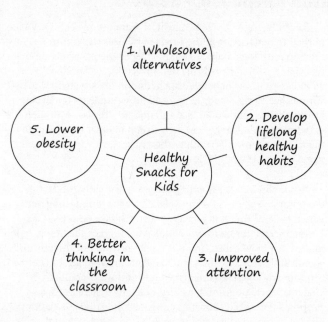

Step 2: Writing

Write your response using the five-paragraph model:

Paragraph 1: Introduction: healthy snacks in vending machines good idea

Paragraph 2: Body (discussion of first point): alternative to unhealthy snacks

Paragraph 3: Body (discussion of second point): creates lifelong habits

Paragraph 4: Body (discussion of third point): enhances learning (improved attention and better thinking)

Paragraph 5: Conclusion (summary): much to gain by eating healthy

---

Consider the "why" approach to develop your thesis statement.

One good way to approach the argumentative essay assignment is to use a "why" format. You can build a "why" response around a thesis statement. The thesis statement begins with your opinion, followed by the word *because,* and then a list of the most important reasons why your opinion is valid, reasonable, or well-founded.

For example, when using the "why" format, a thesis statement might read:

"Healthier snacks in schools are beneficial to students <u>because</u> they provide wholesome alternatives to nutritionally inadequate foods."

Step 3: Proofreading

Remember to allow a few minutes to proofread your essay for errors in spelling and grammar.

Essay 1: Well-Written Response – Score 5

Recently, the U.S. Department of Agriculture (U.S.D.A.) has pushed to replace unhealthy foods in schools with more nutritious options. I agree with the Department's assertion that this change would benefit the nation's children. Specifically, it would assist in the fight against childhood obesity, help ward off various health risks later in life, and allow students to develop healthy habits that would last well into adulthood. Although it may not be a choice that children would make if it were up to them, a move toward healthier food in schools would certainly benefit our youth in the long run.

> The organization of the first paragraph clearly states the writer's position, cites specifics, and previews each of the three supporting paragraphs to follow.

> The writer makes good use of developing ideas to emphasize the benefits of healthy food.

While children enjoy eating fatty, sugary, salty foods, this temporary pleasure is far outweighed by the long-lasting and varied benefits found in a healthy diet. Childhood obesity has become such a threat to our nation's health that the first lady has made it her chief cause, and it is one that would be directly and significantly aided by the U.S.D.A.'s proposal to adopt healthier foods in schools. The benefits would continue even once students reach adulthood, as dietary changes such as those proposed have been shown to mitigate a multitude of health risks later in life, such as heart disease, high cholesterol, and diabetes.

> The writer presents a good supporting argument in the first sentence of the second paragraph. He then adds reinforcing evidence without straying from the main point.

> The writer begins the third paragraph by addressing any potential objections to his position. The writer then immediately addresses those potential objections.

Critics of the proposal may point out that, given the choice, children would likely choose a less healthy option, due to the pleasure they get from a tasty but unhealthy meal. However, children are not yet mature and informed enough to make this sort of decision on their own; it is up to adults to look out for their long-term well-being. Just as a mother would not let her small child play a graphically violent video game that happens to be fun, we must not allow our young to consume junk food every day simply because they enjoy the taste.

> This analogy, "Just as a mother…" draws from a personal observation for ease of understanding the topic.

Our schools take pride in instilling students with positive and helpful habits from an early age, and a healthy diet should be no exception. Nutrition classes should be included in the science and health curriculum. A healthier diet enhances learning by improving cognition, concentration, and attention span. As a child whose parents always packed a healthy lunch, I sometimes looked on enviously at classmates as they wolfed down candy bars at lunch. However, as an adult, I am very thankful for my parents' healthy inclinations; I am now able to maintain excellent health through a naturally nutritious diet, while some of my former classmates struggle with weight issues as they attempt to break their deeply ingrained habits of lunchtime cheeseburgers and afternoon sodas.

> The writer uses personal experience to support his point, and makes sure to directly relate his story to the argument it is intended to support.

> The writer has addressed all parts of the essay question and demonstrates a good use of language variety. The closing paragraph rephrases and summarizes the writer's main arguments and supporting points. He then finishes with a look to the future.

While children may complain about the news, the adoption of the U.S.D.A.'s proposal to replace unhealthy foods in schools with nutritious options would greatly benefit kids in both the short run, by reducing childhood obesity, and in the long run, by fighting a host of health issues late into their lives. As adults tasked with the responsibility of their welfare, we must help our children develop healthy eating habits from an early age, even if they would prefer otherwise. Once our schools start providing students with the foundations of a healthy diet, our youth will be able to look forward to a brighter, healthier future.

Essay 2: Average to Below-Average Response – Score 3

The writer adequately addresses the topic but needs to focus on organizing and developing her position with supporting points.

Use the five-paragraph model instead of three paragraphs. Begin each body paragraph with a unifying sentence, and then provide supporting evidence with specific examples. Each body paragraph should elaborate on and provide examples of the main position discussed in the introductory paragraph.

Remember that essays with brief, undeveloped paragraphs tend to receive low scores.

It is a wonderful idea to provide healthy foods to the students in our schools during lunch. For many of our nation's students this may be the only balanced meal of the day. The image of the stay at home mom cooking 3 nutritious meals for the family daily is now obsolete. Our children eat junk food all day and have "fast food" dinners on a regular basis.

We need to teach children the nutritious food they should eat, because parents aren't providing good food for there children often because of lack of time, money, or not knowing how to provide proper nutrition. Kids come to school eating flaming hot cheetos candy and sugared drinks. No wonder they can't sit still in class. A balance4d breakfast and lunch will probably make them better students and able to concentrate.

Providing nutritious foods in school is a good idea. Our children need this model to learn proper food choices. I applaud the US Department of Education.

Suggestion: Read the argument more than once to organize ideas. Use smooth transitions between paragraphs to form a logical flow of ideas so that the essay dosen't drift to irrelevent matters.

Errors in sentence structure, diction, usage, and spelling are evident (e.g., "there" should be "their" and "kids" should be "children"). Faulty parallelism in the first sentence: "We need to teach...they should eat."

Lacks language consistent with professional educators, "Kids come to school eating flaming hot cheetos candy..."

Overall essay expresses some competency, but it has frequent errors in spelling, punctuation, and sentence structure.

The essay has limited organization and lacks sentence variety. The ideas and reasons for "balanced meals" need to be developed.

Sample Informative/Explanatory (Source-Based) Essay

Now let's try out the strategies given in this chapter to write an informative/explanatory essay. Remember that the informative/explanatory essay requires that you distinguish between two sources (two passages) and identify important points related to the main issue presented.

Sample Topic: Informative/Explanatory Essay

Directions: You will have 30 minutes to read two different passages and then plan and write an informative/explanatory essay using information from BOTH sources provided. Take time organizing your ideas before you discuss the most important concerns regarding the specified issue. Explain the reasons why they are important. You must write on the specified topic. An essay on another topic will not be accepted. When paraphrasing or quoting from the sources, cite each source by referring to the author's last name, the title of the source, or any other clear identifier.

The essay is intended to give you an opportunity to demonstrate your writing skills. Be sure to express your ideas clearly and effectively. The quality of your writing is much more important than the quantity, but to cover the topic adequately, you will likely want to write more than one paragraph. Be specific and provide relevant examples that are related to the topic.

Assignment:

Both of the following passages address the future of desalination and reverse osmosis. Read the two passages carefully and then write an essay in which you identify the most important concerns regarding the issue and explain why they are important. Your essay must draw on information from BOTH of the sources. In addition, you may draw upon your own experiences, observations, and reading. Be sure to correctly cite the sources whether you are paraphrasing or directly quoting.

Source 1:

Adapted from: Adams, Jeanette. *Desalination: Future Water Solutions*. Boston, MA: Houghton Mifflin Harcourt Publishing, 2013. Print.

People have been pulling freshwater out of the oceans for centuries using technologies that involve evaporation, which leaves the salts and other unwanted constituents behind. Salty source water is heated to speed evaporation, and the evaporated water is then trapped and distilled.

This process works well but requires large quantities of heat energy, and costs have been prohibitive for nearly all but the wealthiest nations, such as Kuwait and Saudi Arabia. To make the process more affordable, modern distillation plants recycle heat from the evaporation step.

A potentially cheaper technology called *membrane desalination* may expand the role of desalination worldwide, which today accounts for less than 0.2 percent of the water withdrawn from natural sources. Membrane desalination relies on reverse osmosis. The water on the salty side is highly pressurized to drive water molecules, but not salt and other impurities, to the pure side. In essence, this process pushes freshwater out of saltwater.

Most desalination research over the past few years has focused on *reverse osmosis* because the filters and other components are much smaller than the evaporation chambers used in distillation plants. Reverse osmosis plants are also more compact and energy efficient.

Source 2:

Adapted from: Acosta, Anabel. *Desalination: More Harm than Good?* Boston, MA: Houghton Mifflin Harcourt Publishing, 2015. Print.

The boom in desalination is beginning to alarm environmentalists. One problem is what to do with the salt extracted from the seawater during the process. It emerges as a vast stream of concentrated brine. Most plants, naturally enough, dump it back into the sea. But this salty wastewater also contains the products of corrosion during the desalination process, as well as chemicals added to reduce both the corrosion and the buildup of scale in the plants.

Maybe this pollution can be fixed technically one day. But what can't be fixed is the huge energy demand of desalination. A typical reverse osmosis plant consumes six kilowatt-hours of electricity for every 265 gallons of water it produces. Most of the power, inevitably, comes from burning coal, oil, and other fossil fuels. So, although desalination could conceivably become a viable source of drinking water in coastal regions around the world in the coming decades, it would be at the expense of an extra push toward climate change. At the end of the day, desalination seems like an expensive high-tech solution to a global water problem that is overwhelmingly caused by wasteful use.

Step 1: Pre-Writing

Use a Venn diagram to organize your ideas to show the similarities, differences, and overlapping common elements. Follow the directions on pages 48–49. Insert specific facts, details, concepts, or quotes related to Source 1 in the left circle. Next, write down specific facts, details, concepts, or quotes related to Source 2 in the right circle. If there are any interconnected considerations that you will need to expound upon, write them down in the center space. Remember to put quotation marks around any direct quotes to remind yourself to reference them in your essay.

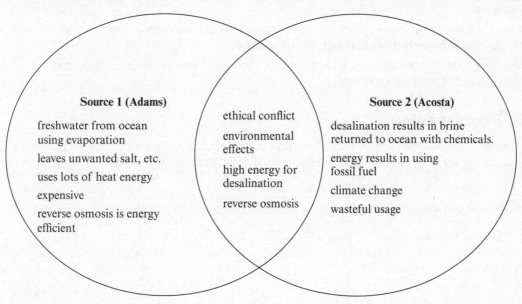

Source 1 (Adams)

freshwater from ocean using evaporation

leaves unwanted salt, etc.

uses lots of heat energy

expensive

reverse osmosis is energy efficient

ethical conflict

environmental effects

high energy for desalination

reverse osmosis

Source 2 (Acosta)

desalination results in brine returned to ocean with chemicals.

energy results in using fossil fuel

climate change

wasteful usage

Step 2: Writing

The informative/explanatory writing process is similar to the argumentative essay, but instead of using the five-paragraph model, try using the four-paragraph model to organize the discussion. Remember that the Praxis readers are looking for how well you address the main concerns in both passages, support your response with examples, and cite sources from your examples from each passage. The four-paragraph model will help you clearly define and compare the issues contained in the two sources.

Paragraph 1: Introduction

   1. Introduce the reader to the general topic of desalination to provide drinking water worldwide.

   2. Restate the question—state important concerns (thesis statement)

      a. Adams—concerned about desalination methods (introduces reverse osmosis)

      b. Acosta—concerned about the environmental impact (is it worth the cost?)

Paragraph 2: Body (discuss important points from Source 1)

   1. Explain the first important concern about the topic/issue (desalination requires a large amount of heat energy and reverse osmosis is a good alternative).

   2. Provide specific examples and cite quotes from one or both passages. (Adams suggests that desalination is "prohibitive" for most nations, reverse osmosis holds promise.)

   3. Include your readings, experiences, or observations, if appropriate.

Paragraph 3: Body (discuss important points from Source 2)

   1. Explain the second important concern about the topic/issue. (Acosta has concerns about costs of desalination and flaws in reverse osmosis.)

   2. Provide specific examples and cite quotes from one or both passages (reverse osmosis "can't be fixed").

   3. Include your readings, experiences, or observations, if appropriate. (Acosta does not address other viable water sources: rainfall and snow in lakes and rivers.)

Paragraph 4: Conclusion (summary of connections between both sources)

   1. Link your explanation to both of the assigned passages. (Both examine possible solutions for providing drinking water.)

   2. Explain the basis for your analysis of the comparison. (Adams emphasizes reverse osmosis; Acosta criticizes reverse osmosis as an alternative to desalination.)

   3. Relate back to your thesis statement. (Neither provides a solid solution to providing drinking water worldwide; future research necessary.)

Step 3: Proofreading

Proofreading is still an essential step to check for spelling and grammatical errors. Remember to check citations (author's last name, title of source, or other identifier) and insert quotation marks around direct quotes.

Essay 1: Well-Written Response – Score 5

This opening paragraph shows that the writer understands the issues and main points of both sources, "conflicts presented by desalination methods." The writer clearly identifies the main points from both sources.

The contrasting perspectives of the two passages, *Desalination: Future Water Solutions* by Jeanette Adams (2013) and *Desalination: More Harm than Good* by Anabel Acosta (2015), address the ethical conflicts presented by desalination methods, the process by which saltwater is converted to drinkable water for communities around the world. Adams is concerned with the problems associated with traditional desalination methods and introduces an efficient method, "reverse osmosis," as a solution. Acosta warns of the environmental impact and asks whether the clean water it produces is worth the cost to our air and water quality.

Notice that the writer begins by citing both sources (titles, authors, dates).

Adams describes the traditional distillation process used for centuries to make drinking water from the ocean and how this process requires a large amount of heat energy. Although Adams notes that costs have traditionally "been prohibitive for nearly all but the wealthiest nations," (para. 2) the affordability and smaller size of reverse osmosis systems suggest a potential use in needy coastal communities desperate for clean drinking water. Adams continues by asserting that the process may be more affordable by recycling the heat used in the processing. The conclusion of the article by Adams explains to the reader that research on reverse osmosis holds promise.

The writer makes use of direct references and quotes from the first and second paragraphs.

Notice that in this four-paragraph essay, paragraph 2 discusses Source 1 and paragraph 3 discusses Source 2.

Acosta does raise valid concerns in the context of developed nations using desalination simply to lower costs; however, she is overly pessimistic in her declaration that the flaws of desalination have a "huge energy demand" (para. 2) at the "expense of climate change" (para. 2). For example, in the same paragraph in which she acknowledges the potential for process refinements leading to the elimination of residual pollution, she flatly dismisses the potential for similar improvements in power (energy) usage. Acosta notes the pollution may be solvable but not the energy costs and the effects on the environment and describes in detail the electrical costs and the sources of electrical costs as fossil fuels. Acosta fails to mention wind and water power as potential renewable electrical sources. Acosta concludes by stating the cause of the global water problem is human "wasteful use." This is an unsupported statement. Acosta does not consider the origins of freshwater sources such as rainfall and snow to feed reservoirs, lakes and rivers. For example, drought conditions such as the ones experienced in California are not controlled by man.

This concluding paragraph summarizes the thesis statement and the primary relationship and conflict between the two sources.

Adams and Acosta examine solutions for providing drinking water to worldwide coastal communities. Adams raises valid concerns about efficiency and proposes reverse osmosis as an energy efficient and compact solution. Acosta criticizes reverse osmosis as energy intensive with adverse effects on the climate. Neither article provides a solution to the problem of drinking water in impoverished coastal communities. Further research is needed to examine the problems cited by these authors for traditional and future desalination solutions.

The essay is well written and responds appropriately to the task. The organization and development of the issues is clear. The writer uses both sources and cites the sources when summarizing the information. The essay uses appropriate vocabulary, sentence variety, and grammar.

Essay 2: Average to Below-Average Response – Score 3

The introductory paragraph describes "desalination," but it is not well developed. It does not explain "why" the authors' concerns are important.

Desalination is the process by which saltwater is converted to freshwater. Passage 1 describes the potential benefits of a new, efficient method called *reverse osmosis*. Passage 2 warns of the environmental impact of even this lower-impact form of desalination, and asks whether the clean water it produces is worth the cost to our air and water quality.

The writer does refer to the passages (passage 1 and passage 2) but does not specifically cite the authors or titles of the passages.

The abrupt change of focus here, without any segue to explain why it is relevant to the main point, is confusing.

Is desalination being used to provide clean drinking water to impoverished communities? If so, I believe desalination would be a worthy use of power. We must not withhold clean drinking water from third-world communities in the name of energy preservation.

This paragraph is brief and does not reference Source 1 or contain any real supporting evidence or citations from Source 1.

These two clauses should be connected by a semicolon or period, not a comma.

"She is wrong" is an overstatement; the essay writer only goes on to discuss *potential* exceptions to the author's claim.

Acosta does raise valid concerns in the context of developed nations using desalination simply to lower costs, however, she is wrong in her declaration that the flaws of reverse osmosis simply "can't be fixed." Plants could become more energy-efficient and power generation could become cleaner over time.

Furthermore, Acosta's conclusion that desalination "seems like an expensive, high-tech solution" seems biased. High-tech solutions to world problems should be encouraged, and I do not understand what she has against them. In addition, just because people are wasteful of water does not mean that alternative sources of clean drinking water should not be pursued.

The writer's personal *opinions* ("We must not withhold clean drinking water…" and "I do not understand what she has against them…") are irrelevant. The informative/explanatory essay does not call for personal opinion or beliefs.

The writer demonstrates good use of quotation marks for Acosta's direct quotes but should also cite the source (Acosta, 2015).

The process of desalination presents a classic climate change dilemma, in which today's benefits must be weighed against tomorrow's costs. While the risks of pollution and excess energy use must be taken seriously, I believe that reverse osmosis desalination could help contribute to a world in which clean drinking water is accessible for all.

The last sentence in paragraph 4 is awkward with a double-negative, and it is unclear what the writer is referring to.

Although the five-paragraph model is acceptable, the four-paragraph model should help the writer develop and organize important details about both sources.

The essay demonstrates some competence, but it requires further development, supporting examples, and appropriate citations.

To receive a higher score, the writer should include important points and examples from Source 2 within the body of the essay, and should avoid personal beliefs and opinions for this type of essay, "I believe that reverse osmosis…"

This is a good final paragraph, although it contains only a very vague summary of the points made in the essay. The writer should explain why the issues presented are important and provide supporting examples with clear links between the two sources.

Tip: Use the strategies and techniques presented on the previous pages to develop and write practice essays in the practice tests. Allow 30 minutes to plan and write each essay. Upon completion of each essay, evaluate (or have a friend evaluate) your writing using the following analysis sheet and the criteria presented on pages 42–44.

Evaluating Your Essays

Use the following checklist to evaluate your practice essays.

Evaluating Your Essay

Questions	Completely	Partially	No
1. Does the essay respond directly to the specific directions for the assignment?			
2. Does the essay identify the relevant aspects of the assignment and develop an insightful analysis?			
3. Does the essay include supporting examples and details? For informative/explanatory essays, does it cite sources?			
4. Does the essay include examples from personal experiences, observations, or readings (argumentative essays)?			
5. Is the essay well organized with clear transitions?			
6. Is the essay written using correct standard written English, and does it use a variety of vocabulary words and sentence openings with varied lengths and structure?			

Chapter 3

The Core Writing Test (5722): Selected Response Questions

As discussed in chapter 2, the Core Writing Test examines your ability to apply the rules of standard written English as you write clear, coherent essays and answer selected response questions. This chapter will identify selected response question types and present strategies and practice exercises that will assist you in reading, evaluating, and identifying errors in grammar and sentence structure.

Note: Selected response questions include both traditional multiple-choice questions with one answer and multiple-choice questions with more than one answer.

Overview of the Selected Response Writing Section

40 minutes • 40 selected response questions

The selected response writing section of the Core Writing Test emphasizes the rules and conventions of standard written English and tests how well you can demonstrate the ability to think critically under time constraints. Many of the grammatical and usage concepts that you will review in this chapter will also help you write a strong, effective essay.

The following table represents an overview of these types of questions.

Category	Selected Response Question Type	Description	*Approximate Number of Questions	*Approximate Percentage
Language and Research Skills for Writing	*Usage	Read, evaluate, and identify errors in grammar, sentence structure, word choice, idiomatic expressions, and mechanics. Some questions have no errors.	18–20	50%
	*Sentence Correction	Identify and correct errors in standard written English. Some questions have no errors.	11–13	25%
	Research Skills	Read a question and select the answer that best identifies strategic approaches to research.	3–6	10%
Text Types, Purposes, and Production	Revision-in-Context	Consider the organization, development, and word choices to read, evaluate, and revise sentences in written passages. Some sentences may have no corrections.	6	15%

*Note: The number of questions on the actual Praxis Core may vary for each test administration. Since approximately 75 percent of the Core Writing selected response questions consist of usage and sentence correction errors, you should spend additional time reviewing, understanding, and practicing these types of questions.

Skills and Concepts Tested

Questions are derived from the *context* of a sentence and will never ask you to define or explain specific grammar and usage rules. You will be tested on how well you can think decisively under time constraints and how well you can fix errors that break the rules of grammar and standard written English.

The rules of correct grammar and usage that have been emphasized in your high school English classes will help you on selected response questions. Remember that most questions—usage, sentence correction, and revision-in-context—require you to look for errors in standard *written* English, not *conversational* English.

Question Types

Selected response writing questions are presented as four specific question types.

- Usage
- Sentence correction
- Research skills
- Revision-in-context

Usage Questions

English usage questions will ask you to recognize errors in grammar, sentence structure, word choice, and mechanics.

Directions

Four portions of each sentence will be underlined. The words not underlined in the sentence are correct and cannot be changed. Read the sentence and decide whether any underlined parts of the sentence contain an error in grammar, punctuation, capitalization, or word choice. No sentence contains more than one error, and some sentences may contain no error.

Identify the underlined portion of the sentence that must be changed to make the sentence correct and click on it to select it as your answer. If the sentence contains no error, click on <u>No error</u>. In this book, we letter the underlined portions of the sentence as choices A, B, C, and D, and then letter <u>No error</u> as choice E.

Example:

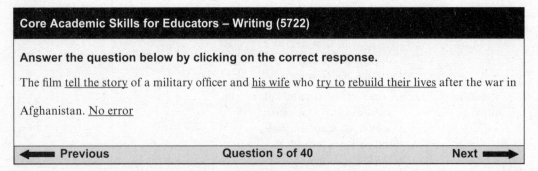

Sentence Correction Questions

Sentence correction questions will test your knowledge of correct and effective English expression. Focus on the meaning of the sentence using correct grammar, sentence construction, punctuation, and word choices. Your answer should make the sentence clear and concise.

Directions

In the question below, some or all of each sentence is boldfaced. The first answer choice repeats the boldfaced portion of the original sentence, while the next four choices offer alternative answer choices. Choose the answer choice that best expresses the meaning of the original sentence and at the same time is grammatically correct and stylistically superior. If an answer choice changes the meaning of the original sentence, do not select it.

Example:

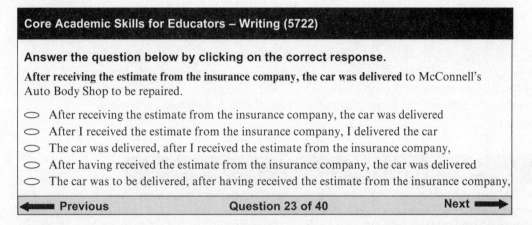

Core Academic Skills for Educators – Writing (5722)

Answer the question below by clicking on the correct response.

After receiving the estimate from the insurance company, the car was delivered to McConnell's Auto Body Shop to be repaired.

- After receiving the estimate from the insurance company, the car was delivered
- After I received the estimate from the insurance company, I delivered the car
- The car was delivered, after I received the estimate from the insurance company,
- After having received the estimate from the insurance company, the car was delivered
- The car was to be delivered, after having received the estimate from the insurance company,

← **Previous**   **Question 23 of 40**   **Next** →

Reminder: In sentence correction questions, the first answer choice (choice A in this book) repeats how the sentence currently appears. Select the first answer choice if no changes are required.

Research Skills Questions

Research skills questions test your ability to effectively use a wide variety of print and electronic research sources. Candidates should be familiar with the proper documentation and bibliographic citation of print and electronic research for books, academic papers, academic journals, periodicals, and encyclopedias.

Directions

The following question will test your familiarity with basic research skills. Each question is followed by five suggested answers. Choose the answer that best identifies strategies for appropriate research skills.

Example:

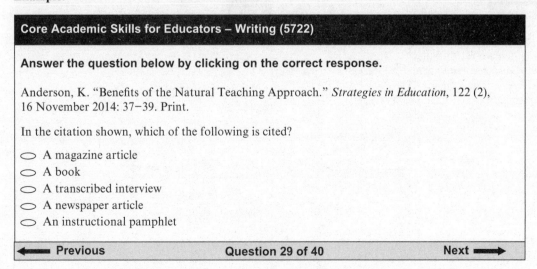

Core Academic Skills for Educators – Writing (5722)

Answer the question below by clicking on the correct response.

Anderson, K. "Benefits of the Natural Teaching Approach." *Strategies in Education*, 122 (2), 16 November 2014: 37–39. Print.

In the citation shown, which of the following is cited?

- A magazine article
- A book
- A transcribed interview
- A newspaper article
- An instructional pamphlet

← **Previous**   **Question 29 of 40**   **Next** →

Revision-in-Context Questions

The revision-in-context question type will ask you to analyze paragraphs on a variety of topics and logically revise incorrect sentences in the *context* of each paragraph. These questions test your ability to identify, edit, or revise errors in paragraphs by following and applying the guidelines of standard written English. There are one or two sets of questions based on short samples of faulty writing. As a rule, each selection contains approximately three paragraphs and consists of approximately 200 to 300 words. There are approximately five to seven questions following each passage.

Directions

The following passage represents a draft of an essay. Some portions of the passage need to be strengthened through editing and revising. Read the passage and choose the best answer for each question that follows. The correct answer addresses the development, organization, word choice, style, and tone of the passage. If the indicated portion of the original sentence is the most effective, no changes will be required.

Example:

Core Academic Skills for Educators – Writing (5722)

(1) Since its beginning, America was basically a rural society, with most people living on farms or in villages. (2) They made their living off the land or from small businesses. (3) In the 19th century, however, the economy underwent major changes, and these changes were often disruptive due to the fact that they disturbed people. (4) The Industrial Revolution brought factories and mass production, which meant that many people had to move to larger towns and cities in order to support themselves. (5) In addition to creating a large working class of people who had to endure low wages, long hours, and sometimes dangerous conditions, an upper class of wealthy individuals who owned the new factories and businesses, were created. (6) For example, men like John D. Rockefeller and Andrew Carnegie, who became major figures. (7) In 1894 Henry Demarest Lloyd wrote a vicious attack on John D. Rockefeller and Standard Oil Company. (8) For the working class, the slower pace and simpler pleasures of the countryside vanished. (9) In the 1890s and early 1900s, vocal critics worried that individual democracy was in danger. (10) Some of them lashed out in articles and books at the new industrialists for introducing corruption and exploitation into the American economy. (11) Theodore Roosevelt coined the term "muckrakers" to describe many of the writers who he believed were "wallowing in the mud" and exaggerating their stories.

Answer the question below by clicking on the correct response.

In context, which is the best version of the underlined portion of Sentence 6 (reproduced below)?

For example, men like John D. Rockefeller and Andrew Carnegie, who became major figures.

- ○ Carnegie became
- ○ Carnegie, both of whom became
- ○ Carnegie, both of who became
- ○ Carnegie, and they both became
- ○ Carnegie, who will become

◄━━ **Previous**   **Question 33 of 40**   **Next** ━━►

General Strategies

Test-taking strategies can accelerate your learning by teaching you time management, organizational skills, and test-taking techniques. This section describes four general strategies to practice as you review the example questions in this chapter. These proven strategies have helped hundreds of test-takers improve their performance on the Core Writing Test by helping them respond to questions quickly and efficiently.

- **Observe the rules of standard written English.** This study guide is consistent with the rules of standard written English, which can be slightly different from spoken English. As you work through the example questions, silently read the words to yourself to *hear* how they sound. Take into account that if a sentence "sounds" accurate, it may still be incorrect if it contains one of the common grammatical or structural errors outlined in this chapter. Always remember that the guidelines of standard written English prevail over spoken English.
- **Focus on the boldfaced words or parts of the sentence.** Read the entire sentence actively and focus your attention on the task at hand. After reading the sentence, read all of the possible answer choices. Do not make a hasty assumption that you know the correct answer without reading all of the possible choices.
- **Manage your time wisely.** Spend about 1½ minutes per question. This will enable you to have enough time to read and answer all of the questions. With sufficient practice, you will know, almost automatically, when a question is taking too much time and when to take an educated guess and move on to the next question. *Remember:* You can mark a question for review and go back to it if there is time.
- **Use the *elimination strategy.*** Eliminate one or more answer choices whenever possible by using the elimination strategy described on page 6. If you get stuck on any one question, you may want to re-read the question. The answer may become apparent when you take a second look. If not, take an educated guess by eliminating any of the choices that you believe are incorrect and proceed to the next question.

Parts of Speech

It is useful to know the meaning of several of the more important grammatical terms and to recognize their distinctive features. With this information, you will be better able to tell the obvious and subtle differences as you evaluate sentences in selected response questions. For example, you should know a noun from a verb and an adverb from an adjective.

Basic Parts of Speech	Definition	Examples
Noun	A word used to name a person, a place, or a thing.	woman, boy, student, New York, airplane
Pronoun	A word used as a substitute for a noun.	I, you, he, she, it, me, him, her, we, they, who, whom, which, what, this, that, one, none, someone, somebody, myself, anything, nothing
Verb	A word used to express action, occurrence, or a state of being.	eat, speak, fall, is, are, remain, think, become
Adjective	A word used to modify a noun or pronoun. To modify is to describe, to qualify, or to limit or restrict in meaning. In the phrase *a small, red rose,* both "small" and "red" are adjectives that modify the noun (rose).	large, sweet, petite, hot, cold, old, new, sad, lucky, green
Adverb	A word used to modify a verb, an adjective, or another adverb. In the phrase *to sing a very long song very slowly,* "very" and "slowly" are adverbs. The first "very" modifies an adjective (long); the second modifies an adverb (slowly); and "slowly" modifies a verb (sing).	very, rather, quickly, quite, easily, carefully

Common Language Skills Errors

Praxis Core candidates should focus on understanding the basic knowledge of grammar, word choice (usage), sentence structure, and punctuation. The table below and the subsequent "Language Skills Review" section are intended to familiarize you with common errors that may appear on the exam.

Language Skills Errors

Content Category	Type of Error	Example of Error	Corrected Example
Grammatical Relationships	Agreement Errors	Houston and Philadelphia are a city in the United States.	Houston and Philadelphia are cities in the United States.
		The teachers of science is taking the test.	The teachers of science are taking the test.
	Pronoun Errors	James was late, so we left without them.	James was late, so we left without him.
		He is the coach that trained the students for the Academic Decathlon.	He is the coach who trained the students for the Academic Decathlon.
	Verb Tense Errors	Last week John buys school supplies and a new computer.	Last week John bought school supplies and a new computer.
	Adjective/Adverb Errors	His writing is carelessly, because he writes too rapid.	His writing is careless, because he writes too rapidly.
Structural Relationships	Parallel Structure Errors	She is studying biology, Spanish, and how to draw.	She is studying biology, Spanish, and drawing.
	Misplaced or Dangling Modifier Errors	The foreman saw a tarantula's nest near the loading dock that was moving.	The foreman saw a tarantula's nest moving near the loading dock.
	Sentence Fragment Errors	Children's books with large, colorful pictures.	Children's books with large, colorful pictures are popular.
	Run-on Sentence Errors	The student grades are ready to be recorded in the computer files and please input them promptly.	The student grades are ready to be recorded in the computer files. Please input them promptly.
	Comparative Errors	Don is the tallest of his two brothers.	Don is taller than his two brothers.
		The student was more older than her sibling.	The student was older than her sibling.
	Coordination Errors	Smartphones first appeared in public use in 1993. They are indispensable communication devices.	Smartphones first appeared in public use in 1993, and now they are indispensable communication devices.

continued

Content Category	Type of Error	Example of Error	Corrected Example
Structural Relationships	Subordination Errors	It is unlikely that the radio signals came from alien life forms, <u>although others have hypothesized to the contrary</u>.	Although it is unlikely that the radio signals came from alien life forms, others have hypothesized to the contrary.
	Word Choice Errors	When disciplining students, do not <u>evoke</u> children to anger.	When disciplining students, do not provoke children to anger.
Word Choice	Redundancy Errors	The student's response was <u>erroneous</u> and <u>incorrect</u>.	The student's response was incorrect.
	Idiomatic Expression Errors	The poetry of Robert Frost is different <u>than that of</u> any other American poet.	The poetry of Robert Frost is different from that of any other American poet.
Mechanics	Punctuation Errors	Anabel has three brothers <u>two of them are doctors</u>.	Anabel has three brothers, and two of them are doctors.
	Capitalization Errors	Thanksgiving falls on the fourth <u>thursday</u> in the <u>Month</u> of November every year.	Thanksgiving falls on the fourth Thursday in the month of November every year.

Language Skills Review

This review section is divided into six Core Writing Test content categories: grammatical relationships, structural relationships, word choice (diction), mechanics, research skills, and revision-in-context.

Grammatical Relationships

The review and example questions that follow provide you with information about grammatical errors that may appear in both usage and sentence correction questions. Not all of these errors will appear on the exam, but many of them have appeared on previous exams.

Note: The answer choices for questions on the actual computer version of the Praxis Core are not labeled with letters A, B, C, D, or E that correspond with your answer choice. The examples and practice tests in this book label each answer choice with a letter for clarity. These letters will not appear on the computer screen when you take the actual test. Instead, you will click on the oval or square(s) next to the choice you select.

Agreement Errors

Grammatical agreement is based on the concept that words in a sentence must match in *number* (singular or plural), *gender* (feminine or masculine), and *person* (first, second, or third person). When words and phrases do not match, or are separated by other words, agreement errors may occur. This section covers the rules for fixing the most common types of Core Writing Test agreement errors: (a) subject-verb, (b) noun-noun, (c) pronoun-noun, and (d) pronoun case.

Types of Agreement Errors	Description
Subject-verb agreement	Errors occur when the verb(s) that refer to noun(s) in a sentence don't agree in singular or plural number and gender.
Noun-noun agreement	Errors occur when nouns that refer to other nouns in a sentence don't agree in singular or plural number.
Pronoun-noun agreement	Errors occur when the number of the pronoun (singular or plural) doesn't agree with the antecedent (the word, phrase, or clause to which it refers).

Subject-Verb Agreement Errors

A subject-verb agreement error is the faulty combination of a *singular* and a *plural* in a sentence. A singular subject must agree with a singular verb, and a plural subject must agree with a plural verb. Nouns ending in –*s* are often plural, and verbs ending in –*s* are often singular.

The <u>computer runs</u> efficiently. (*singular*)

The <u>computers run</u> efficiently. (*plural*)

You should have no trouble with this type of problem as long as you do not let the intervening words distract you from identifying the subject as singular or plural.

Examples:

> **1.** The books of Hill Harper <u>tackles</u> the need for positive role models for youth in the black community
> A
> through <u>affirmations in a colloquial style</u>, <u>quotes from African-American celebrities</u>, and <u>examples of</u>
> B C
> <u>personal experiences</u>. <u>No error</u>
> D E

Although it is separated from the noun by the modifier *of Hill Harper,* the subject *books* is plural. To agree, the verb should be the plural *tackle.* Choices B, C, and D are all correct as is because each item in the list is a noun; this displays proper parallelism. The correct answer for this usage question is A.

> **2.** The **criteria for admission to graduate school includes** two years of work experience.
>
>   **A.**   criteria for admission to graduate school includes
>   **B.**   criteria for admission to graduate school include
>   **C.**   criterion for admission to graduate school include
>   **D.**   criteria for admission to graduate school is
>   **E.**   criteria for admission to graduate school is at least

Watch for nouns with Greek or Latin endings that form plurals with an –*a.* Words like *data* (plural of *datum*), *phenomena* (plural of phenomenon), *media* (plural of *medium*), and *criteria* (plural of *criterion*) are plural forms that can cause subject-verb agreement errors. In this case, *criteria* (plural) must be paired with the verb *include.* Remember that even though the verb *includes* appears to be plural because it ends in an –*s*, it is singular, making choice A incorrect. Choice C, *criterion,* is singular, but *include* is plural. Choices D and E show *criteria* (plural), which does not match *is* (singular). The correct answer for this sentence correction question is B.

Noun-Noun Agreement Errors

On the Core Writing Test, noun-noun agreement errors are not as common as subject-verb agreement errors and pronoun-noun agreement errors. However, you should be familiar with how a noun works in order to understand how pronouns function in a sentence.

Nouns can be *singular,* denoting one item, or *plural,* denoting two or more items.

> The <u>coyote</u> is part of our outdoor ecosystem and digs <u>its</u> own <u>den</u>. (*singular*)

> <u>Coyotes</u> are part of our outdoor ecosystem and dig <u>their</u> own <u>dens</u>. (*plural*)

The type of noun-noun agreement question you may see on the exam is a singular noun *group* question. A singular noun must always agree with another singular noun in a sentence, even when the noun refers to a singular *group* (club, company, family, team, Senate, audience, etc.). When groups imply multiple individuals within a single unit, the collective noun is considered singular. When groups imply two or more groups (or the individuals within the group), the collective nouns are considered plural.

> The Senate <u>committee</u> collaborated to develop a <u>solution</u> to the budget cut. (*singular*)

> The Senate <u>committees</u> collaborated to develop <u>solutions</u> to the budget cut. (*plural*)

Example:

---

3. The Board of Governors expressed **their full support to the CEO and her team, but also indicated that such** patience would not be infinite.

   A. their full support to the CEO and her team, but also indicated that such
   B. their full support to the CEO and her team, indicating that such
   C. its full support to the CEO and her team, but also indicated that such
   D. its full support to the CEO and her team, and also indicated that such
   E. full support to the CEO and her team, but also indicating that such

---

The given sentence contains a problematic pronoun reference, as "Board of Governors" is a singular noun. Replacing "their" with "its" corrects the error and does not introduce further errors, as in choice C. Choices B and D connect the two clauses, but do so without a connector that appropriately expresses the contrast between the two clauses. Choice E mixes tenses (*expressed … indicating*). The correct answer for this sentence correction question is C.

Pronoun-Noun Agreement Errors

Before discussing pronoun-antecedent errors, let's cover pronoun-noun agreement errors in general because this is a common type of error on the Core Writing Test.

A pronoun takes the place of a word or phrase so that writers can avoid using that word or phrase over and over again.

> Angel left <u>Angel's</u> workplace, and forgot to take <u>Angel's</u> iPad. (*without pronouns*)

> Angel left <u>his</u> workplace, and forgot to take <u>his</u> iPad. (*substituting pronouns*)

Pronouns can be either singular or plural and must agree with the noun, verb, or other pronoun to which they refer. Remember that the *number* of a pronoun (i.e., whether it is singular or plural) must agree in number with its *antecedent* (the word, phrase, or clause to which it refers). Personal pronouns have distinctive singular and plural forms (he/they, his/their, him/them).

Pronoun Cases

Nouns and pronouns have a *subjective* (nominative) case, a *possessive* case, and an *objective* case (see the following table). Thus, nouns and pronouns can be used as *subjects* (The *cell phone* is small. *I* am tired.), as *objects* (Justin watered the *lawn*. Justin met *him*.), and as *possessors* (*Blake's* guitar is large. *His* arm is broken.). Because the form of a noun in the subjective case is no different from the form of the same noun in the objective case (The bat hit the ball. The ball hit the bat.), case errors do not occur with nouns.

Pronoun Cases

	First Person	Second Person	Third Person
Subjective Case			
Singular	I	you	he, she, it, who
Plural	we	you	they, who
Possessive Case			
Singular	mine, my	your, yours	his, hers, its, whose
Plural	our, ours	your, yours	their, theirs, whose
Objective Case			
Singular	me	you	him, her, it, whom
Plural	us	you	them, whom

Personal Pronouns and Intensive Pronouns

Several personal pronouns have different forms as subjects and objects that can sometimes be confusing. Here are three basic rules:

- Use *I, he, she, we,* and *they* in place of the *subject* of a sentence. (*the subject is the doer*)

    <u>Blake</u> wrote an essay. (*without pronoun*)

    <u>He</u> wrote an essay. (*substituting pronoun*)

- Use *me, him, her, us,* and *them* in place of the *object* of a sentence. (*the object is the receiver*)

    Ida greeted <u>Chuck</u>. (*without pronoun*)

    Ida greeted <u>him</u>. *or* Ida greeted <u>me</u>. (*substituting pronoun*)

- Use *myself, yourself, herself, himself, itself, ourselves, yourselves,* and *themselves* to reflect or emphasize the subject of the sentence. These types of pronouns are called *intensive (reflexive) pronouns;* they combine personal pronouns with *–self* or *–selves.*

    Take your time to learn this about intensive pronouns because these types of errors have appeared on previous exams. An easy way to identify an intensive pronoun is to remove it from the sentence. When an intensive pronoun is removed from the sentence, the original meaning remains unchanged.

    He will do it <u>himself</u>.

    It is only through faithful endeavor, by the girl <u>herself</u>, that the goal eventually is reached.

Examples:

---

4. **When one reaches the first plateau, it** does not guarantee that you will complete the climb to the summit.

    A.   When one reaches the first plateau, it
    B.   Because one reaches the first plateau, it
    C.   One's reaching the first plateau
    D.   Upon reaching the first plateau, it
    E.   Reaching the first plateau

This sentence contains an inconsistency in the pronouns; the clause that cannot be changed uses *you,* but the boldface section uses *one.* A correct answer must either use *you* or eliminate the pronoun altogether; choices A, B, and C are incorrect because they use the pronoun *one.* Choice D eliminates the pronoun but is incorrect because it contains a dangling modifier (*upon reaching…*) that mistakenly refers to the pronoun *it.* Choice E eliminates the pronoun without introducing any additional errors into the sentence. The correct answer in this sentence correction question is E.

> **5.** After extensive trials, the coach chose four swimmers to make up the relay **team: Kiera, Alicia, Nicole, and me**.
>
> **A.** team: Kiera, Alicia, Nicole, and me
> **B.** team: Kiera, Alicia, Nicole, and I
> **C.** team: Kiera and I, Alicia and Nicole
> **D.** team: I, Kiera, Alicia, and Nicole
> **E.** team, and they are Kiera, Alicia, Nicole, and me

The original version is correct. The pronoun should be of the objective form (*me*) because the four names are in apposition to *swimmers*—meaning that they are directly following and modified by the noun *swimmers*—which, in turn, is the object of the verb *chose*. Therefore, the *I/me* pronoun should be consistent with the verb *chose*, so the subjective *I* in choices B, C, and D is incorrect. Choice E revises the sentence so that the subject of the second clause is *they*; therefore, the pronoun in choice E should be the subjective *I*, not *me*. The correct answer in this sentence correction question is A.

Pronoun-Antecedent and Ambiguous Pronoun Errors

Like pronouns and nouns, pronouns and antecedents must agree in number. As mentioned in the previous section, a pronoun is a word that takes the place of a noun. The antecedent ("ante" means "before") of a pronoun is the word to which the pronoun refers. In the following example, the pronoun *his* refers to the antecedent *Dr. Martin Luther King, Jr.*

> <u>Dr. Martin Luther King, Jr.</u> delivered <u>his</u> famous "I Have a Dream" speech in 1963.

In spoken conversation and in informal writing, we often use ambiguous pronouns that have no single word as their antecedent. For example, "This happens all the time." The word *This* is problematic because it refers to a general idea of the preceding sentence, but not to a specific subject. On the Core Writing Test, you should immediately regard an ambiguous pronoun that does not have a specific noun (or word used as a noun) as its antecedent as an error. *Note:* Sentences in which a pronoun could have two or more possible antecedents should be rewritten.

Examples:

> **6.** The greatest strength of the American political system <u>is</u> each voter's right <u>to determine</u> which way <u>they</u>
>   A   B   C
> <u>will vote</u>. <u>No error</u>
>   D   E

The singular *is* agrees with the singular *strength;* therefore, there is no error in choice A. Choice C contains an error in agreement. The plural *they* does not agree with the singular *each voter*. Remember that the number (singular or plural) of a pronoun is always determined by its antecedent. The correct answer in this usage question is C.

> **7.** <u>In recent years,</u> Anne Perry <u>wrote the Victorian Christmas books</u> *A Christmas Homecoming* and
>   A   B
> *A Christmas Odyssey: A Novel,* <u>but it did not</u> attain the <u>popularity of</u> her Victorian crime series involving
>   C   D
> Thomas and Charlotte Pitt. <u>No error</u>
>   E

There are two possible antecedents to the singular pronoun *it: A Christmas Homecoming* and *A Christmas Odyssey: A Novel.* If the pronoun is meant to refer to both books, it should be the plural *they.* Choice A correctly uses the preposition *in* and correctly modifies the following clause, and choice B contains no errors. Choice D correctly uses the preposition *of.* The correct answer in this usage question is C.

8. Climatologists warn that erosion in North Carolina's Outer Banks presents a severe **threat, which is to be taken** seriously.

    A. threat, which is to be taken
    B. threat which is to be taken
    C. threat, that is to be taken
    D. threat, whose opinions should be taken
    E. threat, and their opinions are to be taken

The pronoun *which* has no specific antecedent here, making choices A and B incorrect; it could refer to either the climatologists' warning or to the *severe threat* posed by erosion. Choice E corrects the sentence by inserting *and their opinions* to provide clarity. Choice D also attempts to provide clarity, but incorrectly refers to the antecedent *severe threat* with the pronoun *whose*. The correct answer in this sentence correction question is E.

Who and Whom

The pronouns *who* and *whom* are subject and object pronouns. When the pronoun functions as a subject, the doer of an action, use the subjective pronoun *who*. When the pronoun functions as an object, the receiver of an action, use the objective pronoun *whom*. If you have trouble with *who* and *whom*, change the question to a statement and replace *I/me* or *he/him* for *who/whom*.

    Who did that? (*He did that.*)
    Whom do you favor to win the tennis tournament? (*I favor him to win the tennis tournament.*)

Example:

9. Ravi Vakani, with <u>whom</u> John Abraham created the omnipresent app, *Crafty Bird,* <u>possesses</u> a net worth
               A   B

reportedly <u>in</u> excess <u>of</u> one billion dollars. <u>No error</u>
         C   D   E

In this sentence, *whom* correctly plays the role of an object. Watch for *who/whom* directly following a preposition; this indicates the need for the object form (*whom*). The singular verb *possesses* in choice B correctly agrees with *Ravi Vakani,* and *in excess of* (choices C and D) is idiomatically correct. The correct answer in this usage question is E, No error.

Verb Tense Errors

Verb tense (past, present, future) errors are common on the Core Writing Test. A verb is a part of speech that expresses a state of being or action.

    Past: I <u>walked</u> yesterday.
    Present: I <u>walk</u> today.
    Future: I <u>will</u> walk tomorrow.

Verb tenses are formed according to person, number, voice, and tense.

- **Person** refers to the subject (or object) of the verb. The three persons of a verb are first (*I, we*), second (*you*), and third (*he, she, it, they*).
- **Number** simply refers to whether a verb is singular (*she goes*) or plural (*they go*).
- **Voice** refers to whether the verb is active or passive: active (*I hit the ball.*) and passive (*The ball was hit by me.*). If the subject of a verb performs the action of the verb, the verb is *active*. If the subject receives the action, the verb is *passive*.

■ **Tense** refers to the time of the action or state of being. The tenses (past, present, and future) of the verbs in a sentence must be logical and consistent. Many of the verb tense errors on the Core Writing Test occur in sentences with two verbs and with past and past participle forms of irregular verbs. Always look carefully at the tenses of the verbs in a sentence and ask yourself, "Does the time scheme make logical sense?" The time scheme will determine the tense. Look carefully at the verbs and the other words in the sentence to establish the time scheme. Adverbs such as *then, subsequently, before, yesterday,* and *tomorrow,* plus prepositional phrases such as *in the last decade* and *in the future,* work with verbs to make the time of the actions clearer.

Examples:

10. When the bell rang, I <u>grabbed</u> my backpack and <u>run</u> <u>as fast as I could</u> <u>to catch</u> the first bus. <u>No error</u>
                A   B   C   D   E

The first two verbs here (*rang* and *grabbed*) are in the past tense. To be consistent, *run* in choice B should be *ran.* Changing choice A could make the verb tense of *grab* consistent with the current tense of *run,* but it would still be inconsistent with *rang.* The preposition usage is correct in both choice C and choice D. The correct answer for this usage question is B.

11. Facebook users love to update their status and converse with friends, **but frequent changes in its privacy policies are often made by the company, which frustrates users**.

    A.   but frequent changes in its privacy policies are often made by the company, which frustrates users
    B.   but the company has often made frequent changes to its privacy policies, which frustrates users
    C.   and frequent changes in its privacy policies are often made by the company, which frustrates users
    D.   but the company makes frequent privacy policy changes, which frustrate users
    E.   but frequent changes in its privacy policies have often been made by the company, which frustrates users

The first clause is in the preferred active voice, in that the subjects (*Facebook users*) are acting upon the verbs (*love, update,* and *converse*). However, the second clause is in the passive voice, in that the subject (*changes*) are being acted upon by the verb (*are often made*). When possible, passive voice should be avoided. Choice D is the best answer because it rephrases the second clause in the active voice without introducing any additional errors. Choice B uses the active voice but changes the verb tense to past tense and is redundant. Choice C does not correct the use of the passive voice, while choice E ambiguously and redundantly rephrases the sentence in the passive voice. The correct answer for this sentence correction question is D.

12. Although he had appeared as a guest on several popular cable news shows in recent months, yesterday's interview **is the first time the governor has admitted** his interest in running for senator.

    A.   is the first time the governor has admitted
    B.   was the first time the governor admitted
    C.   will be the first time the governor will admit
    D.   had been the first time the governor had admitted
    E.   shall be the first time the governor admitted

The description of the interview as *yesterday's* places the action in the past. Logically, it follows that the tense of the main verb must then be past tense; therefore, the correct answer is choice B. Choice A uses the present tense of the verb, and choice C uses the future tense of the verb. Choice D uses the past perfect tense of the verb, which should be used to indicate that an event preceded another event in the past. Choice E is not only future tense, but *shall* is a nonstandard form of expression (except with first person). The correct answer for this sentence correction question is B.

Adjective/Adverb Errors

Another common type of error is using an adjective when an adverb is required or vice versa. The difference between an adjective and an adverb relates to how each functions in a sentence. Adjectives and adverbs are similar because they are both *modifiers* (words or groups of words that describe other words).

While **adjectives** describe nouns and pronouns (*a red balloon, a quick trip*), **adverbs** describe verbs or actions (*the balloon sailed high, I traveled quickly*). Adverbs also describe adjectives (*the balloon was very red*) and other adverbs (*I traveled extremely quickly*), but their primary use is in answering questions about actions. Several special rules apply to adjectives and adverbs.

Adjective and Adverb Rules

Rule 1 Most adverbs end in *–ly*	Most, but not all, adverbs end in *–ly* (*quickly, happily, clearly*) and point to the place, time, or degree. Adverbs tell you: • how an action occurred (*I traveled quickly*) • when an action occurred (*I traveled immediately*) • where an action occurred (*I traveled there*) • to what extent or how much an action occurred (*I traveled long before I stopped*) On the Core Writing Test, watch for exceptions to this rule (see Rule 2).
Rule 2 Some adjectives end in *–ly*	Be aware that some adjectives end in *–ly* (*friendly* cat, *deadly* snake), but keep in mind that it is how the word is being used that makes it an adjective or adverb. For example, in the sentence *The man treated her kindly.*, *kindly* is an adverb; but in the sentence *The kindly man helped her.*, *kindly* is an adjective. Here is another example to help you remember that adverbs answer the question "How?" It is a common error to say, "That's real sad." Since *real* modifies *sad,* the modifier usage is incorrect because *real* is an adjective. To understand this rule, ask yourself "*How* sad is it?" The answer is, "It is *very* sad." Therefore, the phrase should use the adverb *really* to modify the adjective. The correct usage is, "That's *really* sad."
Rule 3 Use *–ly* when verbs (linking verbs) are senses	Some verbs (called linking verbs) are usually followed by an adjective rather than an adverb. Among these are verbs of the senses, such as *taste, smell, feel,* and other commonly used verbs such as forms of *to be* (*am, is, are,* etc.), *become, seem, grow,* and *appear.* Linking verbs don't express an action, but rather help to make a statement by describing a state of being. The question to ask when considering whether to use an adjective or an adverb in describing a verb is, "Does the verb express an action, or is it describing a state of being or one of the senses?" If the verb is used to express an action, then use *–ly.* If not, do not use *–ly.* Here are some examples: {{TABLE}}

Action: Use an adverb.	Linking: Use an adjective.
The man <u>looked angrily</u> at the girl.	He <u>looked angry</u> when he saw her.
The man <u>felt</u> the fabric <u>carefully</u>.	He <u>felt bad</u> about his error.
The corn grew <u>quickly</u>.	He <u>grew sad</u> after their meeting.

Example:

---

13. Though the game was in Los Angeles, **most every fan in the stands was cheering loud** for the Oregon Ducks.

    A.   most every fan in the stands was cheering loud
    B.   almost every fan in the stands was cheering loudly
    C.   almost every fan in the stands was cheering loud
    D.   most fans in the stands were cheering loud
    E.   most every fan in the stands was cheering loudly

Adjectives modify nouns, and adverbs modify verbs, adjectives, and other adverbs. In this example, there are two adjective-adverb errors. *Most* is an adjective, but in this case it is meant to modify the adjective *every,* not the noun *fan.* This means it must take its adverb form *almost. Loud* can be used as an adjective, but here it is meant to modify a verb (*was cheering*). Therefore, it must take the form of an adverb—*loudly.* Choice B is the only choice that corrects both of these errors. The correct answer for this sentence correction question is B.

Structural Relationships

The review and example questions that follow provide you with information about structural errors that may appear in both usage and sentence correction questions.

Errors in structural relationships occur in the following situations:

- When the parts of a sentence are not arranged in a logical order
- When there is an abrupt shift in clauses
- When an essential part(s) has been omitted from the sentence

Usage questions testing for misplaced parts will usually have grammar errors or be unclear, awkward, or ambiguous. Watch for sentences that seem odd or have an unnatural word order. Common sentence structure errors can appear as faulty parallelism, misplaced or dangling modifiers, sentence fragments, run-on (wordy) sentences, comparative errors (comparing two items that are not comparable), and misuse of coordinating or subordinating conjunctions.

Parallel Structure Errors

Phrases in a sentence are parallel when they have the same grammatical structure. The basic rule is that when there are two or more linked constructs, they must show the same grammatical construction.

Incorrect: The young college graduate held future goals of <u>staying happy</u>, <u>keeping fit</u>, and <u>prosperity</u>.

Correct: The young college graduate held future goals of <u>happiness</u>, <u>fitness</u>, and <u>prosperity</u>.

Parallel structure errors may also include unnecessary shifts in verb tense (past to present, for example) or voice (active to passive, for example). They may also include shifts in pronouns (*you* to *one*, for example). Watch for these errors in lists or series. Be especially careful with sentences that use correlatives (*both … and, no … but, not only … but also, not … but, either … or,* and so on). Make sure the construction that follows the second of the correlative conjunctions is the same construction as the one that follows the first.

Examples:

---

14. People <u>who</u> experience the neurological phenomenon known as "number form synesthesia" <u>have</u> specific
       A   B

spatial associations <u>with</u> particular months of the year, days of the week, and <u>when thinking of certain</u>
              C   D

numbers. <u>No error</u>
        E

The list at the end of the sentence displays faulty parallelism; while the first two items listed are nouns (*months of the year* and *days of the week*), the last item is not (*when thinking of…*). Eliminating the underlined portion in choice D would correct this error. *Who* is the correct pronoun in choice A; the plural *have* in choice B correctly refers to the plural *people;* and *with* in choice C is the proper preposition to follow *associations.* The correct answer to this usage question is D.

---

15. **To strive, to seek, to find, and not yielding** are the heroic goals of Ulysses in Alfred Lord Tennyson's famous poem by the same name.

    A.   To strive, to seek, to find, and not yielding
    B.   To strive, to seek, finding and not yielding
    C.   To strive, to seek, to find, and to not yield
    D.   To strive, seeking, to find, and not yielding
    E.   Striving, seeking, finding, and not to yield

Not yielding is incorrect because it should have the same infinitive form (*to* _____) as the other items in the series. Choices A, B, D, and E all have faulty parallelism, mixing infinitives (verbs with *to*) and gerunds (verbs with *–ing*). Choice C correctly shows all three verbs in the infinitive form. The correct answer for this sentence correction question is C.

Misplaced or Dangling Modifiers

Misplaced or dangling modifiers are often awkward, and the meaning of the sentence becomes confusing to the reader. Watch for this kind of error in sentence correction questions. Look for sentences that seem odd or have an unnatural word order. If a sentence is unclear or if a phrase or a clause has nothing to modify, then the error is a misplaced modifier. Also watch for phrases that have nothing to modify, called dangling modifiers.

Incorrect: Hoping to score the winning touchdown, Don Brown's performance must be first-rate.

Correct: If Don Brown hopes to score the winning touchdown, his performance must be first-rate.

In this example, the incorrect sentence begins with a dangling participial phrase that appears to modify *winning touchdown* instead of *Don Brown*. The revised sentence eliminates the error.

Example:

---

16. **Looking at the tiny image on the screen of her iPhone,** Mount Rushmore seemed much smaller and farther away than it had only seconds before.

    A.   Looking at the tiny image on the screen of her iPhone

    B.   With her iPhone in hand

    C.   Via the image displayed by the screen of the iPhone she was looking at

    D.   When she looked at the tiny image of it on the screen of her iPhone

    E.   Against the screen of her iPhone

Literally interpreted, the original sentence seems to say that Mount Rushmore, rather than the woman, was looking at the iPhone screen because the modifier (*Looking*) modifies *Mount Rushmore* instead of the woman who was looking at her iPhone. In other words, the modifier dangles. Choice D eliminates this dangling modifier in a clear and concise way, unlike choice C, which is extremely wordy. By beginning the sentence with *When she looked at the tiny image of it*—a clause that modifies *Mount Rushmore,* rather than the woman—choice D makes the remainder of the sentence flow logically. Choices A and B contain dangling modifiers, and choice E changes the meaning of the sentence. The correct answer for this sentence correction question is D.

Sentence Fragments

The word *fragment* means "incomplete part." A sentence fragment might look like a sentence, but it cannot stand by itself because it is incomplete. Do not assume that a subject and verb automatically make a complete sentence. Sentences must contain an *independent clause* (a group of words that include a subject, a predicate, and a complete thought).

After the movie is over. (*fragment*)

After the movie is over, we will enjoy a late dinner. (*complete sentence*)

Example:

> **17.** By the early eleventh century, Muslim scientists **knowing the rich medical literature of ancient Greece, as well as** arithmetic and algebra.
>
>   **A.**   knowing the rich medical literature of ancient Greece, as well as
>   **B.**   knew the rich medical literature of ancient Greece, as well as
>   **C.**   know the rich medical literature of ancient Greece, as well as
>   **D.**   having learned the rich medical literature of ancient Greece, as well as
>   **E.**   having been given knowledge of the rich medical literature of ancient Greece, as well as

This question is a sentence fragment; it contains a participle (*knowing*) but no main verb. Choices B and C supply the missing verb, but only choice B is correct because it replaces this participle with a verb in the proper past tense. Choice C eliminates the sentence fragment, but incorrectly uses the verb in the present tense. Choices D and E are participles in a different tense than in the question. The correct answer for this sentence correction question is B.

Run-on Sentences

Run-on sentence errors occur when two complete sentences blend together without the correct punctuation. Comma errors are common in run-on sentence questions (see page 85).

Example:

> **18.** Each year about fifty thousand books are **published in Great Britain that is as many as in** the United States, which is four times larger.
>
>   **A.**   published in Great Britain that is as many as in
>   **B.**   published in Great Britain; that is as many as in
>   **C.**   published in Great Britain; as many as in
>   **D.**   published in Great Britain; which is as many as in
>   **E.**   published in Great Britain as many as in

The original sentence is a run-on sentence; the two independent clauses (or complete sentences) are joined without punctuation. The error can be corrected by using a period, a comma with a conjunction, or, as in choice B, a semicolon. Although choices C and D use semicolons, they no longer have independent second clauses, while choice E, which has made the second clause dependent, omits the comma. The correct answer for this sentence correction question is B.

Comparative Errors

Make sure you are relating the items you are intending to compare. Sentence clarity suffers if two items being compared are not alike.

> **Incorrect:** His iridescent <u>jogging suit</u> was much more distracting than the other <u>athletes</u>.
> **Correct:** His iridescent <u>jogging suit</u> was much more distracting than <u>those of</u> the other athletes.

In the incorrect sentence, the jogging suit is compared to athletes, but these items are not alike. A clear and correct comparison compares the *jogging suit* to *other jogging suits*.

When comparing two items, make sure to use the proper comparative and insert *more* before the quality being compared or put the suffix *–er* on the end of it, as is appropriate for the adjective or adverb being used.

Example:

> **19.** Dr. Bishop's comments after the lecture **were more clear than the lecture itself, and the students inferred** that he felt more comfortable when talking to a smaller group.
>
>   A.   were more clear than the lecture itself, and the students inferred
>   B.   were more clear than the lecture itself, and the students infer
>   C.   were clearer than the lecture itself, and the students inferred
>   D.   was more clear than the lecture itself, and the students inferred
>   E.   were clearer than the lecture itself, and the students infer

The comparative form of *clear* is *clearer,* not *more clear.* To form the comparative form of most one-syllable adjectives, such as *clear,* add *–er.* Some adjectives of two or more syllables can form the comparative with *–er* (*happier*), but often the comparative is formed with *more* (*more eager*). *Inferred* is correct here; therefore, choices B and E can be eliminated. Choice C is correct because *clearer* is used and *were* is in agreement with *comments* (plural). When in doubt about the comparative and superlative forms of an adjective, check a dictionary. The correct answer for this sentence correction question is C.

Coordination and Subordination Errors

An independent clause is a grammatically complete sentence. To combine two or more independent clauses, you need to balance and control the elements in each sentence using coordinating conjunctions (*and, but, for, or, nor, so, yet,* etc.) and *subordinating conjunctions* (*as, although, despite,* etc.). To coordinate is to make equal; to subordinate is to place something in a less important position.

Coordination: If the relationship between two thoughts is equally significant, use a coordinating conjunction that best expresses this relationship.

> The clouds turned black, <u>and</u> the storm was looming.

Subordination: If one thought is more important, use a subordinating conjunction.

> <u>As</u> the clouds turned black, the storm was looming. (*storm* is the focus)
>
> <u>As</u> the storm was looming, the clouds turned black. (*clouds* are the focus)

Practice different ways of combining sentences, especially sentences that seem awkward to you. It will help you with this type of question.

Coordinating Conjunctions That Express Equal Relationships

and	for	so
but	or, nor	yet

Subordinating Conjunctions That Express Unequal Relationships

after	despite	though
although	how	unless
as	if	yet
as … as	in order that	until
as if	provided that	when
as long as	since	whenever
as soon as	so … as	where
as though	so that	wherever
because	than	whereupon
before	that	while

Examples:

> **20.** A growing number of athletes <u>are</u> turning to <u>so-called</u> energy bracelets, <u>as believing</u> them to be beneficial
>   A   B   C
>
> <u>in</u> various areas of competition. <u>No error</u>
> D   E

The sentence displays faulty subordination (*as believing*); *as* is incorrect to include in this context. The prepositions *are* (choice A) and *in* (choice D) are used correctly, as is the compound adjective *so-called* (choice B). The correct answer for this usage question is C.

> **21.** While Congress **believe the sanctions to be severe, yet the separatists'** campaign of violence continues as strongly as ever.
>
> **A.** believe the sanctions to be severe, yet the separatists'
> **B.** believe the sanctions to be severe, the separatists
> **C.** believes the sanctions are severe, yet the separatist's
> **D.** believes the sanctions to be severe, the separatists'
> **E.** believes the sanctions to be severe the separatists'

The given sentence displays two errors: (1) incorrect agreement between the singular noun *Congress* and the plural verb *believe,* and (2) faulty subordination (either of *While…* or *…yet* would have been correct, but not both). Choice D corrects both errors without introducing any new errors. The correct answer for this sentence correction question is D.

Word Choice (Diction)

Word choice errors are caused by not knowing exactly what each word means, resulting in pairs of words that are commonly confused. Errors in word choice are likely to appear on the Core Writing Test with a word that you know, which looks or sounds very much like another word you know; for example, *sit* and *set* or *retain* and *detain*. Word choice errors consist of words that you already know, but that you may confuse easily with one another.

Listed below are examples of commonly misused words with their definitions for easy reference. Don't try to memorize the list, just remember to read *each word* carefully before you answer a question.

Pairs of Commonly Misused Words

accept (to agree)	except (excluding)
adapt (to adjust or modify)	adept (proficient, skilled)
affect (verb—to influence; noun—expression of feeling or emotion)	effect (noun—a result; verb—to bring about)
afflict (cause suffering to)	inflict (impose)
allude (to mention indirectly)	elude (to physically or mentally escape from)
allusion (reference)	illusion (false or misleading appearance)
between (when there are only two)	among (three or more)
break (noun—a rest; verb—to fracture)	brake (a device to decelerate)
cite (mention as the source)	site (a place)
complement (to make complete or improve)	compliment (to praise or flatter)
elicit (to bring forth or arrive at by reasoning)	illicit (prohibited by law)
farther (more distant)	further (more time or quantity)
imply (to express indirectly)	infer (to conclude from evidence)

continued

Pairs of Commonly Misused Words (continued)	
its (belonging to it)	it's (it is)
lie (to be in a horizontal position), or lie (to tell something that is not true)	lay (to cause something to be in a certain place, or to produce eggs; past tense form of lie)
precede (to go before)	proceed (to go on, advance, or continue)
principle (a standard rule)	principal (a head of a school, or the initial investment in an account, or first in order of importance)
raise (to elevate or move up)	rise (to get up from lying or sitting)
that (refers to an understood thing or place)	which (refers to a specific thing or place), or who (refers to an understood person)
then (at another time, or next in order)	than (a comparison of unequal parts)
there (in that place)	their (belonging to them) they're (they are)

Lie/Lay

When using *lie* and *lay,* you need to remember that *lie* means "to rest or to recline." It does not take an object—it does not place an object. *Lay* means "to put or to place"; it moves an object.

"I could <u>lie</u> in bed for hours."

"He <u>lays</u> the book down." (In this example, notice that <u>he</u> moves the object—the book.)

The confusion between the two verbs arose because the past tense of *lie* is the same as the present tense of the verb *lay.* On the Core Writing Test, be on the alert for the past tense and past participle of *lie.*

Present Tense – Lie

Past Tense – Lay

Past Participle – Lain

Present Participle – Lying

"Yesterday I <u>lay</u> in bed for hours." (past tense for *lie*)

Example:

---

22. In a half-canvassed business suit, some glue is used to connect the outer fabric **to the inner fabric; however, a third piece of fabric lays** between the two layers in the chest and lapel area.

    A.   to the inner fabric; however, a third piece of fabric lays

    B.   to the inner fabric. However, a third piece of fabric lays

    C.   to the inner fabric; however, a third piece of fabric lies

    D.   to the inner fabric, but a third piece of fabric lays

    E.   to the inner fabric. However, a third piece of fabric was lain

---

The intransitive verb *lie* needs to be used here because the verb is meant to describe the subject rather than transfer action to an object. Therefore, choices A, B, and D are incorrect. Choice E is also incorrect, as the tense of *was lain* is not parallel with the present tense of the rest of the sentence. The correct answer for this sentence correction question is C.

Redundancy Errors

In certain contexts, using the same words and phrases twice can serve a purpose to convey a particular meaning. On the Core Writing Test, however, the unnecessary use of repeating words and phrases in sentences is considered an error. Remember that the correct answer is always clear and concise.

The snow skier <u>descended</u> <u>down</u> the slope at a 38-degree angle. (*redundant*)

The snow skier <u>descended</u> the slope at a 38-degree angle. (*correct*)

The Board of Supervisors agreed to <u>cooperate</u> <u>together</u> to reach a decision. (*redundant*)

The Board of Supervisors agreed to cooperate to reach a decision. (*correct*)

Example:

---

23. Although a complete understanding **of how slaves in the region that is now called Turkey lived in their day-to-day lives is most likely impossible, a recently discovered manuscript is providing new evidence** for a higher rate of literacy than was previously imagined.

    A. of how slaves in the region that is now called Turkey lived in their day-to-day lives is most likely impossible, a recently discovered manuscript is providing new evidence

    B. is most likely impossible of how slaves in the region that is now called Turkey lived their day-to-day lives, recently, a manuscript was discovered that provides new evidence

    C. of the day-to-day lives of slaves in the region that is now called Turkey is most likely impossible, a recently discovered manuscript provides new evidence

    D. of the day-to-day lives of slaves in the region that is now called Turkey is most likely impossible, new evidence is provided in a recently discovered manuscript.

    E. is most likely impossible of the day-to-day lives of slaves in the region that is now called Turkey a manuscript discovered recently provides new evidence

---

The phrasing *lived in their day-to-day lives* is awkward and redundant; therefore, eliminate choice A. Choice B also redundantly uses the words *lived* and *lives,* compounding the awkwardness by splitting up the words *understanding* and *of.* Choice D is incorrect because it includes the passive construction *is provided.* Eliminate choice E because it awkwardly separates the words *understanding* and *of.* Choice C removes the redundancy, streamlines the sentence, and avoids the use of passive construction. The correct answer for this sentence correction question is C.

Idiomatic Expression Errors

To native English speakers, certain expressions "sound right" because they are commonly used. Such expressions are called idiomatic expressions and are correct because they are so widely accepted.

Some Core Writing Test questions will test your ability to recognize errors in nonstandard expressions. There are no general rules, but most idiomatic errors arise from the use of prepositions (*to, from, of, on, by, than,* and so on). For example, depending upon the sentence, you might say *agree with, agree to,* or *agree upon.* The meaning of the sentence will determine the correct usage.

    agree with (people): The teachers agreed with the principal.

    agree to (do something): The students agree to complete the assignment.

    agree upon or **agree on** (something): The school district administrator agreed with the board upon the new academic calendar.

Here is a list of common idiomatic errors.

Correct	Incorrect
except for	excepting for
try to	try and
plan to	plan on
prior to	prior than
type of	type of a
by accident	on accident

continued

Correct	Incorrect
on account of	on account that
fewer things	less things
ashamed of	ashamed about
amused by	amused at
at any rate	in any rate
at fault	of fault
is intent on	is intent to
in reference to	in reference of
regarded as	regarded to be
preoccupied with	preoccupied by
used to	use to
should have	should of
supposed to	suppose to

Example:

---

24. The law prohibits passengers **to bring liquids in excess of 3 ounces in the plane**.

    A.   to bring liquids in excess of 3 ounces in the plane
    B.   from bringing liquids in excess of 3 ounces in the plane
    C.   to bring liquids in excess of 3 ounces on the plane
    D.   from bringing liquids in excess of 3 ounces onto the plane
    E.   to bring liquids in excess of 3 ounces to the plane

The original sentence contains two idiomatic errors. First, the parallel idiom for the verb *prohibits* is *from bringing* rather than *to bring,* eliminating choices A, C, and E. Second, the idiomatic preposition in this sentence should be *onto* or *on* rather than *in* or *to;* this eliminates choice B. Choice D is the only choice that corrects both of these errors; the correct answer for this sentence correction question is D.

Mechanics

Conventions in mechanics that govern the organization of a sentence include correct punctuation and capitalization. The review and example questions that follow provide you with information about punctuation and capitalization errors that may appear in both usage and sentence correction questions.

Punctuation Errors

Look carefully at the punctuation and capitalization in each sentence. Before you take the practice tests, make sure you know the proper way to use commas, semicolons, and apostrophes.

Commas

It is common for comma errors to appear on the Core Writing Test. A general rule to keep in mind is that commas are often used to signal a subtle pause within a sentence. Therefore, if you are uncertain about using a comma, try reading the sentence silently. If the sentence sounds better with a pause, add the comma. If not, omit the comma. Review the table below to test your knowledge of the common uses of commas.

Type of Comma	Description	Example
Coordinating Conjunctions	Two independent clauses may not be simply joined by a comma. They must be connected by a comma, followed by a coordinating conjunction (*and, but, so*) or a period.	Brown bears tend to roam over large areas of land, but they are not very territorial.
Introductory	To separate introductory words or phrases.	Yes, I can attend the football game.
Nonrestrictive Clauses	To set off nonrestrictive clauses. In nonrestrictive clauses, commas are used to add a phrase (clause) to the sentence. In a way, the commas interrupt the sentence to add extra information.	In 2004, when Facebook was launched, college students were eager to become socially connected.
Series Commas	To separate words, phrases, or clauses in a series.	Lily bought white, yellow, and lavender flowers.
Parenthetical Commas	To set off parenthetical phrases. A parenthetical phrase can be removed without changing the meaning of a sentence. Commas are used on both sides of the phrase to set it off from the sentence.	The check, you will be happy to know, was mailed on Tuesday.
Appositive Commas	To set off appositives. An appositive is a noun phrase that renames another noun and is set off by commas on each side.	LeBron James, the forward for the Cleveland Cavaliers, scored a three-point basket in the first minute of the playoffs.

Example:

> **25.** George Eliot did not begin to write fiction until she was nearly **40 years old, this** late start accounts for the maturity of even her earliest works.
>
>   **A.** 40 years old, this
>   **B.** 40 years old this
>   **C.** 40 years old, and this
>   **D.** 40 years old, a
>   **E.** 40 years old, such a

This is a run-on sentence created by a comma splice. It can be corrected by changing the comma to a semicolon, or by adding a conjunction such as *and,* such as in choice C. None of the other choices corrects the run-on sentence; the correct answer for this sentence correction question is C.

Semicolons

The semicolon is like a balance scale. It helps the writer connect closely related ideas. Semicolons always separate elements of equal power of meaning: two or more words, phrases, or sentences. They should never separate main clauses from subordinate clauses.

Use a semicolon to separate main clauses when the separation is not done by a coordinating conjunction (*and, but, or, nor, for*) and a comma.

    Ask Cindy for the lecture notes; she still has them.

Use a semicolon to separate main clauses joined by a conjunctive adverb (*therefore, however, moreover, nevertheless,* etc.).

    We had plenty of time; nevertheless, we felt we should begin.

Use a semicolon to separate items in a series when there are commas within the items.

Maya's dress was red, blue, and green; Alyssa's was lilac and white; and Marcella's was black, turquoise, and white.

Example:

---

26. Research indicates that trusting one's first instinct is not always the best **test-taking strategy, instead, they** should attempt to think through the reasons behind this instinct before trusting it.

    A.   test-taking strategy, instead, they
    B.   test-taking strategy, instead, one
    C.   test-taking strategy; instead, one
    D.   test-taking strategy. Instead, they
    E.   test-taking strategy, instead students

The given sentence consists of two complete clauses connected by a conjunctive adverb, which requires a semicolon rather than a comma. It also displays faulty parallelism between *one's* and *they*. Choice C corrects these errors and does not introduce further errors. The correct answer for this sentence correction question is C.

Apostrophes

The placement of an apostrophe depends upon its function. Apostrophes are used to indicate the omission of a letter or letters in a contraction (*it's, I've, I'm, don't, we're, who's*), but they can also show possession.

Apostrophes show possession of *singular nouns* by adding *'s*.

This is the student's term paper. (One student wrote the term paper.)

Apostrophes show the possession of *plural nouns*. If the plural noun ends in *–s*, just add an apostrophe to the end.

This is the students' term paper. (More than one student wrote the term paper.)

If a plural noun (regular) ends in *–s*, add an apostrophe after the *–s*.

These are the students' term papers. (More than one student wrote more than one term paper.)

Example:

---

27. Studies have shown that the blood of young mice <u>helps</u> reduce the <u>effects</u> of aging in older mice; although,
                                                     A   B

some pundits have criticized the potential use of healthier, younger <u>peoples'</u> blood for the purpose of
                                                         C   D

vanity. <u>No error</u>
         E

Despite not ending with an *–s*, the noun *people* is plural; therefore, its possessive form is *people's*. Choice D incorrectly places the apostrophe after the letter *s*. The verb in choice A correctly agrees with the singular noun *blood*, and the noun *effects* is correctly used in choice B. The comma in choice C correctly separates two adjectives directly preceding the noun to be modified. The correct answer for this usage question is D.

Capitalization Errors

Follow these four key rules for capitalization:

- Capitalize the first letter of the first word at the beginning of each sentence.
- Capitalize proper nouns and titles. **Remember:** Nouns are a person, place, or thing. For example, although the word *president* is not capitalized when used within a sentence, it is capitalized when it is paired with a name (*President Obama*). Remember to capitalize both words in a hyphenated compound proper noun (for example, *Lorenzo Lamas-Craig*).
- The word *north* is not capitalized when used as a direction on a compass; but when it refers to a name, such as a region of the country, it is capitalized (*Northwest*).
- Capitalize the first word within quotations if the quotation is a complete sentence or if the quotation is a direct quote:

In an international study of climate change, scientific researchers concluded by affirming that "Global warming is the result of humankind's reliance on fossil fuels."

Example:

---

28. A group of inventors <u>has</u> created a system of hexagonal<u>,</u> interlocking solar panels that could be used to
                             A   B

build <u>energy-producing</u> <u>Highways</u>. <u>No error</u>
        C   D   E

The noun *Highways* in choice D does not require capitalization unless it is part of a proper noun (e.g., *Highway 42*), and neither does its plural form. The verb *has* in choice A correctly agrees with the singular noun *group,* the comma in choice B correctly separates two adjectives directly preceding the noun to be modified, and the compound adjective *energy-producing* in choice C is correctly hyphenated. The correct answer to this usage question is D.

Research Skills

Core Writing Test candidates will need to demonstrate their knowledge of research methods and techniques used for books, academic papers, academic journals, periodicals, and encyclopedias. The research you have conducted for your previous college writing assignments should help you with this type of question. Unlike usage and sentence correction questions, which require you to look for errors, research skills questions require that you select the *correct* response from five answer choices.

Strategies for effective research include the following:

- **Focus on the topic.** When gathering information from print or electronic sources, it is easy to become distracted by irrelevant information. Work from general to specific as you refine your topic and generate subtopics, but try to stay focused on specific information relevant to your topic.
- **Run a key word search.** Conduct a key word search that is focused on authoritative contributions in the field of your topic. Authoritative research findings help to provide credible evidence, claims, reasoning, data, and details that strengthen your research paper. Start your search by identifying the exact words related to your topic (author, title, and subject). Use as many sources as possible (books, journals, articles, magazines, newspapers, the Internet, and electronic academic resources). If you feel stuck, use a thesaurus to assist in locating synonymous key words that describe your topic.
- **Look for authoritative bibliographic references.** When searching for additional sources related to your topic, remember to skim through the bibliography of textbooks, academic papers, and journals. The bibliographic reference section can often lead you to research-based scholarly articles related to your topic.

- **Know the difference between primary and secondary sources.** The original creator of the material (book, article, film, letter, speech, poem, art, etc.) is considered the *primary source*. The *secondary source* is the person who interprets or writes about the primary source. Secondary sources are included in many journal articles, encyclopedias, dictionaries, reviews, newspaper articles, dissertations, and essays.

- **Know how to document in-text citations.** Citations are the *direct, indirect,* and *paraphrased* words and phrases inserted in your paper from another person's body of work (source). To avoid plagiarism, you should be able to distinguish your personal ideas from another author's ideas by crediting the original source. Always quote and cite sources that help to clarify, illustrate, or support your point of view.

  Citations are listed in two areas of a research paper: *in text* and on the *reference* (or *bibliography*) list. Make sure that your research paper includes the most up-to-date citations, and that citations inserted in the body of your paper match your reference (bibliography) list.

- **Know the difference between a reference and a bibliography.** A reference or bibliography is an alphabetical list of sources used in your paper. The two lists are often mistaken to be the same since both are inserted at the end of the paper, but there is significant distinction in their function.

  A *reference* list covers the sources that are directly or indirectly "cited" in the text of your research paper. A reference list is often used in high school and college classes that require APA (American Psychological Association) or MLA (Modern Language Association) style guidelines for research papers. A *bibliography* is an extensive list of all works (books, articles, websites, etc.) that you consulted in preparing your paper, even if the material is "not cited" in your paper. A bibliography list is often required for class assignments, essays, and reports so the instructor will be able to see what sources informed your thinking on the topic.

- **Identify elements in the reference and bibliography lists.** On the Core Writing Test, you will be asked to identify the exact order of each element of bibliographic reference elements such as the author, title, date of publication, place of publication, publishing company, volume number, and page number.

  Guidelines for inserting citations in academic papers are consistent with MLA style, APA style, or CMS (Chicago Manual of Style). Formatting preferences are regulated by individual schools, but most K-12 schools use the following MLA formatting guidelines for the reference (or bibliography) section of academic papers.

Book with one author:

Greenspan, Dorie. *Around My French Table: More Than 300 Recipes from My Home to Yours.* Boston: Houghton Mifflin Harcourt, 2010. Print.

Book with more than one author:

Campbell, J., P. Cousineau, and S.L. Brown. *The hero's journey: Joseph Campbell on his life and work.* Novato: New World Library, 2003. Print.

Academic journal article:

Kafka, Ben. "The Demon of Writing: Paperwork, Public Safety, and the Reign of Terror." *Representations* 98 (2007): 1–24. Print.

Journal article from a website:

Eberle, Scott G. "Playing with the Multiple Intelligences: How Play Helps Them Grow." *American Journal of Play* 4: 19–51, 1 June 2011. Web. 3 December, 2014.

Newspaper article:

Brubaker, Bill. "New Health Center Targets County's Uninsured Patients." *Washington Post* 24 May 2007: (add section and page number here). Print.

Magazine article:

Cummins, Carrice. "Celebrating Teachers: Using Children's Literature to Make a Difference." *Reading Today*, 30, no. 2, October 2012: 2–4. Print.

Note: Research questions may appear in the format of APA style. For example,

Academic journal article:

Kafka, Ben. (2007). The demon of writing: Paperwork, public safety, and the reign of terror. *Representations*, 98(1), 1–24.

Examples:

---

29. Anderson, K. "Benefits of the Natural Teaching Approach." *Strategies in Education*, 122 (2), 16 November 2014: 37–39. Print.

In the citation shown, which of the following is cited?

A. A magazine article
B. A book
C. A transcribed interview
D. A newspaper article
E. An instructional pamphlet

The publication name (*Strategies in Education*), the specific date of publication (*16 November 2014*), the volume/issue numbers (*122 (2)*), and the title of the work (*"Benefits of the Natural Teaching Approach"*) indicate that a magazine article is being cited following MLA style guidelines. The correct answer for this research skills question is A.

---

30. A student is researching Pablo Picasso for a paper. Which of the following would be considered a secondary source for the paper?

A. Rare nature photographs taken by Picasso
B. A biography based primarily on Picasso's personal journal
C. Descriptions of Picasso from his friends and contemporaries
D. A letter written by Picasso to his family
E. An unpublished essay written by Picasso on communist politics

---

A primary source is a contemporary account of the person or event in question, produced by someone who witnessed or experienced it directly. A secondary source, on the other hand, is secondhand—often a description or analysis based on another source, rather than the person or event itself. Thus, while the journal of Picasso would be considered a primary source, a biography based on it would be a secondary source. The other four answer choices represent direct evidence or descriptions of Picasso and his activities. The correct answer for this research skills question is B.

Revision-in-Context

The final selected response writing question type is called revision-in-context. At first glance, you may think this question type looks like a reading comprehension passage, but it is not. In revision-in-context questions, *you* become the editor as you proofread and revise sentences to improve paragraphs within a passage.

Your task is to read and evaluate a short passage and then apply your knowledge of sentence structure, organization, word choice, and style to choose the best answer among five choices. Some questions have no errors and do not require changes. On the Core Writing Test, structurally incorrect sentences must be revised so that the organizational flow is not *choppy* or *wordy*.

For example, select the "best version" sentence below.

Elizabeth is twenty. She is getting married in June. She is designing a dress. It is white.

Elizabeth is twenty, and she is getting married in June, and she is designing a dress, and the dress is white.

Twenty-year-old Elizabeth is designing a white dress for her June wedding.

The third sentence is the best revision: *Twenty-year-old Elizabeth is designing a white dress for her June wedding.* In choppy sentences, you are expected to organize and simplify them so that the reader will not be forced to stop and start when reading. In sentences that are wordy, you are expected to economize the writing and eliminate unnecessary words.

The most common types of revision-in-context questions will ask you to do the following:

- Combine sentences.
- Find the best version of the sentence.
- Improve the organizational flow.
- Eliminate unnecessary words and phrases.
- Reorder sentences.

Examples:

Questions 31–35 refer to the following passage.

(1) The nature of human relationships has intrigued mankind for centuries. (2) Sometimes one person considers another to be a friend, but in fact the other person doesn't feel the same way. (3) This is called relationship inequality. (4) The second person may act in a friendly way, but the friendliness is only in a superficial way on the surface. (5) Researchers have observed relationship inequality in adults, but have also observed relationship inequality among children in elementary school.

(6) Social researchers working with third to sixth graders in an elementary school that was affiliated with a university found that 12 percent of relationships between the children followed patterns of relationship disparity. (7) Although it may seem surprising, that was a higher percentage than the relationships in which the two children disliked each other.

(8) Two-way friendships made up only about a fourth of the over 2,300 relationships the researchers studied.

(9) Aggressive and socially awkward children in the study often believed they were friends with peers who actually disliked them, which probably isn't surprising. (10) On the other hand, children who were identified as "buddies" by a classmate they didn't like got along well with others and had a large number of real friends.

(11) Social reciprocity among children requires well-developed interpersonal skills that may be difficult for children who have underdeveloped social skills. (12) It appears that the conclusion could be that socially disadvantaged children are drawn to peers who are well liked, though the feeling isn't always mutual.

(13) Most research with children has focused on pairs who either like or dislike each other and not on pairs that are unequal.

---

31. Which of the following is the best way to revise and combine sentences 2 and 3 (reproduced below)?

Sometimes one person considers another to be a friend, but in fact the other person doesn't feel the same way. This is called relationship inequality.

A. In an unequal relationship, one person considers another person a friend, but the feeling is not mutual.

B. When one person considers another person a friend, but the second person doesn't consider the first to be a friend, is an example of an unequal relationship.

C. If one person considers another person to be a friend, but that person doesn't consider the first person to be a friend, that is an unequal relationship.

D. When one person considers another person a friend, it is an unequal relationship if the other person doesn't consider the first person in the same way.

E. A relationship is unequal when a person considers another person to be a friend, and yet the other person doesn't consider the first person to be a friend.

Of the choices, choice A is the most efficient and succinct revision. The other choices are wordy and not as clear. Choice B is an incorrect construction. The correct answer is A.

32. Which of the following is the best change to make in sentence 4 (reproduced below)?

> *The second person may act in a friendly way, but the friendliness is only in a superficial way on the surface.*

- **A.** Change *friendly* to *affable.*
- **B.** Replace the comma after *way* with a semicolon.
- **C.** Change *second person* to *other person.*
- **D.** Eliminate *in a superficial way.*
- **E.** Change *the friendliness* to *it.*

In a superficial way and *on the surface* say the same thing; therefore, one of the phrases should be eliminated. The correct answer is D.

33. The best place for sentence 8 (reproduced below) is

> *Two-way friendships made up only about a fourth of the over 2,300 relationships the researchers studied.*

- **A.** where it is now.
- **B.** as the last sentence in paragraph 2.
- **C.** after sentence 4 in paragraph 1.
- **D.** after sentence 13.
- **E.** after sentence 12 in paragraph 5.

Facts about the research findings are covered in paragraph 2, making the end of paragraph 2 the best place for sentence 8. A paragraph should consist of more than one sentence, so choice A is not a good choice. The correct answer is B.

34. The underlined part of sentence 12 (reproduced below) should be

> *It appears that <u>the conclusion could be that</u> socially disadvantaged children are drawn to peers who are well liked, though the feeling isn't always mutual.*

- **A.** changed to *the conclusion would be.*
- **B.** changed to *the unavoidable conclusion is.*
- **C.** eliminated.
- **D.** changed to *conclusively.*
- **E.** changed to *the conclusion might be.*

The phrase adds nothing to the meaning of the statement and should be eliminated. The correct answer is C.

35. The passage would be most improved by

- **A.** moving the last sentence of the passage to paragraph 2.
- **B.** including information about the researchers and their goals.
- **C.** presenting and discussing conflicting data.
- **D.** including interviews with psychologists.
- **E.** explaining the criteria for identifying aggressive students.

The last sentence of the passage should be moved to paragraph 2, choice A. Of the choices, this change would most improve the passage. As it stands in the draft, it is tacked on and not developed into a conclusion. It belongs in the paragraph concerned with facts about the research. The correct answer is A.

Chapter 4

The Core Mathematics Test (5732)

The Core Mathematics Test (5732) is designed to test your mathematical reasoning skills and cumulative knowledge of numbers and quantity (arithmetic), algebra and functions, geometry, and statistics and probability. This chapter will introduce these math content areas, review the question type setups, and present strategies with practice exercises to help you understand how to solve problems.

To enhance your learning experience, we have organized a comprehensive math review of the Praxis content topics in chapters 5 through 8. These chapters will present a review of each content topic starting with basic arithmetic and ending with statistics. Each chapter includes a diagnostic test, terminology, formulas, concepts, step-by-step examples, and a short practice test. Each stage of your learning will build upon your previous understanding of a math concept. As you work through the example questions, you will be steadily increasing your comfort level with the test format and increasing your ability to solve more challenging questions.

Overview of the Core Mathematics Test

85 minutes • 56 questions (selected response and numeric entry)

As illustrated below, the Core Mathematics Test focuses on four content categories:

- Numbers and quantity (arithmetic)
- Algebra and functions
- Geometry
- Statistics and probability

Category	Topics Covered	Description	Approximate Number of Questions	Approximate Percentage
Numbers and Quantity (Arithmetic)	A. Ratios and Proportional Relationships B. The Real Number System C. Quantities	Questions include basic mathematical numeric reasoning problems involving operations with whole numbers, decimals, fractions, integers, rational and irrational numbers, positive exponents, square roots, approximations, percentages, ratios and proportions, factors and multiples of integers, and multi-digit numbers.	17 Questions	30%
Algebra and Functions	A. Seeing Structure in Expressions B. Reasoning with Equations and Inequalities C. Functions	Questions under this content area include topics such as algorithmic thinking; using numeric and algebraic variables to express relationships; properties of operations; proportional relationships, lines, and linear equations; solving problems by the process of reasoning; solving one-variable equations; solving linear inequalities in one variable; solving equations and inequalities graphically; and interpreting functions.	17 Questions	30%

continued

Category	Topics Covered	Description	Approximate Number of Questions	Approximate Percentage
Geometry	A. Congruence and Similarity B. Right Triangles C. Circles D. Geometric Measurement and Dimension E. Modeling with Geometry	Questions under this content area are based on the properties of plane figures, lines, angles, triangles (Pythagorean theorem), rectangles, and circles; congruence and similarity; *xy*-coordinate plane; and measurements such as angle measure, area, surface area, and volume.	11 Questions	20%
Statistics and Probability	A. Basic Statistics and Probability B. Interpreting Categorical and Quantitative Data C. Making Inferences and Justifying Conclusions D. Using Probability to Make Decisions	Questions under this content area are grounded in basic statistics, data interpretation, and probability. Topics include interpreting bivariate data (two variables); drawing statistical inferences based on numeric or graphic displays; measuring central tendency (mean, median, mode); interpreting frequency distributions, random sampling, and chance processes; and using probability to evaluate outcomes.	11 Questions	20%

Skills and Concepts Tested

To do well on the Core Mathematics Test, you must demonstrate competence in math Common Core State Standards (CCSS). According to the CCSS, math proficiency extends beyond memorizing math formulas and terms to finding the correct solution to a problem. CCSS focuses on your ability to be an effective "math problem solver." You will be asked to apply critical thinking skills to everyday scenarios as you "reason abstractly and quantitatively" to solve multi-step math problems.

These critical thinking skills include the following:

- Your ability to use basic math skills in arithmetic, algebra, geometry, and basic statistics
- Your ability to use math insight and reasoning skills to solve real-world math word problems
- Your ability to make sense of problems quantitatively and abstractly while using numeric and symbolic mathematical operations
- Your ability to use an on-screen calculator to solve problems

Calculator Use

A simple four-function **on-screen calculator** is available to help you perform computations. The calculator will look something like this:

Use the Calculator for Time-Consuming Problems

The general rule of thumb is that you should only use the on-screen calculator for time-consuming computations (square roots, long division, and problems with several digits). Although the calculator will help you save time compared to handwritten calculations, you must have a basic knowledge of mathematics to be able to determine whether your calculation results make logical sense. Remember that the Core Mathematics Test is a reasoning test, not a computation test. The calculator will help to reduce your chance of calculation errors, but keep in mind that if you use the on-screen calculator for every math problem, it is unlikely that you will complete the test in the allotted time.

Transfer Display

After you have determined that your calculated results are the best answer choice for the numeric entry questions, you can transfer your results to your answer box with one click. Keep in mind, however, that you will need to transfer calculated results in the correct form that the question asks. For example, some numeric entry questions may require you to round off to a certain decimal place, and others may ask you to convert your answer to a percent. Be sure to adjust your on-screen calculator results before transferring your answer to the answer box.

Practice Before the Exam Date

To help you become familiar with the on-screen calculator, use a calculator similar to the on-screen calculator while working through example problems and taking the practice tests in this book. The TI-108 (Texas Instruments 108) calculator has functions that are similar to the on-screen calculator. If you have a computer with a calculator function, it may also help you to become more familiar with the on-screen type of calculator. Familiarize yourself with the best keystrokes to accomplish certain math tasks as you work through the math content in this book.

Question Types

Mathematics questions are presented within selected response (multiple choice) and numeric entry (fill in the blank) question types that require you to "click on" or "fill in" your answer. If a question has answer choices with **ovals,** then the correct answer requires a single choice. If a question has answer choices with **square boxes,** then the correct answer requires one or more answer choices. If a question has no answer choices, you are provided with a **blank rectangular box** (or two stacked boxes for answers with fractions) and must manually enter your answer. Read the directions carefully before you answer each question.

Ovals	⬯	Selected response question (select one answer choice)
Square Boxes	☐	Selected response question (select one or more answer choices)
Rectangular Boxes	▭	Numeric entry question (fill in your answer)
Two Stacked Boxes	▭ / ▭	Numeric entry question (fill in your fraction answer)

The importance of understanding the question types and test content cannot be overstated. Research has shown that there is a significant increase in score results when test-takers learn test format and directions prior to taking the exam. This is why this chapter begins with familiarizing you with the Core Mathematics question types. As you understand and memorize the three question-type setups, you should be able to effectively apply the appropriate strategy to become proficient with any type of problem.

Note: The example questions and practice tests in this book label each answer choice with a letter for clarity. These letters will not appear on the computer screen when you take the actual test. Instead, you will click on the oval or square(s) next to the answer you choose.

Selected Response (Select One Answer Choice) Questions

The selected response (select one answer choice) questions require you to use math insight, reasoning approximations, and simple calculations to solve math problems.

Directions

Answer each problem by using the information given and your own mathematical calculations. Select *one* correct answer from the five given choices by clicking on the corresponding oval.

Example:

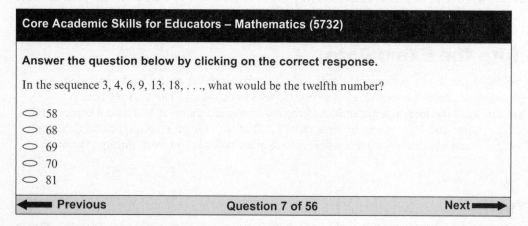

Core Academic Skills for Educators – Mathematics (5732)

Answer the question below by clicking on the correct response.

In the sequence 3, 4, 6, 9, 13, 18, . . ., what would be the twelfth number?

- ○ 58
- ○ 68
- ○ 69
- ○ 70
- ○ 81

◄══ Previous   Question 7 of 56   Next ══►

Selected Response (Select One or More Answer Choices) Questions

Selected response (select one or more answer choices) questions require you to solve math problems using math insight, approximations, reasoning, and calculations to choose ALL of the correct answers from among a list of three to five choices. If you do not mark *all* of the correct answer choices, you will not be given credit for a correct response. There is no partial credit.

Directions

Answer each problem by using the information given and your own mathematical calculations. Select *all* of the correct answers from the given choices by clicking on the corresponding box(es).

Example:

Core Academic Skills for Educators – Mathematics (5732)

Click on your choices.

Which of the following decimals lie between 0.53 and 0.842 on the real number line?

Select **all** that apply.

☐ 0.394

☐ 0.4

☐ 0.5314

☐ 0.71

☐ 0.85

| ◀━━ Previous | Question 10 of 56 | Next ━━▶ |

Numeric Entry (Fill in the Blank) Questions

The numeric entry (fill in the blank) questions require you to solve math problems by using math insight and simple calculations to fill in the blank space with the correct answer.

Directions

Answer each problem by using the information given and your own mathematical calculations. Enter your answer in the space provided.

- Arrive at a numeric answer based on the guidelines provided in each given problem.
- If answering a question with a single answer, use the mouse to click on the rectangular answer box; then use the keyboard to type in your answer.
- If answering a question with a common fraction answer, use the mouse to click on each separate answer box (one for the numerator and one for the denominator); then use the keyboard to type in your answers. Unless indicated in the question, fractional answers do not have to be reduced. For example, if an answer is *three-fourths,* then the answer could be entered as $\dfrac{3}{4}$ or $\dfrac{9}{12}$.

- If answering a question using a decimal response, do not forget to include the decimal point, if required. For example, if the answer is 23, then answers such as 23, 23., or 23.0 are all correct. If the answer is 5.2, then answers such as 5.2, 5.20, or 05.2 are all correct.
- If using the on-screen calculator to compute your answer, your numeric answer can be transferred from the calculator to the answer box by using the "transfer display."

Example:

Core Academic Skills for Educators – Mathematics (5732)

Click on each box and type in a number. Backspace to erase.

If you flip a fair coin four times, what is the probability of getting at least two heads?

☐
☐

◀━━ **Previous**　　　　　**Question 19 of 56**　　　　　**Next** ━━▶

General Strategies

Test-taking strategies can accelerate your learning and help you respond to questions quickly and efficiently.

- **Make assumptions about the math problems.** You can make the following assumptions about all math problems:
  1. All numerical values used are real numbers.
  2. Figures or diagrams are not necessarily drawn to scale and should not be used to estimate sizes by measurement.
  3. On a number line, positive numbers are to the right of zero and increase to the right and negative numbers are to the left of zero and decrease to the left.
  4. Lines that appear straight can be assumed to be straight.
- **Do scratch work.** All scratch work with your notes and computations must be done on the scratch paper or writing board provided by the test administrators.
- **Memorize the question types.** Memorize and practice using the three possible mathematics question types *before* your test day to save valuable testing time. As you become more familiar with the three question types, on the day of the test you will only need to scan the directions to confirm that you understand the question.
- **Manage your time wisely.** Spend about 1½ minutes per question. This will enable you to have enough time to read and answer all the questions. With sufficient practice, you will know almost automatically when a problem is taking too much time and when to take an educated guess and move on to the next question. Remember that you can mark a question for review and go back to it if there is time.
- **Use the *elimination strategy*.** Eliminate one or more answer choices whenever possible by using the elimination strategy described on page 6. If you get stuck on any one question, you may want to re-read the question. The answer may become apparent when you take a second look. If not, take an educated guess by eliminating any of the choices that you believe are incorrect and proceed to the next question.
- **Guess if you don't know the answer.** There is no penalty for guessing. Although it may be difficult to answer a numeric entry question correctly by writing in a wild guess, fill in your answer anyway (even if you think it's probably wrong). Never leave an answer blank. If you don't know the answer to a selected response problem but you can make an educated guess to get a general range for your answer, you may be able to eliminate one or more answer choices. You have nothing to lose and, quite possibly, something to gain.
- **Be on alert for the "attractive distracter" answer choice.** Watch out for an attractive distracter—an answer choice that looks good but is not the *best* answer choice. Just because an answer choice is a true statement does not mean that it is the best choice. The facts and concepts presented on the exam are often in subtle variations of selected answer choices that make it difficult for test-takers to narrow down the correct answer.

Suggested Strategies with Example Questions

Consider the following list of suggested test-taking strategies when preparing for the Core Mathematics Test:

- Focus on reasoning.
- Write down key words to pull out information.
- Avoid unnecessary calculations.
- Substitute simple numbers.
- Work backward from the answer choices.
- Approximate.
- Look for relationships among the answer choices.
- Make comparisons.
- Draw a simple diagram.
- Try "possibilities" in probability problems.
- Determine the most efficient method to solve the problem.
- Accurately interpret data—graphs, charts, tables, and diagrams.

Focus on Reasoning

It's important to remember that the Praxis Core Mathematics Test focuses on your ability to reason quantitatively. Many reasoning problems appear in a word problem format that combines both numbers and descriptive text. Sometimes word problems can be confusing because you are required to take words and translate them into a math equation.

Try not to over-think reasoning questions. Focus on the words used, their meaning, and how they are connected to solve the problem. Because this type of problem can be confusing, try to practice as often as time permits and follow these steps:

1. Read the problem entirely.
2. Write down key words.
3. Translate the wording into an organized numeric equation.
4. Solve the problem.
5. Check your work to make sure your answer is reasonable.

Example:

1. If the price of apples is changed from two dozen for $5 to three dozen for $6, how many more apples can be purchased for $30 now than could be purchased before?

   A. 36
   B. 48
   C. 72
   D. 144
   E. 180

Reasoning can help you solve this problem. Let's start by looking at the first part of the problem. If the price of apples is $5 for two dozen, then $30 will allow you to purchase six groups of two dozen apples, or $6 \times 2 \times 12 = 144$ apples.

The second part of the problem shows that when the price of apples is changed to three dozen for $6, then $30 will allow you to purchase five groups of three dozen apples, or $5 \times 3 \times 12 = 180$ apples.

Now let's put these two together and look at the question again. "How many <u>more</u> apples can be purchased for $30 now than could be purchased before?" Therefore, 180 − 144 = 36 more apples can be purchased now. The correct answer to this arithmetic problem is choice A.

Write Down Key Words to Pull Out Information

Writing down key words on your scratch paper (or writing board) is an effective test-taking technique, especially for math word problems that require reasoning abilities. Pulling out information from the word problem can often give you additional insight and help you focus on precisely what you are being asked to calculate.

Example:

> **2.** If 3 yards of fabric cost $12.96, what is the price per foot?
>
> A. $1.44
> B. $4.32
> C. $5.32
> D. $4.00
> E. $12.96

The key word here is *foot*. It is important to immediately make a mental note or write down the word *foot* to help you stay focused on what is being asked in the problem. Dividing $12.96 by 3 will tell you only the price per *yard*. By quickly glancing over the question and not writing down key words, you may have selected choice B. This is because $12.96 divided by 3 equals $4.32. However, choice B is incorrect because you need to divide by 3 again (since there are 3 feet per yard) to find the cost per foot. Choice D is incorrect because it's an approximation of $4.32, and choices C and E are both incorrect. To solve the problem:

$$\$12.96 \div 3 \text{ yards} = \$4.32 \text{ per yard}$$

$$\$4.32 \div 3 \text{ feet} = \$1.44 \text{ per foot}$$

The correct answer to this arithmetic problem is choice A.

Avoid Unnecessary Calculations

Click on the icon found at the top of the screen to use the on-screen calculator, but try to avoid unnecessary calculations. Remember that the calculator should only be used for time-consuming computations (square roots, long division, and problems with several digits).

Example:

> **3.** What is the final cost of a scarf that sells for $49 if the sales tax is 7%?
>
> A. $49.07
> B. $49.70
> C. $52.00
> D. $52.43
> E. $56.00

First, write down or make a mental note of the words *final cost*. Since the sales tax is 7% of $49, (.07)($49) = $3.43. The total cost of the scarf is $49.00 + $3.43 = $52.43. The correct answer to this arithmetic problem is choice D.

Substitute Simple Numbers

Substituting numbers for variables can often be an aid to understanding a problem. Try not to use zero and negative numbers when substituting numbers because these numbers can be used to compare variables and may change your answer. Sometimes you will immediately recognize a simple method to solve a problem when substituting numbers.

Example:

---

4. If x is a positive integer in the equation $2x = y$, then y must be

    A.   a positive even integer.
    B.   a negative even integer.
    C.   zero.
    D.   a positive odd integer.
    E.   a negative odd integer.

At first glance, this problem appears quite complex. But let's plug in some numbers and see what happens. For instance, first plug in the number 1 (the simplest positive integer) for x.

$$2x = y$$
$$2(1) = y$$
$$2 = y$$

Now try 2.

$$2x = y$$
$$2(2) = y$$
$$4 = y$$

Try it again. No matter what positive integer is plugged in for x, y will always be positive and even. Therefore, the correct answer to this algebra problem is choice A.

Work Backward from the Answer Choices

Working backward from the answer choices is an accepted method to find the solution, although it usually takes longer than reasoning to find the correct answer. If you don't immediately recognize a method or formula, or if a method will take you a great deal of time, work backward from the answer choices. This method will at least eliminate some of the choices and may help lead you to the correct answer.

Since the answer choices are frequently given in ascending or descending order, always start by plugging in the middle answer choice first if values are given. Then you'll know whether to go up or down with your next try. (Sometimes you might want to plug in one of the simple answer choices first.)

Example:

---

5. Which of the following is a value of r for which $r^2 - r - 20 = 0$?

    A.   4
    B.   5
    C.   6
    D.   7
    E.   8

You should first underline or circle "value of r." If you've forgotten how to solve this equation, work backward by plugging in answers. Start with choice C, plugging in 6.

$$6^2 - 6 - 20 \stackrel{?}{=} 0$$
$$36 - 6 - 20 \stackrel{?}{=} 0$$
$$10 \neq 0$$

Since this answer is too large, try choice B, a smaller number. Plugging in 5 is shown below.

$$5^2 - 5 - 20 \stackrel{?}{=} 0$$
$$25 - 5 - 20 \stackrel{?}{=} 0$$
$$0 = 0$$

This is a true statement. Working backward from the answer choices is a valuable technique.

You could also work this problem by factoring into $(r - 5)(r + 4) = 0$ and then setting $(r - 5) = 0$ and $(r + 4) = 0$, leaving $r = 5$ or $r = -4$.

The correct answer to this algebra problem is choice B.

Approximate

Some questions may only require approximation. It may be useful to look at the answer choices and see how close together or far apart the answers are. This will guide you in determining how close your approximation needs to be to choose the correct answer. Some questions require accurate computations. For others, estimation may be all you need to arrive at the correct answer.

Example:

6. The value of $\sqrt{\dfrac{7,194}{187}}$ is approximately

    A.   6
    B.   9
    C.   18
    D.   35
    E.   72

First, round off both numbers to the hundreds place. The problem then becomes $\sqrt{\dfrac{7,200}{200}}$.

Now this problem is much easier to work. The next step is to divide 7,200 by 200 so that the problem becomes $\sqrt{36}$. Thus, $\sqrt{36}$ can be simplified to the value 6. The correct answer to this arithmetic problem is choice A.

Look for Relationships Among the Answer Choices

In some questions, you are asked which answer choice meets certain requirements. This usually involves examining each answer choice individually. You may find a relationship or pattern among the answer choices that allows you to settle on the correct answer more quickly.

Example:

> **7.** In the sequence 3, 4, 6, 9, 13, 18, . . ., what would be the twelfth number?
>
> A. 58
> B. 68
> C. 69
> D. 70
> E. 81

In the sequence, the difference between the first and second number is 1. The difference between the second and third number is 2. The difference between the third and fourth number is 3, and so forth. Following the same pattern, the first eleven numbers of the sequence are 3, 4, 6, 9, 13, 18, 24, 31, 39, 48, 58, and the twelfth number is 69. The correct answer to this arithmetic problem is choice C.

Make Comparisons

At times, questions will require you to compare the sizes of several decimals or of several fractions. If decimals are being compared, make sure that the numbers being compared have the same number of digits. (Remember that zeros to the far right of decimal point can be inserted or eliminated without changing the value of the number.)

Example:

> **8.** Put these numbers in order from smallest to largest: $0.6, 0.16, 0.66\frac{2}{3}, 0.58$
>
> A. $0.6, 0.16, 0.66\frac{2}{3}, 0.58$
>
> B. $0.58, 0.16, 0.6, 0.66\frac{2}{3}$
>
> C. $0.16, 0.58, 0.6, 0.66\frac{2}{3}$
>
> D. $0.66\frac{2}{3}, 0.6, 0.58, 0.16$
>
> E. $0.58, 0.6, 0.66\frac{2}{3}, 0.16$

First, make a mental note (or write down) "smallest to largest," then rewrite 0.6 as 0.60 so all of the decimals now have the same number of digits:

$$0.60, 0.16\ 0.66\frac{2}{3}, 0.58$$

Now treat these as though the decimal point were not there (this can be done only when all of the numbers have the same number of digits to the right of the decimal). Put in number order:

$$0.16, 0.58, 0.60, 0.66\frac{2}{3}$$

Note: A quick method is to look for the largest place value. In this case it would be the tenths place. Since 1 is the smallest number, we can rule out choices A, B, D, and E.

The correct answer to this arithmetic problem is choice C.

Draw a Simple Diagram

Although it is not time-efficient to draw a diagram for every geometry problem, drawing simple diagrams can help you visualize the facts that have been given and may tip off a simple solution.

Example:

---

9. The perimeter of the isosceles triangle shown below is 42 inches. Each of the two equal sides is three times as long as the third side. What are the lengths of each side, in inches?

$\triangle ABC$ is isosceles

$AB = AC$

- **A.** 21, 21, 21
- **B.** 6, 6, 18
- **C.** 18, 21, 3
- **D.** 18, 18, 6
- **E.** 4, 19, 19

Draw and mark the equal sides of the triangle. $\overline{AB}$ and $\overline{AC}$ are both three times as long as $\overline{BC}$.

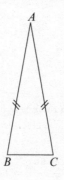 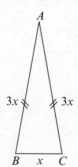

The equation for perimeter is

$$3x + 3x + x = 42$$
$$7x = 42$$
$$x = 6$$

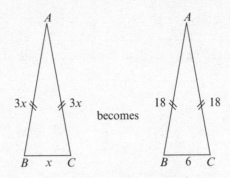

Note: This problem may have been solved by eliminating the wrong answers. Choices A and B are incorrect because they do not have a perimeter of 42″. Choice C is incorrect because it is not an isosceles triangle (it does not have two sides of equal length). Choice E is incorrect because it does not have long sides that are three times the short side. The correct answer to this geometry problem is choice D.

Try "Possibilities" in Probability Problems

Some questions will involve probability. If you can't remember a formal method, try some reasonable "possibilities" by setting up possible combinations. Remember to set up only what is necessary to solve the problem.

Example:

10. What is the probability of throwing two dice in one toss so that they total 11?

- A. $\dfrac{1}{6}$
- B. $\dfrac{1}{11}$
- C. $\dfrac{1}{18}$
- D. $\dfrac{1}{20}$
- E. $\dfrac{1}{36}$

In this problem, you should simply list all of the possible combinations resulting in 11 (5 + 6 and 6 + 5) and realize that the total possibilities are 36 (6 × 6). Thus, the probability equals

$$\frac{\text{possibilities totaling 11}}{\text{total possibilities}} = \frac{2}{36} = \frac{1}{18}$$

The correct answer to this probability problem is choice C.

Determine the Most Efficient Method to Solve the Problem

Some problems may not ask you to find a correct numerical answer. Rather, you may be asked "how to work" the problem.

Example:

---

11. Which of the following methods is the most efficient way to calculate 51 × 6?

    A.   50 × 6 + 6

    B.   51 + 51 + 51 + 51+ 51 + 51

    C.   (50 × 6) + (1 × 6)

    D. $(50 \times 6) + \dfrac{1}{6}$

    E.   adding 51 sixes

The most efficient method of calculating 51 × 6 is to first multiply 50 × 6 (resulting in 300), then multiply 1 × 6 (resulting in 6), and then add the two answers together (300 + 6 = 306). Choices B and E provide the correct answer (306), but neither is the most efficient method to quickly calculate the answer. Although choice C is a variation of the correct answer, choice A, it is not the most efficient. The correct answer to this arithmetic problem is choice A.

Accurately Interpret Data—Graphs, Charts, Tables, and Diagrams

Some math questions are based on interpreting data provided in graphs, charts, tables, and diagrams. To answer questions, you must accurately read and draw conclusions about graphic illustrations before performing calculations. A solid understanding of arithmetic and the ability to make sound decisions by interpreting and calculating numbers will help you solve these types of problems.

Your familiarity with a wide range of graphic illustrations discussed in chapter 5 (see "Graph Interpretation Problems," page 145) will help you answer these types of questions. Spend a few moments studying the title, labels/categories, and numeric values *before* reading the question.

- **Title:** The title always provides an overview of the graph.
- **Labels/categories:** Each category provides information about the whole picture.
- **Numeric values:** The visual illustration of each category quickly distinguishes variations in data (greatest and lowest numerical values).

Examples:

Questions 12 and 13 refer to the following graph.

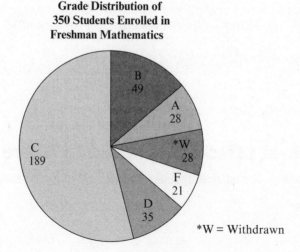

**Grade Distribution of
350 Students Enrolled in
Freshman Mathematics**

*W = Withdrawn

12. If a grade of C or better is required to take the next level mathematics course, what percent of the students qualify?

    A. 54%

    B. 22%

    C. 16%

    D. 76%

    E. 83%

The number of students who received a grade of C or better is:

$$28 + 49 + 189 = 266$$

Next, you should take 266 over the "total number of students." Since $\dfrac{266}{350} = 0.76 = 76\%$, 76% of the students qualify to take the next level mathematics course. The correct answer to this arithmetic problem is choice D.

13. What is the ratio of students who received a grade of B to the total number of students who completed the course?

    A. $\dfrac{7}{50}$

    B. $\dfrac{6}{46}$

    C. $\dfrac{6}{50}$

    D. $\dfrac{49}{350}$

    E. $\dfrac{7}{46}$

Since 28 students withdrew from the class and did not receive a letter grade, $350 - 28 = 322$ students completed the course, of which 49 earned a grade of B.

$$\text{The ratio is: } \frac{\text{students who received a B}}{\text{total number of students who completed the course}} \quad \frac{49}{322} = \frac{7}{46}$$

The correct to this arithmetic problem answer is choice E.

Questions 14 and 15 refer to the following graph.

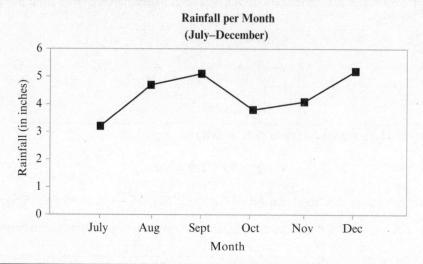

14. Which two months saw the greatest increases in rainfall compared to the months before them?

    A.   July and August
    B.   July and December
    C.   August and September
    D.   September and December
    E.   August and December

In this example, notice that the information is plotted along vertical and horizontal axes. The fastest way to find the greatest increase between data points that are equally spaced on the *x*-axis is to identify the steepest upward slope on the chart.

Note that the sharpest upward trajectory comes before the month of August, and the second sharpest comes before the month of December, as in choice E. The months of September and November also saw increases in rainfall compared to the months before them, but both increases were much smaller.

The correct answer to this arithmetic problem is choice E.

15. Approximately how many inches of rain fell during the month with the second-lowest amount of rainfall?

    A.   3.0
    B.   3.2
    C.   3.8
    D.   4.2
    E.   5.0

The first step in solving this problem is to identify the month with the second smallest amount of rainfall, which is October (the lowest was in July). The data point for October is clearly below the marker for 4 inches, so choices D and E can be eliminated.

However, the data point is also much closer to the marker for 4 inches than to the marker for 3 inches, which eliminates choices A and B. Choice C, at 3.8 inches, is the only answer choice that fits these observations.

Note: A tip for estimating charts is to place a pencil (or your finger) on the horizontal axis and move it upward to the point you want to determine the value of. This way you would realize that October rainfall was just below the 4″ marker.

The correct answer to this arithmetic problem is choice C.

Questions 16 and 17 refer to the following graph.

City Academy Students Playing on the Baseball, Basketball, and Football Teams

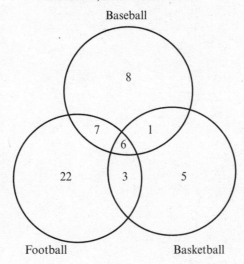

---

16. How many students play on both the football and baseball teams, but not on the basketball team?

    A. 1
    B. 3
    C. 6
    D. 7
    E. 13

The number of students playing on both the football and baseball teams, but not on the basketball team, is found in the overlapping area of the football and baseball circles, but outside of the basketball circle. The number is 7.

The correct answer to this arithmetic problem is choice D.

---

17. How many students play on exactly two of the three teams?

    A. 7
    B. 10
    C. 11
    D. 17
    E. 18

The number of students who play on exactly two of the three teams can be found by adding all of the numbers in overlapping regions *except* for the number in the center region in which all three teams overlap.

Therefore, the number of students who play only football and baseball (7) + the number of students who play only football and basketball (3) + the number of students who play only basketball and baseball (1) = 11 total students who play exactly two sports.

The correct answer to this arithmetic problem is choice C.

Chapter 5
Arithmetic Review (Numbers and Quantity)

Arithmetic (Numbers and Quantity) is the foundation for all mathematical concepts and shares the basic properties of counting: adding, subtracting, multiplying, and dividing. These fundamental concepts, along with Core Standard quantitative reasoning concepts, are covered in this chapter.

Since all math reasoning is best understood through orderly stages of sequential learning, basic arithmetic review is a normal step toward building interconnected associations to help make sense of more advanced quantitative concepts. By studying arithmetic first, you will be strengthening your ability to tackle more challenging problems in algebra, geometry, and statistics.

Start with the arithmetic diagnostic test and use the following chart to work through the topics. As you study the material, check off the topics and focus your attention on one math topic at a time. Then, assess your strengths to evaluate areas in which you feel may need improvement. Even if your cumulative knowledge of math is strong, you should at least skim through each topic heading to help trigger your memory of forgotten math concepts.

Arithmetic Study Guide Checklist

Math Category	Topic	Chapter Review Page Number	Worked Examples	Further Study Required
	Diagnostic Test	pp. 112–113		
The Real Number System	Sets of numbers	pp. 115–117		
	Integers	p. 117		
	Math operation symbols	p. 118		
	Number grouping symbols	pp. 118–119		
	Order of operations	p. 119		
	Math properties and operations	pp. 119–121		
	Basic math properties	pp. 119–121		
	Addition and subtraction	p. 120		
	Multiplication and division	pp. 120–121		
	Distributive properties	p. 121		
	Math operations and number rules	pp. 121–124		
	Addition	pp. 121–122		
	Subtraction	pp. 122–123		
	Multiplication	p. 123		
	Division	pp. 123–124		
	Fractions (negative, proper, improper, mixed, reducing, equivalent denominators)	pp. 124–132		
	Factors	pp. 126–127		
	Multiples	pp. 127–128		
	Decimals	pp. 133–136		
	Place value and multi-digit numbers	p. 133		
	Rounding off (approximation)	p. 133		
	Expanded notation	p. 134		
	Adding and subtracting decimals	p. 134		
	Multiplying decimals	pp. 134–135		
	Dividing decimals	p. 135		
	Changing a decimal to a fraction	pp. 135–136		
	Changing a fraction to a decimal	p. 136		

continued

Math Category	Topic	Chapter Review Page Number	Worked Examples	Further Study Required
Ratios and Proportional Relationships	Ratios and proportional relationships	pp. 136–138		
	Ratio	pp. 136–137		
	Proportion	pp. 137–138		
	Percents	pp. 138–142		
	Changing decimals to percents	pp. 138–139		
	Changing fractions to percents	p. 139		
	Fraction-decimal-percent equivalents	p. 139		
	Solving percentage problems	p. 140		
	Solving percentage problems using proportion	pp. 140–141		
	Percent change: increase or decrease	pp. 141–142		
Quantitative Reasoning (Quantities)	Quantitative word problems	pp. 142–143		
	Units of measurement problems	pp. 143–145		
	Graph interpretation problems	pp. 145–148		

Now let's get started and see what arithmetic skills you remember. Take the arithmetic diagnostic test that follows to help you evaluate how familiar you are with the selected arithmetic topics. The diagnostic test will give you valuable insight into the topics you will need to study.

Arithmetic Diagnostic Test

Directions: Solve each problem in this section by using the information given and your own mathematical calculations.

1. Which of the following are integers?
$\frac{1}{2}, -2, 0, 4, \sqrt{25}, -\frac{15}{3}, 7.5$

2. Which of the following are rational numbers?
$5.8, -4, \sqrt{7}, \pi, 2\frac{5}{8}$

3. List the prime numbers between 0 and 50.

4. List the perfect cubes between 1 and 100.

5. $3\left[3^2 + 2(4+1)\right] =$

6. $-4 + 8 =$

7. $-12 - 6 =$

8. $(-6)(-8) =$

9. $\frac{-48}{3} =$

10. Change $\frac{59}{6}$ to a mixed number in lowest terms.

11. Add: $\frac{2}{7} + \frac{3}{5} =$

12. Add: $1\frac{3}{8} + 2\frac{5}{6} =$

13. Subtract: $6\frac{1}{8} - 3\frac{3}{4} =$

14. Multiply: $-\frac{1}{6} \times \frac{1}{3} =$

15. Multiply: $2\frac{3}{8} \times 1\frac{5}{6} =$

16. Divide: $-\frac{1}{4} \div \frac{9}{14} =$

17. Divide: $2\frac{3}{7} \div 1\frac{1}{4} =$

18. What is $0.08 + 1.3 + 0.562$?

19. What is $0.45 - 0.003$?

20. What is the product of 8.001 and 2.4?

21. What is $0.147 \div 0.7$?

22. Change $\dfrac{3}{20}$ to a decimal.

23. Change 7% to a decimal.

24. Round 96,372 to the nearest thousand.

25. Round -3.6 to the nearest integer.

26. Solve the proportion for x: $\dfrac{4}{x} = \dfrac{7}{5}$

27. Change $\dfrac{1}{8}$ to a percent.

28. What is 79% of 64?

29. 40% of what is 20?

30. What percent of 45 is 30?

31. What is the percent increase of a rise in temperature from 80° to 100°?

32. Find the simple interest on $15,000 borrowed for 4 years at an annual rate of 5%.

33. If an item is marked down from $75 to $50, what is the percent decrease?

34. Convert 972 inches to yards.

35. Convert 17 gallons to pints.

Scoring the Diagnostic Test

The following section assists you in scoring and analyzing your diagnostic test results. Use the answer key and the analysis worksheet that follows to help you evaluate specific problem types. Corresponding topic headings can be found in the arithmetic review section following the diagnostic test. In fact, most of the diagnostic problems are covered in the review, with details on how to solve them.

Answer Key

Sets of Numbers

1. $-2, 0, 4, \sqrt{25}, -\dfrac{15}{3}$

2. $5.8, -4, 2\dfrac{5}{8}$

3. 2, 3, 5, 7, 11, 13, 17, 19, 23, 29, 31, 37, 41, 43, 47

4. 8, 27, 64

Order of Operations and Grouping Symbols

5. 57

Integers

6. 4

7. -18

8. 48

9. -16

Fractions

10. $9\dfrac{5}{6}$

11. $\dfrac{31}{35}$

12. $4\dfrac{5}{24}$

13. $2\dfrac{3}{8}$

14. $-\dfrac{1}{18}$

15. $\dfrac{209}{48} = 4\dfrac{17}{48}$

16. $-\dfrac{7}{18}$

17. $\dfrac{68}{35} = 1\dfrac{33}{35}$

Decimals

18. 1.942

19. 0.447

20. 19.2024

21. 0.21

22. 0.15

23. 0.07

Rounding Off

24. 96,000

25. −4

Ratios and Proportions

26. $x = \dfrac{20}{7}$ or $2\dfrac{6}{7}$

Percents

27. $12\dfrac{1}{2}\%$ or 12.5%

28. 50.56

29. 50

30. $66\dfrac{2}{3}\%$

31. 25%

32. $3,000

33. $33\dfrac{1}{3}\%$

Units of Measure

34. 27 yards

35. 136 pints

Charting and Analyzing Your Diagnostic Test Results

Record your diagnostic test results in the following chart and use these results as a guide to assist you in planning your arithmetic review goals and objectives. Mark the problems that you missed, paying particular attention to those that were missed in Column (C) because they are unfamiliar math concepts. These are the areas you will want to focus on as you study the arithmetic topics.

Analysis Worksheet

Topic	Total Possible	Number Correct	Number Incorrect (A) Simple Mistake	(B) Misread Problem	(C) Unfamiliar Math Concept
Sets of Numbers	4				
Order of Operations	1				
Integers	4				
Fractions	8				
Decimals	6				
Rounding Off	2				
Ratios and Proportions	1				
Percents	7				
Units of Measure	2				
Total Possible Explanations for Incorrect Answers: Columns A, B, and C					
Total Number of Answers Correct and Incorrect	35	Add the total number of correct answers here: ____	Add columns A, B, and C: _____ Total number of incorrect answers		

Arithmetic Review

The Real Number System

Proficiency with numbers is not just about finding the solution to an equation. It is the ability to see how numbers relate to one another when applied to real-world problems. On the Core Mathematics Test, these types of problems appear as word problems. To help you deconstruct and translate word problems into numeric equations, this section contains references with examples that you can refer to again and again during your math preparation. The basic references in this chapter contain terms, symbols, formulas, and general information.

Sets of Numbers

Numbers can be represented in a variety of ways and have special rules to express how they relate to other quantities. This section introduces these basic sets of numbers and their definitions. On the Core Mathematics Test, you will see references to integers and rational numbers.

Type of Number	Main Features	Description
Natural or counting numbers	• Positive numbers • No zero	{1, 2, 3, 4, 5 …} Natural numbers are the most basic counting numbers. Natural numbers are used when counting objects and can continue to infinity. For example, natural numbers are used when you are counting the number of copies you need to print for handouts to give to your students in class. Zero is *not* a natural number.
Whole numbers	• Positive numbers • Includes zero	{0, 1, 2, 3, 4, …} Whole numbers are all of the natural numbers, but what makes them different is that they include zero. Whole numbers cannot be a fraction and cannot be a decimal. They are simply whole numbers.

Integers	• Positive and negative whole numbers (and zero)
	• Even and odd
	• Cannot be a fraction
	• All integers are rational numbers
		Integers are positive whole numbers, but they can also be negative whole numbers and zero. (***Note:*** Zero is neither positive nor negative.) Integers *cannot* be fractions. The terms *even* and *odd* apply only to integers:
		  Even integers: All integers that are perfectly divisible by 2. {… −6, −4, −2, 0, 2, 4, 6 …}
		  Odd integers: All integers that are *not* perfectly divisible by 2. {…, −5, −3, −1, 1, 3, 5, …}

Rational numbers	• Positive and negative whole numbers (and zero) • Includes fractions, decimals, and repeating decimals	*All integers are rational numbers, but not all rational numbers are integers.* A rational number is a number value that can be expressed as a fraction of the form $\frac{a}{b}$, where a is any integer and b is any nonzero integer. In a decimal form, rational numbers can be expressed as a terminating or repeating decimal. For example: $\frac{1}{4} = 0.25$, $\frac{1}{12} = 0.08333... = 0.08\overline{3}$.

continued

Type of Number	Main Features	Description

Irrational numbers	• Not integers and not fractions	Irrational numbers are not integers and are not fractions. Some examples of irrational numbers are π and $\sqrt{2}$.
		
		 In decimal form, an irrational number neither terminates nor has any block of repeating digits. For example:
		
		     π: The decimal name for *pi* starts out 3.14159265… The decimal name for *pi* does not terminate, nor does it have a repeating pattern.
		
		     $\sqrt{2}$: The decimal name for the square root of 2 starts out 1.141421356… The decimal name for the square root of 2 does not terminate, nor does it have a repeating pattern.

Real numbers	• Most of the numbers you will encounter are real numbers	Real numbers are natural numbers, whole numbers, integers, rational numbers, and irrational numbers. Real numbers are the union of sets of rational and irrational numbers and include fractions and decimal numbers.
Prime numbers	• Integers greater than 1 • Divisible ONLY by 1 and itself	Prime numbers are all integers greater than 1 that are divisible only by 1 and the number itself (prime numbers have exactly two different divisors). Zero and 1 are *not* prime numbers. The only even prime number is 2. The first 10 prime numbers are 2, 3, 5, 7, 11, 13, 17, 19, 23, and 29. For example: 23 is a prime number because it can be divided by only 23 and 1. On the other hand, the integer 16 is *not* a prime number because it can be divided by 1, 2, 4, 8, and 16.
Composite numbers	• Integers greater than 1 (that are not prime)	Composite numbers are any integers greater than 1 that are not prime. The first 10 composite numbers are 4, 6, 8, 9, 10, 12, 14, 15, 16, and 18. A composite number is divisible by more than just 1 and itself. *Note:* 1 is neither prime nor composite.

Square numbers		Square numbers are nonzero integers that are multiplied by themselves. Square numbers are the result of multiplying numbers times themselves. The first seven square numbers are 1, 4, 9, 16, 25, 36, and 49. For example:
		
		     16 is a square number because it can be written as 4^2 or 4×4.
		     $\{(\pm 1)^2, (\pm 2)^2, (\pm 3)^2, (\pm 4)^2, …\} = \{1, 4, 9, 16, …\}$
		 Note: Multiplying two negative numbers always gives a positive answer. For example: $(-1)^2 = (-1)(-1) = 1$.

Cube numbers		Cube numbers are nonzero integers that are the result of cubing a number. For example:
		
		     8 is a cube number because it can be written as 2^3 or $2 \times 2 \times 2$.
		     -27 is a cube number because it can be written as $(-3)^3$ or $-3 \times -3 \times -3$.
		     Cubes can be positive or negative. $\{(\pm 1)^3, (\pm 2)^3, (\pm 3)^3, (\pm 4)^3, …\} = \{\pm 1, \pm 8, \pm 27, \pm 64, ….\}$

Examples:

---

1. Which of the following are integers? $\frac{1}{2}, -2, 0, 4, \sqrt{25}, -\frac{15}{3}, 7.5$

Integers are only whole numbers or their opposites. Only the numbers $-2, 0, 4, \sqrt{25} = 5$, and $-\frac{15}{3} = -5$ are integers.

---

2. Which of the following are rational numbers? $5.8, -4, \sqrt{7}, \pi, 2\frac{5}{8}$

Any value that can be expressed as $\dfrac{\text{integer}}{\text{nonzero integer}}$ or as a decimal that either ends or has a repeating pattern is a rational number. Only the numbers $5.8, -4$, and $2\frac{5}{8}$ are rational numbers.

---

3. List the prime numbers between 0 and 50.

A prime number is an integer greater than 1 that can be divided only by itself or 1. Only the numbers 2, 3, 5, 7, 11, 13, 17, 19, 23, 29, 31, 37, 41, 43, and 47 satisfy this definition for integers between 1 and 50.

---

4. List the perfect cubes between 1 and 100.

Perfect cubes are integers raised to the third power (see "Exponents," chapter 6, page 159). The perfect cubes between 1 and 100 come from $2^3 = 8$, $3^3 = 27$, and $4^3 = 64$. The value 1 is not between 1 and 100, thus $1^3 = 1$ is not included in this list. The perfect cubes between 1 and 100 are, therefore, 8, 27, and 64.

Integers

Number Line

On a **number line,** the numbers to the right of 0 are *positive*. Numbers to the left of 0 are *negative,* as follows:

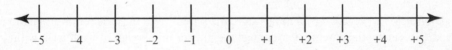

Given any two integers on a number line, the integer located the farthest to the right is always larger, regardless of its sign (positive or negative). Note that fractions may also be placed on a number line and can be similarly compared.

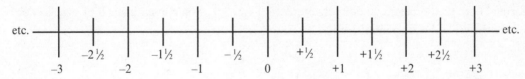

Examples:

For each pair of values, select the one with the greater value.

---

1. $-8, -3$

$-3 > -8$ since -3 is farther to right on the number line.

---

2. $0, -3\frac{1}{4}$

$0 > -3\frac{1}{4}$ since 0 is farther to the right on the number line.

Math Operation Symbols

Math symbols represent a quick method for identifying math operations of numbers. Below is a list of commonly used math symbols.

Symbol	Definition	Example	Written Examples
$=$	is equal to	$x = 5$	x is equal to 5
$\neq$	is not equal to	$x \neq 5$	x is not equal to 5
$\approx$	is approximately equal to	$x \approx y$	x is approximately equal to y
$>$	is greater than	$6 > 5$	6 is greater than 5
$\geq$	is greater than or equal to	$x \geq 5$	x is greater than or equal to 5
$<$	is less than	$4 < 5$	4 is less than 5
$\leq$	is less than or equal to	$x \leq 5$	x is less than or equal to 5
$\sqrt{}$	the square root of, or "radical"	$\sqrt{9}$	the square root of 9
$\perp$	is perpendicular to	$a \perp b$	line a is perpendicular to line b
$\parallel$	is parallel to	$a \parallel b$	line a is parallel to line b
$\sim$	is similar to	$\triangle ABC \sim \triangle DEF$	triangle ABC is similar to triangle DEF
$\cong$	is congruent to	$\angle A \cong \angle C$	angle A is congruent to angle C

Number Grouping Symbols

Parentheses ( ), brackets [ ], and braces { } are frequently needed to group numbers in mathematics. Generally, parentheses are used first, followed by brackets and then braces. Operations inside grouping symbols must be performed before any operations outside of the grouping symbols (see "Order of Operations" on page 119).

1. **Parentheses** are used to group numbers or variables. Calculations inside parentheses take precedence and should be performed before any other operations.

    $$50(2 + 6) = 50(8) = 400$$

    If a set of parentheses is preceded by a minus sign, the parentheses must be removed before calculations can be performed. To remove the parentheses, change the plus or minus sign of each term within the parentheses.

    $$6 - (-3 + a - 2b + c) = 6 + 3 - a + 2b - c = 9 - a + 2b - c$$

2. **Brackets** and **braces** are also used to group numbers or variables. Operations inside parentheses should be performed first, then brackets, and finally braces: $\left\{ \left[\left(\ \right) \right] \right\}$. Sometimes, instead of brackets or braces, you'll see the use of larger parentheses:

    $$\left((3+4) \cdot 5 \right) + 2$$

    An expression using all three grouping symbols might look like this:

    $$2\left\{ 1 + \left[4(2+1) + 3 \right] \right\}$$

This expression can be simplified as follows (notice that you work from the innermost set of the parentheses):

$$2\{1+[4(2+1)+3]\} = 2\{1+[4(3)+3]\}$$
$$= 2\{1+[12+3]\}$$
$$= 2\{1+[15]\}$$
$$= 2\{16\}$$
$$= 32$$

Order of Operations

If multiplication, division, exponents, addition, subtraction, or parenthetical (grouping symbols) are all contained in one problem, the **order of operations** is as follows:

1. Parentheses (or other grouping symbols)
2. Exponents
3. Multiplication or division in the order it occurs from left to right
4. Addition or subtraction in the order it occurs from left to right

---

Tip: An easy way to remember the order of operations is **P**lease **E**xcuse **M**y **D**ear **A**unt **S**ally (**P**arentheses, **E**xponents, **M**ultiplication, **D**ivision, **A**ddition, and **S**ubtraction).

Examples:

---

1. $3\left[3^2 + 2(4+1)\right] = 3\left[3^2 + 2(5)\right]$ — Innermost parentheses first.

$3\left[3^2 + 2(5)\right] = 3\left[9 + 2(5)\right]$ — Exponents next.

$3\left[9 + 2(5)\right] = 3[9+10]$ — Multiply and divide in order from left to right inside the brackets first.

$3[9+10] = 3[19]$ — Add and subtract in order from left to right.

$3[19] = 57$

2. $10 - 3 \times 6 + 10^2 + (6+1) \times 4 = 10 - 3 \times 6 + 10^2 + 7 \times 4$ — Parentheses first.

$10 - 3 \times 6 + 10^2 + 7 \times 4 = 10 - 3 \times 6 + 100 + 7 \times 4$ — Exponents next.

$10 - 3 \times 6 + 100 + 7 \times 4 = 10 - 18 + 100 + 28$ — Multiply and divide in order from left to right.

$10 - 18 + 100 + 28 = -8 + 100 + 28$ — Add and subtract in order from left to right.

$-8 + 100 + 28 = 92 + 28$ — Add and subtract in order from left to right.

$92 + 28 = 120$

3. $-3^2 + (-2)^3 = -1(3)^2 + (-2)^3$ — The exponent 2 only applies to the 3, while

$= -1(9) + (-8)$ — the exponent 3 applies to the entire (-2).

$= -9 + (-8)$

$= -17$

Math Properties and Operations

Before we introduce the basic operating steps to add, subtract, multiply, and divide, let's discuss the fundamental mathematical properties you should know to be successful in solving these types of problems.

Basic Math Properties

The "Sets of Numbers" section earlier in this chapter (pages 115–116) described the different types of numbers. The numerical value of every real number fits between the numerical values of two other real numbers, and the result of adding or multiplying real numbers is always another real number. This fact is described as a **closure property.** For example, if you add two even numbers, the answer will always be an even number: $8 + 6 = 14$. Therefore, the set of even numbers is called "closed for addition." This section helps you understand these basic properties of mathematical operations, makes it easier for you to work with real numbers, and helps you conceptually understand how sets of numbers fit together.

Properties of Addition and Subtraction

There are four mathematical properties of addition that are fundamental mathematical building blocks: commutative, associative, identity, and inverse.

Property	Operation	Examples
Commutative property	The word *commute* means "move around or exchange." In the commutative property of addition, when you change the order, it does not affect the sum of two or more numbers.	$a + b = b + a$ $2 + 3 = 3 + 2$ *Note:* The commutative property is NOT true for subtraction: $2 - 3 \neq 3 - 2$
Associative property	The word *associate* means "grouping." In the associative property of addition, grouping does not affect the sum of three or more numbers. Notice that even though the grouping changes (parentheses move), the sums are still equal.	$(a + b) + c = a + (b + c)$ $(2 + 3) + 4 = 2 + (3 + 4)$ *Note:* The associative property is NOT true for subtraction: $(2 - 3) - 4 \neq 2 - (3 - 4)$
Identity property	The sum of 0 and any number is always the original number.	$a + 0 = 0 + a = a$ $5 + 0 = 0 + 5 = 5$
Inverse property	The sum of any number and its additive inverse (opposite) is always 0.	$a + (-a) = (-a) + a = 0$ $5 + (-5) = (-5) + 5 = 0$ *Note:* Zero is its own inverse.

Properties of Multiplication and Division

The four mathematical properties of multiplication (commutative, associative, identity, and inverse) make it easier to solve problems. Before we discuss these properties, notice the different ways to show multiplication.

Multiplication Notation

The operation of multiplication may be represented in a number of ways. For example, the product of two numbers, a and b, may be expressed as

$$a \times b \qquad a \cdot b \qquad ab \qquad (a)(b)$$

Property	Operation	Examples
Commutative property	The order does not affect the product of two or more numbers.	$a \cdot b = b \cdot a$ $2 \cdot 3 = 3 \cdot 2$ *Note:* The commutative property is NOT true for division: $a \div b \neq b \div a$ $2 \div 3 \neq 3 \div 2$

continued

Property	Operation	Examples
Associative property	Grouping does not affect the product of three or more numbers.	$(a \cdot b) \cdot c = a \cdot (b \cdot c)$ $(2 \cdot 3) \cdot 4 = 2 \cdot (3 \cdot 4)$ *Note:* The associative property is NOT true for division: $(a \div b) \div c \neq a \div (b \div c)$ $(2 \div 3) \div 4 \neq 2 \div (3 \div 4)$
Identity property	The product of 1 and any number is always the original number.	$a \cdot 1 = 1 \cdot a = a$ $2 \cdot 1 = 1 \cdot 2 = 2$
Inverse property	The product of any nonzero number and its multiplicative inverse (reciprocal) is always 1.	$a \cdot \dfrac{1}{a} = \dfrac{1}{a} \cdot a = 1 \qquad (a \neq 0)$ *Note:* 0 is the only real number that does NOT have a reciprocal. $2 \cdot \dfrac{1}{2} = \dfrac{1}{2} \cdot 2 = 1$ or $-2 \cdot -\dfrac{1}{2} = -\dfrac{1}{2} \cdot -2 = 1$

Distributive Properties

The distributive property is one of the most used properties in math and is considered a basis for understanding mental operations of math. To *distribute* means to "spread out," and this basic operation makes it easier for you to work with numbers as you separate them into component parts. In the distributive property, it is possible to take a number and separately distribute it across the sum of two or more other numbers before it is either added or subtracted. The following examples show two important distributive properties: multiplication over addition and multiplication over subtraction.

Property	Operation	Examples
Multiplication over addition	This distributive property shows the process of distributing the number on the outside of the parentheses to each term on the inside.	$a \cdot (b + c) = a \cdot b + a \cdot c$ or $a(b + c) = a \cdot b + a \cdot c$ $2 \cdot (3 + 4) = 2 \cdot 3 + 2 \cdot 4$ or $2(3 + 4) = 2 \cdot 3 + 2 \cdot 4$ and $a \cdot b + a \cdot c = a \cdot (b + c)$ $2 \cdot 3 + 2 \cdot 4 = 2 \cdot (3 + 4)$
Multiplication over subtraction	This distributive property shows the process of distributing multiplication over subtraction.	$a \cdot (b - c) = a \cdot b - a \cdot c$ $2 \cdot (3 - 4) = 2 \cdot 3 - 2 \cdot 4$ and $a \cdot b - a \cdot c = a \cdot (b - c)$ $2 \cdot 3 - 2 \cdot 4 = 2 \cdot (3 - 4)$

Math Operations and Number Rules

Math fluency begins with understanding the basic rules for real number operations: addition, subtraction, multiplication, and division.

Addition

Steps to Adding Integers

1. If the two integers have the same sign (either both positive or both negative), add their absolute values and keep the same sign.
2. If the two integers have different signs (one positive and one negative), subtract their absolute values and keep the sign of the integer with the greater absolute value.
3. If the two integers are opposites, their sum is zero.

Examples:

Two Integers with the Same Sign

1. $(-15) + (-8) = -23$

2.
$$\begin{array}{r} -8 \\ +\,-3 \\ \hline -11 \end{array}$$
$\quad |-8| = 8, \quad |-3| = 3, \quad 3 + 8 = 11$

Two Integers with Different Signs

3. $-38 + 25 = -13$

4.
$$\begin{array}{r} +5 \\ +\,-7 \\ \hline -2 \end{array}$$
$\quad |+5| = 5, \quad |-7| = 7 \quad 7 - 5 = 2 \quad |-7| > |+5|$

Two Integers that Are Opposites

5. $14 + (-14) = 0$

Subtraction

Steps to Subtracting Integers

1. To subtract two integers (positive and/or negative), first change the sign of the number being subtracted.
2. Then add.

Examples:

1. $-12 - 6 = -12 + -6 = -18$

2.
$$\begin{array}{r} +12 \\ -\,+4 \\ \hline \end{array} \quad \text{becomes} \quad \begin{array}{r} +\;\;12 \\ +\,-4 \\ \hline +8 \text{ or } 8 \end{array}$$

3.
$$\begin{array}{r} -14 \\ -\,-4 \\ \hline \end{array} \quad \text{becomes} \quad \begin{array}{r} -14 \\ +\,+4 \\ \hline -10 \end{array}$$

Note: When number values are positive, the "+" is dropped: +5 = 5.

Steps to Subtracting Integers if the Minus Sign Precedes Parentheses

1. If a minus sign precedes parentheses, it means everything within the parentheses should be subtracted. Therefore, using the same rule as in the subtraction of integers, change every sign within the parentheses to its opposite.
2. Then add.

As a formula, $a - b = a +$ (the opposite of b).

Examples:

> **1.** $16 - (-7) = 16 + 7 = 23$
>
> **2.** $(-22) - 23 = (-22) + (-23) = -45$

Multiplication

Steps to Multiplying Integers

1. If the two integers have the same sign, multiply their absolute values, and their product will be positive.
2. If the two integers have different signs, multiply their absolute values, and their product will be negative.

Note: Zero times any integers always equals zero.

Examples:

> **1.** $(-3)(8)(-5)(-1)(-2) = 240$
>
> **2.** $(-3)(8)(-1)(-2) = -48$
>
> **3.** $(0)(5) = 0$
>
> **4.** $(8)(9)(0)(3)(-4) = 0$

Division

Steps to Dividing Integers

1. If the two integers have the same sign, divide their absolute values, and their quotient will be positive.
2. If the two integers have different signs, divide their absolute values, and their quotient will be negative.
3. If the first integer is zero and the divisor is any nonzero integer, the quotient will always be zero.

Important note: Dividing by zero is "undefined" and is not permitted. $\dfrac{6}{0}$ **and** $\dfrac{0}{0}$ **are not permitted because there are no values for these expressions. The answer is *not* zero.**

Examples:

> **1.** $\dfrac{-64}{-2} = 32$
>
> **2.** $\dfrac{-64}{2} = -32$
>
> **3.** $0 \div 5$, also written as $\dfrac{0}{5}$, $= 0$

Divisibility Rules

Divisibility rules are shortcuts that help you to quickly determine whether a number can be divided with no remainder. Memorizing these rules can help you immediately evaluate and rule out incorrect answer choices.

If a Number Is Divisible By	Divisibility Rules
2	it ends in 0, 2, 4, 6, or 8.
3	the sum of its digits is divisible by 3.
4	the number formed by the last two digits is divisible by 4.
5	it ends in 0 or 5.
6	it is divisible by 2 and by 3 (use the rules for both).
7	N/A (no simple rule)
8	the number formed by the last three digits is divisible by 8.
9	the sum of its digits is divisible by 9.
10	the last digit is 0.

Examples:

1. Which integers between 1 and 10 divide into 2,730?

2 — 2,730 ends in a 0.

3 — The sum of the digits is 12, which is divisible by 3.

5 — 2,730 ends in a 0.

6 — The rules for 2 and 3 both work.

7 — 2,730 ÷ 7 = 390.

Even though 2,730 is divisible by 10, 10 is not between 1 and 10.

2. Which integers between 1 and 10 divide into 2,648?

2 — 2,648 ends in 8.

4 — 48, the number formed by the last two digits, is divisible by 4.

8 — 648, the number formed by the last three digits, is divisible by 8.

Fractions

Fractions compare two values, written as

$$\frac{1}{2} \quad \frac{\text{numerator}}{\text{denominator}} \quad \text{or } 1 \div 2$$

The **numerator** is written above the fraction bar, and the **denominator** is written below the fraction bar. The denominator cannot be zero since it is undefined. The fraction bar indicates division. All rules for the arithmetic operations involving integers also apply to fractions.

Negative Fractions

Fractions may be *negative* as well as *positive*. However, negative fractions are typically written with the negative sign next to the fraction bar. For example: $-\frac{3}{4}$. You may sometimes see negative fractions expressed as $\frac{-3}{4}$ or $\frac{3}{-4}$.

Proper Fractions and Improper Fractions

Proper Fraction—a fraction where the numerator is less than the denominator, such as $\frac{2}{3}$.

Improper Fraction—a fraction where the numerator is greater than or equal to the denominator, such as $\frac{19}{7}$ or $\frac{8}{8}$. Note that when the numerator and the denominator are equal, the fraction is equal to 1.

Mixed Numbers

When a fraction expression contains both a whole number and a fraction, it is called a **mixed number.** For instance, $7\frac{2}{4}$ and $180\frac{3}{4}$ are both mixed numbers. To change an improper fraction to a mixed number, you divide the denominator into the numerator to get the whole number portion and then place the remainder over the divisor to get the fraction portion. For example:

$$\frac{18}{7} = 2\frac{4}{7} \quad \begin{array}{l} \leftarrow \text{remainder} \\ \leftarrow \text{divisor} \end{array} \qquad \begin{array}{r} 2 \\ 7\overline{)18} \\ \underline{14} \\ 4 \end{array} \quad \begin{array}{l} \longleftarrow \text{2 is the whole number} \\ \\ \text{4 (the remainder)} \\ \longleftarrow \text{becomes the numerator} \end{array}$$

To change a mixed number to an improper fraction, you multiply the denominator of the fraction portion with the whole number and then add the numerator portion to that product. Then put that total over the original denominator.

$$4\frac{1}{2} = \frac{9}{2} \qquad \frac{2 \times 4 + 1}{2} = \frac{9}{2}$$

Examples:

1. Change $5\frac{3}{4}$ to an improper fraction.

$$5\frac{3}{4} = \frac{23}{4} \qquad \frac{4 \times 5 + 3}{4} = \frac{23}{4}$$

2. Change $\frac{59}{6}$ to a mixed number.

$$\frac{59}{6} = 9\frac{5}{6} \qquad \begin{array}{r} 9 \\ 6\overline{)59} \\ \underline{54} \\ 5 \end{array}$$

Reducing/Simplifying Fractions

On the Core Mathematics Test, selected response answer choices containing fractions should be expressed in the lowest terms. However, in numeric entry (fill in the blank) questions, fractions do not need to be reduced to the lowest terms.

To reduce to the lowest terms, divide both the numerator and the denominator by the largest number that will divide them both evenly.

Examples:

1. $\dfrac{30}{50} = \dfrac{30 \div 10}{50 \div 10} = \dfrac{3}{5}$

2. $\dfrac{8}{40} = \dfrac{8 \div 8}{40 \div 8} = \dfrac{1}{5}$

3. $\dfrac{9}{15} = \dfrac{9 \div 3}{15 \div 3} = \dfrac{3}{5}$

Equivalent Denominators in Fractions

The denominator of a fraction can be enlarged by multiplying both the numerator and the denominator by the same number to generate an equivalent fraction.

Examples:

1. Change $\dfrac{1}{2}$ into tenths.

First, determine what number you would multiply 2 by to get 10. The answer is 5. Then multiply both the numerator and the denominator by 5. By multiplying by $\dfrac{5}{5}$, you are making an equivalent fraction because $5 \div 5 = 1$.

$$\frac{1}{2} = \frac{1 \times 5}{2 \times 5} = \frac{5}{10}$$

2. Change $\dfrac{3}{4}$ into fortieths.

$$\frac{3}{4} = \frac{3 \times 10}{4 \times 10} = \frac{30}{40}$$

Factors

Factors of a number are the whole numbers that divide the number with no remainder.

Examples:

1. What are the factors of 8?

$$8 = 1 \times 8 \text{ and } 8 = 2 \times 4$$

Therefore, the factors of 8 are 1, 2, 4, and 8.

2. What are the factors of 24?

$$24 = 1 \times 24,\ 2 \times 12,\ 3 \times 8,\ 4 \times 6$$

Therefore, the factors of 24 are 1, 2, 3, 4, 6, 8, 12, and 24.

Common Factors

Common factors are those factors that are the same for two or more numbers.

Examples:

1. What are the common factors of 6 and 8?

Number	List of factors
6	1 2 3 6
8	1 2 4 8

The common factors of 6 and 8 are 1 and 2.

Note: Some numbers may have many common factors.

2. What are the common factors of 24 and 36?

Number	List of factors
24	1 2 3 4 6 8 12 24
36	1 2 3 4 6 9 12 18 36

The common factors of 24 and 36 are 1, 2, 3, 4, 6, and 12.

Greatest Common Factor

The **greatest common factor** (GCF), also known as the greatest common divisor, is the largest factor common for two or more numbers.

Example:

1. What is the greatest common factor of 24 and 36?

Number	List of factors
24	1 2 3 4 6 8 12 24
36	1 2 3 4 6 9 12 18 36

Notice that while 1, 2, 3, 4, 6, and 12 are all common factors of 24 and 36, 12 is the greatest common factor.

Multiples

Multiples of a number are found by multiplying that number by 1, by 2, by 3, by 4, by 5, and so on.

Examples:

1. Multiples of 3 are 3, 6, 9, 12, 15, 18, 21, and so on.

2. Multiples of 4 are 4, 8, 12, 16, 20, 24, 28, 32, and so on.

3. Multiples of 7 are 7, 14, 21, 28, 35, 42, 49, 56, and so on.

Common Multiples

Common multiples are those multiples that are the same for two or more numbers.

Example:

> **1.** What are the common multiples of 2 and 3?

Number				Multiples						
2		2	4	6	8	10	12	14	16	18	etc.
3		3		6	9		12	15		18	etc.

The common multiples of 2 and 3 are 6, 12, 18,... Notice that common multiples go on indefinitely.

Least Common Multiple

The **least common multiple** (LCM) is the smallest multiple that is common to two or more numbers.

Example:

> **1.** What is the least common multiple of 2 and 3?

Number				Multiples						
2		2	4	6	8	10	12	14	16	18	etc.
3		3		6	9		12	15		18	etc.

The least common multiple of 2 and 3 is 6.

Least Common Denominator

When adding or subtracting fractions, the denominators must be the same. If the denominators are not the same, you must change all denominators to their **least common denominator** (LCD). The LCD is also known as the least common multiple of the denominators. After all the denominators are the same, add fractions by adding the numerators (notice the denominator remains the same).

Examples:

1. $\dfrac{2}{7}+\dfrac{3}{5}=\left(\dfrac{5}{5}\right)\left(\dfrac{2}{7}\right)+\left(\dfrac{7}{7}\right)\left(\dfrac{3}{5}\right)=\dfrac{10}{35}+\dfrac{21}{35}=\dfrac{31}{35}$

35 is the LCD and $\dfrac{2}{7}=\dfrac{10}{35}$, $\dfrac{3}{5}=\dfrac{21}{35}$.

2. $\dfrac{3}{8}=\dfrac{3}{8}$ 8 is the LCD and $\dfrac{3}{8}=\dfrac{3}{8}$

$+\dfrac{1}{2}=\dfrac{4}{8}$ 8 is the LCD and $\dfrac{1}{2}=\dfrac{4}{8}$

$\dfrac{7}{8}$

3. $\dfrac{4}{11}+\dfrac{9}{11}=\dfrac{13}{11}$ or $1\dfrac{2}{11}$

Since the denominators are the same, it is not necessary to find an LCD.

Adding and Subtracting Positive and Negative Fractions

The rules for integers apply to adding or subtracting positive and negative fractions.

$$\text{Addition:} \quad \frac{a}{c} + \frac{b}{c} = \frac{a+b}{c}$$

$$\text{Subtraction:} \quad \frac{a}{c} - \frac{b}{c} = \frac{a-b}{c}$$

Examples:

1. $-\dfrac{1}{2} + \dfrac{1}{3} = -\dfrac{3}{6} + \dfrac{2}{6} = \dfrac{-3}{6} + \dfrac{2}{6} = \dfrac{-3+2}{6} = -\dfrac{1}{6}$

2.
$$\begin{array}{r} \dfrac{3}{4} = \dfrac{9}{12} \\[2mm] +\left(-\dfrac{1}{3}\right) = +\left(-\dfrac{4}{12}\right) \\[1mm] \hline \dfrac{5}{12} \end{array}$$

3. $-\dfrac{7}{8} - \dfrac{2}{3} = -\dfrac{7}{8} + \left(-\dfrac{2}{3}\right)$

$\qquad = \left(\dfrac{3}{3}\right)\left(\dfrac{-7}{8}\right) + \left(\dfrac{8}{8}\right)\left(\dfrac{-2}{3}\right)$

$\qquad = \dfrac{-21}{24} + \dfrac{-16}{24}$

$\qquad = \dfrac{-37}{24} \text{ or } -1\dfrac{13}{24}$

Adding Mixed Numbers

The rules for adding and subtracting integers also apply to mixed numbers. To add mixed numbers, add the fraction portions together, add the whole numbers, and then combine the two results.

Example:

1. $1\dfrac{3}{8} + 2\dfrac{5}{6} = (1+2) + \left(\dfrac{3}{8} + \dfrac{5}{6}\right)$

$\qquad = 3 + \left(\dfrac{9}{24} + \dfrac{20}{24}\right)$

$\qquad = 3 + \dfrac{29}{24}$ $\qquad\qquad \dfrac{3}{8} = \dfrac{9}{24}$ and $\dfrac{5}{6} = \dfrac{20}{24}$

$\qquad = 3 + 1\dfrac{5}{24}$

$\qquad = 4\dfrac{5}{24}$

Subtracting Mixed Numbers

When you subtract mixed numbers, sometimes you may have to "borrow" from the whole number, just as you sometimes borrow from the next column when subtracting ordinary numbers.

Examples:

1. $8\dfrac{1}{4}$

    $-\ 3\dfrac{7}{8}$

    $8\dfrac{1}{4}=8\dfrac{2}{8}=\qquad 7\dfrac{10}{8}$

    $-3\dfrac{7}{8}=3\dfrac{7}{8}=\qquad -3\dfrac{7}{8}$

    $\qquad\qquad\qquad\quad =4\dfrac{3}{8}$

2. $\quad 6=\ 5\dfrac{5}{5}\ \leftarrow$ Borrow 1 in the form of $\dfrac{5}{5}$ from the 6.

    $-3\dfrac{1}{5}=-3\dfrac{1}{5}$

    $\qquad\quad 2\dfrac{4}{5}$

3. $\quad 11=10\dfrac{3}{3}\ \leftarrow$ Borrow 1 in the form of $\dfrac{3}{3}$ from the 11.

    $-\dfrac{2}{3}=-\dfrac{2}{3}$

    $\qquad 10\dfrac{1}{3}$

4. $6\dfrac{1}{8}-3\dfrac{3}{4}=6\dfrac{1}{8}-3\dfrac{6}{8}=\cancel{6}\ \overset{\overset{9}{8}}{\cancel{\dfrac{1}{8}}}-3\dfrac{6}{8}=2\dfrac{3}{8}$

5. $-\dfrac{7}{8}-\dfrac{5}{9}=-\dfrac{63}{72}+\left(-\dfrac{40}{72}\right)\qquad\qquad \dfrac{7}{8}=\dfrac{63}{72},\ \dfrac{5}{9}=\dfrac{40}{72}$

    $\qquad\qquad =-\dfrac{103}{72}\ \text{or}\ -1\dfrac{31}{72}$

Multiplying Fractions

The rules for multiplying and dividing integers also apply to multiplying and dividing fractions when working with positive and negative terms. To multiply fractions, multiply the numerators and then multiply the denominators. Simplify if possible.

Examples:

1. $-\dfrac{1}{6}\times\dfrac{1}{3}=-\dfrac{1\times 1}{6\times 3}=-\dfrac{1}{18}$

2. $\left(-\dfrac{3}{4}\right)\left(-\dfrac{5}{7}\right)=+\dfrac{3\times 5}{4\times 7}=\dfrac{15}{28}$

3. $\dfrac{2}{3}\times\dfrac{5}{12}=\dfrac{10}{36}\qquad$ Simplify $\dfrac{10}{36}$ to $\dfrac{5}{18}$.

    Notice the answer was simplified because $\dfrac{10}{36}$ was not in lowest terms.

Whole numbers can be written as fractions: $3 = \dfrac{3}{1}$, $4 = \dfrac{4}{1}$, and so on.

---

4. $3 \times \dfrac{3}{8} = \dfrac{3}{1} \times \dfrac{3}{8} = \dfrac{9}{8} = 1\dfrac{1}{8}$

When multiplying fractions, it is often possible to simplify the problem by **cross canceling.** To cross cancel, find a number that divides into one numerator and one denominator. In the next example, 2 in the numerator and 12 in the denominator are both divisible by 2.

---

5. $\dfrac{2}{3} \times \dfrac{5}{12} = \dfrac{\overset{1}{\cancel{2}}}{3} \times \dfrac{5}{\underset{6}{\cancel{12}}} = \dfrac{5}{18}$

6. $\dfrac{1}{4} \times \dfrac{2}{7} = \dfrac{1}{\underset{2}{\cancel{4}}} \times \dfrac{\overset{1}{\cancel{2}}}{7} = \dfrac{1}{14}$

Remember: You can cancel only when multiplying fractions.

Multiplying Mixed Numbers

To multiply mixed numbers, change any mixed numbers or whole numbers to improper fractions and then multiply as previously shown.

Examples:

---

1. $2\dfrac{3}{8} \times 1\dfrac{5}{6} = \dfrac{19}{8} \times \dfrac{11}{6} = \dfrac{209}{48}$ or $4\dfrac{17}{48}$

2. $\left(-3\dfrac{1}{3}\right)\left(2\dfrac{1}{4}\right) = -\left(\dfrac{\overset{5}{\cancel{10}}}{\underset{1}{\cancel{3}}}\right)\left(\dfrac{\overset{3}{\cancel{9}}}{\underset{2}{\cancel{4}}}\right) = -\dfrac{15}{2}$ or $-7\dfrac{1}{2}$

Dividing Fractions or Mixed Numbers

To divide fractions or mixed numbers, invert (turn upside down) the second fraction (the one "divided by") and multiply. Simplify where possible.

Examples:

---

1. $-\dfrac{1}{4} \div \dfrac{9}{14} = \left(-\dfrac{1}{\underset{2}{\cancel{4}}}\right)\left(\dfrac{\overset{7}{\cancel{14}}}{9}\right) = -\dfrac{7}{18}$

2. $6 \div 2\dfrac{1}{3} = \dfrac{6}{1} \div \dfrac{7}{3} = \dfrac{6}{1} \times \dfrac{3}{7} = \dfrac{18}{7}$ or $2\dfrac{4}{7}$

Complex Fractions

Sometimes a division of fractions problem may appear in the following form, called **complex fractions.**

$$\dfrac{\dfrac{3}{4}}{\dfrac{7}{8}}$$

The line separating the two fractions means "divided by." This problem may be rewritten as $\dfrac{3}{4} \div \dfrac{7}{8}$. Now follow the same procedure as previously shown.

$$\frac{3}{4} \div \frac{7}{8} = \frac{3}{\cancel{4}_1} \times \frac{\cancel{8}^2}{7} = \frac{6}{7}$$

Some complex fractions require applying the order of operations.

Example:

1. $\quad \dfrac{1}{3 + \dfrac{2}{1 + \dfrac{1}{3}}}$

This problem can be rewritten using grouping symbols.

$$\frac{1}{3 + \dfrac{2}{1 + \dfrac{1}{3}}} = 1 \div \left\{ 3 + \left[2 \div \left(1 + \frac{1}{3} \right) \right] \right\} \quad \text{Start with the most inside grouping.}$$

$$= 1 \div \left\{ 3 + \left[2 \div \left(\frac{4}{3} \right) \right] \right\} \quad \text{Do the next most inside grouping.}$$

$$= 1 \div \left\{ 3 + \left[\frac{\cancel{2}^1}{1} \times \frac{3}{\cancel{4}_2} \right] \right\}$$

$$= 1 \div \left\{ 3 + \left[\frac{3}{2} \right] \right\} \quad \text{Do the next most inside grouping.}$$

$$= 1 \div \left\{ \frac{9}{2} \right\}$$

$$= 1 \times \frac{2}{9}$$

$$= \frac{2}{9}$$

Decimals

As you work with real numbers, it is also important to understand the *value* of numbers assigned.

Place Value

Each position in any decimal number has **place value.** For instance, in the number 485.03, the 4 is in the hundreds place, the 8 is in the tens place, the 5 is in the ones place, the 0 is in the tenths place, and the 3 is in the hundredths place. The following chart will help you identify place value and visually identify the positions of decimal points.

millions	hundred thousands	ten thousands	thousands	hundreds	tens	ones	tenths	hundredths	thousandths	ten thousandths	hundred thousandths
							1/10	1/100	1/1,000	1/10,000	1/100,000
1,000,000	100,000	10,000	1,000	100	10	1	0.1	0.01	0.001	0.0001	0.00001
10^6	10^5	10^4	10^3	10^2	10^1	10^0	10^{-1}	10^{-2}	10^{-3}	10^{-4}	10^{-5}
				4	8	5	0	3			

Rounding Off (Approximation)

To round off any positive number:

1. Underline the place value to which you're rounding off.
2. Look to the immediate right (one place) of the underlined place value.
3. Identify the number (the one to the right). If it is 5 or higher, round the underlined place value up by 1. If the number (the one to the right) is 4 or less, leave your underlined place value as it is and change all the other numbers to the right of it to zeros or drop them if the place value is to the right of the decimal point.

To round off any negative number:

1. Take the absolute value of the number.
2. Do the three steps as previously listed.
3. Re-place the negative sign on the number.

Examples:

> **1.** Round 4.4584 to the nearest thousandth.

The 8 is in the thousandth place. To its right is a 4. Thus, the 8 is left unchanged and the digits to the right are dropped. The rounded-off answer becomes 4.458.

> **2.** Round 3,456.12 to the nearest ten.

The 5 is in the tens place. To its right is a 6. Thus, the 5 is increased by 1, and the digit in the ones place becomes zero. Then, the remaining digits to the right of the decimal point are dropped. The rounded-off answer is 3,460.

> **3.** Round −3.6 to the nearest integer.

|−3.6| = 3.6. Rounding to the nearest integer is the same as rounding to the nearest whole number one. The 3 is in the ones place and to its right is a 6. Thus, 3.6 rounded to the nearest one is 4. Therefore, −3.6 rounded to the nearest integer is −4.

Expanded Notation

Numbers can be expressed in expanded notation to emphasize the place value for each digit. The number 629.453 can be written in expanded notation as

$$600 \quad + \quad 20 \quad + \quad 9 \quad + \quad 0.4 \quad + \quad 0.05 \quad + \quad 0.003$$

$$(6 \times 100) + (2 \times 10) + (9 \times 1) + \left(4 \times \frac{1}{10}\right) + \left(5 \times \frac{1}{100}\right) + \left(3 \times \frac{1}{1,000}\right)$$

Using exponents, 629.453 can be written as

$$(6 \times 10^2) + (2 \times 10^1) + (9 \times 10^0) + (4 \times 10^{-1}) + (5 \times 10^{-2}) + (3 \times 10^{-3})$$

Adding and Subtracting Decimals

To add or subtract decimals, line up the decimal points and place values; then add or subtract in the same manner that you would add or subtract other numbers. It is often helpful to place zeros to the right of the decimal point before adding or subtracting to make the problem more readable.

Examples:

1. $0.08 + 1.3 + 0.562 = 0.080$
    $$1.300$$
    $$\underline{+\ 0.562}$$
    $$1.942$$

2. $0.45 - 0.003 = 0.4\,\overset{4\ 10}{\cancel{5}\ \cancel{0}}$
    $$\underline{-\ 0.0\ 0\ 3}$$
    $$0.4\ 4\ 7$$

A whole number has an understood decimal point to its right.

3. $17 - 8.43 = 1\overset{6\ \ 9\ 10}{7}.\cancel{0}\,\cancel{0}$
    $$\underline{-\ 8.\ 4\ 3}$$
    $$8.5\ 7$$

Multiplying Decimals

To multiply decimal numbers, perform multiplication as usual as if there were no decimal points in the numbers. As you perform the multiplication calculations, you will notice that the decimal points are *not* aligned. Now that you have a numeric answer, it's time to insert the decimal point. To accomplish this, count the total number of digits to the right of the decimal point in all the numbers being multiplied.

Place the decimal point in your answer so that there are the same number of digits to the right. For example, 8.001 has three digits to the right of the decimal point, and 2.4 has one digit to the right of the decimal point. Now add these digits together (3 + 1 = 4). You will place the decimal point four digits from the right in the answer.

Examples:

1.   8.001 ← 3 digits to the right of the decimal point.
   × 2.4 ← 1 digit to the right of the decimal point.
   ─────
   32004
   16002
   ─────
   19.2024 ← Decimal point placed so there are 4 digits to the right of the decimal point.

In Example 2, notice that it is sometimes necessary to insert zeros immediately to the right of the decimal point in the answer to have the correct number of digits.

2.   3.02 ← 2 digits to the right of the decimal point.
   × 0.004 ← 3 digits to the right of the decimal point.
   ─────
   0.01208 ← Zero inserted on the left so there are 5 digits to the right of the decimal point.

Dividing Decimals

To divide decimals, divide as usual. Note that the **divisor** (the number you're dividing by) should always be a whole number. If the divisor is not a whole number and has a decimal, move the decimal point to the right as many places as necessary until it's a whole number. Then move the decimal point to the right the same number of places in the **dividend** (the number being divided into).

Note that sometimes you may have to insert zeros in the dividend (the number inside the division bracket).

Examples:

$$0.147 \div 0.7 \text{ becomes } 0.7\overline{)0.147} = 7\overline{)1.47}^{\,0.21}$$

The decimal point was moved to the right one place in each number.

$$0.002\overline{)26.} = 2\overline{)26000.}^{\,13000.}$$

The decimal point was moved three places to the right in each number. This required inserting three zeros in the dividend.

Changing a Decimal to a Fraction

When changing a decimal to a fraction, numbers to the left of the decimal point are whole numbers and numbers to the right of the decimal point are expressed as fractions determined by their place value.

Read it: 0.8 (eight-tenths)

Write it: $\dfrac{8}{10}$

Reduce it: $\dfrac{4}{5}$

Move the decimal point two places to the right, place that number over 100, and reduce if necessary.

Read it:	0.28 (twenty-eight hundredths)
Write it:	$\dfrac{28}{100}$
Reduce it:	$\dfrac{7}{25}$

Examples:

1. $0.19 = \dfrac{19}{100}$

2. $0.084 = \dfrac{84}{1{,}000} = \dfrac{21}{250}$

3. $8.6 = 8\dfrac{6}{10} = 8\dfrac{3}{5}$

Changing a Fraction to a Decimal

When changing a fraction to a decimal, divide the numerator by the denominator.

For example: $\dfrac{13}{20}$ means 13 divided by 20, or $20\overline{)13.00}^{\,.65} = .65$.

Zeros may be written to the right of the decimal point in the numerator without changing its value. Every fraction, when changed to a decimal, either terminates (ends) or has a number or block of numbers that repeat indefinitely. To indicate a repeating decimal, a bar is used over only the number or block of numbers that repeat.

Examples:

Change each fraction into its decimal name.

1. $\dfrac{3}{20}$ becomes $20\overline{)3.00}^{\,0.15} = 0.15$

2. $\dfrac{5}{8}$ becomes $8\overline{)5.000}^{\,0.625} = 0.625$

3. $\dfrac{7}{12}$ becomes $12\overline{)7.00000}^{\,0.58333} = 0.58333...$ or $0.58\overline{3}$

Ratios and Proportional Relationships

Ratios and proportional relationships are important concepts on the Core Mathematics Test.

Ratio

A **ratio** is a comparison of two quantities and is usually written as a fraction. The ratio of 3 to 5 can be expressed as 3:5 or $\dfrac{3}{5}$.

Examples:

---

1. The ratio of 9 to 20 is $\dfrac{9}{20}$ or 9:20.

2. The ratio of 32 to 40 is $\dfrac{32}{40} = \dfrac{4}{5}$ or 4:5.

3. An SAT preparatory program advertises a student-teacher ratio of no more than five students for every teacher. Which of the following numbers of students and teachers would exceed the program's advertised ratio?

   A. 10 teachers and 5 students
   B. 14 teachers and 3 students
   C. 4 teachers and 18 students
   D. 5 teachers and 26 students
   E. 6 teachers and 29 students

In question 3, the ratio in choice A simplifies to 5 to 1 (5 teachers for every 1 student), and choices B, C, and E all contain ratios of fewer than 5 students per teacher. The ratio in choice D can be simplified to 1 teacher for every 5.2 students, which exceeds the stated maximum ratio. The correct choice is D.

Proportion

A **proportion** is an equation that states that two ratios are equal. Because $\dfrac{5}{10}$ and $\dfrac{4}{8}$ both have values of $\dfrac{1}{2}$, it can be stated that $\dfrac{5}{10} = \dfrac{4}{8}$, or $\dfrac{5}{10}$ is proportional to $\dfrac{4}{8}$.

Proportions and the Cross-Multiplication Rule

To prove that two ratios are equal, use the cross-multiplication rule. The cross-multiplication rule (multiplying across the equal sign) should always produce equal answers.

You can use this cross-multiplication rule to solve any proportion problems. For example, you can test to see if $\dfrac{5}{10} = \dfrac{4}{8}$ by multiplying across the equal sign.

$$\frac{5}{10} \searrow \frac{4}{8} = \frac{5}{10} \nearrow \frac{4}{8}$$
$$5 \times 8 = 10 \times 4$$
$$40 = 40$$

Therefore, $\dfrac{5}{10} = \dfrac{4}{8}$ is a true proportion.

Examples:

---

1. $\dfrac{32}{40} = \dfrac{4}{5}$ is a true proportion since $32 \times 5 = 40 \times 4$.

2. $\dfrac{12}{18} = \dfrac{3}{4}$ is *not* a true proportion since $12 \times 4 \neq 18 \times 3$.

On the Core Mathematics Test, you will be asked to analyze proportional relationships to solve real-world problems.

---

3. The chart below shows Katie's scores on her weekly problem sets through the first 6 weeks of her junior year. In which of the following weeks did she achieve a score proportionate to her score in Week 6?

Week	Questions Correct	Total Questions
1	18	22
2	16	26
3	14	19
4	15	18
5	7	13
6	20	24

   A.   Week 1
   B.   Week 2
   C.   Week 3
   D.   Week 4
   E.   Week 5

Katie scored 20 correct out of 24 total questions in Week 6, which can be simplified to $\frac{5}{6}$. In Week 4, Katie scored 15 correct out of 18 total questions, which can also be simplified to $\frac{5}{6}$. The correct choice is D.

---

4. In researching her genealogy for a class project, Ashley discovers that one of her great-grandparents was Paraguayan. Assuming Ashley has no other Paraguayan lineage, which of the following percentages is proportionate to Ashley's Paraguayan ancestry?

   A.   8%
   B.   12.5%
   C.   16.7%
   D.   18%
   E.   25%

The first step to solving this problem is to figure out how many total biological great-grandparents Ashley has. Assuming each biological parent has two biological parents, and so forth, Ashley has $2 \times 2 \times 2 = 8$ biological great-grandparents. Therefore, the proportion of Ashley's Paraguayan ancestry is $\frac{1}{8}$. Converted into percentage form, this value is 12.5%. The correct choice is B.

Percents

A **percent** is a ratio of a number compared to 100 (hundredths). The symbol for percent is %. For example, the expression 23% is read as 23 hundredths and can be expressed either as a fraction or decimal: $23\% = \frac{23}{100} = 0.23$.

Changing Decimals to Percents

Steps to Change Decimals to Percents	Examples
1. Move the decimal point two places to the right. 2. Insert a percent sign. 3. Add zeros if necessary.	1. $0.75 = 75\%$ 2. $0.005 = 0.5\%$ 3. $1.85 = 185\%$ 4. $20.3 = 2,030\%$

Steps to Change Percents to Decimals	Examples
1. Eliminate the percent sign.	1. 7% = 0.07
2. Move the decimal point two places to the left.	2. 23% = 0.23
3. Add zeros if necessary (see Examples 1 and 3).	3. 0.2% = 0.002

Changing Fractions to Percents

There are two steps for changing a fraction to a percent:

1. Change the fraction to a decimal.
2. Change the decimal to a percent.

Examples:

Change each fraction into a percent.

1. $\frac{1}{8}$ $\quad \frac{1}{8} = 0.125 = 12.5\%$ or $12\frac{1}{2}\%$

2. $\frac{2}{5}$ $\quad \frac{2}{5} = 0.4 = 40\%$

3. $\frac{5}{2}$ $\quad \frac{5}{2} = 2.5 = 250\%$

Fraction-Decimal-Percent Equivalents

A time-saving tip is to try to memorize some of the following equivalents before you take the test to eliminate unnecessary computations on the day of the exam.

$\frac{1}{100} = 0.01 = 1\%$

$\frac{1}{10} = 0.1 = 10\%$

$\frac{1}{5} = \frac{2}{10} = 0.2 = 0.20 = 20\%$

$\frac{3}{10} = 0.3 = 0.30 = 30\%$

$\frac{2}{5} = \frac{4}{10} = 0.4 = 0.40 = 40\%$

$\frac{1}{2} = \frac{5}{10} = 0.5 = 0.50 = 50\%$

$\frac{3}{5} = \frac{6}{10} = 0.6 = 0.60 = 60\%$

$\frac{7}{10} = 0.7 = 0.70 = 70\%$

$\frac{4}{5} = \frac{8}{10} = 0.8 = 0.80 = 80\%$

$\frac{9}{10} = 0.9 = 0.90 = 90\%$

$\frac{1}{4} = \frac{25}{100} = 0.25 = 25\%$

$\frac{3}{4} = \frac{75}{100} = 0.75 = 75\%$

$\frac{1}{3} = 0.33\frac{1}{3} = 33\frac{1}{3}\%$

$\frac{2}{3} = 0.66\frac{2}{3} = 66\frac{2}{3}\%$

$\frac{1}{8} = 0.125 = 0.12\frac{1}{2} = 12\frac{1}{2}\%$

$\frac{3}{8} = 0.375 = 0.37\frac{1}{2} = 37\frac{1}{2}\%$

$\frac{5}{8} = 0.625 = 0.62\frac{1}{2} = 62\frac{1}{2}\%$

$\frac{7}{8} = 0.875 = 0.87\frac{1}{2} = 87\frac{1}{2}\%$

$\frac{1}{6} = 0.16\frac{2}{3} = 16\frac{2}{3}\%$

$\frac{5}{6} = 0.83\frac{1}{3} = 83\frac{1}{3}\%$

$1 = 1.00 = 100\%$

$2 = 2.00 = 200\%$

$3\frac{1}{2} = 3.50 = 350\%$

Solving Percentage Problems

Percentage problems are frequent on the Core Mathematics Test. Before attempting to solve a percentage problem, change the percent to a fraction or decimal, depending upon what seems appropriate. Keep in mind that the word "of" means to multiply.

For example, A is B% of C. If B and C are known, the process is simply to multiply the B-percent value with the C-value to find A.

Examples:

1. What is 79% of 64?

Using decimals: 79% of $64 = (0.79)(64) = 50.56$

Using fractions: 79% of $64 = \dfrac{79}{100} \times \dfrac{64}{1} = \dfrac{5,056}{100}$ or 50.56

2. What is 15% of 50?

Using decimals: 15% of $50 = 0.15 \times 50 = 7.5$

Using fractions: 15% of $50 = \dfrac{\cancel{15}^{3}}{\cancel{100}_{20}} \times \dfrac{\cancel{50}^{5}}{1} = \dfrac{15}{2} = 7\dfrac{1}{2}$ or 7.5

3. What is $33\dfrac{1}{3}\%$ of 36?

The fraction method works best in this case.

$$33\dfrac{1}{3}\% \text{ of } 36 = \dfrac{1}{\cancel{3}_{1}} \times \dfrac{\cancel{36}^{12}}{1} = \dfrac{12}{1} = 12$$

4. 24 is 30% of what number?

$$0.30(x) = 24$$
$$x = \dfrac{24}{0.3}$$
$$x = 80$$

Solving Percentage Problems Using Proportion Methods

Use the following steps to solve percentage problems using the proportion method:

1. Use x to replace the unknown value.
2. Replace *is* with an *equal sign* (=) and replace *of* with *multiplication*. The proportion will look like this: $\dfrac{\%\text{-number}}{100} = \dfrac{\text{"is"-number}}{\text{"of"-number}}$

Examples:

---

1. 40% of what is 20?

$$\frac{40}{100} = \frac{20}{x}$$
$$40x = 2,000$$
$$x = 50$$

Therefore, 40% of 50 is 20.

---

2. What percent of 45 is 30?

$$\frac{x}{100} = \frac{30}{45}$$
$$45x = 3,000$$
$$x = \frac{3,000}{45}$$
$$x = \frac{200}{3} \text{ or } 66\frac{2}{3}$$

Therefore, $66\frac{2}{3}$% of 45 is 30.

Percent Change: Finding Percent Increase or Percent Decrease

Percentage word problems are especially common on the Core Mathematics Test and will test your ability to analyze problems as you translate English words into numeric equations. Make sure that you are familiar with solving this type of problem. To find the percent increase or decrease, use one of the following two formulas. ***Note:*** The terms *percentage increase* (rise), *percentage decrease* (fall), and *percentage change* are the same as percent change.

To find **percent change,** use this formula:

$$\frac{\text{amount of change (increase or decrease)}}{\text{starting amount}} \times 100\% = \text{percent change}$$

Examples:

---

1. Find the percent increase from scoring 12 points to scoring 16 points.

The amount of change from 12 to 16 equals 4, therefore

$$\frac{\text{amount of change}}{\text{starting amount}} \times 100\% = \frac{\cancel{4}^{1}}{\cancel{12}_{3}} \times 100\% = 33\frac{1}{3}\% \text{ increase}$$

---

2. What is the percent increase of a rise in temperature from 80° to 100°?

The amount of change is the difference between 100 and 80, or 20.

$$\frac{\text{amount of change}}{\text{starting amount}} \times 100\% = \frac{\overset{1}{\cancel{20}}}{\underset{4}{\cancel{80}}} \times 100\% = 25\% \text{ increase}$$

3. What is the percent decrease of Jordan's salary if it went from $150 per hour to $100 per hour?

$$\frac{\text{amount of change}}{\text{starting amount}} \times 100\% = \frac{\overset{1}{\cancel{50}}}{\underset{3}{\cancel{150}}} \times 100\% = \left(\frac{100}{3}\right)\% = 33\frac{1}{3}\% \text{ decrease}$$

4. What is the percent change in the monthly sales from 2,100 to 1,890?

$$\frac{\text{amount of change}}{\text{starting amount}} \times 100\% = \frac{\overset{1}{\cancel{210}}}{\underset{10}{\cancel{2,100}}} \times 100\% = 10\% \text{ change}$$

Quantitative Reasoning (Quantities)

This section covers math problems that focus on quantitative reasoning. You will be required to use reasoning and logic skills as you analyze different quantities represented by multiple sources:

- Numbers (numbers, symbols, and variables)
- Word problems (text statements)
- Units of measurement (feet, yards, pounds, etc.)
- Graph interpretation (graphs, charts, tables, and diagrams)

These types of problems may challenge your thinking process, but remember that they may also provide you an opportunity to excel. Once you learn the key strategies to solving these types of problems, you will be able to use your analytical skills to logically make sense of questions.

Consider these steps when approaching quantitative reasoning questions:

Steps to Solving Quantitative Reasoning Questions

1. **Identify what you are trying to solve**. Write down key terms to better understand what the question is asking. For example, "How much **time** does it take to get to the airport **30 miles away**?" or "What is the cost of **two** cell phones at **$124.75** each, plus **one** adapter at **$36.55**?"
2. **Watch for key words**. Watch for key words in the word statement, graph title, or graph labels. For example, look for words or symbols that require an operation (add, subtract, multiply, divide); look for words that signal the unit of measurement (length, width, volume); and look at all labels in the context of a graphic illustration (title, headings, values, categories).
3. **Follow the order of operations**. Always follow the order of operations when setting up your equation, and perform the calculations carefully.
4. **Use the calculator**. Take advantage of the on-screen calculator for time-consuming questions.
5. **Restate**. Restate your answer in a sentence to verify that it makes sense and that it is reasonable.

Quantitative Word Problems

Core math questions often appear as quantitative word problems. To solve word problems, you must be able to translate English words that describe a situation or scenario into a math equation. A common mistake is that the hurried test-taker quickly reads the question and rushes to a solution. Word problems can be misleading unless you carefully organize words into math symbols and numbers.

Words that Signal Math Operations

Use the following list of math operation words to help you decipher word problems.

Operation	Words Signaling an Operation	Written Examples
Addition	• Sum • Plus • Is increased by… • More than…	What is the sum of 5 and 28? What is 5 plus 28? What is 28 increased by 5? What is 4 more than 8?
Subtraction	• Difference • Minus • Is decreased by… • Less/fewer than…	What is the difference between 28 and 5? What is 28 minus 5? 28 decreased by 5 is what? What is 4 fewer than 8?
Multiplication	• Product • Times • Of • At	What is the product of 5 and 28? What is 5 × 28? 5% of 15 is what? Four at 8 cents each would cost how much?
Division	• Quotient • Ratio • Is a part of… • Goes into…	What is the quotient of 28 divided by 5? What is the ratio of 12 to 48, or $\frac{12}{48}$? 5% is what part of 15% 2 goes into 30 how many times?

Examples:

1. Maria purchased a new backpack that sells for $39.99. If the sales tax on the purchase was 8.5%, what was the total cost of the backpack?

$$\begin{aligned}
\text{Sales tax} &= 8.5\% \text{ of } \$39.99\\
&= (0.085)(\$39.99)\\
&= \$3.39915\\
&= \$3.40 \text{ (rounded two decimal places because it needs to be rounded to the nearest cent)}
\end{aligned}$$

Total cost $= \$39.99 + \$3.40 = \$43.39$

2. A history class has 24 female students enrolled and 16 male students enrolled. What is the ratio of male students to the total number of students in the class?

$$\begin{aligned}
\text{ratio} &= \frac{\text{number of male students}}{\text{total number of students}}\\
&= \frac{16}{24+16}\\
&= \frac{16}{40}\\
&= \frac{2}{5}
\end{aligned}$$

A ratio of $\frac{2}{5}$ means that there are 2 male students for every 5 students in the class.

> **Tip:** It is important to note that in a ratio, the first number mentioned is always the numerator unless the directions say "What is the ratio of…"

Units of Measurement Problems

Units of measurement problems draw upon your knowledge of arithmetic and reasoning. Review the following measurement equivalents to make sure you are comfortable with the terminology of unit quantities before solving these types of problems.

Unit and Measurement Equivalents

Basic Metric Prefixes

milli (m) = $\dfrac{1}{1,000}$, or 0.001	deca (da) = 10
centi (c) = $\dfrac{1}{100}$, or 0.01	hecto (h) = 100
deci (d) = $\dfrac{1}{10}$, or 0.1	kilo (k) = 1,000

Length

English	Metric
12 inches (in) = 1 foot (ft) 3 feet = 1 yard (yd) 36 inches = 1 yard (yd) 5,280 feet = 1 mile (mi) 1,760 yards = 1 mile (mi)	10 millimeter (mm) = 1 centimeter (cm) 10 centimeters = 1 decimeter (dm) 10 decimeters = 1 meter (m) 10 meters = 1 decameter (dam) 10 decameters = 1 hectometer (hm) 10 hectometers = 1 kilometer (km)
Note: The basic unit of length in the metric system is the meter (m). It is approximately 3 inches more than a yard, or approximately 39 inches.	
1 kilometer is about 0.6 mile.	

Weight

English	Metric
16 ounces (oz) = 1 pound (lb) 2,000 pounds = 1 ton (T)	10 milligram (mg) = 1 centigram (cg) 10 centigrams = 1 decigram (dg) 10 decigrams = 1 gram (g) 10 grams = 1 decagram (dag) 10 decagrams = 1 hectogram (hg) 10 hectograms = 1 kilogram (kg)
Note: The basic unit of weight in the metric system is the gram (g). 1 ounce is approximately 28 grams. A more useful measure of weight is the kilogram (kg), or 1,000 grams, which is approximately 2.2 pounds.	
1,000 kilograms = 1 metric ton.	

Volume (capacity)

English	Metric
1 cup (C) = 8 fluid ounces (fl oz) 2 cups = 1 pint (pt) 2 pints = 1 quart (qt) 4 quarts = 1 gallon (gal)	10 milliliter (ml or mL) = 1 centiliter (cl or cL) 10 centiliters = 1 deciliter (dl or dL) 10 deciliters = 1 liter (l or L) 10 liters = 1 decaliter (dal or daL) 10 decaliters = 1 hectoliter (hl or hL) 10 hectoliters = 1 kiloliter (kl or kL)
Note: The basic unit of volume in the metric system is the liter (L). One liter is approximately 1 quart.	

Time/Calendar

Time	Calendar Days
60 seconds = 1 minute 60 minutes = 1 hour 24 hours = 1 day 7 days = 1 week	365 days = 1 year 12 months = 1 year 52 weeks = 1 year

Units of Measure – English System

Examples:

---

1. How many inches in 9 yards?

Since 1 yard = 36 inches, 9 yards = 9 × 36 = 324 inches.

---

2. How many miles in 7,040 yards?

Since 1 mile = 1,760 yards, 7,040 yards = 7,040 ÷ 1,760 = 4 miles.

---

3. How many pounds in 352 ounces?

Since 1 pound = 16 ounces, 352 ounces = 352 ÷ 16 = 22 pounds.

---

4. How many pints in 7 gallons?

Since 1 gallon = 4 quarts, 7 gallons = 7 × 4 = 28 quarts.

Since 1 quart = 2 pints, 28 quarts = 28 × 2 = 56 pints.

---

5. How many weeks in 343 days?

Since 1 week = 7 days, 343 days = 343 ÷ 7 = 49 weeks.

---

6. How many minutes in 6 days?

Since 1 day = 24 hours, 6 days = 24 × 6 = 144 hours.

Since 1 hour = 60 minutes, 144 hours = 144 × 60 = 8,640 minutes.

Units of Measure – Metric System

Examples:

---

1. 1 kilometer = 1,000 meters

2. 1 milligram = 0.001 gram

3. 1 centiliter = 0.01 liter

4. 1 meter = 100 centimeters

5. 1 liter = 10 deciliters

6. 1 gram = 0.001 kilogram

7. 1 centimeter = 10 millimeters

8. 1 decigram = 10 centigrams

9. 1 deciliter = 100 milliliters

Graph Interpretation Problems

Graph interpretation problems (also called data interpretation problems) draw upon your knowledge of reasoning, descriptive arithmetic, and graph analysis. Visual illustrations of graphs, charts, tables, and diagrams are commonly used to evaluate the numeric values of real-world problems. Visual pictures help to provide a clear picture about the compiled data in order to show patterns and trends and to draw conclusions.

Graph interpretation strategies were introduced in chapter 4 on page 106. Remember that you must accurately read and draw conclusions about graphic illustrations before performing calculations. Always read the title, labels, and values (if available) when interpreting graphs.

Types of Graphic Illustrations

Circle or pie graphs	Circle or pie graphs show comparisons and are used to show relative proportions (fractions) of a whole circle; they are especially good visual representations of percentage problems. For example, a circle graph shows the relationship between a whole circle (100%) and portions (slices) of a circle called *sectors*. The size of each sector compared to the whole circle represents the ratio of the individual categories to the whole circle.
Bar graph	A bar graph (histogram) is commonly used to quickly compare data or frequencies. The bars (columns) can be either vertical or horizontal and can appear as single bars, a group of bars, or stacked bars. The bars should be labeled to indicate the differences between the various categories.
Line graph	A line graph is a common graphic representation on the Core Mathematics Test. The line represents increases or decreases in data information as points on a two-dimensional coordinate system. This type of graph provides a good visual picture of changes or trends in data values and can be valuable in hypothesizing predictions over time.
Charts and tables	A chart or table is often used to organize lists of data in a more readable and organized format. Charts often help to effectively view multiple values of data simultaneously, making it easier to compare and compute *averages* or *ranges*.
Venn diagrams	A Venn diagram is a useful method to visually represent two or more sets and to illustrate whether the sets have any elements in common. Sets are generally represented as circles or ovals, but other geometric figures can be used. Sets that have elements in common will overlap, while sets that have no elements in common are shown disjointed from each other.

Examples:

Question 1 refers to the following graph.

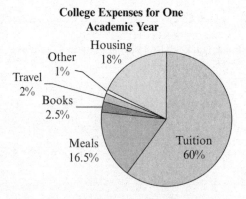

College Expenses for One Academic Year

1.	What is the ratio of the amount spent on housing to the amount spent on tuition?

The circle graph shows a comparison of a student's college expenses for one academic year. Since housing accounted for 18% of college expenses and tuition accounted for 60% of college expenses, the ratio of the amount spent on housing to the amount spent on tuition is $\dfrac{18}{60} = \dfrac{3}{10}$.

Question 2 refers to the following graph.

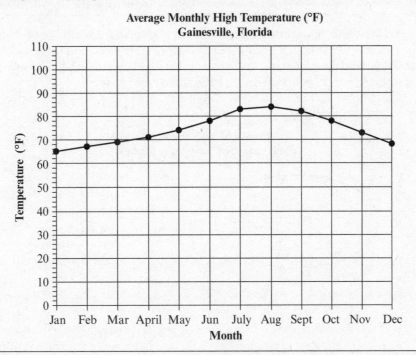

Average Monthly High Temperature (°F)
Gainesville, Florida

2. What was the approximate percent decrease in the average high temperature from August to December? Round the answer to the nearest percent.

$$\text{percent decrease} = \frac{\text{decrease amount}}{\text{original amount}}$$

This line graph shows that the average high temperature dropped from 84° in August to 68° in December for a decrease of 16°.

$$\text{percent decrease} = \frac{16}{84} \approx 0.190 \approx 19\%$$

Question 3 refers to the following graph.

Railroad Track in Use 1875–1915 (in thousands of miles)

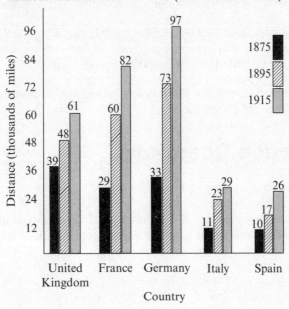

> **3.** In hundreds of miles of track, how much more was in use in France in 1895 than in Spain in 1915?

To answer this bar graph question, be aware that the information given in track miles is in thousands of miles and the question asked for an answer in hundreds of miles. For example, 2 thousand miles would be 20 hundred miles. France in 1895 had 60 thousand miles of track, and Spain in 1915 had 26 thousand miles of track. The difference is 34 thousand miles of track, which, in hundreds, is 340 hundred miles of track.

Question 4 refers to the following diagram.

**Percent of All Students at
Hollywood High Enrolled in Classes**

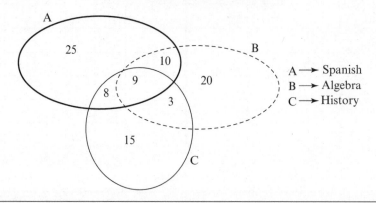

> **4.** What percent of all the students at Hollywood High are not enrolled in history?

Assumptions: In this Venn diagram, region A represents the percent of the students at Hollywood High who are taking Spanish, region B represents the percent of students at Hollywood High taking algebra, and region C represents the percent of students at Hollywood High taking history.

Only looking at region A and the regions it overlaps, we can make the following conclusions from the diagram:

- 25% of the students at Hollywood High take Spanish but do not take either algebra or history.
- 10% of the students at Hollywood High take Spanish and algebra, but not history.
- 9% of the students at Hollywood High take Spanish, algebra, and history.
- 8% of the students at Hollywood High take Spanish and history, but not algebra.

One approach to help you answer this question is to take the percentage of students who are enrolled in history, and then subtract that from 100%. Another approach is to add the percentages indicated outside of history and be sure to add in the 10% who are not taking any of the three classes.

According to the diagram, there are 8% + 9% + 3% + 15% = 35% of the students taking history; thus, there are 100% – 35% = 65% of the students not taking history.

Arithmetic Practice Questions

Now that you have reviewed arithmetic topics and concepts, you can practice on your own. Questions appear in the format of the Core Mathematics Test question types: selected response (select one answer), selected response (select one or more answers), and numeric entry (fill in the blank). These practice questions give you a chance to solve problems in the same format as the actual test. The answers and explanations that follow the questions include strategies to help you understand how to solve the problems.

General Directions: Answer each question by selecting the correct response from the choices given. Practice questions have several different formats. Unless otherwise directed, indicate a single answer choice.

1. Put these fractions in order from smallest to largest: $\dfrac{5}{8}, \dfrac{3}{4}, \dfrac{2}{3}$

   A. $\dfrac{2}{3}, \dfrac{3}{4}, \dfrac{5}{8}$

   B. $\dfrac{2}{3}, \dfrac{5}{8}, \dfrac{3}{4}$

   C. $\dfrac{5}{8}, \dfrac{2}{3}, \dfrac{3}{4}$

   D. $\dfrac{3}{4}, \dfrac{5}{8}, \dfrac{2}{3}$

   E. $\dfrac{3}{4}, \dfrac{2}{3}, \dfrac{5}{8}$

2. Katie wants to buy a block of tickets for a theater play. She can spend $3,500 for the tickets. Tickets for orchestra seats cost $17.50 each, and tickets for balcony seats cost $12.50 each. How many more tickets can Katie buy if she chooses to buy tickets for balcony seats instead of buying tickets for orchestra seats?

   A. 65
   B. 70
   C. 75
   D. 80
   E. 85

3. The following four operations were performed in succession on a given value: divide by 3, multiply by 6, divide by 4, and multiply by 3. Which of the following two operations, when performed in succession, would accomplish the same thing?

   A. Multiply by 9 and then divide by 4.
   B. Divide by 4 and then multiply by 3.
   C. Multiply by 4 and then divide by 3.
   D. Divide by 3 and then multiply by 2.
   E. Multiply by 3 and then divide by 2.

4. A third-grade class is composed of 16 girls and 12 boys. There are 2 teacher aides in the class. What is the ratio of girls to boys to teacher aides?

   A. $16 : 12 : 1$
   B. $8 : 6 : 2$
   C. $8 : 6 : 1$
   D. $8 : 3 : 1$
   E. $4 : 3 : 1$

5. If a product costs $47, which of the following sales tax rates would keep the total cost less than $50?

   Select **all** that apply.

   A. 5.0%
   B. 5.5%
   C. 6.0%
   D. 6.5%
   E. 7.0%

6. A political club is composed of nine members, five men and four women. Of the five men, two are Democrats and three are Republicans. Of the four women, three are Democrats and one is a Republican. What is the ratio of the percentage of men who are Democrats to the percentage of women who are Democrats?

   A. $\dfrac{7}{15}$

   B. $\dfrac{8}{15}$

   C. $\dfrac{2}{3}$

   D. $\dfrac{4}{5}$

   E. $\dfrac{5}{4}$

7. The fastest method to solve $\dfrac{7}{48} \times \dfrac{6}{7}$ is to

   A. invert the second fraction and then multiply.
   B. multiply each column across and then reduce to the lowest terms.
   C. find the common denominator and then multiply across.
   D. divide 7 into the numerator and denominator, divide 6 into the numerator and denominator, and then multiply across.
   E. reduce the first fraction to the lowest terms and then multiply across.

8. Which of the following numbers would lie between $\frac{1}{8}$ and $\frac{1}{9}$ on a real number line?

- A. 0.11
- B. 0.12
- C. 0.13
- D. 0.18
- E. 0.19

9. What is the number of inches in 15 yards?

10. Which of the following decimals lie between 0.53 and 0.842 on the real number line?

Select **all** that apply.

- A. 0.394
- B. 0.4
- C. 0.5314
- D. 0.71
- E. 0.85

11. In the Venn diagram below, circle A represents all multiples of 3 that are below 20 and circle B represents all multiples of 2 that are below 20. How many integers are represented by the shaded portion?

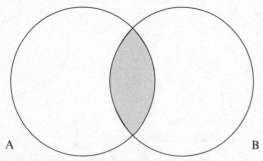

- A. 3
- B. 4
- C. 5
- D. 6
- E. 9

12. The circle graph below represents the Central High School senior prom budget, distributed across five expense categories.

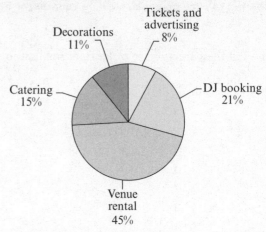

If the total budget is $4,000, how many of the expense categories are budgeted for under $500?

- A. 1
- B. 2
- C. 3
- D. 4
- E. 5

13. Of the following, which is the most likely height of a high school student's desk?

- A. 1 meter
- B. 2 yards
- C. 90 inches
- D. 245 centimeters
- E. 500 millimeters

Answers and Explanations

1. **C.**

   Solution 1: Use the common denominator to help you solve this problem.

   $$\frac{5}{8} = \frac{15}{24}$$
   $$\frac{3}{4} = \frac{18}{24}$$
   $$\frac{2}{3} = \frac{16}{24}$$

   Using this information, you can easily see that the order from smallest to largest is $\frac{5}{8}, \frac{2}{3}, \frac{3}{4}$.

   Solution 2: Use decimal equivalents to help you solve this problem.

   $$\frac{5}{8} = 0.625, \quad \frac{3}{4} = 0.75 \text{ or } 0.750, \quad \text{and } \frac{2}{3} = 0.66\frac{2}{3} \text{ or } 0.666\frac{2}{3}$$

   The order again becomes $\frac{5}{8}, \frac{2}{3}, \frac{3}{4}$.

2. **D.** Although this problem can be done without a calculator, this is one case where use of the calculator would definitely save you time. Divide $3,500 by both $17.50 and $12.50 to determine how many of each type of ticket can be purchased with the $3,500. Then, subtract the two quantities. Katie could buy 280 balcony seat tickets or 200 orchestra seat tickets. Thus, the difference is 80.

3. **E.** Starting with the number x, performing the required four operations would yield $\frac{6 \times 3}{3 \times 4} x$. This simplifies to $\frac{6 \times 3}{3 \times 4} x = \frac{6}{4} x = \frac{3}{2} x$. Therefore, the two required operations to accomplish the same thing as the given four operations is to multiply by 3 and then divide by 2.

4. **C.** Girls to boys to teacher aides are in proportion 16 to 12 to 2. Ratios should be written in reduced form. Dividing each number by 2 gives a ratio of $8 : 6 : 1$.

5. **A, B, and C.**

   To solve, find the total cost using each of the sales taxes given:

   Choice A: 5.0% of $47 = (0.05)($47) = $2.35; $2.35 + $47 = $49.35

   Choice B: 5.5% of $47 = (0.055)($47) = $2.59; $2.59 + $47 = $49.59

   Choice C: 6.0% of $47 = (0.06)($47) = $2.82; $2.82 + $47 = $49.82

   Choice D: 6.5% of $47 = (0.065)($47) = $3.06; $3.06 + $47 = $50.06

   Therefore, the sales tax rates that would keep the total cost less than $50 are 5.0%, 5.5%, and 6.0%. Notice that you do not need to check choice E because the sales tax in choice E is higher than in choice D. Choice E is incorrect because the total price would be higher than $50.06.

6. **B.** The percentage of men who are Democrats is $\frac{2}{5} = 40\%$. The percentage of women who are Democrats is $\frac{3}{4} = 75\%$. Now calculate the ratio of these percentages.

   $$\frac{40\%}{75\%} = \frac{40}{75} = \frac{8}{15}$$

7. D. In this problem, the way to determine the fastest method to solve the problem is to "work the problem" as you would if you were working toward the answer. Then see if that procedure is listed among the choices. You should then compare your answer to the other methods listed. If one of the other methods is faster, select the fastest.

These types of problems are not constructed to test your knowledge of obscure tricks in solving mathematical equations. Rather, they test your knowledge of common procedures used in standard mathematical equations. Thus, the fastest way to solve this problem is to first divide 7 into the numerator and denominator.

$$\frac{\overset{1}{\cancel{7}}}{48}\times\frac{6}{\cancel{7}_1}$$

Then, divide 6 into the numerator and denominator.

$$\frac{\overset{1}{\cancel{7}}}{_8\cancel{48}}\times\frac{\cancel{6}^1}{\cancel{7}_1}$$

Then multiply across.

$$\frac{\overset{1}{\cancel{7}}}{_8\cancel{48}}\times\frac{\cancel{6}^1}{\cancel{7}_1}=\frac{1}{8}$$

8. B. Since $\frac{1}{8}=0.125$ and $\frac{1}{9}=0.\overline{11}$ and 0.12 is between $0.\overline{11}$ and 0.125, 0.12 is between $\frac{1}{8}$ and $\frac{1}{9}$ on a real number line.

9. 540

Since 1 yard = 36 inches, 15 yards = 15 × 36 = 540 inches.

10. C and D. Since 0.394 and 0.4 are less than 0.53, and since 0.85 is greater than 0.842, the only decimals that lie between 0.53 and 0.842 on the real number line are 0.5314 and 0.71.

11. A. The shaded portion of the Venn diagram represents the integers that fall into both circles A and B, or that are multiples of both 2 and 3. Multiples of 3 that are below 20 that are also multiples of 2 (or that are also even numbers) include the integers 6, 12, and 18.

12. B. First, divide $500 by the total budget amount ($4,000) to determine the percent of the total budget that $500 represents: 12.5%. Only two of the expense categories on the graph show a smaller percentage than 12.5%: Tickets and advertising (8%) and Decorations (11%).

13. A. The average high school desk is not six feet tall or taller, so choices B and C can be eliminated. 245 centimeters converts to just under 2.5 meters, which is also over 6 feet, so choice D can also be eliminated. 500 millimeters (choice E) converts to half of a meter, which is less than 2 feet off of the ground—too short for the average high school student. One meter translates to just under 3 feet 4 inches, which seems a logical height for a high school desk.

Chapter 6

Algebra and Functions Review

Algebra is a key branch of mathematics that uses the basic building blocks of the four operations of arithmetic: addition, subtraction, multiplication, and division. This chapter defines key algebraic terms, introduces basic algebraic topics, and walks you through step-by-step practice examples.

Use the following table to chart your progress as you review each topic. Check off topics as you study the material. Focus your attention on one math topic at a time, and assess your strengths to evaluate areas in which you feel you may need improvement. To reinforce what you have learned, work the practice questions at the end of this chapter (answers and explanations are provided).

Algebra and Functions Study Guide Checklist

Math Category	Topic	Chapter Review Page Number	Worked Examples	Further Study Required
	Diagnostic Test	pp. 154–155		
Basic Rules	Exponents	p. 159		
	Scientific notation	pp. 159–160		
	Square roots	pp. 160–161		
Seeing Structure in Expressions	Variables	pp. 161–162		
	Algebraic multiplication	p. 162		
	Order of operations and algebraic expressions	pp. 162–163		
	Algebraic word problems	pp. 163–166		
	Polynomials: Monomials, binomials, and trinomials	pp. 166–167		
Reasoning with Equations and Inequalities	Solving linear equations	pp. 167–169		
	Solving linear inequalities	pp. 169–170		
	Analyzing linear relationships: Coordinate graphs	pp. 170–173		
	Simultaneous linear equations	pp. 173–175		
Functions	Building functions	pp. 175–176		

Take the algebra diagnostic test that follows to help you evaluate how familiar you are with the selected algebra topics. The diagnostic test will give you valuable insight into the topics you will need to study.

Algebra Diagnostic Test

Directions: Solve each problem in this section by using the information given and your own mathematical calculations.

1. $8^3 \times 8^7 =$

2. $9^5 \div 9^{-2} =$

Questions 3 and 4 refer to the following statement.

This year the sales at Acme Widget Factory totaled 120,000. Acme Widget Factory expects sales to grow at a rate of 3% a year for the next 7 years.

3. Write an equation that represents the widget sales for year 7 in exponential form.

4. To the nearest whole widget, how many sales will Acme Widget Factory have in year 7?

5. Express 0.00000023 in scientific notation.

6. The value of $\sqrt{211}$ falls between what two whole numbers?

7. Simplify: $\sqrt{80}$

8. Express algebraically: five increased by three times x.

9. Let x represent the number of sales on Monday at Tech, Inc. Write an algebraic expression that represents the sales on Tuesday when the sales on Tuesday are exactly half of Monday's sales.

10. Evaluate $-3x^2 - 4x - 6$ if $x = -5$.

11. Evaluate $\dfrac{x}{3} - \dfrac{x+2y}{y}$ if $x = 2$ and $y = 6$.

12. Simplify: $\dfrac{1}{2x} + \dfrac{7x}{y}$

13. Solve for x: $2x - 9 = 21$

14. Solve for y: $\dfrac{4}{7}y + 6 = 18$

15. Solve for x: $3x - 5 = -2x - 25$

16. Simplify and graph: $2y + x = 7x + 10$

17. Solve for x: $-3x + 5 > 14$

18. Solve for x: $8x + 4 \geq 6x - 10$

Question 19 refers to the following statement.

Sarah's first three test scores in her English class are 87, 91, and 88. In order for Sarah receive a final grade of A, she must have a combined test average of at least 90% from a total of four equally weighted tests.

19. Write a math equation that illustrates the possible scores Sarah could receive on the fourth test in order to receive an A as her final grade in class.

20. $12x + 4x - 23x - (-3x) =$

21. $(4x - 7z) - (3x - 4z) =$

22. $6x^2y(4xy^2) =$

23. What is the slope of a line that goes through points (3, 4) and (4, 8)?

24. Write the linear equation that represents the chart below.

x	y
0	4
2	8
5	14
10	24

25. A bag of marbles contains 715 marbles. If there are 4 times as many other colors as there are green, how many marbles are green?

26. A chemist must dilute 50 ml of a 40% acid solution into a 30% acid solution. How much pure water must be added?

Question 27 refers to the following graph.

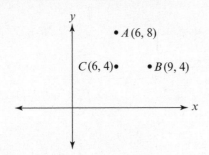

27. What is the distance between A and B?

28. If $f(x) = x^2 - 3x$, then $f(4) - f(1) = ?$

29. Complete the chart below:

$f(x) = -x + 5$

x	$f(x)$
0	
	7
2	
	0

30. Solve the system of equations for x and y:

$$7y + 3 = 21x + 10$$
$$y = 2x + 2$$

Scoring the Diagnostic Test

The following section will assist you in scoring and analyzing your diagnostic test results. Use the answer key and the analysis worksheet that follows to help you evaluate specific problem types. Corresponding topic headings can be found in the algebra review section following the diagnostic test. In fact, most of the problems are covered in the review, with details on how to solve them.

Answer Key

Exponents

1. 8^{10}

2. 9^7

3. $120,000 \cdot (1.03)^7$

4. $147,585$

Scientific Notation

5. 2.3×10^{-7}

Square Roots

6. 14 and 15

7. $4\sqrt{5}$

Variables and Algebraic Expressions

8. $5 + 3x$

9. $\dfrac{1}{2}x$

10. -61

11. $-\dfrac{5}{3}$

12. $\dfrac{y + 14x^2}{2xy}$

Solving and Graphing Linear Equations

13. $x = 15$

14. $y = 21$

15. $x = -4$

16. $y = 3x + 5$

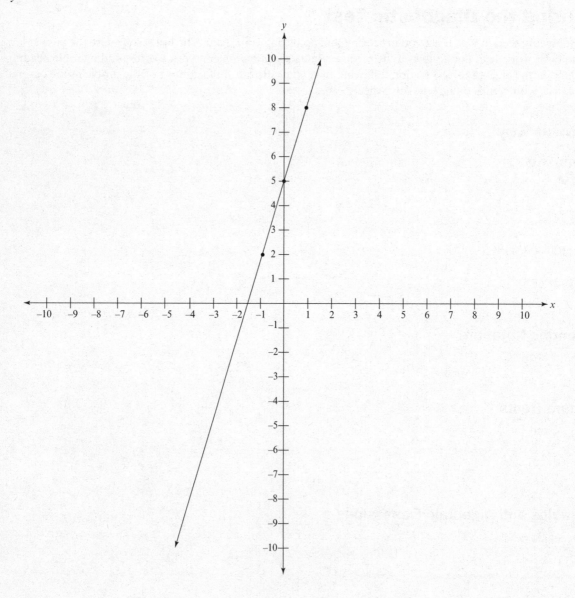

Solving and Graphing Linear Inequalities

17. $x < -3$

18. $x \geq -7$

Polynomials

19. $x \geq 94$

20. $-4x$

21. $x - 3z$

22. $24x^3y^3$

Algebraic Word Problems

23. Slope = 4

24. $y = 2x + 4$

25. 143 green marbles

26. $16\frac{2}{3}$ ml

Linear Relationships: Coordinate Graphs

27. 5

Functions

28. 6

Simultaneous Linear Equations (Systems of Equations)

29.

x	$f(x)$
0	5
−2	7
2	3
5	0

30. $(1, 4)$

Charting and Analyzing Your Diagnostic Test Results

Record your diagnostic test results in the following chart and use these results as a guide to assist you in planning your algebra review goals and objectives. Mark the problems that you missed and pay particular attention to those that were missed in Column (C) because they are unfamiliar math concepts. These are the areas you will want to focus on as you study algebra topics.

Analysis Worksheet

Topic	Total Possible	Number Correct	(A) Simple Mistake	(B) Misread Problem	(C) Unfamiliar Math Concept
			Number Incorrect		
Exponents	4				
Scientific notation	1				
Square roots	2				
Variables and algebraic expressions	5				
Solving and graphing linear equations	4				
Solving and graphing linear inequalities	2				
Polynomials	4				
Algebraic word problems	4				
Linear relationships: Coordinate graphs	1				
Functions	1				
Simultaneous linear equations	2				
Total Possible Explanations for Incorrect Answers: Columns A, B, and C	■■■■■■■				
Total Number of Answers Correct and Incorrect	30	Add the total number of correct answers here: _____	Add columns A, B, and C _____ Total number of incorrect answers		

Algebra and Functions Review

As you approach algebra questions on the Core Mathematics Test, look for patterns and relationships among the numbers, variables, and their operations. You may not be aware of it, but you already use algebraic skills every day. Any time you analyze unknown quantities, you are using a part of your brain that accesses the reasoning skills necessary to perform algebraic equations.

Let's take a look at an everyday scenario to illustrate how the relationships among numbers, variables, and their operations help you solve unknown variables. For instance, suppose you need to attend a school district conference and want to estimate how long it will take (the unknown variable is *time* = t) to get to the conference center. The conference center is 30 miles from your home (*distance* = d), and you travel at a steady rate of 60 mph (rate or speed = r). You could have easily calculated the answer in your head, but the algebraic expression known as the time-distance formula, $d = r \cdot t$ (or $t = d \div r$ or $r = d \div t$) will always help you solve this type of problem. At a steady rate of speed, it will take 30 minutes to travel to the conference center. This is algebra!

Now before we start the algebra review, let's go through some useful rules of exponents, scientific notation, and square roots.

Basic Rules

Exponents

An **exponent** is shorthand to let you know how many times to multiply a quantity by itself. Just like multiplication is repeated addition ($2 + 2 + 2 = 2 \cdot 3$), exponents are repeated multiplication. An exponent is a number placed above and to the right of a quantity (number or variable). In 6^2, 6 is the **base** and 2 is the exponent. This example shows that 6 is to a factor two times: $6^2 = (6)(6)$, and is read as *six to the second power* or *six squared*.

Example:

1. $2^5 = (2)(2)(2)(2)(2) = 32$

2. $(-3)^3 = (-3)(-3)(-3) = -27$

3. $6^1 = 6$

4. $5^0 = 1$; $x^0 = 1$ as long as $x \neq 0$

Solving Exponent Word Problems

The Core Mathematics Test may have word problems that require exponential operations. When solving exponent problems (repeated multiplication), the first step is to determine the base number in the problem. Then find how many times it should be increased times itself.

Example:

1. Sales at Acme Widget Factory totaled 120,000 this year. Acme Widget Factory expects sales to grow at a rate of 3% a year for the next 7 years.

   Write an equation that represents the widget sales for year 7 in exponential form.

In this example, we must take the original amount (120,000), find out how much it is increased each year (3%), and multiply the base number by itself and by the number of years (7). Let x = the number of expected widget sales in year 7.

Multiplying the first year's widget sales by 1.03 provides us with the original amount plus the 3% that sales increase each year. Therefore, 1.03 is our base amount, not 0.03.

Then calculate the original amount of widget sales (120,000) times the base number multiplied by itself for the number of years of sales increase (1.03 raised to the 7th power).

The equation written in exponential form is $x = 120{,}000 \cdot 1.03^7$.

The solution written to the nearest whole widget is $x = 147{,}585$.

Scientific Notation

The Core Mathematics Test may have a problem related to scientific notation. Very large or very small numbers can be written in scientific notation to make the numbers easier to read. A number written in scientific notation is a number between 1 and 10 and multiplied by a power of 10. For example, 2,100,000 written in scientific notation is 2.1×10^6. Simply place the decimal point to get a number between 1 and 10 and then count the digits to the right of the decimal to get the power of 10.

$$2\underset{6\ \ 5\ \ 4\ \ 3\ \ 2\ \ 1}{1\,0\,0\,0\,0\,0}$$

Most calculators have a limited amount of space to display large numbers. When answers are too large, the calculator may convert your answer to scientific notation on the display screen. For example, when $1,000,000 \times 1,000,000$ is entered into your calculator, the answer may appear as 1 E 12. This answer represents the number 1 times 10 raised to the 12th power. The 1 is actually in the 13th place to the left of the decimal point, or 1,000,000,000,000.

Notice that numbers greater than 1 have positive exponents when expressed in scientific notation. Numbers smaller than 1 written in scientific notation will have a negative exponent.

Examples:

Change the following to scientific notation.

> **1.** $35,000 = 3.5 \times 10^4$
>
> **2.** $1,112,000,000 = 1.112 \times 10^9$
>
> **3.** $0.0045 = 4.5 \times 10^{-3}$

Square Roots

To square a number, just multiply it by itself. For example, 5 squared (written exponentially as 5^2) is 5×5 or 25. Conversely, the square root of 25 is 5, written $\sqrt{25} = 5$. Notice the symbol for square root is $\sqrt{}$ (called a **radical** sign).

In another example, $\sqrt{49} = 7$ since $7^2 = (7)(7) = 49$.

Perfect Squares

The value of 25 is called a **perfect square** (the square of a whole number). It is important to be familiar with this partial list of perfect (whole number) square roots to help you quickly answer square root questions.

$$
\begin{array}{lll}
\sqrt{0} = 0 & \sqrt{25} = 5 & \sqrt{100} = 10 \\
\sqrt{1} = 1 & \sqrt{36} = 6 & \sqrt{121} = 11 \\
\sqrt{4} = 2 & \sqrt{49} = 7 & \sqrt{144} = 12 \\
\sqrt{9} = 3 & \sqrt{64} = 8 & \\
\sqrt{16} = 4 & \sqrt{81} = 9 &
\end{array}
$$

Note: $x^1 = x$ and $x^0 = 1$ when x is any number (other than 0).

Approximating Nonperfect Squares

On the Core Mathematics Test, you may be asked to compare a group of numbers, including whole numbers, fractions, decimals, and square roots, and arrange them from least to greatest.

To quickly find the square root of a number that is not a perfect square, you will need to approximate your answer. One advantage you will have is that you will have access to an online calculator to help you easily calculate your results. After calculating the square root, use your knowledge of rounding off to determine the desired place value.

Examples:

---

1. Find the approximate square root of 57, or $\sqrt{57}$.

To solve this problem, you will need to approximate. Refer to the list of perfect squares to find the perfect squares that are closest to $\sqrt{57}$.

$$\sqrt{49} \; < \; \sqrt{57} \; < \; \sqrt{64}$$
$$7 \; < \; ? \; < \; 8$$

By approximating square roots, you will be able to compare your answer to find the solution to the problem. The square root 57 is just about halfway between 49 and 64. Therefore, $\sqrt{57}$ is approximately equal to $7\frac{1}{2}$.

Note that if this question asked you to round to the nearest whole number, the answer would be 8 because $\sqrt{57}$ is approximately 7.549834435. When rounding to the nearest whole number, you must evaluate the number in the tenths place. The number in the tenths place is 5. Therefore, 7.549834435 rounds up to the whole number 8.

---

2. What whole number is closest to $\sqrt{83}$?

Once again you will need to approximate, but there's another step to consider when approximating square roots.

$$\sqrt{81} \; < \; \sqrt{83} \; < \; \sqrt{100}$$
$$9 \; < \; ? \; < \; 10$$

Since $\sqrt{83}$ is slightly more than $\sqrt{81}$ (whose square root is 9), and 83 is only two steps up from the nearest perfect square (81) and 17 steps to the next perfect square (100), 83 is $\frac{2}{19}$ of the way to 100. $\frac{2}{19} \approx \frac{2}{20} \approx \frac{1}{10} = .1$ Therefore, $\sqrt{83} \approx 9.1$.

Note that by using a calculator, you will see that $\sqrt{83}$ is approximately 9.110433579. Since the number 1 is in the tenths place, and because 1 is less than 5, 9.110433579 rounds down to 9.

Seeing the Structure in Algebraic Expressions

Analyzing algebraic expressions depends on your knowledge of arithmetic operations. Your goal should be to have a solid understanding of the arithmetic topics covered in chapter 5 to prepare you for the algebra topics covered on the Core Mathematics Test.

Variables

Think of algebra as a language that uses letters (variables), such as x, y, a, b, m, and n, to represent unknown rational numbers. A **variable,** therefore, is a letter used to represent a number until the numeric value is known. The importance of using variables in real-life scenarios is endless. For example, when ordering student textbooks for your classroom of 25 students, you may need to order an unknown number of additional textbooks (variable x) in the event additional students register the first week of school, or $25 + x$.

Variables are often used to change verbal expressions into algebraic expressions. To solve problems using algebraic expressions, you will need to analyze the structural relationship between variables (unknown quantities) and numbers (known quantities).

In the algebraic expression $x + 4 = 19$, some unknown number (represented by x) plus 4 equals 19. Using basic arithmetic, it is easy to see that $15 + 4 = 19$.

Variable
(Unknown quantity) $\longrightarrow x + 4 = 19 \longleftarrow$ Rational number
(Known quantity)

Algebraic Multiplication

Algebraic multiplication refers to the common multiplication symbols that appear in algebraic equations.

1. Multiplication is implied when two or more variables (or variables and numbers) are placed next to each other. In the first example below, the letter x is the variable and 5 (the coefficient) is the number used to multiply the variable.

$$5x \quad \text{(read 5 times } x\text{)}$$
$$ab \quad \text{(read } a \text{ times } b\text{)}$$
$$4ab \quad \text{(read 4 times } a \text{ times } b\text{)}$$

2. Perform multiplication when there are parentheses around one variable (or number).

$$(a)b \quad \text{or} \quad (a)4$$

$$a(b) \quad \text{or} \quad a(4)$$

$$(a)(b) \quad \text{or} \quad (a)(4)$$

3. Perform multiplication when there is a raised dot between variables and/or numbers.

$$a \cdot b$$

$$5 \cdot 4$$

Order of Operations and Algebraic Expressions

To evaluate an algebraic expression, follow these three steps using arithmetic rules for grouping symbols and order of operations:

1. Replace the unknowns with grouping symbols.
2. Insert the numeric value for the unknown variables. *Note:* It is important to place the values in the grouping symbols (parentheses) to solve the problem correctly.
3. Perform the arithmetic to solve the problem. (Always make sure that you follow the rules for the order of operations introduced in chapter 5 on page 119 when performing arithmetic.)

Examples:

1. Evaluate $-3x^2 - 4x - 6$ if $x = -5$.

$$
\begin{aligned}
-3x^2 - 4x - 6 &= -3(-5)^2 - 4(-5) - 6 \\
&= -3(25) + 20 - 6 \\
&= -75 + 20 - 6 \\
&= -61
\end{aligned}
$$

2. Evaluate $\dfrac{x}{3} - \dfrac{x+2y}{y}$ if $x = 2$ and $y = 6$.

$$\frac{x}{3} - \frac{x+2y}{y} = \frac{(2)}{3} - \left(\frac{(2)+2(6)}{(6)}\right)$$

$$= \frac{2}{3} - \frac{2+12}{6}$$

$$= \frac{2}{3} - \frac{14}{6}$$

$$= \frac{2}{3} - \frac{7}{3}$$

$$= -\frac{5}{3}$$

3. Simplify: $\dfrac{1}{2x} + \dfrac{7x}{y}$

Adding and subtracting fractions with variables follows the same steps for adding and subtracting fractions without variables. Compare these basic steps of adding fractions with and without variables using the sample equation $\dfrac{1}{2} + \dfrac{1}{3}$ side by side with the equation $\dfrac{1}{2x} + \dfrac{7x}{y}$.

| Without Variables | With Variables |

Step 1. Find the common denominator.

$$\frac{1}{2} + \frac{1}{3}$$
$$2 \times 3 = 6$$

$$\frac{1}{2x} + \frac{7x}{y}$$
$$2x \cdot y = 2xy$$

Step 2. Find equivalent fractions with the new denominator.

$$\frac{1}{2}\left(\frac{3}{3}\right) + \frac{1}{3}\left(\frac{2}{2}\right)$$

$$\frac{1}{2x}\left(\frac{y}{y}\right) + \frac{7x}{y}\left(\frac{2x}{2x}\right)$$

Step 3. Multiply each numerator together, and then each denominator together.

$$\frac{3}{6} + \frac{2}{6}$$

$$\frac{1y}{2xy} + \frac{7 \cdot 2 \cdot x \cdot x}{2xy} = \frac{1y}{2xy} + \frac{14x^2}{2xy}$$

Step 4. Add the numerators together.

$$\frac{5}{6}$$

$$\frac{y + 14x^2}{2xy}$$

Algebraic Word Problems

Comparing different real-world relationships in the form of algebraic word problems is common on the Core Mathematics Test.

Translating Word Expressions into Algebraic Expressions

To solve real-life algebraic word problems, you must be able to convert English words that describe a situation or scenario into simple algebraic equations or inequalities. Here are some verbal expressions that signal a math operation:

- **Addition:** sum, plus, more than, greater than, increase, rise
- **Subtraction:** minus, difference, less than, decrease, reduce
- **Multiplication:** times, multiplied by, of, product, twice
- **Division:** divided by, ratio, half, quotient

Examples:

Word Expression	Algebraic Expression
The sum of a number n and 7	$n + 7$
Seven decreased by two times x	$7 - 2x$
Three times a number	$3x$
Four more than the product of 2 and x	$2x + 4$ (Note that the reason $2x$ comes before the 4 is that "four more" must be added to "something," and that something is "$2x$.")
What is a number (x) divided by 8?	$\dfrac{x}{8}$
What number is one-half of x?	$\dfrac{1}{2}x$ or $\dfrac{x}{2}$

Solving Algebraic Word Problems

The most common forms of algebraic word problems are distance and time, work, mixture, motion, and age-related scenarios. The key to solving these types of problems is to identify specific details about what the question is asking. A common mistake is that the hurried test-taker quickly reads the question and rushes to a solution. Algebraic word problems can be misleading unless you carefully organize the words into math variables and numbers.

Examples:

1. Kimberly leaves Atlanta at 9 a.m. and travels at a rate of 55 miles per hour. Two hours later, Maria leaves Atlanta and travels at a rate of 75 miles per hour. How many hours will it take for Maria to catch up to Kimberly?

Use the distance formula to solve this problem: $d = r \times t$ (distance = rate × time).

Kimberly travels a distance of $55(t)$ in t hours and Maria travels a distance of $75(t-2)$ in $t-2$ hours. When Maria catches up to Kimberly, they have traveled the same distance. Therefore,

$$55t = 75(t-2)$$
$$55t = 75t - 150$$
$$55t - 75t = 75t - 150 - 75t$$
$$-20t = -150$$
$$\frac{-20t}{-20} = \frac{-150}{-20}$$
$$t = 7.5 \text{ hours}$$

You should also be able to get an estimate before starting the problem. To travel a certain distance going 55 miles per hour will take longer than going that distance at 75 miles per hour, which means that the average speed will be closer to 55 mi/hr than to 75 mi/hr. Had this been a selected response question and only one answer choice was between 55 and 60, calculations would have been unnecessary.

---

2. Working alone, Mason can do a job in 4 hours. With Angel's help, it takes only $2\frac{2}{9}$ hours. How long should it take Angel working alone to do the job?

If two methods of completing a job are given, to find the length of time it would take working together, take the product of the two lengths of time and divide by the sum of the two lengths of time. If one method undoes the job, then take the product of the two lengths of time and divide by the difference of the two lengths of time.

If the work problem involves more than two methods of either completing or undoing the job, then an algebraic approach to get the answer would look like this:

$$\frac{1\,(\text{one job})}{\text{first person's time}} + \frac{1\,(\text{one job})}{\text{second person's time}} + \frac{1\,(\text{one job})}{\text{third person's time}} + \cdots = \frac{1\,(\text{one job})}{\text{time together}}$$

Method 1. First change $2\frac{2}{9}$ to $\frac{20}{9}$. Let x be how long it would take Angel alone:

$$\frac{1}{4} + \frac{1}{x} = \frac{1}{2\frac{2}{9}}$$

$$\frac{1}{4} + \frac{1}{x} = \frac{1}{\frac{20}{9}}$$

$$\frac{1}{4} + \frac{1}{x} = \frac{9}{20}$$

Multiply by $4x$, which is the LCD of the left side of the equation.

$$4x\left(\frac{1}{4}\right) + 4x\left(\frac{1}{x}\right) = \frac{9}{20}$$

$$\frac{x}{4x} + \frac{4}{4x} = \frac{9}{20}$$

$$\frac{x+4}{4x} = \frac{9}{20}$$

Now you can see that $x = 5$.

$$\frac{5+4}{4(5)} = \frac{9}{20}$$

Method 2. When you have two fractions equal to each other, remember that another way to solve the problem is to cross multiply $\frac{x+4}{4x} = \frac{9}{20}$.

$$\frac{x+4}{4x} = \frac{9}{20}$$

$$4x(9) = 20(4+x)$$

$$36x = 80 + 20x$$

$$\underline{20x \qquad 20x} \quad \text{Subtract } 20x \text{ from both sides to isolate your variable.}$$

$$16x = 80$$

$$\frac{16x}{16} = \frac{80}{16} \qquad \text{Divide both sides by 16.}$$

$$x = 5$$

Method 3. Since we do not know how fast Angel works, this becomes our variable x in the algebraic method.

$$\frac{1}{4} + \frac{1}{x} = \frac{1}{2\frac{2}{9}} \qquad \left(\frac{1}{2\frac{2}{9}} = \frac{1}{\frac{20}{9}} = \frac{9}{20} \right)$$

$$\frac{1}{4} + \frac{1}{x} = \frac{9}{20}$$

Multiply each side by the LCD of $20x$.

$$20x\left(\frac{1}{4} + \frac{1}{x} \right) = 20x\left(\frac{9}{20} \right)$$

$$5x + 20 = 9x$$

$$20 = 4x$$

$$5 = x$$

It would take Angel 5 hours to do the job alone.

---

3. In 6 years, men like Antonio Stradivari were able to build 58 violins. Considering all violin-makers worked at the same speed, how many complete violins could be built in 11 years by one man?

The first step to answering this question is to write down what is known: *how many complete violins* (note the word *complete*). Now, using the information given in the problem, set up a proportion equation and solve for x.

$$\frac{\text{violins}}{\text{years}} = \frac{\text{violins}}{\text{years}}$$

$$\frac{58}{6} = \frac{x}{11}$$

Cross multiply:

$$638 = 6x$$

$$\frac{638}{6} = \frac{6x}{6}$$

$$106.33 = x$$

The questions asks for the number of *complete* violins that one man could build in 11 years. Therefore, you must round down to the nearest whole number. The answer is 106.

Polynomials: Monomials, Binomials, and Trinomials

Polynomials, monomials, binomials, and trinomials are important algebraic terms.

A **polynomial** is an algebraic expression made up of one or more terms. Terms are separated by addition or subtraction signs (no equal signs). For instance, $x + y$, $y^2 - x^2$, and $x^2 + 3x + 5y^2$ are all polynomials.

Polynomials are usually arranged in one of two ways:

- **Ascending order** is when the power of a term increases for each succeeding term. For example, $x + x^2 + x^3$ or $5x + 2x^2 - 3x^3 + x^5$ are arranged in ascending order.
- **Descending order** is when the power of a term decreases for each succeeding term. For example, $x^3 + x^2 + x$ or $2x^4 + 3x^2 + 7x$ are arranged in descending order. Descending order is more commonly used.

A **monomial** is a polynomial that consists of only one term (with no addition or subtraction signs). For instance, $9x$ and $4a^2$ are monomials.

A **binomial** is a polynomial with exactly two terms. For example, $4x + 3y$ and $6z^4 - 11$ are binomials.

A **trinomial** is a polynomial with exactly three terms. For example, $3y^5 + 4y - 9$ and $8a^2b^2 - 9a^2b + 10ab^2$ are trinomials.

Adding and Subtracting Polynomials

To add or subtract polynomials, follow the same rules as with integers introduced in chapter 5. Notice that you add or subtract the coefficients only and leave the variables the same.

Examples:

1. $12x + 4x - 23x - (-3x) = [12 + 4 - 23 - (-3)]x = [12 + 4 - 23 + 3]x = -4x$

2. $(4x - 7z) - (3x - 4z) = 4x - 7z - 3x + 4z = (4 - 3)x + (-7 + 4)z = x - 3z$

Notice that the first step in Example 2 above is to distribute the negative sign in front of the second set of parentheses.

Reasoning with Equations and Inequalities

On the Core Mathematics Test, you may be asked to reason and solve simple one-variable equations and inequalities, analyze graphic representations of linear equations, and analyze pairs of simultaneous linear equations.

Solving Linear Equations

The word *linear* means straight line. If you plot the points on a graph from a linear equation, the result would be a line. Remember that algebraic equations show a relationship between numbers and variables. To solve an algebraic equation, it is necessary to find all the replacement values for the variable that makes the equation a true statement. An equation consists of a left side and a right side separated by an equal sign (=). The goal in solving an equation is to get the variable isolated on one side of the equation and the numerical value on the other side of the equation.

In the equation $2x = 4$, 2 is the **coefficient** (the number before the variable) and x is the variable. **Remember:** For an equation to be completely solved, the coefficient must be 1. Therefore, in this example, $2x = 4$ cannot be the final answer. Both sides of the equation must be divided by 2 (the coefficient) to solve this equation. The correct answer is $x = 2$.

$$2x = 4$$
$$\frac{2x}{2} = \frac{4}{2}$$
$$x = 2$$

A basic rule to follow is to think about equations like a balance scale with the equal sign (=) being the center point, or fulcrum. The relationship between variables and numbers must be kept in balance. In order to maintain the balance, whatever operation is performed on one side of an equation must also be performed on the other side of the equation. In the same manner, you may add, subtract, multiply, or divide both sides of an equation by the same (nonzero) number, and the linear equation will not change. Remember to always perform addition and subtraction first, and then multiplication and division.

Example:

1. Solve for x: $x - 7 = 25$

To solve this equation, first get x by itself on one side. To accomplish this, add 7 to both sides of the equation.

$$x - 7 = 25$$
$$\underline{+7 \quad +7}$$ Add 7 to both sides.
$$x \quad\;\; = 32$$

The next two examples show that sometimes you have to use more than one step to solve for the unknown variable.

---

2. Solve for x: $4x + 6 = 18$

$$4x + 6 = 18$$
$$\underline{\quad -6 \;\; -6}$$ Subtract 6 from both sides.
$$4x \quad\;\; = 12$$

$$\frac{4x}{4} = \frac{12}{4}$$ Divide both sides by 4.

$$x = 3$$

---

3. Solve for x: $2x - 9 = 21$

$$2x - 9 = 21$$
$$\underline{\quad +9 \;\; +9}$$ Add 9 to both sides.
$$2x \quad\;\; = 30$$

$$\frac{2x}{2} = \frac{30}{2}$$ Divide both sides by 2.

$$x = 15$$

---

4. Simplify and graph: $2y + x = 7x + 10$

Step 1. Isolate the y-variables on one side of the equal sign, then move the x-variables and numbers to the other side of the equal sign. Solve for y. This will result in an equation that's in slope-intercept form. Slope-intercept will be discussed on page 174.

$$2y + x = 7x + 10$$
$$\underline{\quad -x \;\; -x}$$ Subtract x from both sides.
$$2y \quad\;\; = 6x + 10$$

$$\frac{2y}{2} = \frac{6x}{2} + \frac{10}{2}$$ Divide each term on both sides by 2.

$$y = 3x + 5$$

Step 2. Now that you have placed the equation in slope-intercept form, you can draw a simple x-y chart to create points on the line. Since lines run forever in each direction, any pair of numbers you choose to place in the equation for x and y will give you a point on the line.

x	$y = 3x + 5$	y
0	$y = 3(0) + 5$	5
1	$y = 3(1) + 5$	8
2	$y = 3(2) + 5$	11

Although you can use any three numbers for x to create the x-y chart, substitute small numbers (0, 1, 2, 3) to help you quickly and easily solve the problem. If the three points are not in a straight line, check your work for any mistakes.

Step 3. Plot the points (0, 5), (1, 8), and (2, 11) from the chart above.

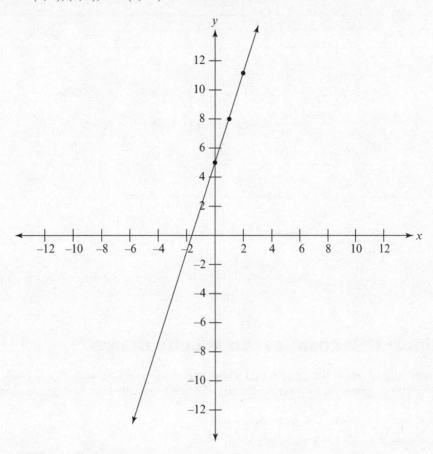

Solving Linear Inequalities

In an **inequality,** the relationships in the statement are not equal. Inequalities have a right side and a left side separated by an inequality symbol:

- \> (greater than)
- \< (less than)
- ≥ (greater than or equal to)
- ≤ (less than or equal to)

The goal in solving an inequality is to find the numerical values (when substituted for the variable) that make the inequality a true statement. To solve an inequality problem, you will need to get the variable isolated on one side of the inequality symbol and the numerical value on the other side. What is done to one side of an inequality must be done to the other side to make it a true statement.

Tip: When working with inequalities, treat them exactly like equations, with one exception: If you multiply or divide both sides by a negative number, then you must reverse the direction of the inequality symbol.

Examples:

---

1. Solve for x: $2x + 4 > 6$

$$
\begin{array}{rl}
2x + 4 &> 6 \\
\underline{-4 \quad -4} & \quad \text{Subtract 4 from both sides.} \\
2x \quad &> 2
\end{array}
$$

$$\frac{2x}{2} > \frac{2}{2} \quad \text{Divide both sides by 2.}$$

$$x > 1$$

---

2. Solve for x: $-3x + 5 > 14$

$$
\begin{array}{rl}
-3x + 5 &> 14 \\
\underline{-5 \quad -5} & \quad \text{Subtract 5 from both sides.} \\
-3x \quad &> 9
\end{array}
$$

$$\frac{-3x}{-3} < \frac{9}{-3} \quad \text{Divide both sides by } -3 \text{, switching the direction of the inequality symbol.}$$

$$x < -3$$

Analyzing Linear Relationships: Coordinate Graphs

A **coordinate graph** provides a visual illustration that shows the relationship between two variables x and y. A basic coordinate graph is formed by two perpendicular number lines called the coordinate axes:

The horizontal line is the **x-axis** (independent variable).

The vertical line is the **y-axis** (dependent variable).

The point of intersection of the two number lines is called the **origin** and is represented by the coordinate pair $(0, 0)$, often marked simply 0 or with an uppercase letter O for "origin."

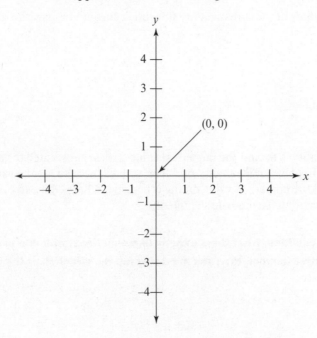

Each point on a coordinate graph is depicted by an ordered pair of numbers called the **coordinates.** Notice that x is always shown as the first numbered value (the independent variable), and y is always shown as the second numbered value (the dependent variable). Some sample coordinates are noted in the following figure.

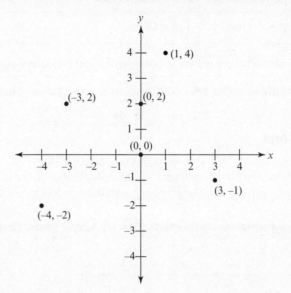

Notice that on the x-axis, numbers to the right of 0 are positive and numbers to the left of 0 are negative. On the y-axis, numbers above 0 are positive and numbers below 0 are negative. The first number in the ordered pair is called the **x-coordinate,** or **abscissa,** and shows how far to the right or left the point is from the origin 0. The second number is the **y-coordinate,** or **ordinate,** and shows how far up or down the point is from the origin 0.

The coordinates, or ordered pairs, are shown as (x, y). The order of these numbers is very important. For example, the point $(3, 2)$ is different from the point $(2, 3)$.

The coordinate graph is divided into four regions (quarters) called **quadrants.** These quadrants are numbered I, II, III, IV, as shown in the following graph.

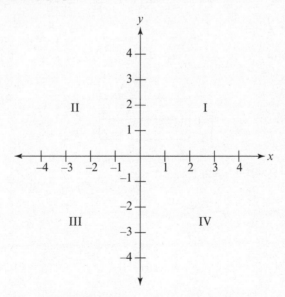

In Quadrant I, x and y are both always positive.
In Quadrant II, x is always negative and y is always positive.
In Quadrant III, x and y are both always negative.
In Quadrant IV, x is always positive and y is always negative.

Examples:

1. In which quadrant(s) do points have positive x-coordinates?

Points have positive x-coordinates in Quadrants I and IV.

2. In which quadrant(s) do points have negative x-coordinates and positive y-coordinates?

Only in Quadrant II do points have negative x-coordinates and positive y-coordinates.

Graphing Linear Equations

To construct a graph of linear equations with two variables (usually x and y), find the ordered pairs that make the equation true, and then plot them on a coordinate graph. The coordinates of the intersection are the solution to the system. If you are unfamiliar with coordinate graphing, carefully review this section.

> **Tip: When giving a value for one variable, start with 0, then try 1, and so on. Then graph the solutions.**

Example:

1. Graph the equation $x + y = 6$.

If x is 0, then y is 6.

$$(0) + y = 6$$
$$y = 6$$

If x is 1, then y is 5.

$$(1) + y = 6$$
$$\underline{-1 \qquad -1}$$
$$y = 5$$

If x is 2, then y is 4.

$$(2) + y = 6$$
$$\underline{-2 \qquad -2}$$
$$y = 4$$

Using a simple x-y chart is helpful.

x	y
0	6
1	5
2	4

Now plot these coordinates and connect them.

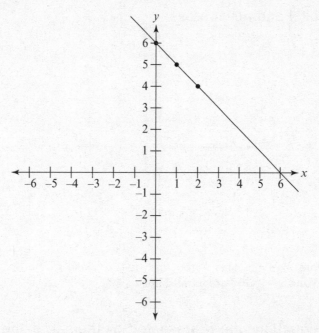

Notice that these solutions form a straight line when plotted. Equations whose solution sets form a straight line are **linear equations.** Equations that have a variable raised to a power, show division by a variable, involve variables with square roots, or have variables multiplied together will not form straight lines when their solutions are graphed. These are called **nonlinear equations.**

Simultaneous Linear Equations

The term **simultaneous linear equations** (also known as **systems of equations**) is used to represent more than one equation with unknown variables located on the same graph. There are three possible types of simultaneous linear equations:

- Lines cross at exactly one point.
- Lines are parallel and never cross.
- Two or more equations are represented by the same line.

Type 1. Lines cross at exactly one point.

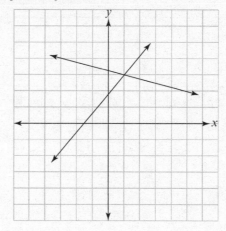

Notice that lines cross at (1, 3). In order for the lines to cross, the slope of one linear equation must be positive and the slope of the second equation must be negative, or both slopes can be positive or both can be negative.

173

Type 2. Lines are parallel and never cross.

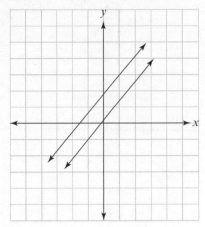

The slopes of the two lines must be identical and cross the x-axis or y-axis (or both) at different points. For example, the lines $y = 2x + 3$ and $y = 2x + 7$ are parallel lines.

Type 3. Two or more equations are represented by the same line.

To see how two equations represent the same line, both need to be in slope-intercept form. Let's look at $y = 3x - 2$ and $4 = -2y + 6x$. Simplify the second equation to be in slope-intercept form.

$$
\begin{array}{ll}
4 = -2y + 6x & \\
\dfrac{+2y \qquad +2y}{2y + 4 = \qquad 6x} & \text{Add } 2y \text{ to both sides.} \\[4pt]
\dfrac{\qquad -4 \quad -4}{2y \quad = 6x - 4} & \text{Subtract 4 from both sides.} \\[4pt]
\dfrac{2y}{2} = \dfrac{6x}{2} - \dfrac{4}{2} & \text{Divide both sides by 2.} \\[4pt]
y = 3x - 2 &
\end{array}
$$

Notice that once you have simplified the second equation, it is identical to the first equation. Therefore, the two equations are represented by the same line.

Example:

> **1.** Solve the system of equations:
> $$7y + 3 = 21x + 10$$
> $$y = 2x + 2$$

Step 1. First reduce the equations to simplified form (if they are not already in simplified form).

$$
\begin{array}{l}
7y + 3 = 21x + 10 \\
\dfrac{\quad -3 \qquad \quad -3}{7y \quad = 21x + 7} \\[4pt]
\dfrac{7y}{7} = \dfrac{21x}{7} + \dfrac{7}{7} \\[4pt]
y = 3x + 1
\end{array}
$$

The two equations now read $y = 3x + 1$ and $y = 2x + 2$.

Step 2. Using the substitution method, substitute one of the equation values for y into the other equation. In this example, take the first equation and replace the y value into the second equation for y. Therefore, substitute $3x + 1$ for y in the second equation.

$$3x + 1 = 2x + 2$$

Step 3. There is now only one variable. Solve for x:

$$\begin{aligned} 3x + 1 &= 2x + 2 \\ \underline{-2x \quad\;\; -2x} & \qquad \text{Subtract the smaller value of } x \text{ from both sides.} \\ x + 1 &= 2 \\ \underline{-1 \;\; -1} & \qquad \text{Subtract 1 from both sides to isolate the variable.} \\ x &= 1 \end{aligned}$$

Step 4. Now that you have solved for x, insert x in either of the original equations to obtain the y-value. (The following example illustrates the second equation, but the first equation could also have been used.)

$$\begin{aligned} y &= 2x + 2 \\ y &= 2(1) + 2 \\ y &= 2 + 2 \\ y &= 4 \end{aligned}$$

The value for $x = 1$ and the value for $y = 4$. Therefore, $(1, 4)$ is the point on the graph where the two lines intersect.

Functions

A **function** is an equation that assigns each acceptable input exactly one output. The equation $y = x^2 + 2$ is the same as $f(x) = x^2 + 2$. Each equation will have the same answer for the same values of x. Follow the same steps as in solving linear equations.

Often the letters f, g, or h are used to denote functions. Consider the function $f(x) = x^2 - 2x$. The English phrase "find the value of the function when x is 6" is expressed as $f(6) = ?$

The function is then evaluated by replacing each x with the value 6.

$$\begin{aligned} f(x) &= x^2 - 2x \\ f(6) &= (6)^2 - 2(6) \\ f(6) &= 36 - 12 \\ f(6) &= 24 \end{aligned}$$

Examples:

1. If $f(x) = x^2 - 3x$, then $f(4) - f(1) = ?$

First find $f(4)$ and $f(1)$. Then solve the subtractions of these results.

$$f(x) = x^2 - 3x$$

$$\begin{array}{ll} f(4) = (4)^2 - 3(4) & \qquad f(1) = (1)^2 - 3(1) \\ f(4) = 16 - 12 & \qquad f(1) = 1 - 3 \\ f(4) = 4 & \qquad f(1) = -2 \end{array}$$

$$f(4) - f(1) = 4 - (-2) = 6$$

2. If $f(x) = 5x + 3$, then $f(4) - f(-2) = ?$

$$f(x) = 5x + 3$$

$$
\begin{array}{ll}
f(4) = 5(4) + 3 & f(-2) = 5(-2) + 3 \\
f(4) = 20 + 3 & f(-2) = -10 + 3 \\
f(4) = 23 & f(-2) = -7
\end{array}
$$

$$f(4) - f(-2) = 23 - (-7) = 30$$

3. If $f(x) = x^3 - 3x^2 + x + 5$, find $f(2)$.

$$
\begin{aligned}
f(2) &= (2)^3 - 3(2)^2 + 2 + 5 \\
&= 8 - 12 + 2 + 5 \\
f(2) &= 3
\end{aligned}
$$

Algebra Practice Questions

Now that you have reviewed the algebra and functions topics, you can practice on your own. Questions appear in the format of the Core Mathematics Test question types: selected response (select one answer), selected response (select one or more answers), and numeric entry (fill-in). These practice questions give you a chance to solve problems in the same format as the actual test. The answers and explanations that follow the questions include strategies to help you understand how to solve the problems.

Remember: Answer choices in this study guide have lettered choices A, B, C, D, and E for clarity, but answer choice letters will not appear on the actual exam. On the actual computer version of the exam, you will be required to click on ovals, click on squares, or fill in your answer.

General Directions: Answer each question by selecting the correct response from the choices given. Practice questions have several different formats. Unless otherwise directed, indicate a single answer choice.

1. Which of the following is the closest approximation of $\sqrt{119}$?
   A. 10.5
   B. 10.7
   C. 10.9
   D. 11.1
   E. 11.2

2. An electrician charges d dollars per minute plus $50 for his travel time to get to the job. What will be the total amount the electrician charges for a job that takes 3 hours?
   A. $28d$
   B. $3d + 50$
   C. $3(d + 50)$
   D. $180d + 50$
   E. $180d$

3. Which of the following are equal to 3^{100}?
   Select **all** that apply.
   A. 9^{25}
   B. 9^{50}
   C. 27^{25}
   D. 81^{25}
   E. 243^{20}

4. If m is an odd integer, which of the following must be an odd integer?
   A. m^2
   B. $(m - 1)^2$
   C. $5m - 1$
   D. $(m + 1)^3$
   E. $2m + 4$

5. Which of the follow linear equations contains the points $(-3, 6)$, $(0, 4)$, $(6, 0)$, and $(9, -2)$?
   A. $2x + y = 0$
   B. $y - 2x = 12$
   C. $2x + 3y = 12$
   D. $x + 3y = 15$
   E. $x + y = 3$

6. Juan can do a certain job in 8 hours alone, while it would take Susan 12 hours to do the same job alone. If they work together, how long should it take to do the job?
   A. 20 hours
   B. 10 hours
   C. At least 5 hours but less than 10 hours
   D. Less than 5 hours
   E. More than 5 hours

7. If $\dfrac{z-2}{z+4} = \dfrac{13}{15}$, then $z =$
   A. 11
   B. 13
   C. 15
   D. 41
   E. 81

8. Twice the sum of a and b less than three times the difference of a and b in simplest form is illustrated by which of the following expressions?
   A. $a - 5b$
   B. $5b - a$
   C. $-a$
   D. a
   E. $5 - a$

9. Which of the following points lie on the line $5x - 3y = 12$?
   A. $(0, 4)$
   B. $(3, 1)$
   C. $(0, -4)$
   D. $(3, -1)$
   E. $\left(\dfrac{2}{5}, \dfrac{-10}{3} \right)$

10. James is 12 years older than Mason. Five years ago, the sum of their ages was 42. What will be the product of their ages in 5 years?

    Write your answer in the box below.

11. If $3x + 1 = 16$, what is the value of $x - 4$?
    A. 19
    B. 16
    C. 5
    D. 1
    E. −1

12. If x and y are prime numbers less than 10, which of the following could be values of xy?
    A. 10
    B. 14
    C. 15
    D. 25
    E. 49

13. If $\dfrac{a+5}{4}$ is an integer, then a must be
    A. a positive integer
    B. an even integer
    C. an odd integer
    D. a multiple of 4
    E. a multiple of 5

14. Sandra spent $125 for a sweater and a jacket. If she spent $25 more on the sweater than the jacket, how much did she pay for the jacket?
    A. $25
    B. $50
    C. $75
    D. $100
    E. $125

15. If $5^x + 5^x + 5^x + 5^x + 5^x = 5^{10}$, what is the value of x?

    Write your answer in the box below.

16. If a point P has coordinates (a, b), which of the following guarantees that $a > b$?
    A. P lies in Quadrant I.
    B. P lies in Quadrant II.
    C. P lies in Quadrant III.
    D. P lies in Quadrant IV.
    E. P lies on the horizontal axis.

17. Which of the following values of z would be in the solution of $5z - 10 < 8z - 6$?
    A. −8
    B. −5
    C. −1
    D. 0
    E. 4

Answers and Explanations

1. **C.** Since $10^2 = 100$ and $11^2 = 121$, $\sqrt{119}$ is between 10 and 11. 119 is very close to, but slightly less than, 121; therefore, $\sqrt{119}$ is very close to, but slightly less than, $\sqrt{121}$. $\sqrt{121} = 11$; hence, a reasonable approximation would be $\sqrt{119} \approx 10.9$. Note that $(10.9)^2 = 118.81$.

2. **D.** The electrician charges by the minute (not the hour), and there are 180 minutes in 3 hours. Since the electrician charges d dollars per minute, he will charge $180d$ dollars for 3 hours. The answer is choice D because the electrician also charges $50 for his travel time, $180d + 50$.

3. **B, D, and E.**

$$9^{50} = \left(3^2\right)^{50} = 3^{2 \cdot 50} = 3^{100}$$

$$81^{25} = \left(3^4\right)^{25} = 3^{4 \cdot 25} = 3^{100}$$

$$243^{20} = \left(3^5\right)^{20} = 3^{5 \cdot 20} = 3^{100}$$

4. **A.** The square of an odd integer is another odd integer, so m^2 is odd since m is odd. The other answer choices will all be even integers.

5. **C.** The only equation that yields a true statement for all four ordered pairs is $2x + 3y = 12$.

$(-3, 6) =$	$(0, 4) =$	$(6, 0) =$	$(9, -2) =$
$2x + 3y = 12$	$2x + 3y = 12$	$2x + 3y = 12$	$2x + 3y = 12$
$2(-3) + 3(6) = 12$	$2(0) + 3(4) = 12$	$2(6) + 3(0) = 12$	$2(9) + 3(-2) = 12$
$-6 + 18 = 12$	$0 + 12 = 12$	$12 + 0 = 12$	$18 - 6 = 12$
$12 = 12$	$12 = 12$	$12 = 12$	$12 = 12$

6. **D.** Use common sense to eliminate choices A and B since together these choices, 20 hours and 10 hours, will require more time than the person who already completes the job in the least amount of time.

   Using algebra: Let x be the amount of time it takes together.

   If Juan needs 8 hours to do the job, then in 1 hour he does $\frac{1}{8}$ of the job. If Susan needs 12 hours to do the job, then in 1 hour she does $\frac{1}{12}$ of the job. If together they need x hours to do the job, then if they have 1 hour together, they will be able to complete $\frac{1}{x}$ of the job.

   Therefore, $\frac{1}{8} + \frac{1}{12} = \frac{1}{x}$. Now solve this equation.

   $$\frac{1}{8} + \frac{1}{12} = \frac{1}{x} \qquad \text{Multiply both sides by the least common denominator, } 24x.$$

   $$24x\left(\frac{1}{8} + \frac{1}{12}\right) = 24x\left(\frac{1}{x}\right)$$

   $$3x + 2x = 24$$

   $$5x = 24$$

   $$x = \frac{24}{5} = 4.8 \text{ hours}$$

   Together they will need less than 5 hours, choice D.

   Using a fast method: $\dfrac{(8)(12)}{8 + 12} = \dfrac{96}{20} = 4\dfrac{4}{5}$ or 4.8

7. D. If $\dfrac{z-2}{z+4} = \dfrac{13}{15}$, cross multiplying yields

$$15(z-2) = 13(z+4)$$
$$15z - 30 = 13z + 52$$
$$15z - 30 - 13z = 13z + 52 - 13z$$
$$2z - 30 = 52$$
$$2z - 30 + 30 = 52 + 30$$
$$2z = 82$$
$$\frac{2z}{2} = \frac{82}{2}$$
$$z = 41$$

8. A. "Twice the sum of a and b less than three times the difference of a and b" is translated into the following expression, which is then simplified.

$$3(a-b) - 2(a+b) = 3a - 3b - 2a - 2b$$
$$= (3a - 2a) - (3b + 2b)$$
$$= a - 5b$$

9. B, C, and E.

For the given equation $5x - 3y = 12$,

Choice A at $(0, 4)$: $5(0) - 3(4) = 0 - 12 = -12 \neq 12$

Choice B at $(3, 1)$: $5(3) - 3(1) = 15 - 3 = 12$

Choice C at $(0, -4)$: $5(0) - 3(-4) = 0 + 12 = 12$

Choice D at $(3, -1)$: $5(3) - 3(-1) = 15 + 3 = 18 \neq 12$

Choice E at $\left(\dfrac{2}{5}, \dfrac{-10}{3}\right)$: $5\left(\dfrac{2}{5}\right) - 3\left(\dfrac{-10}{3}\right) = 2 + 10 = 12$

10. 925

Let x be Mason's age now and $12 + x$ be James' age now.

Person	Current Age	Age 5 Years Ago
Mason	x	$x - 5$
James	$12 + x$	$12 + x - 5$ or $x + 7$

Translate "Five years ago, the sum of their ages was 42" into an algebraic equation.

$$(x - 5) + (12 + x - 5) = 42$$
$$2x + 2 = 42$$
$$2x = 40$$
$$x = 20 \quad \text{and} \quad 12 + x = 32$$

Therefore, Mason is currently 20 years old, and James is 32 years old. In 5 years, Mason will be 25, and James will be 37 years old. The product of their ages will be $(25)(37) = 925$.

11. D. To help you focus on the question, you may have jotted down "$x - 4$." Note that solving the original equation only tells you the value of x.

$$
\begin{aligned}
3x + 1 &= 16 \\
-1 \quad &-1 \\
\hline
3x \quad\;\; &= 15 \\
\frac{3x}{3} &= \frac{15}{3} \\
x &= 5
\end{aligned}
$$

Notice that choice C is 5, but this is incorrect because the question asks, "What is the value of $x - 4$," not just x. To continue the problem, replace x with 5 and solve.

$$
\begin{aligned}
x - 4 &= ? \\
5 - 4 &= 1
\end{aligned}
$$

12. A, B, C, D, and E.

Since x and y are prime numbers that are less than 10, their possible values are 2, 3, 5, and 7. Among the values that xy could be are

$$2 \cdot 5 = 5 \cdot 2 = 10$$

$$2 \cdot 7 = 7 \cdot 2 = 14$$

$$3 \cdot 5 = 5 \cdot 3 = 15$$

$$5 \cdot 5 = 25$$

$$7 \cdot 7 = 49$$

13. C. If $\dfrac{a+5}{4}$ is an integer, $a + 5$ is divisible by 4 and $a + 5$ must be an even integer. Since $a + 5$ is an even integer, a must be an odd integer.

14. B. This problem can be done using algebra or using a trial-and-error method.

Algebra method: Let x = the cost of the jacket. Then $x + 25$ = the cost of the sweater.

$$
\begin{aligned}
x + (x + 25) &= 125 \\
2x + 25 &= 125 \\
2x &= 100 \\
x &= 50
\end{aligned}
$$

Trial-and-error method:

Tip: The trial-and-error method can save you a great deal of time by working backward from the answers. Answers are usually given in ascending or descending order. If you start with the middle value (choice C), you will immediately know if the correct answer is higher (choices D and E), or lower (choices A and B).

Each answer represents the cost of the jacket, and the sweater costs $25 more than the jacket for a total of $125. Start with choice C, as it is the middle value among the answer choices.

Choice C: The jacket would be $75 and the sweater $100 ($75 + $25 = $100) for a total of $175, not $125. The value in choice C is too large, so you now know the answer must be a smaller value (choice A or B).

Choice A: The jacket is $25, would make the sweater $50 ($25 + 25 = $50), for a total of $75, not $125. Choice A is too low.

Choice B: The jacket is $50, which would make the sweater $75 ($50 + $25 = $75), for a total of $125, which is correct.

You can stop here since you found the correct answer. For reference, here are the checks for choices D and E.

Choice D: The jacket would be $100 and the sweater $125 ($100 + $25 = $125) for a total of $225, not $125.

Choice E: The jacket would be $125 and the sweater $150 ($125 + $25 = $150) for a total of $275, not $125.

15. 9

$$5^x + 5^x + 5^x + 5^x + 5^x = 5^{10}$$
$$5(5^x) = 5^{10}$$
$$5^{x+1} = 5^{10}$$
$$x + 1 = 10$$
$$x + 1 - 1 = 10 - 1$$
$$x = 9$$

16. D. Any point in Quadrant IV will have a positive x-coordinate and a negative y-coordinate. Therefore, if the point $P(a, b)$ is in Quadrant IV, $a > b$.

17. C, D, and E.

$$5z - 10 < 8z - 6$$
$$5z - 10 - 8z < 8z - 6 - 8z$$
$$-3z - 10 < -6$$
$$-3z - 10 + 10 < -6 + 10$$
$$-3z < 4$$
$$\frac{-3z}{-3} > \frac{4}{-3}$$
$$z > \frac{-4}{3}$$

Hence, -1, 0, and 4 are in the solution of $5z - 10 < 8z - 6$.

Chapter 7

Geometry Review

Geometry literally means "measurement of the earth." The Core Mathematics exam tests your ability to apply measurement and geometric concepts to solve problems within the context of math and spatial reasoning in four critical areas:

- Understanding common geometry terms, concepts, properties, and their relationships
- Drawing conclusions about basic geometric figures based on the use of congruence, similarity, symmetry, and transformation
- Identifying important theorems for right triangles and circles
- Solving real-life geometry word problems using math and deductive reasoning skills to measure angles, perimeter, area, surface area, and volume

Use the following table to chart your progress as you review each topic. Check off topics as you study the material. Focus your attention on one math topic at a time, and assess your strengths to evaluate areas in which you feel you may need improvement. To reinforce what you have learned, work the practice questions at the end of this chapter (answers and explanations are provided).

Geometry Study Guide Checklist

Praxis Core Math Category	Topic	Chapter Review Page Number	Worked Examples	Further Study Required
	Diagnostic Test	pp. 184–185		
Geometric Formulas	Perimeter and area: Square, rectangle, parallelogram, triangle, rhombus, trapezoid, circle, and right triangle	pp. 186–187		
Geometry Terms	Point, line, line segment, and ray	pp. 188–189		
	Angles			
	Types and measurements of angles	pp. 189–191		
	Single angles (acute, right, obtuse, and straight)	pp. 189–190		
	Pairs of angles (adjacent, complementary, supplementary, congruent, alternate interior, and alternate exterior)	pp. 190–191		
Congruence and Similarity	Congruence	p. 192		
	Symmetry and Transformation	pp. 192–193		
	Similarity	pp. 194–195		
Polygons	Special polygons	p. 195		
	Triangles: Common facts and area of a triangle	pp. 195–200		
	Triangle inequality theorem and exterior angle theorem	p. 197		
	Opposite angles and opposite sides	p. 198		
	Types of triangles (equilateral, right, isosceles, and scalene)	pp. 198–199		
	Angle measures (equilateral, acute, obtuse, and right)	pp. 199–200		
	Pythagorean Theorem	pp. 200–201		
	Pythagorean triples	p. 201		
	30-60-90 right triangles	pp. 201–202		
	45-45-90 right triangles	pp. 202–203		
	Quadrilaterals (trapezoid, parallelogram, rectangle, and square)	pp. 203–204		
	Circles: Circumference and area	pp. 205–206		

continued

Geometry Study Guide Checklist

Praxis Core Math Category	Topic	Chapter Review Page Number	Worked Examples	Further Study Required
Geometric Measurement and Dimension	Perimeter Surface area Volume	pp. 206–207 p. 208 pp. 208–209		
Modeling with Geometry	Visual and spatial reasoning	pp. 209–210		

Take the geometry diagnostic test that follows to help you evaluate how familiar you are with the selected geometry topics. The diagnostic test will give you valuable insight into the topics you will need to study.

Geometry Diagnostic Test

Directions: Solve each problem in this section by using the information given and your own mathematical calculations.

1. A(n) _____ angle measures more than 0°, but less than 90°.

2. A(n) _____ angle measures exactly 90°.

3. A(n) _____ angle measures more than 90°, but less than 180°.

4. In the figure below, find the measures of ∠1, ∠2, and ∠3.

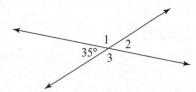

5. If $\triangle ABC \cong \triangle EFG$ and $m\angle A = 35°$ and $m\angle B = 75°$, then $m\angle G =$ _____?

6. If $m\angle A = 59°$ and $m\angle B = 58°$ in $\triangle ABC$, what is the longest side of the triangle?

Question 7 refers to the figure below.

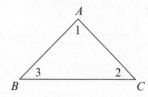

7. $m\angle 1 + m\angle 2 + m\angle 3 =$ ____°.

8. In the following figure, $MP = NP$ and $m\angle N = 57°$. Find the measure of ∠1.

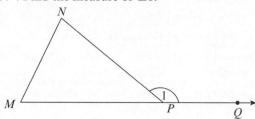

9. An isosceles right triangle has a leg with a length of 15. Find the length of its hypotenuse.

10. A(n) _____ triangle has three congruent sides. Therefore, each interior angle measures _____°.

11. In the following figure, if $b = 8$ and $a = 15$, find c.

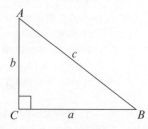

12. Find the perimeter and area of the following trapezoid.

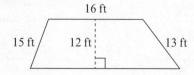

13. Find the area of a rectangle if one of its sides has a length of 30 and one of its diagonals has a length of 34.

14. In the following circle, X is a point on the circle and $m\angle X = 50°$. Find the measure of $\overset{\frown}{YXZ}$

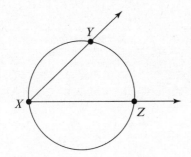

15. Find the volume of a right circular cylinder with a radius of 6 inches and a height of 14 inches.

16. Find the volume of a cardboard box whose base is a rectangle of 3 feet by 4 feet and whose height is 2 feet.

17. Find the volume of a circular cylinder can of popcorn with a base radius of 12 inches and a height of 10 inches.

Scoring the Diagnostic Test

The following section will assist you in scoring and analyzing your diagnostic test results. Use the answer key and the analysis worksheet that follows to help you evaluate specific problem types. Corresponding topic headings can be found in the geometry review section following the diagnostic test. In fact, most of the problems are covered in the review, with details on how to solve them.

Answer Key

Geometry Terms: Lines, Segments, Rays, and Angles

1. acute

2. right

3. obtuse

4. $m\angle 1 = m\angle 3 = 145°$; $m\angle 2 = 35°$

Congruence and Similarity

5. $m\angle G = 70°$

Triangles

6. $\overline{AB}$

7. 180°

8. $m\angle 1 = 114°$

9. $15\sqrt{2}$

10. equilateral triangle; 60

11. 17

Quadrilaterals

12. perimeter = 74 ft: area = 276 ft²

13. 480

Circles

14. $\overset{\frown}{YXZ} = 260°$

Geometric Measurement and Dimension: Perimeter, Surface Area, and Volume

15. 504π cubic inches

16. 24 cubic feet

17. volume = $1,440\pi$ in³

Charting and Analyzing Your Diagnostic Test Results

Record your diagnostic test results in the following chart and use these results as a guide to assist you in planning your geometry review goals and objectives. Mark the problems that you missed, paying particular attention to those that were missed in Column (C) because they are unfamiliar math concepts. These are the areas you will want to focus on as you study the geometry topics.

Analysis Worksheet

Topic	Total Possible	Number Correct	Number Incorrect		
			(A) Simple Mistake	(B) Misread Problem	(C) Unfamiliar Math Concept
Geometry terms: Lines, segments, rays, and angles	4				
Congruence and similarity	1				
Triangles	6				
Quadrilaterals	2				
Circles	1				
Geometric measurement and dimensions: Perimeter, surface area, and volume	3				
Total Possible Explanations for Incorrect Answers: Columns A, B, and C					
Total Number of Answers Correct and Incorrect	17	Add the total number of correct answers here: ____	Add columns A, B, and C: _____ Total number of incorrect answers		

Geometry Review

Understanding geometry is more than memorizing formulas. It is about applying logic, reasoning, and math strategies to various geometric shapes, angles, and other configurations to solve problems. As you work through this review section, notice that geometry concepts are linked to the corresponding topics of arithmetic and algebra. Use your prior learning of the math topics discussed in chapters 5 and 6 to help you answer geometry questions.

Always base your answer on geometric logic, not on estimating or comparing quantities by sight. Lines shown in the figures are straight and points on a line occur in the order shown, but geometric figures are *not* necessarily drawn to scale. Some shapes may appear larger, while others may appear smaller.

Basic Geometric Formulas

Use the following geometric formula table as a reference guide for basic shapes that may appear on the Core Mathematics Test: perimeter and area. The Pythagorean theorem illustrates how the lengths of the sides of a right triangle relate to one another.

Shape	Illustration	Perimeter	Area
Square		$P = 4a$	$A = a^2$
Rectangle		$P = 2b + 2h$ or $P = 2(b + h)$	$A = bh$
Parallelogram		$P = 2a + 2b$ or $P = 2(a + b)$	$A = bh$
Triangle		$P = x + y + b$	$A = \dfrac{bh}{2}$ or $A = \dfrac{1}{2}bh$
Rhombus		$P = 4a$	$A = ah$
Trapezoid		$P = b_1 + b_2 + x + y$	$A = \dfrac{h(b_1 + b_2)}{2}$ or $A = \dfrac{1}{2}h(b_1 + b_2)$
Circle		Circumference $C = \pi d$ or $C = 2\pi r$	$A = \pi r^2$
Right triangle		Pythagorean theorem: The sum of the squares of the legs of a right triangle equals the square of the hypotenuse.	$a^2 + b^2 = c^2$

Geometry Terms

Term	Description	Written Symbol	Example
Point	A **point** shows a location in space. It is represented by a dot and usually named with a capital letter. This example is called "point A."	•	• A
Line	A **line** is always considered to be straight. In the example shown, the two arrows illustrate that the line has no beginning point and no endpoint. The line continues indefinitely in both directions. A line consists of an infinite number of points and is named by any two points on it. Notice the symbol ↔ is written on top of the two letters to represent a line.	$\overleftrightarrow{AB}$, $\overleftrightarrow{BA}$, or m	The line in the figure below can be called line AB, line BA, or line m. 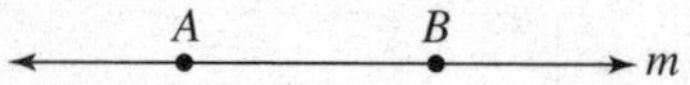
Line Segment	A **line segment** (often called just a **segment**) connects two points on a line. It is a "part" of a line consisting of two endpoints. A line segment has one length, and its length *can* be measured. The example shows line segment CD. A bar is written on the top of the letters CD to represent a line segment. *Note:* A **midpoint** of a line segment is the halfway point.	$\overline{CD}$ or $\overline{DC}$	 Notice in the figure shown below, the segment $\overline{CD}$ is only a "part" of line $\overleftrightarrow{AB}$. 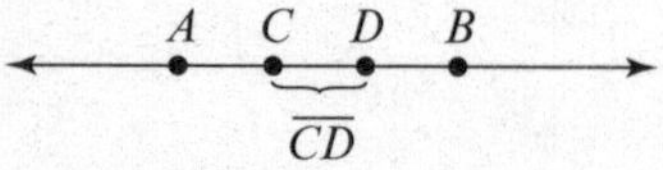 The sides of all triangles are line segments. 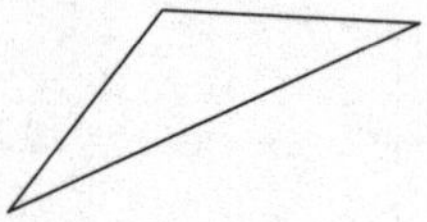
Ray	A **ray** is a part of a line that begins at one specific endpoint (called a **vertex**). A ray can continue indefinitely in one direction, but its length *cannot* be measured. The symbol → is written on top of two letters used to represent the ray.	$\overrightarrow{AB}$	Ray $\overrightarrow{AB}$: 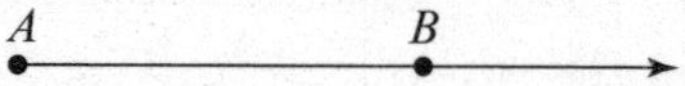 Ray $\overleftarrow{BC}$: 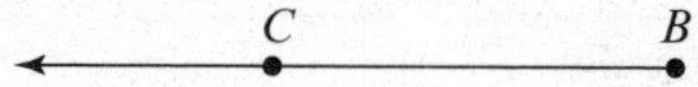 Note the order of the letters—the endpoint is always mentioned first.

continued

Term	Description	Written Symbol	Example
Angle	An **angle** is formed by two sides (two rays) that intersect at a point (the **vertex** of the angle). The angle symbol ∠ is often used to represent an angle instead of the word *angle*.	∠Q	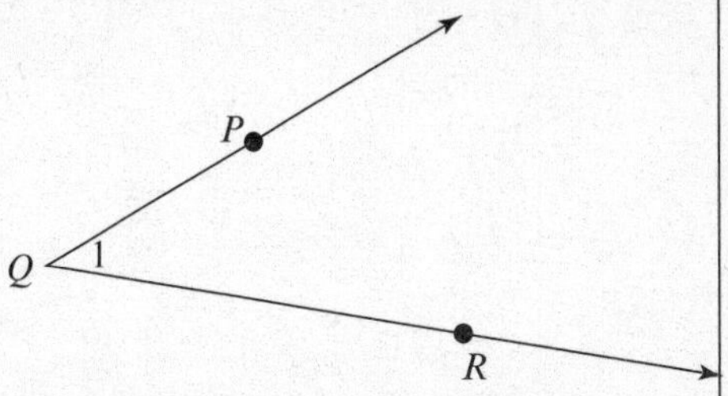 In the figure above, the angle is formed by rays QP and QR. $\overrightarrow{QP}$ and $\overrightarrow{QR}$ are sides of the angle. You can name the angle in several ways: • by the letter of the vertex, ∠Q • by the number in its interior, ∠1 • by three letters with the middle letter the vertex of the angle, ∠PQR or ∠RQP

Types and Measurements of Angles

The Core Mathematics Test calls attention to math problems presented in real-life scenarios. Before we review the types of angles and their measurements, take a moment to think about lines and angles that you encounter in your daily life. Angles are everywhere in our real-world environment and can vary in size and measure. Many objects inside and outside of your home have geometric shapes (roofs, windows, furniture, phones, children's toys, etc.). All of these objects were designed by using lines that formed angles of different shapes and measurements.

In general, there are two groups of geometric angles:

- **Single angles:** acute, right, obtuse, and straight
- **Pairs of angles:** adjacent, complementary, supplementary, congruent, alternate interior, and alternate exterior angles

Single Angles: Acute, Right, Obtuse, and Straight

Single Angle Measurements

Acute Angle	Right Angle	Obtuse Angle	Straight Angle
Single angles are measured in units called degrees (°) from 0 to 360. The number of degrees indicates the size of the angle.			
An **acute** angle is an angle whose measure is greater than 0° and less than 90°.	A **right** angle has a measure of 90°. The small square symbol ◻ in the interior of the angle shows that it is a right angle.	An **obtuse** angle is an angle whose measure is greater than 90°, but less than 180°.	A **straight** angle is an angle whose measure is 180°.
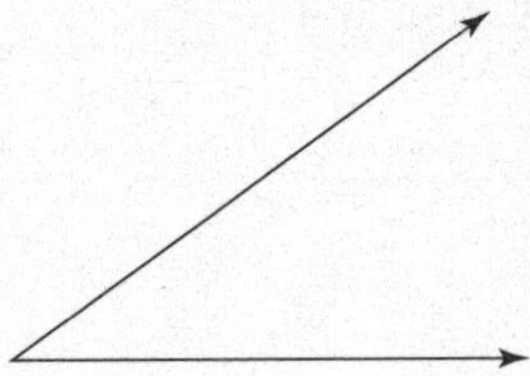			

For example, in the figure below, ∠PQR is an acute angle, ∠PQS is an obtuse angle, and ∠RQS is a straight angle.

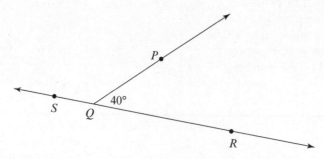

Pairs of Angles: Adjacent, Complementary, and Supplementary Angles

There are six pairs of angles. The following figure illustrates the first three pairs of angles: adjacent, complementary, and supplementary.

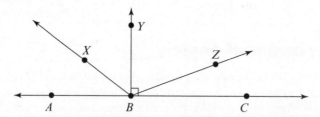

Adjacent Angles	Complementary Angles	Supplementary Angles
Adjacent angles are two angles that share the same vertex and a common side.	**Complementary** angles are two angles whose sum is 90°.	**Supplementary** angles are two angles whose sum is 180°.
∠XBY and ∠YBZ	∠YBZ and ∠ZBC	∠ABZ and ∠ZBC

Pairs of Angles: Congruent Angles

The following figure illustrates congruent vertical angles.

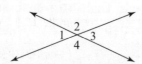

Congruent (Vertical) Angles	
An important property of congruent angles is that they have the same measure and are always equal. **Congruent vertical angles** are formed by two intersecting lines. They have the same vertex whose sides are opposite each other. Vertical angles are sometimes referred to as opposite angles.	In the figure above, ∠1 and ∠3 are congruent angles, and ∠2 and ∠4 are congruent angles. $m\angle 1 = m\angle 3$ and $m\angle 2 = m\angle 4$. Therefore, these angles are congruent and you can write, ∠1 ≅ ∠3 and ∠2 ≅ ∠4.

Pairs of Angles: Alternate Interior and Exterior Angles

Angles are often formed by two lines and a **transversal** (a straight line that cuts through two or more lines at different points). Corresponding angles are formed when the transversal cuts through two or more lines. In the figure below, ∠1 and ∠5, ∠4 and ∠8, ∠2 and ∠6, and ∠3 and ∠7 are corresponding angles. The figure illustrates **alternate interior** and **exterior angles.**

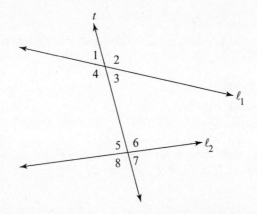

Alternate Interior Angles	Alternate Exterior Angles
If two lines are intersected by a third line (called a **transversal**), they form two pairs of **alternate interior** angles. These angles will be inside the two lines and on alternate sides of the transversal.	If two lines are intersected by a third line, then two pairs of **alternate exterior** angles are formed. These angles will be outside the two lines and on alternate sides of the transversal.
In the figure above, ℓ_1 and ℓ_2 are cut by the transversal, t, forming two pairs of alternative interior angles: $\angle 3$ and $\angle 5$, and $\angle 4$ and $\angle 6$.	In the figure above, two pairs of alternate exterior angles are formed: $\angle 1$ and $\angle 7$, and $\angle 2$ and $\angle 8$.

The following figure illustrates a special case of alternate exterior angles.

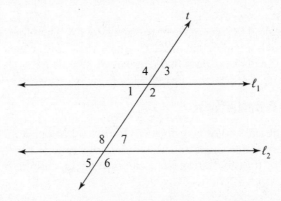

If the corresponding angles are equal, lines l_1 and l_2 are parallel ($\ell_1 \parallel \ell_2$) and they are cut by a transversal, t.

Therefore, the alternate interior angles are equal: $m\angle 1 = m\angle 7$ and $m\angle 2 = m\angle 8$, and the alternate exterior angles are equal as well: $m\angle 3 = m\angle 5$ and $m\angle 4 = m\angle 6$. If you have a question on the Core Mathematics Test that shows the measure of these angles, the measures of the remaining seven angles can be determined. Also note that there are four pairs of vertical angles and sixteen pairs of supplementary angles in the figure.

For example, if $m\angle 2 = 140°$, find the measures of the other seven angles.

$m\angle 2 = m\angle 8 = m\angle 6 = m\angle 4 = 140°$

$m\angle 1 = m\angle 7 = m\angle 5 = m\angle 3 = 40°$

Congruence and Similarity

Look for congruent and similar relationships among geometric figures on the Core Mathematics Test.

Congruence

Two figures are **congruent** if their corresponding parts (angles and line segments) have the same size and measure. For example:

- Two line segments that have identical lengths
- Two angles that have equal measurements
- Two circles that have the same diameters

When congruent figures are named, their vertices are listed in order of corresponding angles. This indicates which angles and sides have the same measure. The symbol $\cong$ shows that a figure "is congruent to" another figure.

Example:

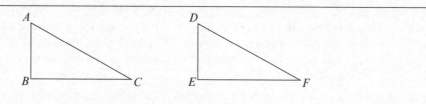

$$\triangle ABC \cong \triangle DEF$$
$$m\angle A = m\angle D,\ m\angle B = m\angle E,\ m\angle C = m\angle F$$
$$AB = DE,\ AC = DF,\ BC = EF$$

1. In the example above, triangle *ABC* is congruent to triangle *DEF*. Therefore, the measures of angle *A* equals angle *D*, angle *B* equals angle *E*, and angle *C* equals angle *F*. The measures of line segment *AB* equals *DE*, line segment *AC* equals *DF*, and line segment *BC* equals *EF*.

Symmetry and Transformation

Congruent objects can be symmetrical and/or transformed. In the table on page 193, notice that the second congruent object (image) appears identical in shape and size to the original object (pre-image). If an original pre-image generates a second image by transformation (flipping, turning, or sliding), both images are understood to be congruent.

Symmetry	Transformation
Symmetry occurs when two congruent halves of an image are in exact balance. If one half of an image has an exact reflection of the other half, they are symmetrical. The line of symmetry divides the images into two congruent halves.	A **transformation** occurs when an object (pre-image) is repositioned by flipping, turning, or sliding the object without changing its shape or size. The new object is called the **image** of the transformation when the new, or second image, is reoriented to a different position. There are three basic motions to transform a figure: ■ reflection – when a pre-image is *flipped* into a new image ■ rotation – when a pre-image is *turned* into a new image ■ translation – when a pre-image is *slid* into a new image

continued

Symmetry	Transformation
Line of symmetry	The following figure illustrates transformation. When an original pre-image is rotated, a second image appears in a different position.

Examples:

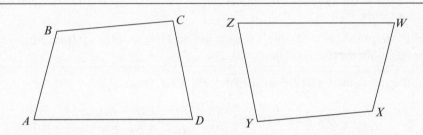

1. In the figures above, if quadrilateral $ABCD \cong$ quadrilateral $WXYZ$, then the following are true:

$m\angle A = m\angle W$ and $\quad AB = WX$

$m\angle B = m\angle X \qquad\qquad BC = XY$

$m\angle C = m\angle Y \qquad\qquad CD = YZ$

$m\angle D = m\angle Z \qquad\qquad AD = WZ$

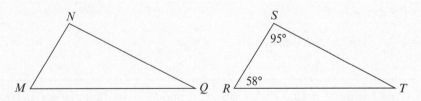

2. Given: $\triangle MNQ \cong \triangle RST$ with $m\angle R = 58°$ and $m\angle S = 95°$. Find the measures of all three angles in $\triangle MNQ$.

In $\triangle RST$, $\quad m\angle R + m\angle S + m\angle T = 180°$

$$58° + 95° + m\angle T = 180°$$

$$153° + m\angle T = 180°$$

$$m\angle T = 27°$$

Since $\triangle MNQ \cong \triangle RST$,

$$m\angle M = m\angle R = 58°$$

$$m\angle N = m\angle S = 95°$$

and $m\angle Q = m\angle T = 27°$

Similarity

Two objects are **similar** if they have exactly the same shape and congruent angles, *but are not necessarily the same size*. Similar objects have corresponding angles that are equal in measure, and have corresponding sides that are *proportional* in measure. The symbol ~ shows that an object "is similar to" another object.

Examples:

1. When resizing a picture, two photographs may be similar because their angles are equal and their sides are proportional in measure.

    Analyze the photographs above and write a proportion problem to solve *x*. (***Hint:*** Strategies for proportion problems are explained in chapter 5).

In the figures above, if quadrilateral *ABCD* ~ quadrilateral *WXYZ*, then:

$$m\angle A = m\angle W \text{ and } \frac{AB}{WX} = \frac{BC}{XY} = \frac{CD}{YZ} = \frac{DA}{ZW}$$

$$m\angle B = m\angle X$$

$$m\angle C = m\angle Y \text{ or } \frac{WX}{AB} = \frac{XY}{BC} = \frac{YZ}{CD} = \frac{ZW}{DA}$$

$$m\angle D = m\angle Z$$

Therefore,

$$\frac{x}{8} = \frac{6}{12} \quad \text{Side } AB \text{ corresponds to side } WX, \text{ and side } CD \text{ corresponds to side } YZ.$$

$$x \cdot 12 = 8 \cdot 6$$

$$\frac{x \cdot 12}{12} = \frac{8 \cdot 6}{12} \quad \text{Divide each side by 12.}$$

$$x = 4$$

2. Given: $\triangle DEF \sim \triangle RST$ with $DE = 18$, $EF = 24$, $DF = 30$, and $ST = 16$. Find the perimeter of $\triangle RST$.

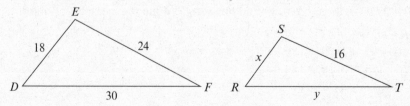

Since $\Delta DEF \sim \Delta RST$, their corresponding sides are proportional:

$$\frac{DE}{RS} = \frac{EF}{ST} = \frac{DF}{RT}$$

$$\frac{DE}{RS} = \frac{EF}{ST} \qquad \text{and} \qquad \frac{EF}{ST} = \frac{DF}{RT}$$

$$\frac{18}{x} = \frac{24}{16} \qquad\qquad\qquad \frac{24}{16} = \frac{30}{y}$$

$$24x = (18)(16) \qquad\qquad 24y = (16)(30)$$

$$24x = 288 \qquad\qquad\qquad 24y = 480$$

$$x = \frac{288}{24} = 12 \qquad\qquad y = \frac{480}{24} = 20$$

Hence, the perimeter of $\Delta RST = 16 + 12 + 20 = 48$.

Polygons

A **polygon** is a "many-sided figure" (*poly* means "many" and *gon* means "side"). A polygon is a closed plane figure made up of line segments that intersect only at their endpoints. The minimum number of sides, angles, or vertices of a polygon is three, but there is no maximum number.

Special Polygons

Pictured below are different types of polygons, but the Core Mathematics Test commonly references two types of polygons: triangles and quadrilaterals.

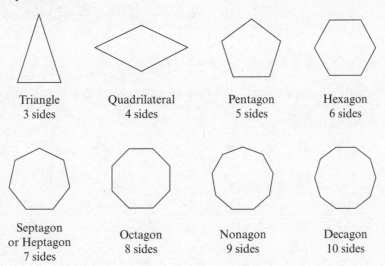

| Triangle | Quadrilateral | Pentagon | Hexagon |
| 3 sides | 4 sides | 5 sides | 6 sides |

| Septagon or Heptagon | Octagon | Nonagon | Decagon |
| 7 sides | 8 sides | 9 sides | 10 sides |

Triangles

Questions about triangles are common on the Core Mathematics Test. A triangle has three sides, angles, and vertices. The symbol for a triangle is Δ.

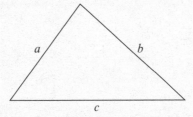

The perimeter P of a triangle = sides $a + b + c$

$$P = a + b + c$$

Common Facts about Triangles

The sum of the interior angles in a triangle is always 180°. Every triangle can be drawn showing a **base** (bottom side) and a **height** (altitude). Every height is the *perpendicular* segment from a vertex to its opposite side (the base), forming two right angles unless the triangle is obtuse with the altitude drawn to an extended side.

In the $\triangle ABC$ below, $\overline{AC}$ is the base and $\overline{BD}$ is the height. $\overline{BD} \perp \overline{AC}$ ($\overline{BD}$ is perpendicular to $\overline{AC}$).

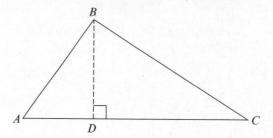

A **median** is the line segment drawn from a vertex to the midpoint of the opposite side. *Note:* Every triangle has three medians. In this figure, $\overline{BD}$ is a median of $\triangle ABC$. Therefore, $AD = DC$ and $\overline{BD}$ is a median of $\triangle ABC$.

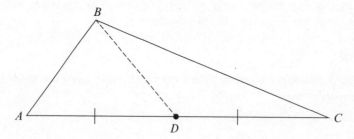

Area of a Triangle

The formula for the area A of a triangle is $A = \dfrac{1}{2}bh$, where the base b is any one of the sides of the triangle and h is the height (altitude) drawn to the base.

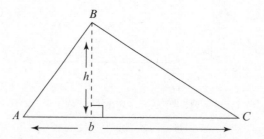

Example:

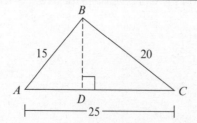

1. Find the perimeter P and area of $\triangle ABC$ above, where $BD = 12$ and $\overline{BD} \perp \overline{AC}$.

The perimeter P of $\triangle ABC$ is the sum of the lengths of its sides: $15 + 20 + 25 = 60$.

$$\begin{aligned}
\text{The area of } \triangle ABC &= \frac{1}{2}bh \\
&= \frac{1}{2}(AC)(BD) \\
&= \frac{1}{2}(25)(12) \\
&= 150
\end{aligned}$$

Triangle Inequality Theorem

The **triangle inequality theorem** states that the sum of the lengths of any two sides of a triangle must be greater than the length of the remaining side.

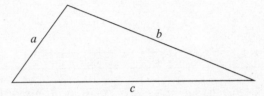

In the preceding figure,

$a + b > c$

$a + c > b$

$b + c > a$

Exterior Angle Theorem

If one side of a triangle is extended in either direction, the exterior angle formed by that extension is equal to the sum of the other two interior angles.

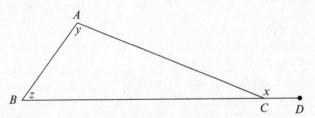

In the preceding $\triangle ABC$, side $\overline{BC}$ is extended to D. The exterior angle formed is $\angle ACD$. Note that every triangle has six possible exterior angles.

Example:

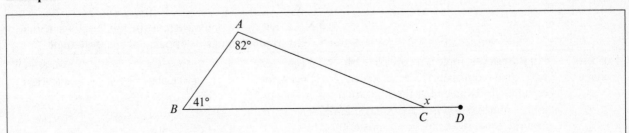

1. In $\triangle ABC$, find the measure of angle x.

$$\begin{aligned}
m\angle x &= m\angle A + m\angle B \\
x &= 82° + 41° \\
x &= 123°
\end{aligned}$$

197

Opposite Angles and Opposite Sides

The largest (or smallest) side of a triangle is opposite its largest (or smallest) angle. Conversely, the largest (or smallest) angle of a triangle is opposite its largest (or smallest) side. If two sides of a triangle are equal, then the angles opposite these sides are equal. Conversely, if two angles of a triangle are equal, then the sides opposite these angles are equal.

Example:

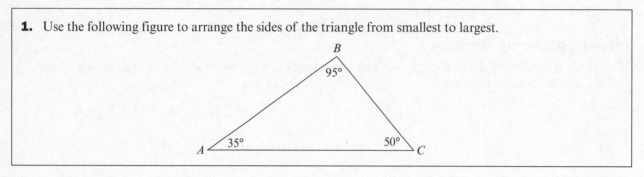

1. Use the following figure to arrange the sides of the triangle from smallest to largest.

Since $\angle A$ is the smallest angle of $\triangle ABC$, the smallest side of $\triangle ABC$ is $\overline{BC}$, opposite $m\angle A = 35°$. The next largest side is $\overline{AB}$, opposite $m\angle C = 50°$. The largest angle of $\triangle ABC$ is $m\angle B = 95°$, so the side opposite $\angle B$, $\overline{AC}$, is the largest side of $\triangle ABC$.

Types of Triangles

Triangles are categorized by either their side lengths or their angle measures.

Side Lengths That Classify Triangles		
Equilateral triangle	An **equilateral** triangle has all three sides of equal length, and all three angles measure 60° each. Therefore, all three sides and angles are congruent. Since all three angles are also equal, the triangle is also known as an *equiangular* triangle.	**Equilateral, Isosceles, Acute**
Right triangle	A **right** triangle is a triangle with one right angle. The two sides that form the right angle are called **legs,** and the side opposite the right angle is called the **hypotenuse.**	Note that the hypotenuse must be the longest side in a right triangle since it is opposite the largest angle.
Isosceles triangle	An **isosceles** triangle is a triangle with two equal (congruent) sides and two equal angles. Remember that the equal angles must be opposite the equal sides, and the equal sides must be opposite the equal angles.	**Isosceles and Acute** **Isosceles and Obtuse** **Isosceles and Right**

continued

Side Lengths That Classify Triangles			
Scalene triangle	A **scalene** triangle is a triangle with no equal (congruent) sides and no equal (congruent) angles.	**Scalene and Right**	**Scalene and Obtuse**

Examples:

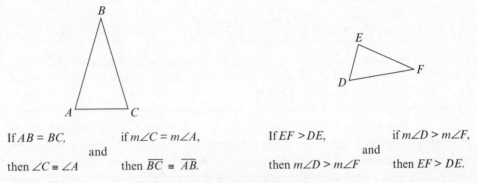

If $AB = BC$,	if $m\angle C = m\angle A$,	If $EF > DE$,	if $m\angle D > m\angle F$,
	and		and
then $\angle C \cong \angle A$	then $\overline{BC} \cong \overline{AB}$.	then $m\angle D > m\angle F$	then $EF > DE$.

Angle Measures That Classify Triangles

Triangle	Description	Interior Angle Degree Measures
Equiangular triangle	An **equiangular** triangle has all of its angles of equal measure of 60°. An equiangular triangle is also an equilateral triangle.	Equal measures of 60° (all angles)
Acute triangle	An **acute** triangle is a triangle with interior angles measuring less than 90°. If $c^2 < a^2 + b^2$, then the triangle is an acute triangle and the angle opposite c is less than 90°, and c is the longest side. The converse is also true. If the angle opposite c is less than 90°, the triangle is an acute triangle and $c^2 < a^2 + b^2$.	Less than 90° (all angles)
Obtuse triangle	An **obtuse** triangle is a triangle with one interior angle measuring greater than 90°. If $c^2 > a^2 + b^2$, then the triangle is an obtuse triangle and the angle opposite c is greater than 90°, and c is the longest side. The converse is also true. If the angle opposite c is greater than 90°, the triangle is an obtuse triangle and $c^2 > a^2 + b^2$.	Greater than 90° (one angle)
Right triangle	A **right** triangle has one interior angle with an exact measure of 90°. If $c^2 = a^2 + b^2$, then the triangle is a right triangle and the angle opposite c is 90°, and c is the longest side. The converse is also true. If the angle opposite c is 90°, the triangle is a right triangle and $c^2 = a^2 + b^2$.	Measure of 90° (one angle)

Examples:

---

1. In the diagram that follows, *ABC* is an isosceles triangle with base $\overline{BC}$ and $m\angle B = 38°$. Find $m\angle A$ and $m\angle C$.

Since line segment *BC* is the base of the isosceles triangle, that means that line segment *AC* is congruent with line segment *AB* or *AC* = *AB*. This means that $\angle B \cong \angle C$. Hence, $m\angle C = 38°$. The sum of the angles of a triangle is 180°; thus, $m\angle A + 38° + 38° = 180°$, then $m\angle A = 104°$.

---

2. A(*n*) _____ triangle has three congruent sides. Therefore, each interior angle measures ____°.

An equilateral triangle has all three congruent sides of equal length. Since the sum of the angles of any triangle is 180°, and congruent length sides means opposite angles are congruent in measure in a triangle, then each angle measures 60°.

Pythagorean Theorem

In any right triangle, the sum of the squares of the two legs is equal to the square of the hypotenuse.

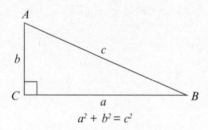

$$a^2 + b^2 = c^2$$

In any right triangle, if the lengths of any two sides are known, then the length of the third side can be determined using the Pythagorean theorem.

Examples:

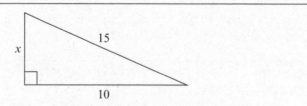

1. Using the Pythagorean theorem, find the missing side in this right triangle.

$$a^2 + b^2 = c^2$$
$$x^2 + 10^2 = 15^2$$
$$x^2 + 100 = 225$$
$$x^2 = 125$$
$$x = \sqrt{125}$$
$$x = \sqrt{25 \cdot 5}$$
$$x = 5\sqrt{5}$$

2. Find the missing hypotenuse, c, in the right triangle below.

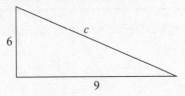

$$c^2 = a^2 + b^2$$
$$c^2 = (6)^2 + (9)^2$$
$$c^2 = 36 + 81$$
$$c^2 = 117$$
$$c = \sqrt{117}$$
$$c = \sqrt{9 \cdot 13}$$
$$c = 3\sqrt{13}$$

Pythagorean Triples

It is useful to note that certain integer values work in the Pythagorean theorem; these integers are called **Pythagorean triples.** Any multiples of these triples will also satisfy the Pythagorean theorem. For example:

- 3, 4, 5 and any multiple of these, such as 6, 8, 10 and 9, 12, 15
- 5, 12, 13 and any multiple of these, such as 10, 24, 26 and 15, 36, 39
- 8, 15, 17 and any multiple of these, such as 16, 30, 34 and 24, 45, 51

Other Right Triangles

There are two other right triangles whose side relationships you should know. One is called the **30-60-90 right triangle,** and the other is the **45-45-90 right triangle.**

The 30-60-90 Right Triangle

- The side opposite the 30° is the shortest side.
- The hypotenuse is twice as long as the shortest side.
- The side opposite the 60° is the shortest side times $\sqrt{3}$.

This is shown in the following figure.

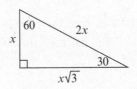

Example:

---

1. As shown below, a 30-60-90 right triangle is formed by cutting an equilateral triangle in half. Find the length of b.

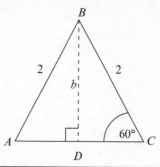

Since $\triangle ABC$ is an equilateral triangle, all sides are the same length. Therefore, side $AB = BC = AC = 2$. If $AC = 2$, then each of the short segments on line segment AC has a length of 1, as shown in the following figure.

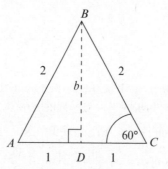

Now consider only $\triangle ABD$. Angle ABD has a measure of 30°, angle A has a measure of 60°, and angle ADB has a measure of 90°. This triangle has a hypotenuse twice as long as the short side, the side opposite the 30° angle. Using the Pythagorean theorem, we can find the measure of the side opposite the 60° angle.

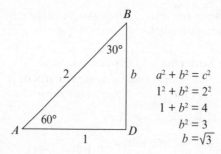

$$a^2 + b^2 = c^2$$
$$1^2 + b^2 = 2^2$$
$$1 + b^2 = 4$$
$$b^2 = 3$$
$$b = \sqrt{3}$$

The 45-45-90 Right Triangle

This right triangle is an isosceles right triangle. If each of the sides that forms the right angle has a measure of 1, then using the Pythagorean theorem, the hypotenuse has the value of $\sqrt{2}$. This is shown in the following figure.

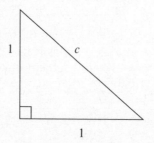

$$a^2 + b^2 = c^2$$
$$1^2 + 1^2 = c^2$$
$$2 = c^2$$
$$\sqrt{2} = c$$

If the legs of a right triangle are equal (i.e., x), then the hypotenuse is a factor of x (i.e., $\sqrt{2}x$).

Quadrilaterals

Quadrilateral problems are not common on the Core Mathematics Test, but you should be familiar with classifying their basic types, measurements, and general properties. A **quadrilateral** is a polygon with four sides, angles, and vertices. The sum of the interior angles in a quadrilateral is always 360°. If the sides of a quadrilateral have lengths a, b, c, and d, then the perimeter, P, is $P = a + b + c + d$.

Quadrilateral

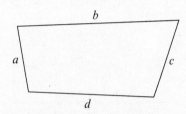

Basic Types of Quadrilaterals		
Trapezoid	A **trapezoid** is a quadrilateral with only one pair of parallel sides. The parallel sides are called the **bases** of the trapezoid and the nonparallel sides are called the *legs.* The **height** or **altitude** of a trapezoid is a segment perpendicular to the two parallel sides. **Area of a Trapezoid** The area A of a trapezoid is $A = \dfrac{1}{2}h(b_1 + b_2)$, where h is the altitude or height and b_1 and b_2 are the bases of the trapezoid.	
Parallelogram	A **parallelogram** has both pairs of opposite sides that are parallel. In parallelograms, opposite sides are congruent and opposite angles are congruent. Also, consecutive angles are supplementary. **Area of a Parallelogram** The area A of a parallelogram is $A = b \cdot h$, where the base b is any one of the sides of the parallelogram and the height h is the height of that side.	
Rectangle	A **rectangle** is a parallelogram with four 90° right angles. In rectangles, opposite sides are congruent and consecutive angles are supplementary. **Area of a Rectangle** The area of a rectangle is $A = b \cdot h$, where b is the base (any one of its sides) and h is the height (any side adjacent to the base) of the rectangle. Another formula that is sometimes used for the area is $A = l \cdot w$, where l is the length and w is the width of the rectangle.	

continued

Basic Types of Quadrilaterals		
Square	A **square** is a rectangle. In squares, all four sides are congruent and all four angles are 90° right angles. Therefore, all angles are equal. **Area of a Square** The area of a square is $A = s^2$, where s is the length of one of the four equal sides of the square.	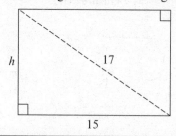

Examples:

1. Find the height of a rectangle with a base length of 15 and a diagonal length of 17.

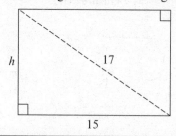

The height, h, can be determined using the Pythagorean theorem.

$$c^2 = a^2 + b^2$$
$$17^2 = h^2 + 15^2$$
$$289 = h^2 + 225$$
$$h^2 = 289 - 225$$
$$h^2 = 64$$
$$h = \sqrt{64} = 8$$

2. Find the area of a parallelogram whose sides have lengths of 20 and 36 and with one of its angles having a measure of 30°.

To solve, make a sketch of the information given.

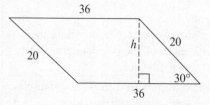

As you can see, the base of the parallelogram is 36 and the height is 10 since it is opposite the 30° angle; therefore, it is half the hypotenuse of a 30-60-90 triangle. The area A is

$$A = b \cdot h$$
$$= (36)(10)$$
$$= 360$$

Circles

A **circle** is a shape whose side is a curved line. A circle is the set of all points in a plane that are the same distance from a fixed point, called the **center** of the circle.

Parts of a Circle

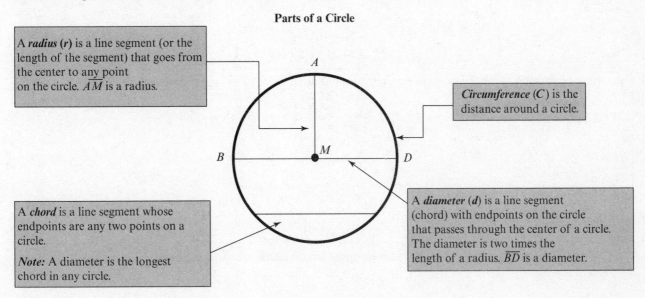

A *radius* (*r*) is a line segment (or the length of the segment) that goes from the center to any point on the circle. $\overline{AM}$ is a radius.

Circumference (*C*) is the distance around a circle.

A *chord* is a line segment whose endpoints are any two points on a circle.

Note: A diameter is the longest chord in any circle.

A *diameter* (*d*) is a line segment (chord) with endpoints on the circle that passes through the center of a circle. The diameter is two times the length of a radius. $\overline{BD}$ is a diameter.

Circumference and Area

Circumference is the distance around the circle. Since there are no sides to add together, a formula is needed.

First, let's discuss the Greek letter π (pi), $\pi \approx 3.14$ or $\pi \approx \frac{22}{7}$. Therefore, the formula for circumference is

$$C = \pi \cdot d \text{ or } C = 2\pi r$$

In many cases, the circumference may be expressed in terms of π with no decimal or fractional approximation. The area A of a circle with a radius r is $A = \pi r^2$, where $\pi \approx 3.14$ or $\pi \approx \frac{22}{7}$.

Examples:

1. In the circle below, find the circumference and area of the circle.

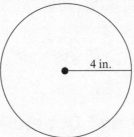

4 in.

First, note that since $r = 4$, $d = 8$.

Therefore, the circumference of the circle is

$$\begin{aligned}
C &= \pi d \\
&= \pi(8) \\
&\approx 3.14(8) \\
&\approx 25.12 \text{ inches}
\end{aligned}$$

Remember: The formula for the area of the circle can be determined by $A = \pi(r^2)$. Since the diameter of the circle is 8, the radius is 4 and the area of the circle is

$$A = \pi r^2$$
$$= \pi(4^2)$$
$$\approx 3.14(16)$$
$$\approx 50.24 \text{ sq. inches}$$

---

2. In the following circle, X is a point on the circle and $m\angle X = 50°$. Find the measure of $\widehat{YXZ}$.

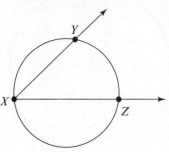

Since X is a point on the circle, $\angle X$ is an inscribed angle whose measure is half of the measure of its intercepted arc, $\widehat{YZ}$:

$$m\angle X = \frac{1}{2}(\widehat{YZ})$$
$$50° = \frac{1}{2}(\widehat{YZ})$$
$$2 \cdot 50° = 2 \cdot \frac{1}{2}(\widehat{YZ})$$
$$m\widehat{YZ} = 100°$$

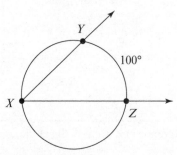

Since a circle is an arc whose measure is 360°,

$$m\widehat{YXZ} = 360° - \widehat{YZ}$$
$$= 360° - 100°$$
$$m\widehat{YXZ} = 260°$$

Geometric Measurement and Dimension

Perimeter

Perimeter is the distance around the outside of a figure. For example, if you add the four sides of a rectangle, the result is the perimeter.

Top side + bottom side + right side + left side = perimeter

20 + 20 + 9 + 9 = 58

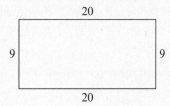

The formula for the perimeter of a rectangle is $P = 2l + 2w$.

Example:

1. Find the perimeter and area of the trapezoid shown here.

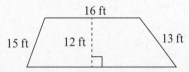

In order to make this question easier to solve, draw the perpendicular segments from the ends of the upper base to the lower base, creating two right triangles. Then use the Pythagorean theorem to find the missing lengths.

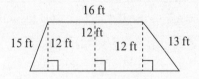

$$x^2 + 12^2 = 15^2 \qquad y^2 + 12^2 = 13^2$$
$$x^2 + 144 = 225 \qquad y^2 + 144 = 169$$
$$x^2 = 81 \qquad y^2 = 25$$
$$x = 9 \qquad y = 5$$

Now the figure can be redrawn with all the measurements indicated.

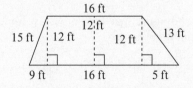

The trapezoid now can be seen as having base lengths of 16 feet and 30 feet (9 + 16 + 5 = 30), and a height of 12 feet.

$$\text{perimeter} = \text{ sum of all the sides} = (15 + 16 + 13 + 30) \text{ ft} = 74 \text{ ft}$$
$$\text{area} = \frac{h(b_1 + b_2)}{2} = \frac{(12)(16 + 30)}{2} \text{ ft}^2 = 276 \text{ ft}^2$$

Surface Area

Surface area is the sum of all the areas of the surfaces of a three-dimensional figure. In three-dimensional shapes, you can determine the surface area of solid figures. To solve surface area problems, find the area of *each* surface and then add them together. For example, in a problem that shows a rectangular figure, you can find the answer by adding all of the six surface areas.

In a rectangular solid, the relationship between the *length* (l), *width* (w), and *height* (h) will find the surface area (SA) using the following formula:

$$SA = 2wh + 2lh + 2lw$$

Example:

1. Find the surface area (SA) of a box with a length of 18 inches, width of 6 inches, and height of 4 inches.

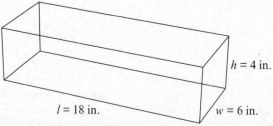

$h = 4$ in.

$l = 18$ in. $w = 6$ in.

The quickest method to solve this problem is to use the surface area formula.

$$SA = 2(6 \cdot 4) + 2(18 \cdot 4) + 2(18 \cdot 6)$$
$$= 48 + 144 + 216 = 408 \text{ sq. inches}$$

You can see that a slower method would give you the same result if you add up the faces of each side.

Top	$18 \times 6 =$	108
Bottom	$18 \times 6 =$	108
Front	$18 \times 4 =$	72
Back	$18 \times 4 =$	72
Left side	$6 \times 4 =$	24
Right side	$6 \times 4 =$	24
		408 sq. inches

Volume

Volume measures the *capacity* inside a solid figure. The formula for volume is different for each shape, but here are a couple of formulas for the most common shapes:

Volume of a rectangular solid: $V = $ (area of the base)(height of the figure), or $V = l \cdot w \cdot h$

Volume of a cylinder with a radius r and height h: $V = \pi r^2 h$

Examples:

1. Find the volume of a shipping box whose base is a rectangle 3 feet by 6 feet and whose height is 4 feet.

$$V = l \cdot w \cdot h$$
$$= 6 \cdot 3 \cdot 4$$
$$V = 72 \text{ cubic feet}$$

2. Find the volume of a circular cylinder can of popcorn with a base radius of 12 inches and a height of 10 inches.

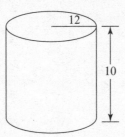

$$\text{Volume} = \pi r^2 h$$
$$= \pi (12)^2 (10)$$
$$= \pi (144)(10)$$
$$= 1,440\pi \text{ cubic inches}$$

Modeling with Geometry

According to scientific research, one of the best indicators of math success is visualization and spatial reasoning. The Common Core State Standards (CCSS) recognizes the importance of illustrating an array of real-life images, physical models, and diagrams to mentally visualize the relationships among geometric shapes and their measurements.

For example, the visual representation of **transformation** will help you distinguish that an original image does not change its size or shape from its second repositioned image. The geometric concept of transformation can be observed in everyday objects. The picture below illustrates the transformation of masonry bricks to construct a walkway.

Modeling and spatial reasoning problems can appear on the Core Mathematics Test as geometry word problems. Because some geometry word problems may not display an accompanying figure, you must carefully organize your thoughts by drawing a visual representation (figure, picture, or diagram) before answering the question.

Example:

1. What is the maximum number of pieces of birthday cake 4 inches by 4 inches in size that can be cut from a cake 20 inches by 20 inches?

    A.   5
    B.   10
    C.   16
    D.   20
    E.   25

First, write down or make a mental note that the question is asking for the "maximum number of pieces." To answer this type of question, it is sometimes helpful to draw and mark a simple diagram.

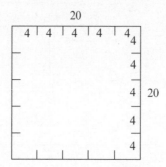

When you visualize the cake drawing, you will notice that five pieces of cake will fit along each side. Therefore, $5 \times 5 = 25$. Finding the total area of the cake and dividing it by the area of one of the 4-inch by 4-inch pieces would also give you the correct answer, choice E.

Geometry Practice Questions

Now that you have reviewed geometry topics and concepts, you can practice on your own. Questions appear in the format of the Core Mathematics question types: multiple-choice (select one answer), multiple-choice (select one or more answers), and numeric entry (fill-in). These practice questions give you a chance to solve problems in the same format as the actual test. The answers and explanations that follow the questions include strategies to help you understand how to solve the problems.

> **Remember: Answer choices in this study guide have lettered choices A, B, C, D, and E for clarity, but answer choice letters will not appear on the actual exam. On the actual computer version of the exam, you will be required to click on ovals, click on squares, or fill in your answer.**

General Directions: Answer each question by selecting the correct response from the choices given. Practice questions have several different formats. Unless otherwise directed, indicate a single answer choice.

---

1. Mrs. Edwards is measuring cloth remnants to create aprons for her art students. The length of each remnant is 36 inches and its diagonal is 39 inches. What is the area of each rectangular remnant in square inches?

    A. 1,404
    B. 702
    C. 540
    D. 108
    E. 75

2. Mr. Delgado is using wooden twigs to demonstrate how to construct miniature Native American teepees. To achieve multiple learning outcomes in history, art, and math, students are asked to mathematically find the angle supplement of two intersecting twigs. What is the supplement of an angle whose measure is 75°?

Write your answer in the box below.

3. In the figure below, $m\angle 1 = 27°$ and $m\angle 3 = 67°$. Find the measure of $\angle 2$.

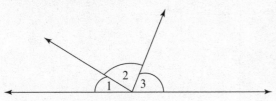

Write your answer in the box below.

4. In the following graph, which of the images is reoriented to form a translation of Figure E?

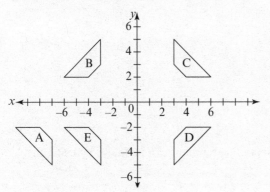

- **A.** Figure A
- **B.** Figure B
- **C.** Figure C
- **D.** Figure D
- **E.** None of the figures

5. In the figure below, $\overline{AB}$ is one edge of a cube. If $AB = 5$, what is the surface area of the cube?

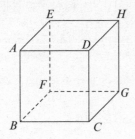

- **A.** 25
- **B.** 100
- **C.** 125
- **D.** 150
- **E.** 300

Question 6 refers to the following statement.

Lucas is laying new rectangular ceramic tiles on his kitchen floor, but the tiles do not fit in one corner of the room. To minimize his expenses, Lucas decides to cut one of the tiles to form another shape—a parallelogram (see below).

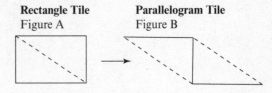

Rectangle Tile
Figure A

Parallelogram Tile
Figure B

6. Which of the following statements correctly expresses the relationship between the ceramic tiles pictured in Figure A and Figure B above?

Select **all** that apply.

- **A.** The two figures have the same perimeter.
- **B.** The two figures do not have the same perimeter.
- **C.** The two figures have the same area.
- **D.** The two figures do not have the same area.
- **E.** The two figures are similar.

7. Dan has a basketball court that measures 30 feet by 50 feet. He needs a grass strip around the perimeter of the court. How wide, in feet, must the strip be to provide 900 square feet of grass?

- **A.** 3
- **B.** 4
- **C.** 5
- **D.** 6
- **E.** 7

8. Find the circumference of a circle whose diameter is 28. Express in terms of π.

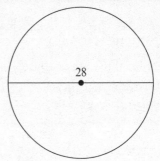

- **A.** 14π
- **B.** 28π
- **C.** 42π
- **D.** 126π
- **E.** 196π

9. An organic juice company is designing a larger aluminum can. The new aluminum can will be designed to hold twice as much juice as the can illustrated in the following figure.

Organic
Juice
16 oz.

Which of the following changes will result in the desired volume of 32 oz?

Reminder: $V = h(\pi r^2)$

- **A.** Double the height of the can.
- **B.** Double the radius of the base.
- **C.** Double the diameter of the base.
- **D.** Double both the height and the radius.
- **E.** Double both the height and the base.

Answers and Explanations

1. **C.** Because a right triangle is formed, the width of the rectangle remnant can be found by using the Pythagorean theorem:

$$w^2 + l^2 = d^2$$
$$w^2 + 36^2 = 39^2$$
$$w^2 + 1,296 = 1,521$$
$$w^2 = 225$$
$$w = 15$$

Since the area of a rectangle is the product of its width and length, the area is (15)(36) = 540, choice C.

You can save time and not use the Pythagorean theorem if you note that the sides of the triangle are multiples of the Pythagorean triple 5, 12, 13. Multiplying each by the factor of 3 gives the sides of 15, 36, and 39. Memorizing the basic Pythagorean triples—(3, 4, 5), (5, 12, 13), and (8, 15, 17)—can save valuable time on the test.

2. **105°** Since the sum of two supplementary angles is 180°, the supplement of an angle that measures 75° is 180° − 75° = 105°.

3. **86°** Since the three angles ∠1, ∠2, and ∠3 form a straight line, their sum is 180° and:

$$m\angle 1 + m\angle 2 + m\angle 3 = 180°$$
$$27° + m\angle 2 + 67° = 180°$$
$$m\angle 2 + 94° = 180°$$
$$m\angle 2 = 180° - 94°$$
$$m\angle 2 = 86°$$

4. **A.** When an image is repositioned by translation, it is slid across without changing its shape or size. A translated image cannot be flipped or turned; the orientation must remain the same in relationship to the original pre-image. Only Figure A maintains this relationship with respect to Figure E.

5. **D.** Since one edge of the cube is 5, all edges equal 5. Therefore, the area of one face of the cube is (5)(5) = 25. Since a cube has 6 equal faces, its surface area will be (6)(25) = 150.

6. B and C. A visual observation of Figure B (parallelogram) shows that the perimeter is different from the perimeter of Figure A (rectangle), choice B. Two widths of Figure A have been replaced by the diagonal sides of Figure B, which are longer. Because the area in Figure B (parallelogram) is unchanged and does not overlap Figure A (rectangle), the two figures have the same area, choice C.

7. C. Sketch the following rectangular diagram to calculate the width of the rectangle's perimeter.

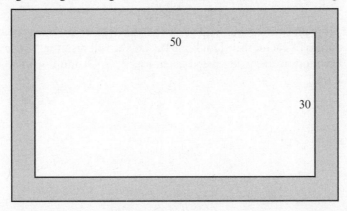

Now you can solve the problem by working from the answer choices. Since the answer choices are in order from smallest to largest, you may want to start from the middle answer and then go up or down as needed. If you use the value in choice C, 5, the diagram looks like this.

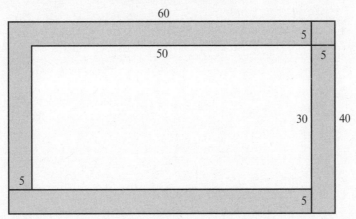

The overall area is 60 feet by 40 feet, or 2,400 square feet. The area of the court is 1,500 square feet. Subtracting the area of the court from the overall area gives the area of the grass strip, which is 900 square feet. So the strip is 5 feet wide, choice C.

An algebraic solution for the problem looks like the following equation (although it is not the quickest method). Working from the answers sometimes yields the correct solution without doing complex arithmetic or algebra. If the width of the strip is x, then

$$(2x + 50)(2x + 30) - 1,500 = 900$$
$$4x^2 + 160x + 1,500 - 1,500 = 900$$
$$4x^2 + 160x - 900 = 0$$
$$x^2 + 40x - 225 = 0$$
$$(x + 45)(x - 5) = 0$$

Because distance cannot be negative, you're left with $x = 5$, choice C.

8. B. The circumference of the circle is

$$C = \pi d$$
$$= \pi(28)$$
$$= 28\pi$$

If you were asked for the area of the circle, the correct answer would have been choice E. Since the diameter of the circle is 28, the radius is 14 and the area of the circle is

$$A = \pi r^2$$
$$= \pi (14)^2$$
$$= 196\pi$$

9. **A.** Visualizing the graphic illustration will help you solve this type of problem. Imagine stacking two identical 16-oz cans on top of each other. Doubling the height will result in "twice as much juice" to achieve the desired volume. The modifications suggested in choices B, C, D, and E would have resulted in a much greater increase in volume.

Chapter 8

Statistics and Probability Review

Core Mathematics statistics and probability questions appear in a unique format compared to other math questions. Many of these types of questions require some basic knowledge of interpreting graphic displays as you draw upon your ability to reason and make inferences. A solid understanding of the arithmetic concepts (fractions, proportion, and data interpretation) covered in chapters 4 and 5 will help you answer these types of questions.

This chapter covers statistics and probability questions that appear in two categories: descriptive and inferential statistics.

- **Descriptive statistics** organizes data with numbers and graphics to describe, inform, and summarize information about real-world populations and phenomena. You may see these types of problems presented in graphic displays with short statements. Questions are frequently related to measures of central tendency (mean, median, mode, and range).
- **Inferential statistics** uses probability to make inferences, justify conclusions, and make predictions about a population based on a random sample of the entire population. You will see these types of problems presented as probability questions.

As you work through this chapter, use the following chart to keep track of the topics to study. Focus your attention on one topic at a time, and assess your strengths to evaluate areas in which you feel may need improvement. To reinforce what you have learned, work the practice questions at the end of this chapter (answers and explanations are provided).

Statistics and Probability Study Guide Checklist

Math Category	Topic	Chapter Review Page Number	Worked Examples	Further Study Required
	Diagnostic test	p. 216		
Basic Statistics	Frequency distribution	pp. 217–218		
	Measures of central tendency	pp. 218–220		
	Mean	pp. 218–219		
	Median	pp. 219–220		
	Mode	p. 220		
	Statistical variability	pp. 220–221		
	Interpreting categorical and quantitative data	pp. 221–222		
	Bivariate data	pp. 221–222		
Probability Review	Making inferences and justifying conclusions	pp. 222–223		
	Random sampling	p. 222		
	Chance	pp. 222–223		
	Probability and methods for counting	p. 223		
	Measuring probability	pp. 223–225		

Take the statistics and probability diagnostic test to help you evaluate how familiar you are with the selected topics. The diagnostic test will give you valuable insight into the topics you will need to study.

Statistics and Probability Diagnostic Test

Directions: Solve each problem in this section by using the information given and your own mathematical calculations.

1. Find the mean of 27, 30, 28, 22, 25, and 28.

2. Find the median of 63, 80, 85, 74, 71, 83, 53, and 82.

3. Find the mode of 18, 19, 13, 17, 18, 16, and 20.

4. Find the mode of 8, 10, 3, 6, 8, 9, 7, and 3.

5. A student has test scores of 83, 95, 91, 86, and 92. What score is needed on the sixth test for the student to have an average of 90?

6. A box contains all 26 letters of the alphabet. What is the probability that the first two letters drawn are the letters a, b, c, d, e, or f?

7. One bag contains 5 white marbles and 4 black marbles. A second bag contains 4 white marbles and 5 black marbles. If one marble is drawn from each bag, what is the probability that both marbles are black?

8. In a single throw of two dice, determine the probability that they will total 6.

9. If a coin is tossed four times, what is the probability that all four tosses will be tails?

10. If one card is drawn at random from a deck of 52 cards, what is the probability that the card will not be a spade?

Scoring the Diagnostic Test

The following section will assist you in scoring and analyzing your diagnostic test results. Use the answer key and analysis worksheet that follows to help you evaluate specific problem types. Corresponding topic headings can be found in the statistics and probability review section following the diagnostic test.

Answer Key

Basic Statistics

1. $26\frac{2}{3}$
2. 77
3. 18
4. 3 and 8
5. 93

Probability

6. $\frac{3}{65}$
7. $\frac{20}{81}$
8. $\frac{5}{36}$
9. $\frac{1}{16}$
10. $\frac{3}{4}$

Charting and Analyzing Your Diagnostic Test Results

Record your diagnostic test results in the following chart and use these results as a guide to assist you in planning your statistics and probability review goals and objectives. Mark the problems that you missed, paying particular attention to those that were missed in Column (C) because they are unfamiliar math concepts. These are the areas you will want to focus on as you study the topics.

Analysis Worksheet

Topic	Total Possible	Number Correct	Number Incorrect		
			(A) Simple Mistake	(B) Misread Problem	(C) Unfamiliar Math Concept
Mean, median, mode, and range	5				
Probability	5				
Total Possible Explanations for Incorrect Answers: Columns A, B, and C					
Total Number of Answers Correct and Incorrect	10	Add the total number of correct answers here: _____	Add columns A, B, and C: _____ Total number of incorrect answers		

Basic Statistics Review

This section introduces the basic concepts of descriptive statistics. **Descriptive statistics** is a mathematical system for organizing, describing, and interpreting numerical data. Statistical results can present a clear picture about everyday events regarding a particular population, event, or situation. Using data and information about the distribution of numbers helps to find patterns that make general and specific statements about many real-life scenarios. For instance, descriptive statistics can be used to evaluate grade point averages, determine college football rankings, predict weather pattern changes, and rate frequently viewed television shows.

Statistics topics that are on the Core Mathematics Test include the fundamentals of frequency distribution, measures of central tendency (mean, median, mode, and range), and statistical variability. Inferential statistics topics of random sampling, chance, and probability will be covered in the Probability Review, starting on page 222.

Frequency Distribution

A **frequency distribution** table is a template used to organize information so that you can make sense of the numerical data collected from lowest to highest (**intervals**). Generally, there is a column on the left (the **data values**) and a column on the right (the **frequency**), which indicate how many of each data value are in the data set.

For example, a survey was taken in an eighth-grade English class at White Oak Middle School. The class of 15 students was asked how many times they were absent during the snowy month of January. The results were recorded as follows: 1, 0, 4, 1, 1, 2, 0, 3, 4, 1, 6, 1, 2, 0, 1. To organize the results, the teacher tallied and recorded the student responses using a frequency table. *Note:* x represents the number of days absent and f represents their frequency.

x	f
0	3
1	6
2	2
3	1
4	2
5	0
6	1

Although frequency distribution tables are useful for gathering and organizing data, they do not provide you with a good visual picture of what the data actually mean. This is why numerical data from a frequency table are often transferred to a graphical display (bar graph, line graph, etc.). Using the data collected in the frequency table above with one variable, the graphic display might look like this.

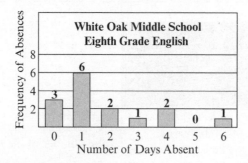

Measures of Central Tendency

A **measure of central tendency** describes any number in the middle of the data. It indicates the "center of a distribution." The three most common measures of central tendency are mean (or arithmetic mean), median, and mode.

Mean

The **mean** (also called the **arithmetic mean**) is what is usually called the **average.** To calculate the arithmetic mean of a group of numbers, take the following steps:

1. Add all of the numbers in the data set.
2. Divide by the total number of items in the set.

Examples:

1. Find the mean of 27, 30, 28, 22, 25, and 28.

$$27 + 30 + 28 + 22 + 25 + 28 = 160$$

Since there are 6 values, the total is divided by 6.

$$160 \div 6 = 26\frac{4}{6} = 26\frac{2}{3}$$

The mean is $26\frac{2}{3}$. If the problem had asked for the answer to be rounded to the nearest whole number, the mean would be 27.

2. What is the average of 2, 2, 5, 6, 5, 7, 9, 8, 8, and 11?

$$2 + 2 + 5 + 6 + 5 + 7 + 9 + 8 + 8 + 11 = 63$$

Since there are 10 values, the total is divided by 10.

$$63 \div 10 = 6\frac{3}{10}$$

The average is $6\frac{3}{10}$.

3. A student has test scores of 83, 67, 92, 88, and 79 in his science class. Find his mean test score.

$$83 + 67 + 92 + 88 + 79 = 409$$

Since there are five test scores, the total is divided by 5, or $\frac{409}{5} = 81\frac{4}{5}$ or 81.8. If the problem had asked for the answer to be rounded to the nearest whole number, the mean would be 82.

4. A student has test scores of 83, 95, 91, 86, and 92. What score is needed on the sixth test for the student to have an average of 90?

Let x = the sixth test score. For the average of the six test scores to equal 90:

$$(83 + 95 + 91 + 86 + 92 + x) \div 6 = 90$$
$$\frac{447 + x}{6} = 90$$
$$\frac{447 + x}{6} \cdot 6 = 90 \cdot 6$$
$$447 + x = 540$$
$$447 + x - 447 = 540 - 447$$
$$x = 93$$

The student needs a score of 93 on the sixth test in order to have an average of 90.

Median

The **median** for a set of data is the middle number when numbers are arranged from smallest to largest, or from largest to smallest. For any set of data, there is only one median. There are two methods to find the median in a group of numbers.

When working with an odd number of values, take the following steps:

1. List all of the numbers from smallest to largest.
2. Find the middle value. (*Note:* The same number of values is on either side.)

Example:

1. What is the median of this group of numbers: 2, 2, 6, 5, 7, 9, 8, 8, 11?

$$2, 2, 5, 6, \underline{7}, 8, 8, 9, 11$$

The median is 7.

Now suppose the number of items in the data set is even. It would be impossible find a middle number. Therefore, the median is determined by finding the mean or average of the two middle numbers.

When working with an even number of values, take the following steps:

1. List all of the numbers from smallest to largest.
2. Look for the middle two numbers and then find their average.

Examples:

> **1.** What is the median of this group of numbers: 2, 2, 6, 6, 5, 9, 8, 8, 8, 11?

$$2, 2, 5, 6, \underline{\mathbf{6, 8}}, 8, 8, 9, 11$$

The middle values are 6 and 8; therefore, you must find the arithmetic mean of the two middle numbers.

$$6 + 8 = 14$$
$$14 \div 2 = 7$$

The median is 7.

> **2.** Find the median of 63, 80, 85, 74, 71, 83, 53, and 82.

Since there is an even number of items in the data, the median is the average of the two middle numbers. Arranging the numbers from smallest to largest (or largest to smallest) yields 53, 63, 71, 74, 80, 82, 83, and 85. The two middle numbers are 74 and 80, whose average is

$$74 + 80 = 154$$
$$154 \div 2 = 77$$

The median is **77**.

Mode

The **mode** for a set of data is the number that appears the most frequently. One difference between the mode, mean, and median is that there may be more than one mode or no mode for any given set of data.

Examples:

> **1.** Find the mode of 18, 19, 13, 17, 18, 16, and 20.

The mode of 18, 19, 13, 17, 18, 16, and 20 is **18.** It is the number that occurs most frequently in the given data.

> **2.** Find the mode of 8, 10, 3, 6, 8, 9, 7, and 3.

The mode of 8, 10, 3, 6, 8, 9, 7, and 3 is **3 and 8** since they both occur twice in the given data.

> **3.** Find the mode of a set of quiz scores: 85, 86, 87, 87, 87, 91, 91, 93, 95, 99

Since the number 87 is repeated most often, the mode in this set of scores is **87**.

Statistical Variability

Variability simply means how "far apart" or "spread out" numbers are from each other. The most common type of a measure of variability that you will see on the Core Mathematics Test is *range*. You have probably calculated the range of numbers many times in your life without knowing that you have calculated the statistical variability.

The **range** for a set of data is the difference (or variance) between the largest and the smallest numbers in the set of data. To find the range, use this formula:

$$\text{largest value} - \text{lowest value} = \text{range}$$

Examples:

1. Find the range of scores: 2, 2, 6, 6, 5, 9, 8, 8, 8, 11

Since the largest number is 11 and the smallest number is 2, the range is $11 - 2 = 9$.

2. According to the graph below, what is the range between the lowest score and highest score on the history pop quiz?

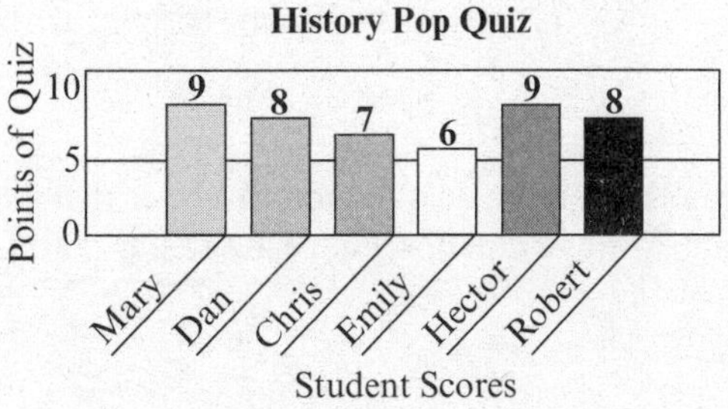

History Pop Quiz

The lowest score is 6 and the highest score is 9. Therefore, the range is $9 - 6 = 3$.

Interpreting Categorical and Quantitative Data

The Core Mathematics Test frequently presents descriptive statistics problems in graphic or pictorial displays containing one or two variables (categories and numbers). Each question presents a brief word problem with a graphic display. Visual graphic displays can simplify problems and make complicated problems easier to solve. A solid understanding of arithmetic and your ability to use reasoning skills to interpret the data are the foundation for solving these types of problems.

As you work through this section, remember to refer to the "Accurately Interpret Data" strategies discussed in chapter 4 (page 106) and to the "Graph Interpretation Problems" section in chapter 5 (page 145).

Bivariate Data

To analyze **bivariate data** means to examine two different variables (categories and/or numerical) in the same population.

Bar graphs (histograms), line graphs, scatter plots, and tables are commonly used to quickly compare numerical data, categories, or frequencies because they provide accurate visual approaches to quickly read, evaluate, and draw conclusions about bivariate data. As you interpret graphs and tables, always read the title, axes labels, and numeric values.

Example:

1. According to the graph below, who is most likely to pursue an advanced degree: men or women?

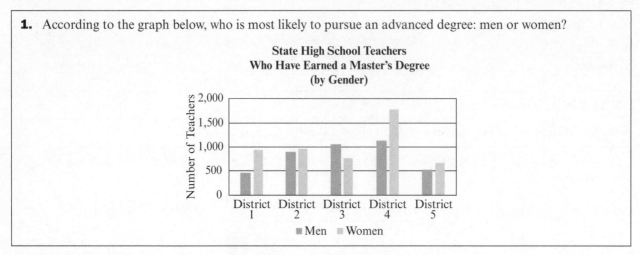

State High School Teachers
Who Have Earned a Master's Degree
(by Gender)

Based on the information provided in the graphic display, you can infer that women are most likely to pursue an advanced degree (in this specific state). After a cursory glance at the bar graph, you should be able to quickly answer this question.

Probability Review

Life events are full of uncertainties, but inferential statistics can explain these events through the study of probability. The term *probability* is used in everyday life to predict the likelihood, odds, or chance that a particular outcome will occur in a specific population or situation. For instance, what is the probability that the New England Patriots will win another Super Bowl, or what is the probability that it will snow tomorrow? On the Core Mathematics Test, the concept of probability is linked to the statistical confidence that a particular outcome may occur in real-life scenarios.

Making Inferences and Justifying Conclusions

Statistical research is more than just describing numerical data. Researchers must use statistical methods to make inferences and draw conclusions. It is important to get a holistic picture of what the statistical numbers actually mean. After the data are collected and analyzed, conclusions can be drawn and applied to answer questions about people or other phenomena being investigated. It is both an art and a science to accurately gather data, organize the data, analyze the data, and then draw inferences with a high level of confidence. Drawing inferences will allow you to make an educated statistical guess based on the numeric and graphic data collected. As you work through statistics and probability problems on the Core Mathematics Test, use the following information about random sampling and probability to help you solve these types of problems.

Random Sampling

Random sampling states that each member of a group (population) has an equal chance of being selected. Random sampling applies the laws of probability to the collected data. Thus, the results of a random sampling are representative of the entire population being studied without bias in the selection process.

Chance

The probability of a **chance** occurrence shows a fair and equal advantage of something being selected. For instance, even when a coin toss is repeated over and over again, there is an equal chance that the coin will be either heads or tails.

Example:

> **1.** If a number between 1 and 100 is drawn at random, what is the chance probability that the number will be divisible by 5?

For a number to be divisible by 5, its last digit must be 0 or 5. There are nine numbers that end in 0 between 1 and 100 and ten numbers that end in 5 between 1 and 100. There are a total of 98 numbers between 1 and 100. Hence, the chance probability P that a number chosen at random will be divisible by 5 is

$$P = \frac{9+10}{98} = \frac{19}{98}$$

Therefore, there are 19 probable chances out of 98 that the number will be divisible by 5.

Probability and Methods for Counting

The **counting principle** states that if a number of successive choices are to be made, and the choices are independent of each other (order makes no difference), the probability of the total number of possible choices is the product of each of the choices at each stage.

Example:

> **1.** How many different probable arrangements of shoes and pants are there if there are 5 pairs of shoes and 3 pairs of pants?

There are 5 choices for shoes and 3 choices for pants; therefore, there are $5 \times 3 = 15$ possible choices. The 15 choices can be illustrated. Let the 5 choices for shoes be called S1, S2, S3, S4, and S5. Let the 3 choices for pants be called P1, P2, and P3.

The 15 probable pairings are as follows:

S1-P1, S1-P2, S1-P3

S2-P1, S2-P2, S2-P3

S3-P1, S3-P2, S3-P3

S4-P1, S4-P2, S4-P3

S5-P1, S5-P2, S5-P3

Measuring Probability

Probability problems are basically "ratio" problems and expressed as fractions. Probability is assigned a measure from 0 to 1, where 0 indicates that the outcome will never happen and 1 indicates that the outcome is sure to occur. As a formula, the probability, P, is expressed by dividing the number of desired outcomes by the number of possible outcomes.

$$\text{Probability } (P) = \frac{\text{number of desired outcomes}}{\text{number of possible outcomes}}$$

If P is the probability that an event will occur, then the probability that the same event will not occur is $1 - P$.

Examples:

> **1.** One bag contains 5 white marbles and 4 black marbles. A second bag contains 4 white marbles and 5 black marbles. If one marble is drawn from each bag, what is the probability that both marbles are black?

The probability that the marble drawn from the first bag is black is $\dfrac{4}{9}$. The probability that the marble drawn from the second bag is black is $\dfrac{5}{9}$. Hence, the probability P that the marbles are both black is $P = \dfrac{4}{9} \cdot \dfrac{5}{9} = \dfrac{20}{81}$.
The probability that both marbles are black is $\dfrac{20}{81}$.

> **2.** A bag of marbles contains 6 red marbles, 9 blue marbles, and 5 white marbles. If a marble is drawn at random from the bag, what is the probability that the marble will be
>
> **(a)** red
> **(b)** blue
> **(c)** not white

(a) The probability (P) that the marble will be red is $P = \dfrac{6}{20} = \dfrac{3}{10}$.

(b) The probability (P) that the marble will be blue is $P = \dfrac{9}{20}$.

(c) The probability (P) that the marble will be white is $P = \dfrac{5}{20} = \dfrac{1}{4}$. Therefore, the probability that it will not be white is $1 - P = 1 - \dfrac{1}{4} = \dfrac{3}{4}$.

> **3.** In the previous example of 20 marbles in a bag, what is the probability that the first two marbles drawn will be blue?

The probability that the first marble will be blue is $\dfrac{9}{20}$. Since there are 8 blue marbles among the remaining 19 marbles, the probability that the second marble will be blue is $\dfrac{8}{19}$. The probability (P) that the first two drawn will be blue is

$$P = \frac{9}{20} \cdot \frac{8}{19} = \frac{72}{380} = \frac{18}{95}$$

> **4.** A box contains all 26 letters of the alphabet. What is the probability that the first two letters drawn are the letters a, b, c, d, e, or f?

The probability that the first letter drawn is a, b, c, d, e, or f is $\dfrac{6}{26}$, while the probability that the second letter is one of the remaining five is $\dfrac{5}{25}$. Hence, the probability P that the first two letters drawn are a, b, c, d, e, or f is

$$P = \frac{6}{26} \cdot \frac{5}{25}$$
$$= \frac{3}{13} \cdot \frac{1}{5}$$
$$= \frac{3}{65}$$

5. The positive integers 4 through 20 are individually written on index cards and placed in a bowl. What is the probability of randomly selecting a prime number?

The integers 4 through 20 are 4, 5, 6, 7, 8, 9, 10, 11, 12, 13, 14, 15, 16, 17, 18, 19, and 20.

There are 17 integers from 4 to 20. The integers that are prime numbers are 5, 7, 11, 13, 17, and 19. There are 6 prime integers from 4 to 20.

$$\text{probability} = \frac{\#\,\text{favorable}}{\#\,\text{total}} = \frac{6}{17}$$

6. In a single throw of two dice, determine the probability that they will total 6.

Since each die contains the numbers 1 through 6, there are $6 \cdot 6 = 36$ possible outcomes when two dice are thrown. There are five possible ways of throwing a total of 6: 1 and 5, 5 and 1, 2 and 4, 4 and 2, and 3 and 3. The probability P of the two dice having a total of 6 is $P = \dfrac{5}{36}$.

7. If a coin is tossed four times, what is the probability that all four tosses will be tails?

Since there are only two possible outcomes, heads or tails, when a coin is tossed, the probability that a toss will result in a tail is $\dfrac{1}{2}$. Hence, the probability P that all four tosses of a coin will be tails is $P = \dfrac{1}{2} \cdot \dfrac{1}{2} \cdot \dfrac{1}{2} \cdot \dfrac{1}{2} = \dfrac{1}{16}$.

8. If one card is drawn at random from a deck of 52 cards, what is the probability that the card will not be a spade?

Since there are 13 spades in a deck of 52 cards, the probability that one card selected from the deck will be a spade is $\dfrac{13}{52}$ or $\dfrac{1}{4}$. The probability P that the card drawn will NOT be a spade is 1 minus the probability that it is a spade: $P = 1 - \dfrac{1}{4} = \dfrac{3}{4}$.

Use the spinner with 12 equally divided sections pictured here for question 9.

9. Using the spinner shown below, what is the probability of spinning a number that is both a multiple of 2 and a multiple of 3 in one spin?

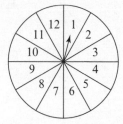

To be a multiple of 2 and 3 means to be a multiple of 6. Of the 12 numbers, only 6 and 12 are multiples of 6.

$$\text{probability} = \frac{\#\,\text{favorable}}{\#\,\text{total}} = \frac{2}{12} = \frac{1}{6}$$

Statistics and Probability Practice Questions

Now that you have reviewed statistics and probability topics, you can practice on your own. Questions appear in the format of the Core Mathematics Test question types: selected response (select one answer), selected response (select one or more answers), and numeric entry (fill in). These practice questions give you a chance to solve problems in the same format as the actual test. The answers and explanations that follow the questions include strategies to help you understand how to solve the problems.

Remember: Answer choices in this study guide have lettered choices A, B, C, D, and E for clarity, but letters will not appear on the actual exam. On the actual computer version of the exam, you will be required to click on ovals, click on squares, or fill in your answer.

General Directions: Answer each question by selecting the correct response from the choices given. Practice questions have several different formats. Unless otherwise directed, indicate a single answer choice.

1. What is the probability of throwing a total of 7 with a single throw of two dice?

   A. $\dfrac{1}{12}$

   B. $\dfrac{1}{6}$

   C. $\dfrac{7}{36}$

   D. $\dfrac{1}{4}$

   E. $\dfrac{1}{2}$

2. Three marbles are drawn at random from a bag of 7 green, 5 blue, and 4 red marbles. What is the probability that all three marbles will be green?

   A. $\dfrac{105}{2,048}$

   B. $\dfrac{1}{16}$

   C. $\dfrac{3}{16}$

   D. $\dfrac{1}{4}$

   E. $\dfrac{7}{16}$

3. Given the data set {2, 2, 3, 3, 3, 4, 6, 7, 7, 7, 7, 8, 10, 12, 12}, which of the following values of x satisfy this relationship: mean < x < median?

   Select **all** that apply.

   A. 6.0

   B. 6.2

   C. 6.4

   D. 6.6

   E. 6.8

4. In anticipation of the upcoming political election, voters are being selected prior to the election date to predict the election outcome. Which of the following methods of selecting registered voters would yield the best statistically significant results to predict who is favored to win the election?

   A. Poll all of the millions of registered voters.

   B. Poll 50 percent of registered voters.

   C. Poll randomly selected smaller groups.

   D. Poll 100 randomly selected registered voter groups who live in 10 different geographic regions.

   E. Poll randomly selected registered voters who live in different geographic regions, have different economic statuses, and are different ages.

Use the spinner with 12 equally divided sections pictured here for question 5.

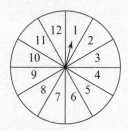

5. What is the probability of NOT spinning a factor of 8 in one spin? Give your answer as a fraction.

Write your answer in the boxes below.

6. A box contains nine cards numbered 1 through 9. If three cards are drawn, one at a time, what is the probability that they will be alternatively odd, even, odd? Give your answer as a fraction.

Write your answer in the boxes below.

Question 7 refers to the following information.

A math teacher organizes a class statistics lesson. To illustrate the concept of probability, Mrs. Allan writes down the hair color of each student in the classroom on a small piece of paper, and then places each paper in a bowl.

The results are provided in the following table:

Hair Color	Number of Students
Black	12
Brown	18
Red	4
Blond	6

7. If Mrs. Allan randomly draws one student's hair color from the random selection of papers in the bowl, what is the probability of selecting a student with black hair or red hair?

A. $\dfrac{2}{5}$

B. $\dfrac{3}{10}$

C. $\dfrac{1}{5}$

D. $\dfrac{3}{20}$

E. $\dfrac{1}{10}$

Question 8 refers to the following table.

1	2	3	4	5	6	7	8	9	10
65	49	32	65	65	82	50	75	60	57

8. The table above gives Justin's test results for the 10 tests given in his mathematics class. Find the mean, median, mode, and range for these values. Use them to calculate the following:

(mean − median) × (mode − range)

A. −37.5

B. 37.5

C. −62.5

D. 62.5

E. None of the above

Question 9 refers to the following table.

Number	Frequency (f)
3	4
4	8
6	2
7	4
8	2

9. Use the frequency table above to determine the mean for the set of data.

    A. 3.5

    B. 4

    C. 5

    D. 5.6

    E. 6

Question 10 refers to the following graph.

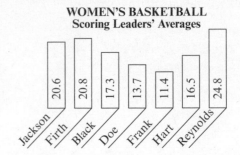

WOMEN'S BASKETBALL
Scoring Leaders' Averages

Jackson 20.6, Firth 20.8, Black 17.3, Doe 13.7, Frank 11.4, Hart 16.5, Reynolds 24.8

10. According to the bar graph above, Reynolds's average score exceeds Doe's average score by how many points?

    A. 13.4

    B. 11.1

    C. 8.3

    D. 7.4

    E. 2.3

Answers and Explanations

1. B. Since each die contains the numbers 1 through 6, there are $6 \cdot 6 = 36$ possible outcomes when two dice are thrown. There are six possible ways of throwing a total of 7: 1 and 6, 6 and 1, 2 and 5, 5 and 2, 3 and 4, and 4 and 3.

Therefore, the probability of the two dice having a total of 7 is $\dfrac{6}{36} = \dfrac{1}{6}$.

2. B. Since there are 7 green marbles out of a total of 16 marbles in the bag, the probability that the first marble drawn will be green is $\dfrac{7}{16}$. The probability that the second marble drawn is green is $\dfrac{6}{15} = \dfrac{2}{5}$, since there are 6 green marbles out of a total of 15 remaining marbles. Similarly, the probability that the third marble drawn is green is $\dfrac{5}{14}$, since there are 5 green marbles out of a total of 14 remaining marbles.

Hence, the probability P that all three marbles are green is $P = \dfrac{7}{16} \cdot \dfrac{2}{5} \cdot \dfrac{5}{14} = \dfrac{1}{16}$.

3. C, D, and E. The median of a set of numbers is the middle number when the numbers in the data set are ranked in order. In this case, since there are 15 numbers in the data set, the eighth number, 7, is the median. The mean is the arithmetic average of the numbers in the data set.

$$\text{mean} = \frac{\text{sum}}{\text{quantity}} = \frac{93}{15} = 6.2$$

Therefore, the values between 6.2 and 7.0 satisfy the relationship.

4. **E.** Robust statistical predictions are dependent upon organizing specific variables related to the research question. Selecting voters of different ages, economic statuses, and geographic regions of the country (choice E) provides the best random sampling among the choices listed. Choices A and B include too many people in the random sampling, and choice D is restricted by geographic regions. Although smaller sample groups can often provide statistically significant results to predict who is favored to win the election, choice C does not provide enough information about the number of voters to be polled.

5. $\frac{2}{3}$ The factors of 8 are 1, 2, 4, and 8. The probability of spinning a factor of 8 becomes

   probability $= \frac{\#\text{favorable}}{\#\text{total}} = \frac{4}{12} = \frac{1}{3}$. Therefore, the probability of *not* spinning a factor of 8 is $1 - \frac{1}{3} = \frac{2}{3}$.

   You could also have found the numbers that were not factors of 8, namely 3, 5, 6, 7, 9, 10, 11, and 12 (there

   are 8 of them), and then said the probability of *not* spinning a factor of 12 is $\frac{8}{12} = \frac{2}{3}$.

6. $\frac{10}{63}$ The probability that the first card drawn will be odd is $\frac{5}{9}$ since there are 5 odd numbers and 4 even

   numbers. The probability that the second card drawn will be even is $\frac{4}{8} = \frac{1}{2}$, and that the third card drawn

   will be odd is $\frac{4}{7}$. The probability (P) that they are drawn alternatively odd, even, odd is:

   $$P = \frac{5}{9} \cdot \frac{1}{2} \cdot \frac{4}{7} = \frac{10}{63}$$

7. **A.** Because you're looking for a probability of selecting a student with black hair or red hair, you must first add:

   $$\begin{array}{ccccc} \text{black hair} & + & \text{red hair} & = \\ 12 & + & 4 & = 16 \end{array}$$

   Then get the total number of students in the class:

   $$12 + 18 + 4 + 6 = 40$$

   And finally set up the fraction $\frac{16}{40}$, which reduces to $\frac{2}{5}$.

8. **A.** The mean of a set of data is the sum of the data values divided by the number of data values.

   $$\text{mean} = \frac{65 + 49 + 32 + 65 + 65 + 82 + 50 + 75 + 60 + 57}{10} = \frac{600}{10} = 60$$

   The median of a set of data values is the middle value when the data is listed from smallest to largest.

Smallest									Largest
32	49	50	57	60	65	65	65	75	82

   Middle values

   Because there is an even number of data values, there are two middle values.

The median becomes the mean of these two values.

$$\text{median} = \frac{60 + 65}{2} = \frac{125}{2} = 62.5$$

The mode of a set of data values is the value repeated most often.

$$\text{mode} = 65$$

The range of a set of data values is the difference between the largest and smallest values.

$$\text{range} = 82 - 32 = 50$$

Now, substitute the values into the equation and solve:

$$(\text{mean} - \text{median}) \times (\text{mode} - \text{range})$$

$$(60 - 62.5) \times (65 - 50) = (-2.5) \times (15) = -37.5$$

9. C. The mean of a set of data is the sum of all its values divided by the number of values. The frequency table indicates how often a value is repeated. This table shows that the number 3 occurs four times, the number 4 occurs eight times, etc. Multiply the number with its frequency and then add these results to find the total of all the numbers. Then add up the numbers in the frequency column to find how many numbers there are.

Number	Frequency (f)	Totals
3	4	12
4	8	32
6	2	12
7	4	28
8	2	16
TOTALS	**20**	**100**

Now you can calculate the mean:

$$\text{mean} = \frac{100}{20} = 5$$

10. B. Reynolds's average score was 24.8, and Doe's average was 13.7.

Therefore, $24.8 - 13.7 = 11.1$.

Chapter 9

Practice Test 1

Reading Test

TIME: 85 Minutes
56 Questions

Directions: A question or number of questions follows each of the statements or passages in this section. Using only the *stated* or *implied* information given in the statement or passage, answer the question or questions by choosing the *best* answer from among the choices given. You are not expected to have any previous knowledge of the topics in the passages or statements.

Remember: Answer choices in this study guide have lettered choices A, B, C, D, and E for clarity, but answer choice letters will *not* appear on the actual exam. On the actual computer version of the exam, you will be required to click on ovals, click on squares, or click on a sentence to highlight your answer in the passage.

Question 1 refers to the following passage.

At the beginning of Queen Victoria's reign (1837), women in England had few rights over their bodies, their property, and their children. Largely because of the suffrage movement,
(5) which came to the public's attention thirty years later, things began to change. John Stuart Mill presented Parliament with the first petition for female suffrage in 1866. The single most important reform passed after this was the
(10) Married Women's Property Act of 1882, which gave women some degree of financial independence. As the writer Virginia Woolf wrote later, financial independence was crucial for all other kinds of independence.

1. In context of the passage, the "Married Women's Property Act of 1882" (line 10) was most important because it

A. gave women full rights over their bodies, property, and children.
B. was a necessary first step toward independence.
C. resulted from women's protesting the status quo.
D. was passed because of John Stuart Mill's petition.
E. made it possible for women to own businesses.

Questions 2–6 refer to the following passage.

Urban legends are a form of modern folklore, a combination of fairy tales, parables, and information from the grapevine. Unlike fairy tales, however, urban legends are intended to be
(5) taken as truth, presented as stories of real events happening to real people, even when the events seem not only unlikely but also bizarre. Usually urban legends are passed on in the form of "I heard it from a friend of a friend." The audience
(10) assumes that while the story isn't firsthand information, it comes from a source close enough to be verified, if one were to choose to verify it— which one seldom does. While some urban legends are elaborate stories filled with gruesome
(15) details, others are succinct. For example, the story that Mrs. O'Leary's cow caused the Great Chicago Fire by knocking over an oil lamp is an urban legend in just one line.

In the digital age, more cyber legends are born
(20) than ever, and cover subjects from massive governmental conspiracies to animals performing incredible feats to medical mishaps and miracles to tear-jerking stories of redemption. Some contain warnings about products (deodorant
(25) causes cancer, for example) or about the end of the world. The Internet has become the backyard fence of the good old days, where gossip and stories are exchanged without the filter of facts and substantiated information.

GO ON TO THE NEXT PAGE

(30)   Like every form of mythology and folklore, urban legends reveal aspects of human nature. A quick look at urban legends in today's world reveals both our fears and suspicions and our need to believe in miracles—both our taste for
(35) shocking details and our need for a good cry.

2. Which of the following is an unstated assumption made by the author of the passage?

A.   Urban legends are part of an oral tradition.

B.   If a story is particularly bizarre, it is untrue.

C.   People will try to verify a story that is passed on to them by a friend.

D.   Urban legends are dangerous and cause serious misunderstandings.

E.   The story of Mrs. O'Leary's cow and the Great Chicago Fire is unlikely but true.

3. In context of the passage, the difference between fairy tales and urban legends is that

A.   fairy tales have individual authors, whereas urban legends do not.

B.   urban legends are produced for adults, whereas fairy tales are for children.

C.   fairy tales don't deal with grotesque behavior, whereas urban legends often relish in bizarre details.

D.   the intention of urban legends is to cause people to change behavior, whereas the intention of fairy tales is to entertain.

E.   fairy tales are intended to be seen as fiction, whereas urban legends are intended to be seen as fact.

4. It can be inferred that the author's primary purpose of the last sentence of the passage (lines 31–35) is to

A.   contrast the modern world with an earlier age.

B.   summarize some of the main themes of modern urban legends.

C.   criticize the quality of urban legends passed on through the Internet.

D.   show that urban legends lack the charm of earlier legends and fairy tales.

E.   ridicule people's need to pass on stories that are not true.

5. In the second paragraph, the author uses the metaphor of the *backyard fence* (lines 26–27) to describe the Internet for which of the following reasons?

A.   Both can be sources of uncensored tales and information.

B.   Both are means by which uneducated people can communicate with each other.

C.   A backyard fence, like the Internet, has a definite purpose.

D.   The Internet, like the backyard fence, encourages casual friendships.

E.   Both are the result of urban existence.

6. The author would most likely agree with which of the following statements?

A.   Urban legends are often exaggerated versions of true stories.

B.   Urban legends are generally without merit or value.

C.   Urban legends are the modern-day equivalent of fairy tales.

D.   Urban legends are more numerous than they were in the past.

E.   Urban legends always take on new details over time and become very elaborate stories as a result.

GO ON TO THE NEXT PAGE

Question 7 refers to the following passage.

Louise Erdrich is an American writer descended from the first Americans. Her mother was part Chippewa and part French, and her grandmother was a tribal chairwoman. Although
(5) Erdrich chronicles Native American ways in her fiction, her novels and short stories include many other sorts of Americans, from a reclusive sculptor in New Hampshire to a small-minded German sister-in-law to a Eurasian doctor.
(10) Erdrich is also thought of as a teller of folk tales and parables, but much of her writing is outside of that category. Erdrich probes emotions between parent and child, man and woman, brother and sister, man and beast.

7. The main idea of the passage is that Erdrich

    A.   successfully uses her Native American heritage in novels and short stories.

    B.   should be considered a master of modern American fiction.

    C.   uses well-known legends throughout her works.

    D.   is an author with themes and concerns beyond Native American culture.

    E.   is a minor but worthwhile author.

Questions 8–10 refer to the following passage.

School lunches have been in the news recently, likely due to the growing nationwide interest in healthy food and good nutrition. A study by the School Nutrition Dietary Assessment has shown
(5) that 70 percent of schools serve lunches that meet guidelines for vitamins, minerals, and protein, but many schools serve meals that are high in salt, sugar, and fat. Lunches for school children must meet a minimum calorie limit set
(10) by the government. But it's up to the individual schools to decide how it should meet that calorie limit. For example, a cook can throw in an extra couple of pieces of bread in order for the lunch to reach the designated calorie limit. One expert,
(15) Dr. Orton of the Rawkings Institute, says that the calorie standard is out of date. According to Dr. Orton, it is more important to make sure children eat healthy food than it is for them to have a certain number of calories in their lunches.
(20) Some schools have vending machines, and some schools do not. Very few include healthy snacks in their vending machines.

8. Which of the following is NOT mentioned by the author as a potential nutritional concern regarding school lunches?

Select **all** that apply.

    A.   Excess calories

    B.   High carbohydrate content

    C.   Overly vague nutritional requirements

9. Which of the following, if true, would most weaken Dr. Orton's argument?

    A.   An increasing number of schools have healthy vending machine options.

    B.   A recent study showed that under-eating was a leading cause of childhood nutritional problems.

    C.   Healthy school lunch initiatives have been unpopular with students.

    D.   Children who receive a healthy dose of vegetables are much less likely to become obese.

    E.   The number of calories needed varies widely, depending on the child.

10. Which of the following best summarizes the School Nutrition Dietary Assessment study?

Select **all** that apply.

    A.   The majority of schools were failing to provide lunches with enough nutrients.

    B.   It is more important for children to eat healthy food than to meet a calorie quota.

    C.   School lunches often tend to be excessively sugary.

GO ON TO THE NEXT PAGE

Question 11 refers to the following passage.

Humpback whales assemble in subtropical or tropical waters to mate and to calve. Researchers don't understand why the whales migrate to these wintering grounds, but it appears to be
(5) more for physical than biological reasons. Most breeding grounds are warmer, shallower, and more protected than summer feeding areas, and these factors may offer more protection for mothers and their newborn calves. The dense
(10) congregation of whales in these wintering grounds also brings together males and females, who may feed in different areas during the summer.

11. Which of the following provides the most likely explanation that humpback whales migrate to warmer waters to mate?

   A. Because a number of whales from different areas congregate in these waters

   B. For the same reason birds migrate in winter

   C. Because the physical characteristics of these waters are more conducive to breeding

   D. Because whales possess a genetic predilection for tropical and subtropical waters

   E. Because food becomes less available in colder waters

Questions 12–14 refer to the following passage.

Mexico gained its independence from Spain in 1822 but put no greater imperative on the development and political control of California than had Spain. Within the region then known
(5) as *Alta California,* a system of feudal estates, which were enlarged by the sale of Spanish mission lands, made local landowners the real power brokers in California. Seeing a future of independence unlikely—with the Russians,
(10) British, French, and Americans all poised to seize their vulnerable territory—some "Californios" looked to Europeans to free them from Mexico's rule. Others rejected the Old World authority of monarchs and instead
(15) favored annexation by the U.S.

12. Select the single clause in the passage that explains why some Californians desired to be ruled under a traditional power.

13. Supporting details in the passage suggest that

   A. the Spanish did not put a significant focus on California's development.

   B. the *Alta California* region was partially located in modern-day Mexico.

   C. the majority of Californians desired to join the U.S. democratic system.

   D. elected officials held a disproportionate amount of power in *Alta California.*

   E. a portion of Californians wanted the territory to pursue its independence.

14. In context of the passage, the author's primary goal is to

   A. explain how Californians came to favor annexation by the United States.

   B. detail the potential moves California could have made to escape Mexican reign.

   C. describe thoroughly the situation faced by Californians under Mexican reign.

   D. provide a comprehensive picture of socioeconomic dynamics of early 19th-century California.

   E. discuss the process by which California gained independence from Spain.

GO ON TO THE NEXT PAGE

Questions 15 and 16 refer to the following passage.

Our atmosphere is composed of 78 percent nitrogen and 21 percent oxygen. However, this atmospheric nitrogen cannot be used by organisms without some assistance. The nitrogen
(5) cycle is unique because it has stages during which bacteria help convert the nitrogen into usable forms. Nitrogen is essential for life because it helps to develop proteins, DNA, and RNA, and also provides for plant growth.

15. The author would most likely agree with which of the following statements?

A. Nitrogen is more important to life than oxygen.

B. The presence of bacteria is a necessary element in the production of life.

C. Fully grown plants consist of a significant portion of nitrogen.

D. Proteins, DNA, and RNA are the only three building blocks for life.

E. Atmospheric nitrogen is more difficult for organisms to use than is non-atmospheric nitrogen.

16. As used in line 4, the term *assistance* refers to

A. the role nitrogen plays in the facilitation of life.

B. the development of proteins, DNA, and RNA in living organisms.

C. the necessary interaction between nitrogen and oxygen.

D. the process by which nitrogen becomes usable.

E. the help needed to begin the nitrogen cycle.

Questions 17 and 18 refer to the following graph.

Breakdown of All Courses at Jordan High School (JHS)

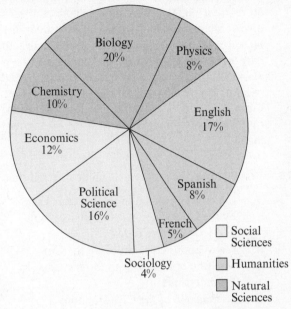

17. In which subject in each of the three divisions was the enrollment lowest at Jordan High School?

A. Physics, French, and Economics

B. Chemistry, English, and Sociology

C. Biology, Spanish, and Political Science

D. Physics, French, and Sociology

E. Spanish, Economics, and Physics

18. Which of the following statements is best supported about the courses at Jordan High School presented in the graph above?

A. JHS students are more interested in social sciences than in humanities.

B. More students take biology than take social sciences.

C. Biology is the most popular subject among high school students nationally.

D. Many students take only natural sciences courses.

E. Humanities courses are the least numerous of any course category at JHS.

GO ON TO THE NEXT PAGE

Question 19 refers to the following passage.

The products of Cro-Magnons, who lived more than 50,000 years ago, include tools of diverse shapes and multi-piece modern weapons. However, of all the Cro-Magnon products that have been unearthed, the best known are their works of art. Anyone who has seen the life-sized paintings of bulls and horses in the Lascaux Cave in southwestern France will acknowledge that their creators were ancestors of modern man.

19. According to the passage, it can be inferred that

   A. the images painted in the Lascaux Cave by the Cro-Magnons are still accessible and recognizable today.

   B. the weapons created during the Cro-Magnon era differ from those created by Neanderthals.

   C. art was one of the Cro-Magnons' primary interests.

   D. the production of art is more important than the production of tools in a civilization.

   E. the Cro-Magnons are the oldest representative of the human species.

Questions 20–22 refer to the following passage.

In *mutualistic interactions,* two or more species benefit from one another, each helping the other. For example, bees and flowers help one another. The bees take nectar and pollen
(5) from the flowers for food while also assisting with the spreading of pollen from one flower to another. Neither organism is harmed during their interactions. Another example is lichens, which are made up of fungi and algae living
(10) together in a symbiotic relationship. The fungi provide shelter for the algae, and the algae provide food for the fungi through their photosynthetic abilities.

20. Which of the following is an example of a *mutualistic interaction,* as defined by the author of the passage?

Select **all** that apply.

   A. A woodsman hunting deer for sustenance

   B. A homeowner hiring a plumber to fix leaking pipes

   C. Birds eating insects off of the backs of elephants

21. Which of the following assumptions is inherent in the passage?

   A. Aside from bees, no other insects assist in the spreading of pollen.

   B. Algae benefit from living in a sheltered environment.

   C. No bees are ever harmed during the process of pollination.

   D. Fungi cannot survive without the presence of algae.

   E. Every species has at least one other species with which it has a mutualistic interaction.

22. What is the primary purpose of the passage?

   A. To educate the reader on the pollination process

   B. To detail the relationship between algae and fungi in lichens

   C. To show that many species are able to coexist without hurting one another

   D. To define and give examples of a term

   E. To argue that mutualistic interactions are a positive phenomenon in nature

GO ON TO THE NEXT PAGE

Questions 23 and 24 refer the following passage.

As a child in Victorian England, Florence Nightingale used to sew up the wounds her sister had inflicted upon her dolls and put splints on her dog's injured paws. Nightingale was a
(5) member of a wealthy and socially prominent family and, as a female, barred from the formal study of the sciences. Nevertheless, as she grew up she pored over the reports of medical commissions and hospitals. She visited hospitals
(10) in England and throughout Europe. In the end, she convinced her conservative family to allow her to become the superintendent of a charitable nursing home in London. Then, in 1854, during the Crimean War, she took a team of nurses to
(15) Scutari in Turkey. The hospital death rate fell from 42 percent to 2 percent.

23. The passage suggests that Florence Nightingale became a nurse because

  A. nursing was a highly respected profession in the early 19th century.

  B. her parents were wealthy enough to sponsor her studies and recognized her strong interest in medicine.

  C. her religious feelings could find no other appropriate outlet.

  D. she was dissatisfied with the usual role of a woman in upper-middle-class Victorian society.

  E. the conventions of the time would not allow her to become a veterinarian.

24. The primary function of the last sentence of the paragraph (lines 15–16) is to

  A. act as a transition to a new idea that will be presented in the next paragraph.

  B. suggest the importance of Florence Nightingale's nurses in the Crimean War.

  C. refute the 19th-century idea that women were incapable of becoming physicians.

  D. dramatize the terrible conditions in military hospitals during the 19th century.

  E. provide a factual detail to support the main idea of the paragraph.

Questions 25–29 refer to the following passage.

Recently, a research group set out to examine the role that sea cucumbers play in the reef environment, and found that the coral reef was dissolving at night, and that sea cucumbers were
(5) playing a crucial part in this process. Sea cucumbers live off the bits of organic matter in the carbonate sand and rubble that they ingest— such as the carbonate materials that form reefs; in this process, their digestive systems produce
(10) acids that dissolve parts of these carbonate minerals. The dissolved carbonate minerals are then released into the surrounding environment. Observing at night, the researchers found that these lowly organisms might be responsible for
(15) half of the calcium carbonate dissolution from the reef.

In addition, burning coal, oil, and gas presents a grave threat to reefs by releasing carbon dioxide into the atmosphere, which is later absorbed by
(20) the ocean, causing the ocean to acidify; this acidification is expected to slow growth of already-scarce reefs. With slower reef growth, the dissolution of calcium carbonate within the guts of sea cucumbers is expected to become
(25) even more important to the reef calcium carbonate budget.

25. The primary purpose of the passage is to

  A. describe the gravest threats currently faced by coral reefs.

  B. encourage action to combat sea cucumbers' damaging effects on reefs.

  C. argue that sea cucumbers are crucial to maintaining balance in the oceans' reefs.

  D. describe the role of sea cucumbers in the destruction of coral reefs.

  E. familiarize the reader with sea cucumbers and their digestive systems.

GO ON TO THE NEXT PAGE

26. According to the passage, which of the following best describes the correct sequence of events by which burning gasoline damages reefs?

   A. Burning gasoline produces carbon dioxide, carbon dioxide is absorbed by the ocean, the ocean becomes more acidic, reef growth slows.

   B. Burning gasoline produces carbon dioxide, carbon dioxide is absorbed by the ocean, carbon dioxide eats away at reefs.

   C. Burning gasoline produces carbon dioxide, carbon dioxide is absorbed by the ocean, carbon dioxide is absorbed by reefs, reef growth slows.

   D. Burning gasoline creates carbon dioxide, carbon dioxide disrupts the local ecosystem, reef growth slows.

   E. Burning gasoline produces carbon dioxide, carbon dioxide is absorbed by the ocean, the ocean becomes more acidic, acid eats away at reefs.

27. In context of the passage, which of the following statements about sea cucumbers is most accurate?

   A. They play a crucial role in maintaining the balance of calcium carbonate in reefs.

   B. They are major contributors to the destruction of reefs.

   C. The acidic byproducts of their digestive systems slow reef growth.

   D. They survive off of inorganic substances like sand and rubble.

   E. Their populations must be reduced if coral reefs are to survive.

28. According to the passage, which of the following best explains how sea cucumbers are contributing to the destruction of reefs?

   A. By increasing the level of acidity in the surrounding ocean water

   B. By decreasing the level of acidity in the surrounding ocean water

   C. By consuming the reefs for sustenance

   D. By dissolving the reefs as part of their digestive process

   E. By releasing carbon dioxide into the atmosphere as part of their digestive process

29. Which of the following best describes the author's overall tone of the passage?

   A. Worried

   B. Hopeful

   C. Panicked

   D. Skeptical

   E. Neutral

Question 30 refers to the following passage.

   Social and cultural beliefs, values, and attitudes influence how people perceive or imagine themselves in relation to other human beings. As a behavioral science, social psychology employs scientific methods to study these types of social influences that impact the behavior of individuals.

30. Which of the following best summarizes the passage?

   A. The primary role of social psychology is to study how social scientists influence the behavior of individuals.

   B. The primary role of social psychology is to study the ways an individual may influence the behavior of others.

   C. The primary role of social psychology is to study the ways in which people in society are affected by their surroundings.

   D. Social psychology provides a better understanding of human behavior, which leads to the eventual betterment a person's beliefs, values, and attitudes about society.

   E. An objective of social psychology is to change how people perceive themselves in social situations.

GO ON TO THE NEXT PAGE

Questions 31 and 32 refer to the following passage.

In future decades, what is actually required is the development of a new type of citizen—an individual who possesses confidence in his or her own potential, a person who is not intimidated by the prospect of actively pursuing a career after the age of forty-five, and an individual who comprehends that technology can produce an easier world but only humans can produce a better one.

31. Which of the following is an unstated assumption made by the author of this passage?

A. Technology is the unrecognized key to a better future.

B. Present citizens are intimidated by the prospect of ending their careers in middle age.

C. Present citizens do not have limitless potentials.

D. Many people in the future will pursue at least two careers in the course of a lifetime.

E. An easier world is not necessarily a safer one.

32. The author of the passage would disagree with which of the following statements?

A. The new type of citizen described in the passage does not presently exist.

B. Future decades may bring about a change in the existing types of citizens.

C. A new type of citizen will become necessary in future decades.

D. Technology should be regarded as a source of a better life.

E. Human potential is not limited, and we should be especially careful not to think of our potential as limited.

Question 33 refers to the following passage.

No matter how significant the speaker's message, and no matter how passionate the speaker feels about the topic, interest will be lost unless the listeners attend to the speech. Attention and perception are key concepts in oral communication.

33. The primary purpose of the statement is to

A. imply that some speakers without strong feelings find an attentive audience.

B. note that some very important messages fall on deaf ears.

C. stress the critical role of listening in oral communication.

D. urge readers to listen more carefully to spoken language.

E. argue that attention and perception are unimportant concepts in communication.

Question 34 refers to the following passage.

Many of today's high school teachers will retire from their careers or professions between the ages of fifty and sixty. Indeed, by 2045, the retirement-related financial difficulties of today's elderly are going to be the problems of the middle-aged.

34. If the above statements are true, which of the following must also be true?

A. People are beginning to age more quickly.

B. People will need to have more money saved or provided for retirement in the future.

C. Today's high school teachers are in careers that require youthful stamina.

D. No one in the future will want to work during the second half of their lives.

E. Retirement will become a more attractive possibility in the future.

Questions 35–37 refer to the following passage.

Fine arts have been dismissed by some legislators as academic entertainment. As we strive not merely to amuse but to reveal the great truths of human nature, we must remember that some regard our performances as "sound and fury, signifying nothing."

35. It can be inferred that the author of this passage is probably

A. a citizen writing to a legislator.

B. an actor writing to other actors.

C. an actor playing a part.

D. a painter writing to other painters.

E. a philosopher writing to political scientists.

GO ON TO THE NEXT PAGE

36. The author of the passage supports a concept of art as

    A. a political activity.
    B. more than entertainment.
    C. empty of entertainment value.
    D. generously subsidized by the government.
    E. of no use to a serious audience.

37. The author most likely repeats the word *some* in the second sentence in order to indicate that

    A. the problem described is a relatively small one.
    B. the legislators may be in the same group that regards performances as signifying nothing.
    C. the actor will never meet with a wholly sympathetic audience.
    D. the "sound and fury" on stage is paralleled in the legislature.
    E. most members of the audience are merely amused.

Questions 38 and 39 refer to following passage.

In modern society, those who are most adaptable to both an inflating economy and the decreasing value of noncreative work will survive in comfort; it is these survivors who will have the most value in the future, rather than the typical "workaholic" who has thrived in the past.

38. According to the passage, it is implied that the kind of "value" that the survivors possess is

    A. inflating.
    B. decreasing.
    C. reliable.
    D. fleeting.
    E. unstated.

39. What conclusion can be drawn about value if we accept the author's statement?

    A. Value transcends the factors of time and place.
    B. Survival is priceless and unrelated to economic forces.
    C. Decreasing value must be tolerated.
    D. Socioeconomic factors affect the definition of value.
    E. Value is inversely proportional to the economy.

Questions 40–46 refer to the following paired passages.

Passage 1

Biodiversity, or "the variability among living organisms from all sources," has recently become a hot topic. Scientists and other experts in the field agree that biological diversity is essential to
(5) the functioning of all ecosystems, and by extension, to the ecosystem services that nature provides to humans. Living organisms play a fundamental role in the cycles of major elements, such as carbon and nitrogen, and in the water of
(10) our environment. Estimates of how many species currently live on earth vary widely, largely because most living species are microorganisms and tiny invertebrates, but roughly 1.5 million have been named.

Passage 2

(15) The unique extinction that occurred in the Late Devonian period was more of a biodiversity crisis than extinction, in that while not many species were lost, very few new species arose. New species usually originate from
(20) "vicariance"—when a population becomes geographically divided by a natural, long-term event. Many species lost substantial diversity during the Late Devonian period as a result of a lack of vicariance; the marine ecosystem in
(25) particular suffered a devastating collapse.

While habitat degradation is an important factor, an influx of invasive species—such as those introduced by humans—can also stop the dominant natural process of new species
(30) formation. The modern extinction rate even exceeds the rate of ancient extinction events.

40. The strongest similarity between Passage 1 and Passage 2 is that they both

    A. define biodiversity.
    B. believe the central issue is protecting the generation of new species.
    C. discuss the effect of vicariance.
    D. present an approach to habitat preservation.
    E. consider the effects of biodiversity loss.

GO ON TO THE NEXT PAGE

41. At least one reason the relationship between Passage 1 and Passage 2 is different is that

  A. the first passage is objective and the second is argumentative.
  B. while the second passage cites the danger of invasive species, the first does not.
  C. the second passage is written by a scientist and the first is not.
  D. the first passage cites habitat degradation as important, while the second does not.
  E. the second passage describes the results of the massive loss of species, while the first passage describes the causes.

42. In the context in which it appears in Passage 1, which of the following is an example of *ecosystem services* (line 6)?

  A. Creation of new species
  B. Regeneration of species
  C. Cycle of nitrogen
  D. Human engineering
  E. Accelerated degradation

43. According to Passage 1, no one knows that exact number of species on earth because

  A. some species are too small to count.
  B. scientists disagree on the exact definition of "species."
  C. the number of species increases continually.
  D. the number of species decreases continually.
  E. species are too widely dispersed.

44. According to Passage 2, the mass extinction occurring in the Late Devonian period was unusual because

  A. the number of species that was lost was greater than in other extinction events.
  B. its primary effect was on the marine ecosystem.
  C. it took place over a longer period than other extinctions.
  D. the cause was the creation of new geographical features.
  E. few new species arose during the period.

45. As used in Passage 2, *vicariance* (line 20) most nearly means

  A. the rate at which new species form.
  B. long-term, natural geographic events that occur from time to time.
  C. the typical method by which new species are formed.
  D. the predictable method of invasive species interfering with new species.
  E. the failure to preserve new species.

46. In Passage 2, the author refers to the Late Devonian period as a *biodiversity crisis* (lines 16–17) rather than a *mass extinction* because

  A. only marine species became extinct.
  B. few new species formed during the period.
  C. habitat degradation grew more common.
  D. those species that became extinct were crucial.
  E. whole ecosystems were destroyed.

Questions 47 and 48 refer to the following passage.

The temperament of a quiet child can be a concern for teachers. In a classroom setting, the psychosocial interactions between teachers and students, and their group dynamics, embody what
(5) Bronfenbrenner calls the *Theory of Ecological Systems*. According to Bronfenbrenner, the classroom is a microcosm within a larger context that influences child development. What impacts one child can impact the entire class. Implementing
(10) classroom strategies that encourage the quiet child to feel "free to talk" promotes a model of support for the entire classroom climate.

GO ON TO THE NEXT PAGE

47. Which of the following is implied by this passage?

- **A.** Teachers who actively encourage quiet students to speak out provide them with a better quality of education.
- **B.** Teachers who allow quiet children to work independently provide them with a better quality of education.
- **C.** Teachers who adhere to Bronfenbrenner's *Theory of Ecological Systems* encourage children to communicate in cooperative peer groups.
- **D.** Teachers who adhere to Bronfenbrenner's *Theory of Ecological Systems* understand that encouraging one child can have a ripple effect in the classroom.
- **E.** Teachers who adhere to Bronfenbrenner's *Theory of Ecological Systems* often see higher test scores from their students.

48. Which of the following best characterizes the *microcosm* referred to in line 7?

- **A.** The social distance between quiet and outgoing children
- **B.** The achievement gap between quiet and outgoing children
- **C.** The classroom experience that influences a student's overall growth
- **D.** The specific classroom referenced that exemplifies Bronfenbrenner's theory
- **E.** The pressure quiet students feel even in small groups

Question 49 refers to the following passage.

Most people think about words and sentences as tools that they have acquired over time used to communicate their thoughts and ideas. People acquire language specific to their respective
(5)   experiences and societies. American linguist Noam Chomsky, however, considers the infinite possibilities of words and sentences as tools for understanding the origins of knowledge. Chomsky's language acquisition device (LAD)
(10) states that language is biologically determined and that all human beings share the same neurological prewiring to learn language.

49. Select the single sentence in the above passage that presents a conflicting viewpoint to Chomsky's language acquisition theory.

Questions 50–56 refer to the following passage.

Throughout human history, predictions of future events have found receptive audiences: During the thirteenth century, the English scientist Roger Bacon discussed the development
(5)   of such things as optical instruments and motor boats. In the fifteenth century, Leonardo da Vinci wrote about tanks and helicopters; in the nineteenth century, Jules Verne described trips to the moon. Humans have always been interested
(10) in where they are going. Since humanity's continued existence is dependent upon its making intelligent decisions about the future, such fascination has taken on a very practical dimension. Along with the changes in social
(15) mores and attitudes, greater numbers of people are demanding a role in planning the future. The social studies curriculum must provide students with an understanding of how significant future challenges will be with regard to our national
(20) survival, social problems, religion, marriage and family life, and political processes.

It is vital that social studies teachers immerse themselves in the new field of futuristics—the study of future prospects and possibilities
(25) affecting the human condition. Futuristics, as an academic area, is already being taught at many major universities for the purpose of encouraging students to achieve an awareness that they can contribute to the development of a much better
(30) national and global society than they ever dreamed of. The perspective of futurism is very important for today's students, since they know they can do nothing about the past.

50. Which of the following best describes the intended audience for the passage?

- **A.** Students planning which courses to take in high school
- **B.** Teachers considering changing or enriching the curriculum
- **C.** Historians interested in the ways that the past reflects the future
- **D.** Politicians drafting future legislation that addresses present social problems
- **E.** Parents concerned about what their children should be learning

GO ON TO THE NEXT PAGE

51. Which of the following types of facts supports the author's point of view that "humans have always been interested in where they are going" (lines 9–10)?

    A. Unfounded

    B. Extraterrestrial

    C. Political

    D. Historical

    E. Scientific

52. Which of the following is an assumption of the passage but is not explicitly stated?

    A. Futuristic studies should take precedence over all other social studies.

    B. Today's students know little about the past and less about the future.

    C. Many social studies curriculums do not adequately acknowledge the importance of futurism.

    D. Some figures in the past have been the equivalent of modern fortune-tellers.

    E. The field of social studies gives little thought to the future.

53. According to the passage, the intended meaning of *global society* as used in line 30 is which of the following?

    A. A society well aware of the contributions of Bacon, da Vinci, and Verne

    B. A society whose students are well schooled in international relations

    C. A society able to communicate with other societies around the globe

    D. A society including planets in other solar systems

    E. A society including all the nations of the earth

54. Which of the following statements, if true, would most weaken the author's argument?

    A. Figures other than Bacon, da Vinci, and Verne might have made even more influential statements about the future.

    B. Apart from Bacon, da Vinci, and Verne, many others who have tried to "see into" the future have voiced prospects and possibilities that did not come true.

    C. Those major universities not offering courses in futuristics are considering them.

    D. Futuristics has been the nonacademic interest of great numbers of people for many centuries.

    E. Futuristic predictions are often used by politicians.

55. The author of this passage is most likely

    A. a historian.

    B. a traditionalist.

    C. a scientist.

    D. an educator.

    E. a pacifist.

56. What purpose does the sentence beginning *Futuristics, as an academic area…* (lines 25–31) primarily serve in the overall context of the passage?

    A. It adds credibility to an argument.

    B. It supports a previous claim made about the current implementation of futurism.

    C. It summarizes the points made up to that point and provides a plan for action.

    D. It provides a conclusion to the passage.

    E. It gives a glimpse into the future of education and how futurism factors into it.

IF YOU FINISH BEFORE TIME IS CALLED, CHECK YOUR WORK ON THIS SECTION ONLY. DO NOT WORK ON ANY OTHER SECTION IN THE TEST.

Writing Test: Selected Response

TIME: 40 Minutes
40 Questions

General Directions: For each question, indicate the best answer using the directions given.

Directions for Questions 1–20: Each of the following questions contains five underlined portions (four with possible errors and one with no error). The parts not underlined in the sentence are correct and cannot be changed. Read the sentence and identify whether any of the first four underlined parts of the sentence contain an error in grammar, diction, punctuation, or capitalization. If the sentence contains no mistake, select choice E, <u>No error</u>. *No sentence has more than one error.*

1. Last <u>year's</u> statistics show that there were <u>less</u> students <u>who</u> applied for law school than in the five <u>previous</u> years. <u>No error</u>
   A — B — C — D — E

2. Galileo discovered that substances expand <u>when heated</u> but contract <u>when cooled</u> <u>,</u> <u>this</u> <u>was</u> an important step in the scientific study of heat.

   <u>No error</u>
   E

3. *The Washington Post* mentioned both you and <u>him</u> in its article about how <u>good</u> the Academic Decathlon team did in the final competition, <u>which</u> was <u>held</u> Monday night. <u>No error</u>
   A — B — C — D — E

4. Bill Gates urged those for <u>whom</u> the lecture <u>was intended</u> to encourage <u>the teaching</u> of mathematics, which <u>are</u> a subject often avoided by students. <u>No error</u>
   A — B — C — D — E

5. The man in charge of the <u>crew</u> that <u>had been</u> <u>sent</u> to clean up the Hurricane Katrina oil spill complained <u>loudly</u> that they worked too <u>slow</u> .
   A — B — B — C — D
   <u>No error</u>
   E

6. <u>Creating a work of art that</u> would inspire people <u>was</u> one aim of the Dada surrealist artists <u>whose</u> primary goal <u>was to motivate</u> social change. <u>No error</u>
   A — B — C — D — E

7. Eating <u>locally grown</u> produce and supporting local business <u>is</u> <u>going to</u> make a difference in California's <u>economic</u> outlook. <u>No error</u>
   A — B — C — D — E

8. Those <u>who had entered the Kentucky Derby race</u> <u>were asked to meet</u> at the <u>fairgrounds an</u> hour before the event <u>was scheduled</u> to begin.
   A — A — B — C — D
   <u>No error</u>
   E

9. The members of the <u>school board</u> agreed to take a <u>vote; but only</u> after <u>they discussed</u> in detail the financial implications of allowing students from outside of the district to register for the <u>advanced mathematics</u> classes. <u>No error</u>
   A — B — C — D — E

10. <u>Sitting on the Susquehanna bank</u>, the river rushed by me and <u>made</u> me think <u>back</u> to the days when my father <u>had taken</u> me here to fish.
    A — B — C — D
    <u>No error</u>
    E

GO ON TO THE NEXT PAGE

11. The <u>present incumbent</u> had promised to reduce
        A
    congestion in the downtown area, increase
    revenues from city parking lots, and prohibit
           B
    delivery trucks from double parking, but he has
    not accomplished any of <u>these</u> things, and,
         C
    <u>therefore</u>, we should not return him to office.
     D
    <u>No error</u>
     E

12. The <u>r</u>evolutionary movement<u>, that</u> had been so
     A   B
    <u>well documented</u> in Gunderson's articles ended
        C
    almost before it <u>began</u>. <u>No error</u>
          D   E

13. The councilman succeeded in telling us what was
    going on in the <u>community, but</u>, in spite of <u>the</u>
        A   B
    seniors in the group wanting to take action, he
    <u>attempted to</u> convince us that nothing we could
     C
    do would <u>effect</u> the council's policy. <u>No error</u>
        D   E

14. If the head of the department <u>would have</u>
        A
    <u>notified</u> the employees <u>who</u> needed to update
     A   B
    their tax forms, the misunderstanding between
    the vice president and <u>him</u> could have been
        C
    avoided, and valuable time <u>could have been</u>
        D
    <u>saved</u>. <u>No error</u>
     D E

15. <u>Except</u> for a few regions in Ireland, the Welsh
     A
    <u>stand apart</u> in retaining their <u>very unique</u> place
     B   C
    names, especially in the <u>north</u>. <u>No error</u>
        D E

16. <u>With a major tropical storm approaching</u>, the
        A
    inhabitants of southwest Kauai were told to
    <u>pack up</u> their most important possessions, lock
     B
    the windows and doors, and <u>to move</u> as fast as
        C
    they could to <u>higher</u> ground. <u>No error</u>
        D E

17. He had arrived in <u>Washington, D.C.</u>, taken a
        A
    taxi to the <u>Lincoln Memorial</u>, and <u>went</u> from
        B   C
    there directly to his hotel, which was near the
    <u>Potomac River</u>. <u>No error</u>
       D E

18. Carl Lewis started <u>quick</u>, ran <u>fast</u>, and, when he
        A   B
    completed the race, felt <u>good</u> about his time
        C
    even though he <u>hadn't</u> won. <u>No error</u>
        D E

19. After the airplane had landed and all the
    passengers <u>had disembarked</u>, the <u>men who</u> were
        A   B
    responsible for removing the baggage <u>arrived</u>
        C
    <u>and</u> began unloading a large <u>amount</u> of
     C   D
    suitcases and boxes in record time. <u>No error</u>
        E

20. The documents were <u>delivered by</u> the messenger
        A
    service after Mr. Dershowitz and Mr. Shapiro
    <u>had left</u> for the day, which meant that <u>they</u> were
     B   C
    unavailable for the trial the next <u>day, and</u>
        D
    <u>therefore</u> the lawyer asked the judge for a
     D
    continuance. <u>No error</u>
        E

GO ON TO THE NEXT PAGE

Directions for Questions 21–30: In each question below, part of the sentence or the entire sentence is boldfaced. The first of these answer choices, Choice A, repeats the boldfaced portion of the original sentence, while the next four choices offer alternative answers. For each sentence, consider the requirements of standard written English. Focus on grammar, word choice, sentence construction, and punctuation. If an answer choice changes the meaning of the original sentence, do not select it. Your answer should be a correct, concise, and effective expression, not awkward or ambiguous.

21. Folic acid **offers prenatal protection, for example numerous studies show** that it reduces the rate of neural tube defects in infants.

   A. offers prenatal protection, for example numerous studies show

   B. offers prenatal protection, for example numerous studies will show

   C. offer prenatal protection, for example numerous studies will have shown

   D. offers prenatal protection. For example, numerous studies show

   E. has offered prenatal protection, for example, numerous studies showed

22. Prince Henry the Navigator of Portugal (1394–1460) actually was a leader who didn't travel much**, in fact he had went overseas only once and that was a mere thirty miles** from the nearest point of Europe.

   A. , in fact he had went overseas only once and that was a mere thirty miles

   B. , in fact having went overseas only once, and that being a mere thirty miles

   C. , in fact he had gone overseas only once, and that was a mere thirty miles

   D. , in fact, he had went only once overseas, which would have been a mere thirty miles

   E. ; in fact, he had gone overseas only once, and that trip had been a mere thirty miles

23. **After receiving the estimate from the insurance company, the car was delivered** to McConnell's Auto Body Shop to be repaired.

   A. After receiving the estimate from the insurance company, the car was delivered

   B. After I received the estimate from the insurance company, I delivered the car

   C. The car was delivered, after I received the estimate from the insurance company,

   D. After having received the estimate from the insurance company, the car was delivered

   E. The car was to be delivered, after having received the estimate from the insurance company,

24. **Mount St. Helens volcano was erupting after one hundred forty dormant years and it spews fountains of lava into the air.**

   A. Mount St. Helens volcano was erupting after one hundred forty dormant years and it spews fountains of lava into the air.

   B. Mount St. Helens volcano was erupting after one hundred forty dormant years, and it spewed fountains of lava into the air.

   C. Mount St. Helens volcano is erupting, after one hundred forty dormant years, and spews fountains of lava into the air.

   D. Mount St. Helens volcano was erupting and it spewed fountains of lava into the air after one hundred forty dormant years.

   E. After one hundred forty dormant years, Mount St. Helens volcano was erupting, spewing fountains of lava into the air.

25. **If Daniel was available to teach summer school, he would have been chosen, but because he had broke his leg** in the accident, he couldn't fill the post.

   A. If Daniel was available to teach summer school, he would have been chosen, but because he had broke his leg

   B. If Daniel was available to teach summer school, he would have been chosen, but because he had broken his leg

   C. If Daniel were available to teach summer school, he would have been chose, but he had broken his leg

   D. If Daniel had been available to teach summer school, he would have been chosen, but because he had broken his leg

   E. If Daniel was available to teach summer school, we would have chose him, but because he broke

GO ON TO THE NEXT PAGE

26. **The schools in the Chicago inner city are more in need of funding than the suburbs.**

   A. The schools in the Chicago inner city are more in need of funding than the suburbs.

   B. The schools in the Chicago inner city need more funding than the suburbs.

   C. The schools in the Chicago inner city are more in need of funding than those schools that are in the suburbs.

   D. The schools in the Chicago inner city, unlike the suburbs, are more in need of funding.

   E. Chicago inner city schools need more funding than suburban schools.

27. **LeBron James discovered that riding a bicycle home from the games, which he had begun doing when the weather was warm, was a good way to get exercise and** have fun with his conditioning program.

   A. LeBron James discovered that riding a bicycle home from the games, which he had begun doing when the weather was warm, was a good way to get exercise and

   B. Riding a bicycle home from the games, LeBron James discovered, which he had begun doing when the weather was warm, was a good way to get exercise, and

   C. In the warm weather when LeBron James began doing it, he discovered, that riding a bicycle home from the games was a good way to get exercise and

   D. LeBron James discovered that riding a bicycle home from the games which he had begun doing when the weather was warm was a good way to get exercise and

   E. Riding a bicycle home from the games which LeBron James discovered when the weather was warm, was a good way to get exercise, and

28. **He had been laying in the sun for hours and his back was more red than** his swimming trunks.

   A. had been laying in the sun for hours and his back was more red than

   B. had been lying in the sun for hours, and his back was redder than

   C. had laid in the sun for hours; and his back was more red than

   D. had lied in the sun for hours, and his back was redder than

   E. had been laying in the sun for hours but his back was redder than

29. **The concert at Lincoln Center and the coverage of the concert in the newspapers was the impetus** that the soprano's career needed.

   A. The concert at Lincoln Center and the coverage of the concert in the newspapers was the impetus

   B. The Lincoln Center concert and its coverage in the newspapers were the impetus

   C. The concert at Lincoln Center as well as the coverage of it in the newspapers was the impetus

   D. The Lincoln Center concert and it's coverage in the newspapers were the impetus

   E. The concert at Lincoln Center, as well as its coverage in the newspapers, were the impetus

30. **The excavations at Cerén reveal the prosperity of the rural Mayans, the staples of their diet, and** the architecture of their homes.

   A. the prosperity of the rural Mayans, the staples of their diet, and

   B. the prosperity of the rural Mayans; the staples of their diet; and

   C. the prosperity of the rural Mayans, and the staples of their diet, and

   D. the rural Mayans, the prosperity and the diet they ate, as well as

   E. how prosperous the rural Mayans were, what their diet was, and

GO ON TO THE NEXT PAGE

Directions for Questions 31–36: The following passage represents an early draft of an essay. Some portions of the essay will require editing and revising. Read the essay carefully and answer the questions that follow. Questions may address the whole essay or selected items from paragraphs. Select the answer that will most effectively express the intended meaning. The correct answer follows the development, organization, word choice, style, and tone of standard written English. If the indicated portion of the original sentence is the most effective, no changes will be required.

Questions 31–36 refer to the following passage.

(1) Mason Locke Weems wrote a biography of George Washington at the beginning of the 19th century. **(2)** He created a picture of our first president that would inspire many generations. **(3)** Weems could be called the father of popular history. **(4)** Weems had been an Anglican minister for eight years, but he didn't like the work or the salary so he became a bookseller.

(5) Weems was a masterful storyteller who understood his audience, and the first edition of his book was an immediate bestseller. **(6)** As an example of its popularity, nineteen more editions of the book appeared, the last one in 1825. **(7)** Weems, according to Edward G. Lengel's book *Inventing George Washington,* sounded like a "grandfather with children at his knee." **(8)** In the biography of Washington, Weems recounts a number of stories that have become part of the myth of our first president, some were already part of the oral tradition, but most came out of his own imagination. **(9)** According to Lengel, virtually no evidence for most of the stories exists. **(10)** Including perhaps the most famous story of all about George Washington as a child cutting down a cherry tree and then bravely confessing the deed to his father. **(11)** Stories like this one are probably what most Americans remember about Washington from their early days in school.

(12) After getting an overnight stay at Mt. Vernon through a relative who was a friend of George Washington's physician, Weems traded on what was only a passing acquaintance with the great man, even claiming to have been a rector at "Mt. Vernon Parish," which in fact didn't exist. **(13)** A shrewd man, he decided to capitalize on Washington's great popularity by writing the biography. **(14)** Although his motive was primarily mercenary, Weems also wanted to use his book to pass on moral lessons. **(15)** In the biography, he emphasizes Washington's Christianity and shows how his piety was the basis for patriotism and public service.

(16) Although biographers who came after Weems relied more on actual evidence for what they wrote and presented a more well-rounded and authentic picture of Washington. **(17)** Mason Locke Weems left an indelible picture that has shaped American opinions of the man and the leader ever since.

31. In context, which of the following is the most effective way to revise and combine Sentences 1 and 2 (reproduced below)?

Mason Locke Weems wrote a biography of George Washington at the beginning of the 19th century. He created a picture of our first president that would inspire many generations.

A. Mason Locke Weems wrote a biography of George Washington at the beginning of the 19th century, and he created a picture of our first president which would inspire many generations.

B. At the beginning of the 19th century, Mason Locke Weems wrote a biography of George Washington, creating a picture of our first president that would inspire many generations.

C. Creating a picture of our first president that would inspire many generations, a biography of George Washington was written by Mason Locke Weems at the beginning of the 19th century.

D. In order to inspire many generations, Mason Locke Weems wrote a biography creating a picture of George Washington.

E. At the beginning of the 19th century, a biography of George Washington was written by Mason Locke Weems and that biography would inspire many generations.

GO ON TO THE NEXT PAGE

32. In context, where is the best placement of Sentence 4 (reproduced below)?

Weems had been an Anglican minister for eight years, but he didn't like the work or the salary so he became a bookseller.

A. Insert it after Sentence 11 in the second paragraph.
B. Insert it after Sentence 2.
C. Add it to the beginning of the third paragraph.
D. Insert it after Sentence 12.
E. Make no changes.

33. In context, which of the following revisions is most needed in Sentence 8 (reproduced below)?

In the biography, Weems recounts a number of stories that have become part of the myth of our first president, some were already part of the oral tradition, but most came out of his own imagination.

A. Insert a period after *president* and begin a new sentence with *Some*.
B. Change *a number of* to *many*.
C. Change *but* to *however*.
D. Replace *that have become* with *that later became*.
E. Insert *although* after *president*.

34. In context, which of the following is the most effective way to revise and combine Sentences 9 and 10 (reproduced below)?

According to Lengel, virtually no evidence for most of the stories exists. Including perhaps the most famous story of all about George Washington as a child cutting down a cherry tree and then bravely confessing the deed to his father.

A. According to Lengel, virtually no evidence for most of the stories exist, and that would include even the most famous story of all about George Washington as a child cutting down a cherry tree and then bravely confessing the deed to his father.
B. According to Lengel, virtually no evidence for most of the stories exists; which includes the most famous story of all about George Washington as a child cutting down a cherry tree and then bravely confessing the deed to his father.
C. Virtually no evidence for most of the stories exists, Lengel says, and he includes perhaps the most famous story of all that is about George Washington as a child cutting down a cherry tree and then bravely confessing the deed to his father.
D. Lengel says that there is virtually no evidence for most the stories about George Washington that exist, and he also says that includes perhaps the most famous story of all, which is about George Washington as a child who chopped down a cherry tree and then bravely confessed to his father.
E. According to Lengel, virtually no evidence for most of the stories exists, including perhaps the most famous one of George Washington as a child cutting down a cherry tree and then bravely confessing the deed to his father.

GO ON TO THE NEXT PAGE

35. In context, which of the following is the best version of Sentences 16 and 17 (reproduced below)?

Although biographers who came after Weems relied more on actual evidence for what they wrote and presented a more well-rounded and authentic picture of Washington. Mason Locke Weems left an indelible picture that has shaped American opinions of the man and the leader ever since.

A. Biographers who came after Weems relied more on actual evidence for what they wrote. These presented a more well-rounded and authentic picture of Washington. However, Mason Locke Weems left an indelible picture that has shaped American opinions of the man and the leader ever since.

B. The biographers who came after Weems relied more on actual evidence and presented a more well-rounded and authentic picture of Washington. Mason Locke Weems, however, left an indelible picture that has shaped American opinions of the man and the leader ever since.

C. Mason Locke Weems left an indelible picture that has shaped American opinion of the man and the leader ever since, however, the biographers who came after him relied more on actual evidence for what they wrote.

D. Relying more on actual evidence for what they wrote, and presenting a more well-rounded and authentic picture of Washington, biographies that came after Weems didn't leave as indelible a picture as Weems did, and therefore Weems shaped American opinion of Washington the man and Washington the leader.

E. Mason Locke Weems, who left an indelible picture that has shaped American opinions of Washington, both the man and the leader, relied less on actual evidence than the biographers who followed him, and therefore didn't present as well-rounded and authentic a picture as these later biographers did.

36. In context, the passage would be most improved by

A. providing information about the period during which Weems wrote.

B. including more details about George Washington.

C. eliminating the final paragraph.

D. summarizing the biographies that followed Weems'.

E. reversing the positions of Paragraphs 2 and 3.

GO ON TO THE NEXT PAGE

Directions for Questions 37–40: For each of the questions below, answer by selecting the correct response.

37. Which of the following Internet search words or terms is the LEAST efficient use of the writer's time when researching a paper about *childhood stuttering?*

    A. Stammer
    B. Speech stutter
    C. Involuntary flow of speech
    D. Pausing before speech
    E. Spasmodic speech repetitions

    > Hall, S. (2015). Solving the autism puzzle. *Technology Review, 118*(1), 36–43.

38. In the above reference, which of the following is cited?

    A. A newspaper article
    B. An academic journal
    C. A dissertation
    D. A book
    E. An Internet article

39. In the reference section of a research paper, why is it necessary to include the date on which the writer obtained an Internet reference but not the date on which the writer obtained a print reference?

    A. To prove that the writer found the reference on the Internet rather than in print
    B. To show that the reference is more up to date than its print counterpart
    C. Because all Internet references are date sensitive
    D. In case the information found on the Internet changes after the date on which the author obtained it
    E. To clarify the information is correct

40. Which of the following best illustrates the correct in-text citation?

    A. "Humanity's deepest desire for knowledge is justification enough for our continuing quest." *A Brief History of Time* by Stephen Hawking.
    B. "Humanity's deepest desire for knowledge is justification enough for our continuing quest." *A Brief History of Time* by Hawking (p. 14).
    C. Stephen Hawking, in his book, *A Brief History of Time,* suggests that "humanity's deepest desire for knowledge is justification enough for our continuing quest." (14).
    D. To illuminate my point, as human beings we have a deep yearning to continue our search for knowledge. Further, it is our goal to be able to investigate and explain the world we live in.
    E. Hawking's book suggests that "humanity's deepest desire for knowledge if justification enough for our continuing quest." (14).

IF YOU FINISH BEFORE TIME IS CALLED, CHECK YOUR WORK ON THIS SECTION ONLY. DO NOT WORK ON ANY OTHER SECTION IN THE TEST.

STOP

Writing Test: Essay

Essay 1: Argumentative Essay

TIME: 30 Minutes

1 Essay

Directions: You will have 30 minutes to plan and write an argumentative essay on the topic specified. You will probably find it best to spend time considering the topic and organizing your thoughts before you begin writing. Do not write on a topic other than the one specified. The essay should be based on your readings, experiences, or observations. You must write on the specified topic. An essay on another topic will not be accepted.

The essay is intended to give you an opportunity to demonstrate your writing skills. Be sure to express your ideas clearly and effectively. The quality of your writing is much more important than the quantity, but to cover the topic adequately, you will likely want to write more than one paragraph. Be specific and provide relevant examples that are related to the topic.

Read the opinion stated below:

"Students who demonstrate exceptional talent should be given increased educational resources, opportunities, and attention."

Assignment: Discuss the extent to which you agree or disagree with this opinion. Support your views with specific reasons and examples from your own experiences, observations, or readings.

IF YOU FINISH BEFORE TIME IS CALLED, CHECK YOUR WORK ON THIS SECTION ONLY. DO NOT WORK ON ANY OTHER SECTION IN THE TEST.

Essay 2: Informative/Explanatory Essay

TIME: 30 Minutes

1 Essay

Directions: You will have 30 minutes to read two different passages and then plan and write an informative/ explanatory essay using information from BOTH sources provided. Take time organizing your ideas before you discuss the most important concerns regarding the specified issue. Explain the reasons why they are important. You must write on the specified topic. An essay on another topic will not be accepted.

The essay is intended to give you an opportunity to demonstrate your writing skills. Be sure to express your ideas clearly and effectively. The quality of your writing is much more important than the quantity, but to cover the topic adequately, you will likely want to write more than one paragraph. Be specific and provide relevant examples that are related to the topic.

Assignment:

Both of the following passages address phonemic awareness, particularly the correlation between learning phonemic awareness and reading success. Read the two passages carefully and then write an essay in which you identify the most important concerns regarding the issue and explain why they are important. Your essay must draw on information from BOTH of the sources. In addition, you may draw upon your own experiences, observations, and readings.

When paraphrasing or quoting from the sources, cite each source by referring to the author's last name, the title of the source, or any other clear identifier.

Source 1:

Adapted from: Bobrow, Jerry et al. *CliffsTestPrep RICA.* Boston, MA: Houghton Mifflin Harcourt Publishing, 2006. Print.

   Phonemic awareness is strongly related to reading achievement and is a precursor for learning to read. Yet a fair amount of misunderstanding, particularly among primary school educators, persists about what this skill is and why it is so important for reading success. Scientific evidence illuminates the importance of teaching phonemic awareness and points to learning deficits in children who fail to acquire phonemic skills in elementary school.

   Phonemic awareness is the understanding that words are made up of sounds. It is the ability to notice, think about, and work with the individual sounds in words. The word *bat,* for example, is made up of three individual sounds (phonemes) /b/ /a/ /t/. During the early stages of reading acquisition, students who learn the conceptual link between blending, deleting, isolating, and segmenting these individual sounds are able to grasp how printed words and individual sounds work together (Ehri et al., 2001). Research shows that students who engage in direct, explicit phonemic instruction through enjoyable activities (i.e., rhyming games) are better equipped to master grade-appropriate language learning (Adams, 1994).

   Phonemic awareness is a reliable predictor of reading achievement (Troia, 1999). As noted in Marilyn Adams' *Beginning to Read: Thinking and Learning about Print,* it is one of the three key predictors of success in early reading. Adams observed that if a student does not attain mastery of phonemic awareness, the student will probably never be able to read at grade level. Stanovich (1994) suggested that phonemic awareness is not only the best predictor of reading success, but is a better predictor of reading achievement than a student's IQ or vocabulary proficiency.

   Linguistic and language experts have established correlations between language abilities and higher order thinking abilities. The link between phonemic awareness mastery and cognitive sophistication distinguishes normal from disabled readers (Adams, 1994). Phonemic awareness competency promotes fluent, independent readers for a lifetime of positive learning experiences.

GO ON TO THE NEXT PAGE

Source 2:

Adapted from: Emmitt, Marie, David Hornsby, and Lorraine Wilson. "The Place of Phonics in Learning to Read and Write." *Australian Journal of Language & Literacy,* 2013. Ebook.

Phonemic awareness instruction in the classroom has significantly increased since the published Report of the National Reading Panel (2000). This well-known report concluded that phonemic awareness instruction significantly improved children's reading abilities compared to instruction without phonemic awareness. The importance of teaching phonemic awareness and phonics continues to be researched, but critics debate whether phonemic awareness is linked to strong reading abilities.

The debate has centered on whether phonemic awareness is a prerequisite for learning to read and write, or whether it develops through reading and writing. Part of the confusion relates to the concepts of correlation and causation. Studies that are used to support explicit, systematic phonemic awareness training are correlational. Correlation is not causation. For example, there is a positive correlation between being dead and being in a cemetery. However, the cemetery did not cause the death. There is a positive correlation between phonemic awareness and ability to read, but no causation should be implied.

Taylor (1998) states that phonemic awareness is based on "written text," rather than "spoken language." Most reading instruction literature only focuses on written text for the foundation of phonemic awareness in decoding words, and has neglected the importance of children's early cognitive learning from spoken language. By age six, children have a "culmination of a long and complex developmental journey in spoken language, which has progressed from meaningful spoken activities to higher levels of abstraction with spoken words and speech sounds" (Walsh, 2009).

Although persuasive research shows that phonemic awareness enhances the decoding of words, there is no evidence concluding that phonemic awareness *causes* reading acquisition. This is true for disabled or second-language readers who experience difficulty learning to read (Ehri et al., 2001). Phonemic awareness may lead to reading knowledge, but other variables should be considered when determining the cause of strong reading abilities.

IF YOU FINISH BEFORE TIME IS CALLED, CHECK YOUR WORK ON THIS SECTION ONLY. DO NOT WORK ON ANY OTHER SECTION IN THE TEST.

Mathematics Test

TIME: 85 Minutes

56 Questions

Directions: Select the best answer of the five choices given. Answer choices have several different formats. Unless otherwise directed, indicate a single answer choice.

Remember: Answer choices in this study guide have lettered choices A, B, C, D, and E for clarity, but answer choice letters will not appear on the actual exam. On the actual computer version of the exam, you will be required to click on ovals, click on squares, or fill in your answer.

1. 24 is x less than half of y. Which of the following expresses this relationship?

   A. $x = 24 - \dfrac{y}{2}$

   B. $24 = \dfrac{y}{2} - x$

   C. $24 = \dfrac{2}{y} - x$

   D. $x = -\dfrac{y}{2} - 24$

   E. $24 < x - \dfrac{1}{2}y$

2. A Zumba fitness class has 48 students enrolled. One-third of the females are less than 6 feet tall, and three-fourths of the class are males. How many females are 6 feet tall or taller?

   A. 4
   B. 8
   C. 12
   D. 16
   E. 36

3. In the context of math reasoning, which of the following directions would correctly express the value 24.7×10^3 in scientific notation?

   A. Add three zeros to the right of the 7.
   B. Move the decimal point to the left one position and increase the exponent by 1.
   C. It already is currently expressed in scientific notation.
   D. Move the decimal point to the left one position and decrease the exponent by 1.
   E. Move the exponent to the right one position and decrease the exponent by 1.

4. Scores on six equally weighted tests are different integers between 70 and 100, inclusive. If the average score on these six tests is 76 and x represents the highest-scoring test, which of the following could be the value of x?

   Select **all** that apply.

   A. 78
   B. 79
   C. 80
   D. 96
   E. 97

5. A bowl contains 18 gumballs. If there are 8 red, 7 white, and 3 green gumballs in the bowl, what is the minimum number of gumballs one must pick from the bowl to be assured of picking one of each color?

   A. 3
   B. 6
   C. 8
   D. 9
   E. 16

6. When 7,500 is written in prime factored form, it becomes $2^x 3^y 5^z$. What is the value of xyz?

   A. 6
   B. 8
   C. 10
   D. 12
   E. 30

GO ON TO THE NEXT PAGE

Question 7 refers to the following two graphs.

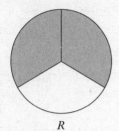 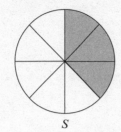

R   S

7. What is the sum of the shaded areas of Figure R and the shaded areas of Figure S above if each circle represents a circle divided into equal parts?

A. $\dfrac{9}{16}$

B. $1\dfrac{7}{9}$

C. $\dfrac{7}{24}$

D. $1\dfrac{1}{24}$

E. $\dfrac{1}{4}$

8. A package of cheese contains *c* cheese slices in each package. A package of turkey contains *t* turkey slices in each package. If you want to buy an equal number of cheese slices and turkey slices so that each slice of cheese will have *exactly* one slice of turkey to make a sandwich, what would be the *least* number of cheese packages and turkey packages that would you need to buy?

In the context of math reasoning, which of the following methods could be used to find the solution to this problem?

A. Add *c* and *t*.

B. Find the greatest common factor of *c* and *t*.

C. Find the least common multiple of *c* and *t*.

D. Divide *c* by *t*.

E. Multiply *c* and *t*.

9. An investor bought 200 shares of Stock A at a price of $16.50 per share and 500 shares of Stock B at a price of $19.50 per share. Later that month, the investor sold the 200 shares of Stock A and the 500 shares of Stock B, all at a price of $20 per share. The profit from Stock B represents what percent of the combined profits from the sales of Stock A and Stock B?

A. 21%

B. 25%

C. 26%

D. 28%

E. 36%

GO ON TO THE NEXT PAGE

Question 10 refers to the following pictograph.

```
 |ıııı|ıııı|ıııı|ıııı|ıııı|ıııı|ıııı|ıııı|ıııı|ıııı|ıııı|ıııı|ıııı|
  1  2  3  4  5  6  7  8  9 10 11 12 13 14 15 16 17 18 19 20 21 22 23 24 25 26
```

10. Use the ruler above and math reasoning to solve this question. A tortoise travels $4\frac{1}{3}$ inches every $\frac{1}{4}$ hour. At this pace, how long will it take the tortoise to move 26 inches?

- **A.** $\frac{1}{2}$ hour
- **B.** $1\frac{1}{12}$ hours
- **C.** $1\frac{1}{2}$ hours
- **D.** 6 hours
- **E.** $6\frac{2}{3}$ hours

11. The width of a rectangle is from one-third to two-thirds of its length. If the perimeter of the rectangle is 40, then which of the following integers could be the area of the rectangle?

Select **all** that apply.

- **A.** 36
- **B.** 64
- **C.** 75
- **D.** 80
- **E.** 96

12. The problem below shows the steps for finding the product of a two-digit number with a three-digit number using the standard multiplication algorithm. The missing digits are represented with the letters x, y, and z.

$$
\begin{array}{r}
2x4 \\
\times \quad 5y \\
\hline
1404 \\
+\ 11z00 \\
\hline
13104
\end{array}
$$

What is the result of $x + yz$?

- **A.** 136
- **B.** 126
- **C.** 63
- **D.** 45
- **E.** 16

13. A U.S. Navy military ship has 250 sailors on board. The ages of the sailors on board range from 20 to 35 years old, and 12% of this population is age 25 or younger. If the remaining population is evenly distributed, how many sailors on this ship are age 30 years old?

- **A.** 22
- **B.** 24
- **C.** 25
- **D.** 27
- **E.** 30

GO ON TO THE NEXT PAGE

Question 14 refers to the following chart.

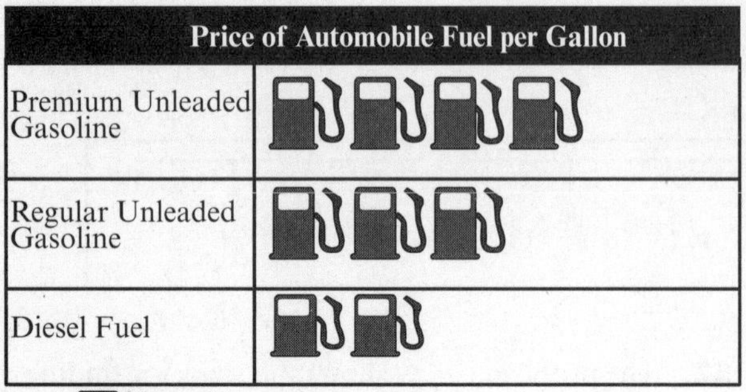

Price of Automobile Fuel per Gallon	
Premium Unleaded Gasoline	⛽⛽⛽⛽
Regular Unleaded Gasoline	⛽⛽⛽
Diesel Fuel	⛽⛽

Each ⛽ represents 50 gallons of fuel.

14. The chart above shows the amount of automobile fuel sold in 1 hour at a local gas station. Regular unleaded gas sold for $3.50 per gallon and diesel fuel sold for $3.45 per gallon. The total sales of all three grades of fuel is $1,612. If each gallon of premium unleaded gas sold for *d* dollars, what is the percent increase in the cost of gasoline if you decide to purchase premium unleaded instead of regular unleaded?

A. 5%
B. 6%
C. 7%
D. 10%
E. 21%

Question 15 refers to the following table.

Annual Teacher Salaries	
Tier 1	$45,256
Tier 2	$57,254
Tier 3	$72,978

15. Carol estimated the sum of these tiered salaries by first rounding each to the nearest thousand. Ivan estimated the sum of these salaries by first rounding each to the nearest ten. By how much do these estimates differ?

A. $110
B. $490
C. $530
D. $600
E. $3,490

Questions 16 and 17 refer to the following data.

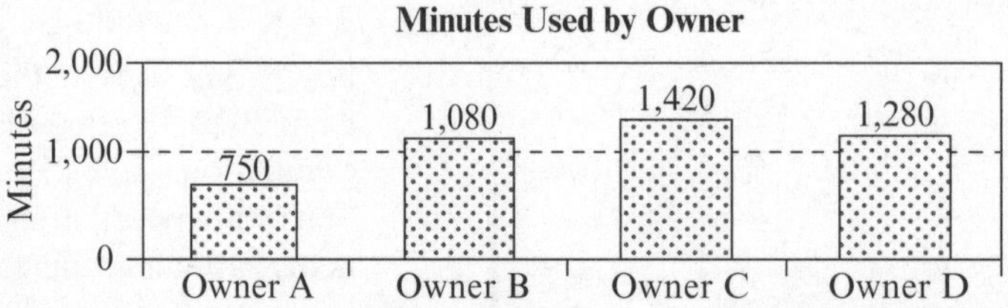

Minutes Used by Owner

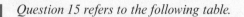

Phone Owner	Plan	Included Minutes	Cost/Extra Minute	Plan Cost/Month
A	Prepaid	700	$0.60	$60
B	Basic	1,000	$0.50	$70
C	Family	1,400	$0.40	$90
D	Smartphone	2,100	$0.25	$120

16. According to the data, Owner B's extra-minute charges for the month exceeded Owner C's extra-minute charges for the month by what percent?

A. 20%
B. 25%
C. 80%
D. 400%
E. 500%

17. According to the data, what would the combined savings of Owners B and D have been if they had used the family plan instead of their current plans?

A. $10
B. $20
C. $30
D. $40
E. $50

GO ON TO THE NEXT PAGE

18. The ordered pair $(-3, 5)$ lies on a line with a slope of $-\dfrac{2}{3}$. Which of the following points will also lie on this line?

A. $(1, 7)$
B. $(-1, 8)$
C. $(-1, 5)$
D. $(-6, 7)$
E. $(-6, 3)$

19. If you flip a fair coin four times, what is the probability of getting at least two heads?

Write the answer as a common fraction in the box below.

Question 20 refers to the following expression.

$$\frac{40}{x} = \frac{70}{y} = \frac{160}{z} = 30$$

20. Which of the following integers is closest to the value of the sum of x, y, and z?

A. 7
B. 8
C. 9
D. 10
E. 11

21. Put the following number values in order from greatest to least:

$$-5.15, \quad -\frac{26}{5}, \quad -5\frac{1}{2}, \quad -5$$

A. $-5.15, \quad -\dfrac{26}{5}, \quad -5\dfrac{1}{2}, \quad -5$
B. $-5 \quad -5\dfrac{1}{2}, \quad -\dfrac{26}{5}, \quad -5.15$
C. $-5\dfrac{1}{2}, \quad -\dfrac{26}{5}, \quad -5.15, \quad -5$
D. $-5, \quad -5.15, \quad -\dfrac{26}{5}, \quad -5\dfrac{1}{2}$
E. $-\dfrac{26}{5}, \quad -5.15, \quad -5\dfrac{1}{2}, \quad -5$

22. If $4A + 20 = B$, then $A + 12 =$

A. $A - 8$
B. $\dfrac{B}{4} - 8$
C. $\dfrac{B}{4} + 7$
D. $4B + 7$
E. $\dfrac{B}{4} + 17$

23. Which of the following steps is the best method to convert the fraction $\dfrac{a}{b}$ into a percent form?

A. Divide a into b, move the decimal point two places to the left, and add a percent sign.
B. Divide a into b, move the decimal point two places to the right, and add a percent sign.
C. Multiply the fraction $\dfrac{a}{b}$ by 100%.
D. Solve the proportion $\dfrac{a}{b} = \dfrac{100}{x}$ and add a percent sign to the value of x.
E. Divide b into a, move the decimal point two places to the left, and add a percent sign.

24. If the natural numbers from 21 to 50 are written individually on index cards and put into a box, and one of the cards is randomly selected, what is the probability that it will be a prime number?

A. $\dfrac{1}{5}$
B. $\dfrac{4}{15}$
C. $\dfrac{7}{29}$
D. $\dfrac{7}{30}$
E. $\dfrac{8}{29}$

GO ON TO THE NEXT PAGE

Qustion 25 refers to the following number line.

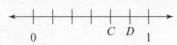

25. Assuming the spaces in the number line above are equal in length, which of the following expressions produces a value that lies between C and D on the number line?

A. $\dfrac{1}{3} \times \dfrac{1}{5}$

B. $\dfrac{2}{3} - \dfrac{1}{5}$

C. $\dfrac{1}{3} + \dfrac{2}{5}$

D. $\dfrac{1}{3} \div \dfrac{2}{5}$

E. $\dfrac{2}{5} \div \dfrac{1}{3}$

26. A patient was told to clean her abrasion with a mixture of $\dfrac{1}{3}$ hydrogen peroxide and $\dfrac{2}{3}$ purified water. She created 600 ml of the solution. After cleaning the abrasion, the patient had 210 ml of the solution left.

After 2 weeks, she was directed to create a second solution of $\dfrac{1}{2}$ hydrogen peroxide and $\dfrac{1}{2}$ purified water. How much hydrogen peroxide should be added to the leftover 210 ml of solution to create the second solution?

A. 70 ml
B. 140 ml
C. 210 ml
D. 280 ml
E. 300 ml

27. A mobile phone battery can last for 3 hours and 30 minutes when charged at 70%. Assuming the phone battery loses its charge at a constant rate, how long can the phone battery last when fully charged?

A. 4 hours
B. 4 hours and 20 minutes
C. 4 hours and 30 minutes
D. 5 hours
E. 5 hours and 30 minutes

Question 28 refers to the following diagram.

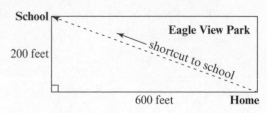

28. Jeremy's usual route to school is about 800 feet by walking around two sides of Eagle View Park. Since Jeremy is late for school, he decides to save time by cutting through the park diagonally.

Which of the following best represents how many feet Jeremy will walk on the shorter route (rounded to the nearest foot)?

A. 400 feet
B. 427 feet
C. 632 feet
D. 747 feet
E. 942 feet

Question 29 refers to the following diagram.

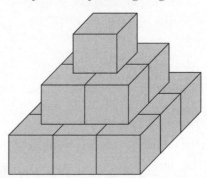

29. To illustrate how pyramids are constructed, sixth-grade students construct pyramids using sugar cubes. The teacher gives each student 55 sugar cubes. If there is only one sugar cube on top and each layer below the top forms a square with one additional cube per side, how many layers of sugar cubes will there be?

The illustration above shows the first three layers.

A. 4
B. 5
C. 6
D. 7
E. 8

GO ON TO THE NEXT PAGE

Question 30 refers to the following equation.

$$7x + 3(x + 5) = 2x - 7$$

30. Which of the following equations would you use as a step in solving the above equation for variable *x*?

  A. $8x = -22$
  B. $8x = -12$
  C. $8x = -15$
  D. $12x = 8$
  E. $12x = -22$

Question 31 refers to the following diagram.

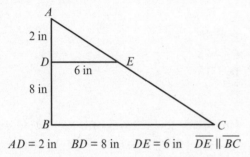

$AD = 2 \text{ in} \quad BD = 8 \text{ in} \quad DE = 6 \text{ in} \quad \overline{DE} \parallel \overline{BC}$

31. What is the length, in inches, of *BC* in the figure above?

  A. 12
  B. 16
  C. 18
  D. 24
  E. 30

32. Triangle *ABC* is obtuse. Angle *A* has a measure of 45°. Which of the following could be the measure of one of the other angles?

  A. 35°
  B. 45°
  C. 55°
  D. 65°
  E. None of the above could be the measure of one of the other angles.

33. A right triangle has legs with lengths of 9 inches and 12 inches. What is the perimeter, in inches, of this triangle?

  A. 15
  B. 21
  C. 36
  D. 42
  E. 54

34. If $1\frac{1}{2}$ dozen machines can produce $1\frac{1}{2}$ dozen screws in $1\frac{1}{2}$ days, how many days would it take 6 dozen machines to produce 12 dozen screws?

  A. $1\frac{1}{2}$
  B. 3
  C. $4\frac{1}{2}$
  D. 6
  E. 9

35. On a map, the scale is given as 1 cm = 25 miles. The map distance between two cities is 15 cm. If you plan to drive between these two cities at an average speed of 35 miles per hour, which of the following is the best estimate for how long the trip should take?

  A. Between 8 and 9 hours
  B. Between 9 and 10 hours
  C. Between 10 and 11 hours
  D. Between 11 and 12 hours
  E. Between 12 and 13 hours

Question 36 refers to the following graph.

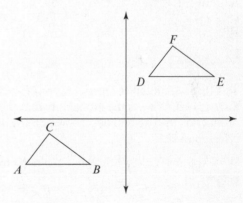

36. In the figure above, $\triangle ABC$ is congruent to $\triangle DEF$. The coordinates of points *A*, *B*, *C*, and *D* are *A* (−7, −5), *B* (−2, −5), *C* (−4, −1), and *D* (1, 6). What are the coordinates of point *F*?

  A. (4, 10)
  B. (6, 10)
  C. (6, 6)
  D. (8, 15)
  E. (6, 11)

GO ON TO THE NEXT PAGE

Question 37 refers to the following Venn diagram.

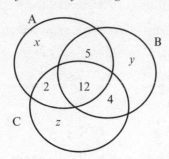

There are 30 teachers participating in *each* of three workshops at the annual teacher's conference:

- 12 teachers are registered in all three workshops.
- 2 teachers are registered in Workshops A and C only.
- 4 teachers are registered in Workshops B and C only.
- 5 teachers are registered in Workshops A and B only.

37. How many teachers are enrolled in Workshop C only?

A. 9
B. 10
C. 11
D. 12
E. 13

38. Two dice with number representations from 1 to 6 are tossed. What is the probability that the product of the two numbers shown on the dice is less than 20?

Write the answer as a fraction in the two boxes below.

39. What should be the next two numbers be in the following sequence?

$$1, 4, 9, 16, 25, \ldots$$

A. 35, 45
B. 35, 46
C. 36, 47
D. 36, 49
E. 37, 50

40. A container weighs 220 pounds. Which of the following is the best approximation of this weight in kilograms? (*Note:* 1 kilogram weighs approximately 2.2 pounds.)

A. 484
B. 220
C. 110
D. 100
E. 48.4

41. If two sides of a triangle have lengths 7 and 15, which of the following could be the length of the third side?

Select **all** that apply.

A. 7
B. 8
C. 15
D. 16
E. 21

42. How many square yards of carpet would be needed to cover a rectangular room that is 100 feet by 180 feet?

A. $222\dfrac{2}{9}$
B. 280
C. 2,000
D. 6,000
E. 18,000

43. Which of the following would NOT change the value of the median of a set of 15 different numbers written in order from smallest to largest or from largest to smallest?

A. Decrease the largest number only.
B. Decrease the smallest number only.
C. Take half of each number.
D. Decrease each number by 1.
E. Double each number.

GO ON TO THE NEXT PAGE

Question 44 refers to the following table.

Quiz Number	1	2	3	4	5	6	7	8	9	10	11	12	13	14	15
Score Percentage	80	70	80	80	70	70	80	70	80	70	80	70	70	70	80

44. The table above shows the results of a student's scores given in his chemistry class for 15 different quizzes. What is the student's average (arithmetic mean) score for the quizzes?

   A.   70

   B. $70\dfrac{7}{15}$

   C. $70\dfrac{1}{2}$

   D. $74\dfrac{2}{3}$

   E.   80

45. How many integers between 10 and 91 are NOT perfect squares?

   A.   6

   B.   40

   C.   73

   D.   74

   E.   75

46. A landscaper purchased $1,000 worth of plants for his business. Some of the plants cost $3 each and the others cost $4 each. If twice as many $3 plants as $4 plants were purchased, what was the total number of plants purchased?

Write your answer in the box below.

> [   ]

47. In an election poll, 84 voters favored candidate x, 65 voters favored candidate y, and 11 voters were undecided. What fraction of those polled favored candidate x?

   A. $\dfrac{13}{32}$

   B. $\dfrac{19}{40}$

   C. $\dfrac{21}{40}$

   D. $\dfrac{85}{149}$

   E. $\dfrac{19}{32}$

48. When purchasing a hybrid car, a buyer can choose from 5 exterior colors and 3 interior colors. How many color combinations are possible?

   A.   4

   B.   6

   C.   8

   D.   11

   E.   15

GO ON TO THE NEXT PAGE

Question 49 refers to the following bar graph.

The graph below shows the distribution for 16 different income brackets in Baltimore. Each bar represents the percentage of the Baltimore population whose yearly income falls within that range.

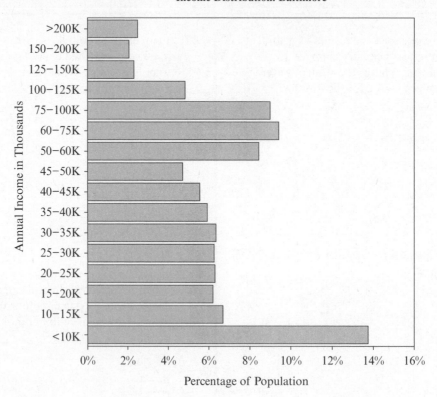

Income Distribution: Baltimore

49. According to the graph, the percent of people in Baltimore earning less than $10,000 per year is approximately how much more than the percent of people in Baltimore earning more than $200,000 per year?

   A. 16%
   B. 11%
   C. 8%
   D. 6%
   E. 4%

50. If $a^2 - 3a < 10$, which of the following CANNOT be a value of a?

Select **all** that apply.

   A. -3
   B. -2
   C. -1
   D. 3
   E. 4

51. If a cabinet refinishing company takes 6 hours to replace 15 dozen hinges, how many minutes will it take to replace 36 hinges?

   A. $1\dfrac{1}{6}$
   B. $6\dfrac{1}{6}$
   C. 66
   D. 72
   E. 370

GO ON TO THE NEXT PAGE

Question 52 refers to the following diagram.

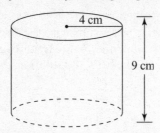

4 cm

9 cm

52. The right cylinder above has a base with a radius of 4 centimeters and a height of 9 centimeters. Between the surface area and the volume of this cylinder, which measurement will have the greater numerical value and by how much?

   A. Volume, 36π
   B. Surface area, 40π
   C. Volume, 40π
   D. Surface area, 72π
   E. Volume, 72π

Question 53 refers to the following chart.

Married men	25
Married women	35
Single men	15
Single women	45

53. The chart above shows the number of men and women in a fitness club and their marital status. If one individual was randomly selected from this fitness club, what is the probability the individual would be male?

   A. $\dfrac{1}{8}$

   B. $\dfrac{5}{24}$

   C. $\dfrac{1}{3}$

   D. $\dfrac{1}{2}$

   E. $\dfrac{2}{3}$

54. Which of the following linear equations have the same slope?

Select **all** that apply.

   A. $4x + 3y = 20$
   B. $3x + 4y = 20$
   C. $4x - 3y = 20$
   D. $3x - 4y = 20$
   E. $9x + 12y = 20$

55. Simplify: $4^4 \cdot 8^3 \cdot 16^2$

   A. 512^{24}
   B. 512^9
   C. 16^{11}
   D. 2^{576}
   E. 2^{25}

56. Round 4,316.136 to the nearest tenth.

   A. 4,320
   B. 4316.14
   C. 4,316.13
   D. 4,316.106
   E. 4,316.1

IF YOU FINISH BEFORE TIME IS CALLED, CHECK YOUR WORK ON THIS SECTION ONLY. DO NOT WORK ON ANY OTHER SECTION IN THE TEST.

STOP

Scoring the Practice Test

The following section will assist you in scoring and analyzing your practice test results. Use the answer key below to score your results, and then carefully review the analysis charts to identify your strengths and weaknesses. Finally, read through the answer explanations starting on page 268 to clarify the solutions to the problems.

Answer Key
Reading Test

1. B		**18.** E		**38.** E	
2. A		**19.** A		**39.** D	
3. E		**20.** C		**40.** E	
4. B		**21.** B		**41.** B	
5. A		**22.** D		**42.** C	
6. D		**23.** D		**43.** A	
7. D		**24.** B		**44.** E	
8. A and B		**25.** D		**45.** C	
9. B		**26.** A		**46.** B	
10. C		**27.** B		**47.** D	
11. C		**28.** D		**48.** C	
12. *Seeing a future of independence unlikely—with the Russians, British, French, and Americans all poised to seize their vulnerable territory*		**29.** A		**49.** *People acquire language specific to their respective experiences and societies.*	
		30. C			
		31. B		**50.** B	
		32. D		**51.** D	
13. A		**33.** C		**52.** C	
14. C		**34.** B		**53.** E	
15. B		**35.** B		**54.** B	
16. D		**36.** B		**55.** D	
17. D		**37.** B		**56.** A	

Writing Test: Selected Response

1. B	11. A	21. D	31. B
2. C	12. B	22. E	32. C
3. B	13. D	23. B	33. A
4. D	14. A	24. E	34. E
5. D	15. C	25. D	35. B
6. E	16. C	26. E	36. E
7. B	17. C	27. A	37. D
8. E	18. A	28. B	38. B
9. B	19. D	29. B	39. D
10. A	20. C	30. A	40. C

Mathematics Test

1. B	15. B	29. B	43. B
2. B	16. D	30. A	44. D
3. B	17. E	31. E	45. D
4. B, C, and D	18. D	32. A	46. 300
5. E	19. $\frac{11}{16}$	33. C	47. C
6. B	20. C	34. B	48. E
7. D	21. D	35. C	49. B
8. C	22. C	36. A	50. A and B
9. C	23. C	37. D	51. D
10. C	24. D	38. $\frac{7}{9}$	52. C
11. C and E	25. C	39. D	53. C
12. D	26. A	40. D	54. B and E
13. A	27. D	41. C, D, and E	55. E
14. B	28. C	42. C	56. E

Charting and Analyzing Your Test Results

The first step in analyzing your test results is to chart your answers. Use the following analysis sheet to identify your strengths and areas needing improvement. Complete the process of evaluating your results and analyzing problems in each area. Re-evaluate your results as you look for trends in the types of errors (repeated errors), and look for low scores in the results of *specific* subject areas. This re-examination and analysis is a tremendous asset to help you maximize your best possible score. The answers and explanations following this analysis sheet will provide you with clarification to help you solve these types of problems in the future.

Practice Test 1 Analysis Sheet					
			Number Incorrect		
Test	Total Possible	Number Correct	**(A)** Simple Mistake	**(B)** Misread Problem	**(C)** Unfamiliar Concept
Reading Test	56				
Writing Test: Selected Response	40				
Mathematics Test	56				
Total Possible Explanations for Incorrect Answers: Columns A, B, and C					
Total Number of Answers Correct and Incorrect	152	Add the total number of correct answers here: _____	Add columns A, B, and C _____ Total number of incorrect answers		

Answers and Explanations

Reading Test

1. **B.** According to Virginia Woolf, financial independence was a crucial first step toward all other forms of independence for women. The Married Women's Property Act gave women some degree of financial independence—but not full rights (choice A), and nothing suggests that it was concerned with women's rights to own businesses (choice E). Choices C and D, while both true, are not why the Married Women's Property Act was important.

2. **A.** The third sentence of the passage indicates that the author sees urban legends as part of an oral tradition (choice A). Choice C is directly contradicted in the passage, and although it is stated that urban legends are often bizarre, no assumption is made that *bizarre* is equal to *untrue,* as suggested by choice B. Choice E is not indicated in the passage, nor does the passage make the judgment in choice D.

3. **E.** The second sentence makes this point. Choices A and B are not supported, and choice C is both unsupported and untrue. Nothing in the passage indicates that the intention of urban legends is to change behavior; in fact, no intention whatsoever is suggested, making choice D incorrect.

4. **B.** The last sentence briefly touches on the main themes of urban legends (choice B). It doesn't contrast modern legends with those of the past to make a point about changes in the world (choice A), nor does it make the judgments in choices C, D, or E.

5. A. According to the passage, both the backyard fence and the Internet are places where information is passed without the filter of facts (choice A). Choice D may be true, but it isn't the reason the metaphor is used. Choice C is vague, and choice E is untrue. Nothing in the passage suggests that people who use the Internet and talk over the backyard fence are uneducated (choice B).

6. D. The author mentions that more urban legends are born than ever before in the digital age, implying that they are more numerous than they used to be (choice D). Choice A is incorrect because the author never implies that there is any truth to urban legends, only that they are *intended to be taken as truth…even when the events seem…unlikely*. Choice B is incorrect because the author discusses how urban legends reveal aspects of human nature. Choice C is incorrect because the author points out aspects in which urban legends differ from fairy tales. Choice E is incorrect because the author discusses how some urban legends are very short, such as the Great Chicago Fire urban legend.

7. D. The passage describes Erdrich's Native American heritage and her use of it in her writing, but the main point is to describe her as an author who goes beyond the Native American culture for her characters and themes (choice D). The passage doesn't make a judgment about her place in American literature (choices A, B, and E), nor does it mention her use of well-known legends (choice C).

8. A and B. The author raises issues with how schools reach the minimum calorie limit but does not express concern regarding excess calories (choice A). The author also does not mention carbohydrates (choice B). However, the author does raise concerns about the lack of specific requirements for how schools meet minimum calorie requirements, making choice C incorrect.

9. B. The study in choice B would underscore the importance of a minimum calorie requirement, and thus weaken Dr. Orton's argument that calorie requirements are outdated and less important than healthy menu items. Choices A and C are irrelevant to Dr. Orton's argument that children would benefit from healthy food more than a required calorie threshold, and choices D and E actually support the doctor's position.

10. C. Only choice C is correct—the author specifically points to lunches that are high in sugar as a concerning finding of the study. Choice A is incorrect because while the study did find flaws with school lunches, it also found that 70 percent of schools provide lunches with sufficient vitamins, minerals, and protein. Choice B confuses an opinion of Dr. Orton with a conclusion of the study.

11. C. The primary assets of the tropical waters are that they are warmer, shallower, and provide more protection for mothers and calves (choice C). The reason the humpback whales mate and calve in warmer waters is physical, not biological, choice D. Choice A is accurate, but it is not cited as the main reason for the whales' migration. No parallel is drawn between whale migration and bird migration, choice B, nor is food supply in colder waters mentioned, choice E.

12. The clause in lines 8–11 beginning with *Seeing a future…* and concluding with *…vulnerable territory* explains why some Californians preferred the Old World Europeans as a viable alternative to Mexico's rule (as independence seemed unlikely).

13. A. Choice A is correct, as the passage implies that Californians were anxious to escape from Mexico's reign yet states that Spain had been no better in terms of its emphasis on the territory's development. Choice B is never implied by the passage, and while the passage suggests that some Californians favored annexation by the U.S., it does not mention a majority, choice C. The passage's reference to landowners as the real power brokers contradicts choice D, and the desire for California to pursue a plan of independence is not mentioned in the passage (choice E).

14. C. The focus of the entire passage is on describing the situation in which Californians found themselves under Mexican reign (choice C). Choice A is incorrect, as the United States is only mentioned in the final sentence, and choices B and E provide only secondary purposes discussed in one to two sentences each. Choice D is an overreach that is only touched on by the reference to the power held by landowners.

15. B. By stating that nitrogen is *essential for life* and that bacteria is required *to convert the nitrogen into usable forms,* the author implies that bacteria must also be essential for life (choice B). Choice A is incorrect because the author makes no reference to the importance of oxygen, and choice C is incorrect because the author does not imply that plants retain the nitrogen they use for growth. Choice D incorrectly interprets the passage as claiming that there are no other building blocks for life, and choice E is incorrect because the author does not mention nonatmospheric nitrogen.

16. **D.** The term *assistance* refers to the points in the nitrogen cycle during which bacteria *help convert the nitrogen into usable forms* (choice D). Choices A and B incorrectly assume that the word refers to nitrogen's assistance in the production of life, while choice C is never mentioned in the passage. Choice E is incorrect because the passage does not mention what causes the nitrogen cycle to begin.

17. **D.** The smallest enrollment in social sciences was in sociology (4%), the smallest enrollment in humanities was in French (5%), and the smallest enrollment in natural sciences was in physics (8%).

18. **E.** The combined percentage representing humanities courses (30%) is smaller than the percentage for both natural sciences (38%) and social sciences (32%), which means that there are fewer humanities classes than there are social studies or natural sciences classes. The graph's title also informs the viewer that the chart represents all classes at JHS; therefore, choice E can safely be concluded. The chart contradicts choices A and B, while choice C is an overreach (the chart does not mention national student preferences). Choice D is not implied by the graph.

19. **A.** The author uses present tense when referring to people seeing the paintings up close, implying that it is possible to currently do so (choice A). Choice B is incorrect because no reference is made to Neanderthals, and choice C is incorrect because no mention is made of art's place on the Cro-Magnons' hierarchy of interests. Choice D makes too significant of a logical jump from the passage's claim that art is the best known of the Cro-Magnons' tools, and choice E is never suggested by the author.

20. **C.** The passage defines a mutualistic interaction as one in which two or more species benefit from one another, each helping the other. Choice C embodies this sort of interaction, as the birds receive food and the elephants enjoy a reduction in the number of insects on their backs. Choice A is incorrect because the deer does not benefit from the interaction, and choice B is incorrect because there are not multiple species interacting.

21. **B.** The example for the benefit gained by algae in its relationship with fungi is shelter; therefore, it must logically follow that algae benefit from living in a sheltered environment, as put forth by choice B. Choice A is incorrect because bees do not need to be the only method of pollen transport for the relationship to be beneficial. Choice C is incorrect because bees could be harmed by outside factors during the otherwise beneficial process of pollination. Choice D is incorrect because the author does not imply that coexisting with algae is the only way for fungi to receive food. Choice E is not an assumption underlying the passage.

22. **D.** Choice D is correct; the purpose of the passage is to define *mutualistic interactions* and then to provide several examples of these interactions. Choices A and B present secondary purposes, while choices C and E present arguments or claims that the author does not attempt to make; rather, the author presents the facts without editorializing.

23. **D.** "Nevertheless" (in line 7) indicates that Nightingale pursued her interest despite social attitudes, suggesting that she was dissatisfied with a woman's usual role. She convinced her family to allow her to do something that was considered off-limits for a woman of her class; they did not sponsor her studies, choice B. Nothing in the passage supports choice A, and Nightingale's religious feelings are not addressed at all, choice C. In spite of her putting splints on her dog's paws, there is no indication in the rest of the paragraph that she wanted to be a veterinarian, choice E.

24. **B.** The author cites the reduction in the hospital death rate immediately after stating that Nightingale took a team of nurses to Turkey. Choice D might seem correct, but the emphasis is on the reduction in the death rate, not on the horrible conditions in hospitals. Choice E might also seem possible, but this detail is used specifically to dramatize the effect of the nurses, which is not the main idea of the paragraph. Choice C is irrelevant because the passage deals with Nightingale's becoming a nurse, not a physician. Finally, the reader has no way of determining whether choice A is true.

25. **D.** Choice D correctly summarizes the main point that the author attempts to get across: that sea cucumbers are contributors to the destruction of coral reefs. Choice A ignores the focus on sea cucumbers, while choice E ignores the focus on coral reefs. Choice B is incorrect because the author never advocates for action, and choice C is incorrect because the passage suggests that sea cucumbers are actually *disrupting* the balance of reefs.

26. A. The sequence described in the final paragraph is best summarized by choice A. Choices B and E are incorrect because the passage claims that the release of carbon dioxide results in slower reef growth, not the *eating away* of reefs. Choice C is incorrect because the passage does not say that carbon dioxide is directly absorbed by reefs, and choice D is too vague.

27. B. The passage states that sea cucumbers are responsible for a major portion of reef dissolution—i.e., destruction (choice B). Choice A is not implied by the passage; to the contrary, it suggests that sea cucumbers are currently *disrupting* the balance of calcium carbonate in reefs. Choice C is incorrect because these digestive byproducts are not said to be acidic, and choice D is incorrect because the passage states that sea cucumbers consume the organic substances *within* sand and rubble. Choice E exaggerates the author's argument to an extreme.

28. D. The passage states that while sea cucumbers do not consume reefs for sustenance (as put forth by choice C), they do indirectly ingest and dissolve carbonate pieces of reefs as part of their digestive process. Choices A and E also include harmful influences on reefs but incorrectly attribute them to sea cucumbers. Choice B is not implied.

29. A. The author presents findings that present danger to coral reefs, and use of language like *already-scarce* and *grave threat* imply that the author is concerned. The author does not present any reasons for hope, as suggested by choice B, nor skepticism of the data presented, as suggested by choice D. Choice C presents an exaggerated interpretation of the passage's tone, while choice E understates the author's apparent concern.

30. C. The passage serves to define social psychology, which choice C accurately does. Choice A conflates *social scientists* with *social influences*. Choice B incorrectly focuses on the influence of *an individual* on behavior, rather than varying influences. Choices D and E overreach and are not implied by the passage.

31. B. By claiming that the kind of citizen who is not intimidated by pursuing careers into middle age will have to be a *new type of citizen,* it must logically follow that present-day citizens are intimidated by such a prospect (choice B). Choice A is incorrect because the author does not suggest that the importance of technology is unrecognized, and choice C conflates confidence in one's potential with actual potential. Choice D is incorrect because the prospect of multiple careers is not brought up, and choice E is incorrect because the issue of safety is not discussed.

32. D. Toward the end of the passage, the author expresses a skeptical, qualified view of the value of technology, making choice D correct. Choice A is implied by the author's argument, and choice B represents the author's hope for the future. Choice C is a summary of the author's main point, and choice E is a rephrasing of a secondary point.

33. C. Both sentences of the passage are focused on the importance of the listener's role in oral communication. Choices A and E embody the opposite of the author's point, while choices B and D are secondary points and overly specific interpretations of the main argument.

34. B. Choice B correctly concludes that if people retire earlier in the future and face the financial burdens of retirement when middle aged, they will need more money to support themselves for the rest of their lives. The passage portrays early retirement as an unattractive, problematic occurrence that will affect many; choices D and E contradict these unattractive connotations of early retirement. Choices A and C state conclusions that are neither expressed nor implied in the passage.

35. B. The *we* in the passage tells us that the author counts himself or herself among those who give performances, which rules out choices A, D, and E. Given that the author is discussing a serious subject, and the perception of acting itself, it is more likely that the author is addressing other actors (choice B), rather than performing for an audience's entertainment (choice C).

36. B. As the author says, art is *not merely to amuse,* meaning it is more than entertainment (choice B). Choices A and C exaggerate the author's emphasis on the serious side of art, while choice D is never suggested. Choice E contradicts the author's main point.

37. B. The repeat of *some* recalls the earlier mention of *some legislators* and indicates that the legislators may be part of the group of people who do not appreciate the full value of art (choice B). The author's tone runs contrary to the implication of choice A, and choices C and E present an overly pessimistic interpretation of the author's point. Choice D is not implied.

38. **E.** The author says that survivors will be adaptable but does not specify the way in which adaptability will be a value (choice E). The author does not suggest that the absolute level of value will increase or decrease (choices A and B), and the author does not imply anything about the staying power of the value, as implied by choices C and D.

39. **D.** Choice D is directly relevant to the author's assertion that the economy is a significant factor in the determination of value. Choices A and B contradict the author's claims, and choices C and E are never suggested by the author.

40. **E.** Both passages consider the effects of biodiversity loss (choice E). See lines 7–10, 22–25, 30–31. The second passage doesn't define biodiversity, choice A, and the first passage doesn't discuss protecting the generation of new species, choice B. Only the second passage discusses vicariance, choice C, and neither passage includes an approach to preventing habitat degradation, choice D.

41. **B.** The second passage is concerned with the process of new species generation and the dangers presented by invasive species; the first passage does not deal with that issue (choice B). Neither passage is argumentative in approach, choice A, and there is no indication that a scientist wrote either passage, choice C. Both passages cite habitat degradation, choice D. Neither passage discusses the causes of habitat degradation, choice E.

42. **C.** Lines 3–10 specifically cite biodiversity as essential for the cycles of major elements such as nitrogen, which the passage refers to as an ecosystem service, making choice C correct. None of the other answer choices refers to an ecosystem service.

43. **A.** See lines 10–14. The implication is that estimates of the number of species are not exact because most are too small to count (choice A). Choice B is not supported in the passage, and choices C, D, and E are not mentioned.

44. **E.** According to Passage 2, the number of species lost in the Late Devonian period was not higher than in other mass extinctions (choice A); the difference was that in the Late Devonian period, few new species arose (choice E). The entire marine ecosystem was affected, but the passage does not compare that effect to other mass extinctions, as suggested by choice B. Neither choice C nor choice D is supported by information in the passage.

45. **C.** According to the passage, vicariance is the method, choice C, rather than the rate, choice A, by which new species are formed. Choice B describes a way that vicariance can occur, but not the process itself. Both choices D and E are irrelevant to vicariance.

46. **B.** The author implies that the extinction was really a *biodiversity crisis* because of the lack of new species formed during the period, as put forth by choice B. Choice A is not supported by the passage; although the marine ecosystem was devastated, it was not only marine species that became extinct. Choice C is irrelevant; habitat degradation is not cited in relation to the biodiversity crisis. Choice D is also not a good choice; no distinction is made between *crucial* and *noncrucial* species. Choice E is inaccurate because although whole ecosystems were destroyed, it was the failure of new species to emerge that was key in the Late Devonian period.

47. **D.** Choice D is directly supported by the sentence *What impacts one child can impact the entire class*. The phrase *free to talk* implies that teachers should not necessarily pressure quiet children to talk, choice A, nor allow them to fade out of the group dynamic, choice B. Choice C is incorrect because *cooperative peer groups* are not mentioned in the passage, nor are the higher test scores suggested by choice E.

48. **C.** The passage puts forth that *the classroom is a microcosm within a larger context that influences child development,* which is rephrased by choice C. Choices A, B, and E misinterpret the definition of the word *microcosm,* while choice D erroneously refers to a specific classroom when the passage only discusses learning dynamics in general terms.

49. The description of language as specific to [people's] respective experiences and societies directly conflicts with Chomsky's theory that language is biologically determined: *People acquire language specific to their respective experiences and societies* (lines 3–5). The first sentence claims that language is learned over time and is used to communicate thoughts and ideas, which does not conflict with the theory, and the final two sentences are descriptions of Chomsky's academic focus and his theory itself.

50. **B.** The passage stresses ways of changing the social studies curriculum, thus designating its audience as those who can effect such changes—teachers (choice B). Since the passage focuses on educating teachers and instituting a proper curriculum rather than urging students to choose certain existing classes, choice A is incorrect. Historians and politicians, as mentioned in choices C and D, are not referenced in the passage. The passage never mentions the role of parents, as posited by choice E, which would make them a secondary audience, at best.

51. **D.** *Humans have always been interested in where they are going* is preceded by a series of supporting historical evidence—facts about occurrences of the past (choice D). Nothing suggests that the supporting claims are unfounded, choice A, and certainly not extraterrestrial, choice B. The evidence does not involve political or scientific systems, so choices C and E are incorrect.

52. **C.** By advocating the addition of futurism to the social studies curriculum, the author assumes that futurism is not adequately acknowledged (choice C). Without that assumption, the author would have no reason to make the argument. Choices A and E exaggerate the author's stance, and the author does not suggest that students know little about the past, as claimed by choice B. Choice D is a non sequitur, as the historical figures discussed are not implied to be similar to modern fortune-tellers.

53. **E.** By distinguishing *global* from *national* in the passage, the author suggests that a global society is larger and more inclusive than a national one, as put forth by choice E. Choices A and B are overly specific and not suggested, and the author does not suggest that global society should include outer space, as in choice D. Choice C seems like an acceptable answer within the context of the overall passage, but it ignores the global/national distinction in its containing sentence.

54. **B.** Choices C and D would strengthen the argument of the value of futurism. Choices A and E are irrelevant to the strength or weakness of the argument. Choice B weakens the passage by calling into question the usefulness and value of futurists of the past, and thus raises questions about the importance of the pursuit.

55. **D.** The overall stress on changes in education indicates that the author is an educator (choice D). The focus on the future rather than the past runs contrary to the conclusions of choices A and B, and the author makes no scientific arguments (as suggested by choice C). Choice E is never implied.

56. **A.** The author claims that futuristics is already being taught at many major universities in an attempt to lend extra credibility and legitimacy to his or her argument that futuristics should be more significantly incorporated into learning curriculums (choice A). Choice B is incorrect because no previous claim was made regarding current university implementation, and the sentence does not summarize the author's arguments or look into the future as implied by choices C, D, and E.

Writing Test: Selected Response

1. **B.** *Less* should be used to refer to one thing only, a singular reference, while *fewer* should be used to refer to a number of things. Use *fewer* if the word it modifies is plural (*students*).

2. **C.** Using a comma here rather than a period or semicolon creates a run-on sentence. Choices A and B are parallel, and choice D is the correct verb.

3. **B.** An adverb (*well*), not an adjective (*good*), is needed to modify the verb *did.* Choice A is the correct pronoun, the object of the verb mentioned. *Which* in choice C correctly refers the *final competition,* and *held* in choice D is the correct tense of the verb *hold.*

4. **D.** Although plural in form, some nouns, such as *mathematics,* sometimes take a singular verb (*is,* not *are*). Other examples of such nouns are *measles, economics, physics,* and *mumps.*

5. **D.** *Slow* should be *slowly* because it is modifying a verb, *worked. Had been sent* is the correct form of the verb, and *loudly* is an adverb modifying the verb complained. There is no error with the noun *crew* in choice A.

6. E. This sentence has no errors, so the correct answer is choice E. The first underlined clause contains no errors, and the singular verb *was* properly agrees with it. *Whose* is the correct possessive pronoun, and the infinitive *to motivate* fits within the context of the sentence.

7. B. The subject of the sentence is compound (*produce* and *business*) and therefore the predicate should be plural (*are* instead of *is*).

8. E. This sentence is correct as is. *Who had entered the Kentucky Derby race* is a restrictive clause, which means that no commas should be used to set it off. The verbs in choices B and D are correct, and *fairgrounds,* choice C, is not a proper noun and therefore shouldn't be capitalized.

9. B. A semicolon is incorrect here and turns the clause that follows it into a fragment. A comma should be used instead.

10. A. This sentence begins with a dangling participle; *the river* is not *sitting on the Susquehanna bank.* The sentence could be changed in various ways to avoid the dangling participle. For example, *As I was sitting on the Susquehanna bank, the river rushed by me…*

11. A. *Present incumbent* is a redundant phrase. *Incumbent* refers to the person currently in office. The comma after *lots,* choice B, is a series comma and is correct. The antecedent of the pronoun *these,* choice C, is the series that precedes it. *Therefore,* in choice D, is correctly placed within the logical progression of the sentence.

12. B. No comma should be used before the modifying clause beginning with *that. Revolutionary,* choice A, is not capitalized because no particular revolutionary movement is identified. *Well documented,* choice C, is correct, and *began,* choice D, is the correct past tense of the verb.

13. D. The correct word here is the verb *affect. Effect* is usually a noun: *the effect of the policy.* When it is a verb, it means "to bring about, to accomplish." The comma between *community* and *but* correctly separates two independent clauses (choice A). *Us* (choice B) is correct here as the object of the preposition *of,* and *attempted to* (choice C) is the correct idiom.

14. A. A common error is to use the conditional *would have* in an *if* clause. Instead, the past perfect should be used here: *If the head of the department had notified* (choice A). *Who,* choice B, is the correct pronoun because it is the subject of a verb (*needed to*), and *him,* choice C, is the correct pronoun because it is the object of the preposition *between.* The conditional *could have been saved,* choice D, is correct because it appears in the clause that states the consequences of the *if* clause.

15. C. *Unique* is a word that cannot be compared; it means "one of a kind" and therefore, it cannot be "very one of a kind."

16. C. This is an error in parallel structure. *To pack up their most important possessions, lock the windows and doors, and move* (not *to move*) corrects the problem (choice C). The initial *to* covers the three items in the series and shouldn't be dropped from the second item and then be repeated with the third item. The sentence could also be corrected by adding the word *to* to the second item in the series: *To pack up … to lock … and to move.*

17. C. *Went* is the past tense of *go,* and to be consistent with the other verbs (*had arrived* and [*had*] *taken*), [*had*] *gone* is required here.

18. A. *Quickly,* not *quick,* is correct here (choice A); it is modifying *started*—an action verb—and therefore, should be an adverb, not an adjective. *Felt* in choice C is a linking verb (as are such words as *seems, is, sound, taste,* etc.); linking verbs do not express action but instead link the subject to a word or idea in the predicate. Adjectives, not adverbs, are used with linking verbs. Choice B is correctly in adverb form, and choice D is an acceptable contraction of *had not.*

19. D. *Amount* refers to a bulk or mass. The correct word here is *number,* which refers to individual countable items. No comma is needed to set off the *who* clause (choice B), which is restrictive. Choices A and C present the respective verbs in their correct tenses.

20. C. The antecedent of the pronoun *they* is not clear here. Does *they* refer to the documents or to Mr. Derschowitz and Mr. Shapiro? The sentence should be rewritten to avoid this possible confusion, or the word *documents* should be repeated instead of using the pronoun.

21. D. The comma after *protection* creates a run-on sentence, or comma splice. *For example* begins an independent clause. It has both a subject and a predicate and can stand alone. Therefore, it should be separated from the first clause by a period or a semicolon. Also, a comma should follow the introductory phrase *For example* (as it does in choice D).

22. E. Choice E corrects the original version, which is a run-on sentence. *In fact* should be preceded by a semicolon, not a comma. Also, the verbs are correct in choice E and the vague word *that* has been clarified with the words *that trip*. Notice that the incorrect past participle *went* is used in choices A, B, and D.

23. B. The original sentence begins with a dangling modifier; it appears that the car received the estimate. Choice B corrects that problem. Choice B also uses the active voice of the verb (*I delivered*), which is preferable to the passive voice (*the car was delivered*). The other choices either do not remedy the basic problem or are awkwardly constructed.

24. E. Choice E corrects the problem of inconsistent tenses in the original sentence and is also the most concise version. It uses subordination well. The comma after *erupting* is correct.

25. D. The problem with the sentence is the use of incorrect verbs. First, in the *if* clause, the subjunctive form of the verb should be used: *had been available*. Second, *would have been chosen* is correct as it is; changing it to *would have been chose* (choice C) or *would have chose* (choice E) would be using the past tense of the verb, not the participle. Finally, the correct past participle of break is *had broken*.

26. E. The original sentence parallels schools in the Chicago inner city with the suburbs rather than with schools in the suburbs, which is a faulty comparison. It is also wordy (*are more in need of*). Choice E corrects both problems.

27. A. This sentence is correct as it is.

28. B. The correct verb is *lie*, not *lay*. *Laying* takes an object: *laying the book down, laying the carpet*, etc. *Lying* does not: *I lie down for a nap, I lie in the sun*, etc. Also, the comparative of *red* is *redder*, not *more red*.

29. B. The main problem with the sentence is that the subject and verb don't agree. The subject is plural (*concert* and *coverage*) and the verb is singular (*was*). Choice B corrects the problem and also eliminates unnecessary words.

30. A. This sentence contains a series; the original version here is the best of the five—parallel, correctly punctuated with commas, and concise. The semicolons of choice B are incorrect; choice C has an extra *and*. Choices D and E break up the parallel construction.

31. B. This choice effectively combines the first two sentences. Choice A is not grammatically incorrect, but it is wordy with the use of *and*. Using a dependent clause to join the sentences, as in choice B, is smoother. The structure of choice C is awkward and uses the passive voice. Choice D mistakenly states Weems's motive for writing. Choice E uses the passive voice and is also wordy.

32. C. This sentence fits best at the beginning of the third paragraph, which deals with the monetary reasons that Weems wrote the biography of Washington. It is tacked on to the first paragraph and doesn't fit well into the second, which characterizes the content of the biography.

33. A. This is the answer that corrects the run-on sentence (or comma splice), which is the biggest problem. The other changes are minor or unnecessary, and choice C would actually create a fragment.

34. E. Choice A is wordy, and *exist* should be *exists* because *evidence* is singular and requires a singular verb. Choice B incorrectly uses a semicolon after *exists,* creating a fragment. Choices C and D are both wordy and awkward.

35. B. This is the best choice because it is concise, contains no grammatical errors, and ends with the emphasis on Weems's influence. Choice A lacks sentence variety, choice C includes a run-on sentence, choice D is awkward, and choice E is exceptionally wordy.

36. E. Details about Weems's background follow the introduction logically and should precede details about the biography's content. Of the choices, choice E would be the best. The passage is about Weems' biography more than about George Washington; more details about Washington himself, choice B, wouldn't improve it. Neither would providing historical background, choice A, or summarizing the biographies that followed, choice D. The final paragraph serves as a conclusion and shouldn't be eliminated, choice C.

37. D. Internet search engines use algorithms to categorize subject matter themes. To retrieve the best Internet results, the researcher must refine the search with specific key words relevant to the topic. Although one of the symptoms of childhood stuttering is *pausing before speech,* choice D, the Internet cannot differentiate between an unintentional pause in speech due to stuttering, and an intentional pause that a skilled speaker might use in a well-crafted speech. Choices A, B, C, and E use well-defined words and phrases related to stuttering.

38. B. "Solving the autism puzzle" follows the format for citing an academic journal:

Author, A. (Year). Title of article. *Title of journal or periodical in italics,* volume number (issue number), pages.

Choice A, a newspaper article, uses an exact date of the publication in parentheses (28 Nov. 2015) and would not list the volume number in parentheses. A dissertation, choice C, would show the words "Doctoral dissertation" and the words "Retrieved from ProQuest Dissertations and Theses." Choice D, a book, would not show the name of the journal and would not show an issue number. Choice E, an Internet article, follows the guidelines for printed articles, but should also show the words "Retrieved from http://www…"

39. D. Articles, papers, and other Internet postings can be updated with new or corrected information or removed from the Internet altogether. Therefore, choice D is the correct answer. (Referencing the copyright date of the reprint of a publication that a writer cites serves the same purpose.) Choice B is incorrect because Internet references are not necessarily more up to date than their print counterparts, and not all Internet references have print counterparts. Choice C is incorrect because not all Internet references are date sensitive. Documenting the date that the writer finds the reference on the Internet does not necessarily prove that the writer found the reference on the Internet any more than indicating the website address proves it, so choice A is incorrect.

40. C. Choice C is the only answer that illustrates the correct usage of MLA (Modern Language Association) style citations. Most academic sources use MLA style, but APA (American Psychological Association) and CMS (Chicago Manual of Style) styles are acceptable references. Choices A and B are incorrect citation formats. Although choice D is a paraphrased version of the original work, the author's work must be cited to avoid plagiarism. Choice E cites the author's words, but it is not the best choice because it does not include the title of his work.

If you reference a direct quote from an original author, always use quotation marks around the author's words. However, if you paraphrase and restate an original author's direct quote, you can exclude the quotation marks.

Writing Test: Essay

Essay 1: Argumentative Essay

A high-scoring strong student response is provided below to help you evaluate your essay. The commentary at the end of this section will further help you identify your areas of improvement.

> Read the opinion stated below:

> "Students who demonstrate exceptional talent should be given increased educational resources, opportunities, and attention."
>
> **Assignment:** Discuss the extent to which you agree or disagree with this opinion. Support your views with specific reasons and examples from your own experiences, observations, or reading.

High-Scoring Strong Response

While many may dismiss the statement above as elitist or patently unfair, I believe it worthwhile to consider the merits of this claim. While it would be unfair to arbitrarily deny less talented students equitable resources, it may prove a wise investment to give some students increased opportunities and attention.

Some may argue that those with exceptional talent will thrive no matter the situation, and that resources should be allocated with an eye to giving all students an equal share of the pie. Specific instances, however, do not bear out this generalization. Great talents such as Albert Einstein and Bill Gates were not successful in school and may have even been overlooked. It wasn't until Gates had the opportunity to participate in an extra-curricular computer club that people recognized his talent and he was able to develop it. If that opportunity had not existed, society may have lost the chance to develop a talented computer engineer. Although it's tempting to believe that all talented students will pursue their gifts regardless of their circumstance, it's important to remember that not all of them will succeed without guidance and attention.

Others may assert that giving some students extra opportunities is unfair and that all students should share equally in resources. This assertion ignores the fact that investing in the most talented students holds a higher probability of greater dividends for the community. One scholarship program identifies high school seniors who show strong academic promise and who wish to become teachers. These students receive scholarships that they repay by fulfilling a commitment to teach in the public schools when they graduate. It's a prime example of giving a resource—money—to a few students who will then be able to help so many more young people. At first blush, it may appear fairer to give all college-bound students a smaller share of scholarship money, but the investment would likely yield a far lower dividend.

The claim that exceptional students should be granted more opportunities, resources, and attention holds true as long as there is an understanding that with greater resources comes greater responsibility. If the exceptionally talented can give back to their communities then it makes sense to offer them greater resources for the ultimate benefit of all.

Commentary

This strong response serves as a reminder that scorers are not looking for test-takers to adopt a specific position on an issue, as this writer defends a perhaps unpopular view. The key is that the writer does a careful job of staking out a clear position by specifying the extent to which the claim is valid and addressing counter-arguments. Notice that the writer clearly and effectively develops his ideas in four paragraphs, rather than five paragraphs. The organizational plan puts each counter-argument at the beginning of a paragraph and then provides an example to support the position. The logical organization and thorough development of examples makes the response both fluent and persuasive.

Essay 2: Informative/Explanatory Essay

> **Assignment:**
>
> Both of the following passages address phonemic awareness, particularly the correlation between learning phonemic awareness and reading success. Read the two passages carefully and then write an essay in which you identify the most important concerns regarding the issue and explain why they are important. Your essay must draw on information from BOTH of the sources. In addition, you may draw upon your own experiences, observations, and readings.
>
> When paraphrasing or quoting from the sources, cite each source by referring to the author's last name, the title of the source, or any other clear identifier.

High-Scoring Strong Response

According to the Report of the National Reading Panel (NRP), phonemic awareness is a fundamental component in the complex process of learning to read. Children enter school with a wide-range of language experiences, and studies show that children must recognize the correlation between sounds and print if they are to succeed in reading (Ehri et al.). Bobrow's (2006) article from CliffsTestPrep RICA, points out that if school-aged children do not learn phonemic awareness in their early years, "learning deficits" in reading may result. Emmitt, Hornsby, and Wilson's (2013) article, "The Place of Phonics in Learning to Read and Write" confirms this viewpoint, but also points out that other variables must be considered when making predictive outcomes. The ability of a student to identify phonemes and relate them to print is integral to developing reading fluency, but it is not an exclusive indicator of a student's future success in reading.

Bobrow references reading experts Adams, Troia, and Stanovich who state that it is a fact that phonemic awareness instruction is a predictor of future reading success "when compared to [reading] instruction without phonemic awareness" (Source 1). Since many students do not enter school with this awareness and vary greatly in their ability to hear individual sounds within words, the systematic instruction of phonemic awareness is necessary. If reading skills are taught in isolation, and out of context, experts agree that student success in reading may be compromised. Students who are taught to isolate, segment, blend, and manipulate phonemes are given the tools to master phonemic awareness and become successful readers (Ehri et al).

Emmitt, Hornsby, and Wilson references reading experts NRP, Taylor, and Walsh who suggest that although phonemic awareness mastery may be a predictor of reading success, it is not the only indicator of a student's future proficiency (Source 2). The authors of the second article distinguish between "correlation," and "causation." Although there is scientific evidence that demonstrates the "correlation" between phonemic awareness and reading success, it does not mean that phonemic awareness instruction "causes" reading success. The value of early language learning before age six cannot be ignored. Integrating skills from spoken language into contextual reading is key to creating meaning and relevancy for the student. Skill-driven models that focus on phonemic awareness exclusively, without presenting these skills in the context of meaningful literature, may not be effective in developing fluent readers. Students may be able to decode words and read well orally in future years through other naturally occurring language and reading instructional variables.

Although it has been asserted that by age six children have a "culmination of a long and complex developmental journey in spoken language, which has progressed from meaningful spoken activities to higher levels of abstraction with spoken words and speech sounds" (Walsh, 2009), it cannot be assumed that all children entering school are equally equipped to engage in the process of learning to read. Some children begin school with a rich base of language, while others do not. Systematic phonemic awareness instruction is widely regarded as an essential component in the success of a student's ability to become a fluent reader. Integrating this important skill into a context of meaning for the student is an essential component in the complex puzzle of becoming a proficient reader.

Commentary

This "informative/explanatory" essay critically analyzes both issues and provides explicit supporting evidence to explain each author's viewpoint. The logical organization of the essay is well developed and follows the four-paragraph model to compare and contrast relevant perspectives of each source. Specific citations are used from both sources to offer details and reasons for each author's line of reasoning. The essay follows the conventions of standard written English with minimal errors in grammar, usage, and sentence structure. The concluding paragraph sums up the supporting connections between both sources and synthesizes important aspects from each source. The key is that the writer does a good job of extracting information from both sources while making clear connections between the two sources related to the issue of phonemic awareness.

Mathematics Test

1. **B.** To solve this problem, make a literal translation of the English words into numbers.

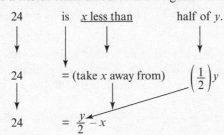

$$24 = \frac{y}{2} - x$$

2. **B.** This arithmetic word problem is straightforward. Simply convert the words into math equations. Of the 48 students, three-fourths are male, or $\frac{3}{4} \times 48 = 36$. Therefore, there are 36 males and 12 females in the class. Of the 12 females, one-third are less than 6 feet tall, or $\frac{1}{3} \times 12 = 4$. Therefore, $12 - 4 = 8$, or 12 total females minus 4 females who are less than 6 feet tall equals 8 females who are at least 6 feet tall. Therefore, 8 females are 6 feet tall or taller.

3. **B.** If you expand the value 24.7×10^3, it would read 24,700 (move the decimal point to the right three positions). Now rewrite 24,700 in scientific notation. It is 2.47×10^4. Hence, the decimal point in the original expression is moved to the left one position, and the exponent is increased by 1.

4. **B, C, and D.** To determine how large the largest score can be, let the other five scores be as small as possible; that is, 70, 71, 72, 73, and 74. Since the average of the score for the six tests is 76, the total of the six tests must be $(76)(6) = 456$. The smallest five scores add up to $70 + 71 + 72 + 73 + 74 = 360$. This leaves $456 - 360 = 96$ for the most that the largest test score can be. This fact eliminates answer choice E, 97. Choice A is incorrect because if 78 is the highest score, the other five different test scores would be 77, 76, 75, 74, and 73. All six tests would then total 453, not 456 (which is the average of all six tests).

   Now determine how small the largest score can be. Since the average of the six scores is 76, the six tests must be centered about 76. This means the scores have to be 73, 74, 75, 77, 78, and 79. Therefore, the smallest the largest score can be is 79. This eliminates 78 as a possible choice. Therefore, the range of values for the largest test is $79 \le x \le 96$.

5. **E.** Since there are 8 red gumballs in the bowl, picking just 8 could result in all 8 being red, and therefore, not choosing one of each. Since there are 8 red and 7 white, picking 15 gumballs could result in getting only red and white gumballs. Therefore, at least 16 must be chosen to be sure of getting at least one of each color.

6. **B.** Factor 7,500 into the product of primes.

$$
\begin{aligned}
7,500 &= 75 \times 100 \\
&= (3 \times 25) \times (4 \times 25) \\
&= 3 \times 5 \times 5 \times 2 \times 2 \times 5 \times 5 \\
&= 2^2 \times 3^1 \times 5^4
\end{aligned}
$$

Therefore, $x = 2$, $y = 1$, and $z = 4$. Then $xyz = (2)(1)(4) = 8$.

7. **D.** Figure R has 2 of 3 parts shaded, so it represents the fraction $\frac{2}{3}$. Figure S has 3 of 8 parts shaded, so it represents the fraction $\frac{3}{8}$. The word *sum* means "addition." Therefore, $\frac{2}{3} + \frac{3}{8} = \frac{16}{24} + \frac{9}{24} = \frac{25}{24} = 1\frac{1}{24}$.

8. **C.** Use math reasoning and simple calculations to answer this question. Let's look at a real-life example to illustrate the correct answer, choice C. Suppose a package of cheese contains 8 slices and a package of turkey contains 6 slices. The least number of packages of cheese and of turkey that you would need to buy is 24 (the least common multiple of 6 and 8). The quantity of 24 packages will ensure that you will not have any leftovers of cheese or turkey.

9. **C.** Stock A was purchased at $16.50 per share and sold at $20 per share, a profit of $3.50 per share. Stock B was purchased at $19.50 per share and sold at $20 per share, a profit of $0.50 per share. The profit from Stock A is (200)($3.50) = $700. The profit from Stock B is (500)($0.50) = $250.

    $$\text{Stock B represents } \frac{250}{700+250} = \frac{250}{950} \approx 0.263 \approx 26\% \text{ of the total profit.}$$

10. **C.** This problem can be solved by using math reasoning or math proportion.

    Method 1: Using math reasoning with the visual graphic.

    The first step is to divide the total distance, 26 inches, by the distance that the tortoise travels.

    The graph below will help you visualize the distance and answer the question using math logic.

    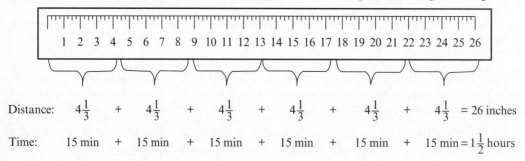

    Distance: $4\frac{1}{3}$ + $4\frac{1}{3}$ + $4\frac{1}{3}$ + $4\frac{1}{3}$ + $4\frac{1}{3}$ + $4\frac{1}{3}$ = 26 inches

    Time: 15 min + 15 min + 15 min + 15 min + 15 min + 15 min = $1\frac{1}{2}$ hours

    Method 2: Using a math proportion equation.

    $$\frac{\text{inches}}{\text{hours}} : \frac{4\frac{1}{3}}{\frac{1}{4}} = \frac{26}{x} \quad \text{Step 1: Set up a proportion.}$$

    $$4\frac{1}{3}x = \frac{1}{4} \times 26 \quad \text{Step 2: Convert } 4\frac{1}{3} \text{ into an improper fraction.}$$

    $$\frac{13}{3}x = \frac{13}{2}$$

    $$x = \frac{3}{2} = 1\frac{1}{2} \quad \text{Step 3: Multiply each side of the equation by } \frac{3}{13}.$$

11. **C and E.** Remember, we are looking for integer values. Since the perimeter of the rectangle is 40, the length plus the width of the rectangle is 20. The width and length values of 1 and 19, 2 and 18, 3 and 17, and 4 and 16 are all eliminated since the width is less than one-third the length. A width of 5 and a length of 15 produces an area of 75. A width of 6 and a length of 14 would work, but the product is not one of the answer choices. The same is true for 7 and 13. A width of 8 and a length of 12 produces an area of 96, which is the other correct answer choice. The width of 8 and the length of 12 are acceptable since 8 is two-thirds of 12.

12. D. Start by solving the "y." Since $y \times 4$ produces a 4, y is either a 1 or a 6. ($1 \times 4 = 4$, $6 \times 4 = 24$.) If y is a 1, the first product line would have to be the repeat of $2x4$. Since this is not the case, the y must be 6.

Original problem	**Solving the "y," the problem looks like this:**
$2x4$	$2x4$
$\times\ \ \ 5y$	$\times\ \ \ 56$
$\overline{1404}$	$\overline{1404}$
$+11z00$	$+11z00$
$\overline{13104}$	$\overline{13104}$

The "x" has to be a number that when multiplied by 6 (remember, $y = 6$) and 2 is added to that ($6 \times 4 = 24$, carry the 2) the result ends in a zero. Only the values 3 or 8 can work. If $x = 8$, then $284 \times 6 = 1,704$, but the problem says it will be 1,404; hence, $x \neq 8$. Therefore, $x = 3$ and $234 \times 6 = 1,404$, as expected. Finally, since 4 adds with z to make a number that ends in a 1, z must be 7.

Therefore, $x = 3$, $y = 6$, and $z = 7$.

$$x + yz = 3 + (6)(7)$$
$$= 3 + 42 \qquad \text{Recall order of operations.}$$
$$= 45$$

13. A. To answer this problem, first find 12% of 250: $0.12 \times 250 = 30$, which means that 30 sailors are 20 to 25 years old. The remaining sailors are ages 26 to 35, which represents 10 age groups. Since there are 250 sailors total, and 30 sailors are 25 years old and younger, then 220 sailors are 26 to 30 years old. Knowing that the remaining sailors are evenly distributed, divide the 220 by the 10 age groups remaining: $220 \div 10 = 22$.

14. B. Start by finding the sum of the sales of regular unleaded gasoline and diesel fuel.

$$150 \text{ gallons of regular unleaded gasoline} \times \$3.50 \text{ per gallon} = \$525 \qquad \$525$$
$$100 \text{ gallons of diesel fuel} \times \$3.45 \text{ per gallon} = \$345 \qquad\qquad \underline{+\ \$345}$$
$$\$870$$

Next, find the difference between the total sales and the sum of regular and diesel fuel to calculate the total sales of premium unleaded gasoline.

$$\$1,612 \quad \text{(total sales of all three grades of gasoline)}$$
$$\underline{-\ \$870} \quad \text{(total sales of regular and diesel)}$$
$$\$742$$

Divide $742 by the amount sold to arrive at the price per gallon of premium unleaded gasoline, $742 \div 200 = \$3.71$.

The percentage change $= \dfrac{\text{amount of change}}{\text{starting amount}} \times 100\%$.

The change from \$3.50 to \$3.71 is \$0.21. The starting amount was \$3.50.

$$\frac{0.21}{3.50} = .06 = 6\%$$

15. B. Carol rounds to the nearest thousand and then adds up the values:

$$\$45,000 + \$57,000 + \$73,000 = \$175,000$$

Ivan rounds to the nearest ten and then adds up the values:

$$\$45,260 + \$57,250 + \$72,980 = \$175,490$$

The difference between these amounts is $\$175,490 - \$175,000 = \$490$.

16. **D.** Owner B used 1,080 minutes, 80 more than the basic plan allows. These extra minutes cost $0.50 each, or a total of (80)($0.50) = $40. Owner C used 1,420 minutes, 20 more than the family plan allows. These extra minutes cost $0.40 each, or a total of (20)($0.40) = $8. Owner B's extra-minute cost exceeded Owner C's extra-minute cost by $40 − $8 = $32. To calculate the percentage, divide this difference by Owner C's extra-minute cost, or $32 ÷ $8 = 4 = 400%.

17. **E.** Calculate Owner B's savings:

Existing basic plan: $70 + (1,080 − 1,000)($0.50) = $70 + $40 = $110
Using the family plan: $90 + (0)($0.40) = $90
Savings using the family plan instead of the basic plan: $110 − $90 = $20

Calculate Owner D's savings:

Existing smartphone plan: $120 + (0)($0.25) = $120
Using the family plan: $90 + (0)($0.40) = $90
Savings using the family plan instead of the smartphone plan: $120 − $90 = $30

Combined savings: $20 + $30 = $50

18. **D.** A slope of $-\frac{2}{3}$ means either $\frac{-2}{3}$ or $\frac{2}{-3}$. Slope means $\frac{rise}{run}$. Therefore, from one point to another point, you can either have a "rise" of −2 and a "run" of +3, or a "rise" of +2 and a "run" of −3. If you start at (−3, 5) on a graph, and do a "rise" of −2 and a "run" of +3, you would be at the point (0, 3), which is not one of the answer choices. If you start at (−3, 5) and do a "rise" of +2 and a "run" of −3, you would be at (−6, 7), choice D.

19. $\frac{11}{16}$

Method 1: The long (time-consuming) method would be to write out all the possible outcomes for flipping a coin four times and count how many consist of at least two heads.

$$\text{HHHH} \quad \text{HHHT} \quad \text{HHTH} \quad \text{HHTT}$$
$$\text{HTHH} \quad \text{HTHT} \quad \text{HTTH} \quad \text{HTTT}$$
$$\text{THHH} \quad \text{THHT} \quad \text{THTH} \quad \text{THTT}$$
$$\text{TTHH} \quad \text{TTHT} \quad \text{TTTH} \quad \text{TTTT}$$

Eleven out of the sixteen possibilities contain at least two heads. Therefore, the probability of getting at least two "heads" is $\frac{11}{16}$.

Method 2: The faster method.

This is a binomial probability method. The values are 1, 4, 6, 4, 1. So, there is 1 way of getting all four heads, 4 ways of getting three heads and one tail, 6 ways of getting two heads and two tails, 4 ways of getting one head and three tails, and 1 way of getting all four tails. Add 1 plus 4 plus 6 to get 11 out of 16 possible outcomes.

20. **C.** To help you solve this problem, separate the three equations and solve individually for each variable.

$$\frac{40}{x} = 30 \qquad \frac{70}{y} = 30 \qquad \frac{160}{z} = 30$$

$$40 = 30x \qquad 70 = 30y \qquad 160 = 30z$$

$$\frac{40}{30} = x \qquad \frac{70}{30} = y \qquad \frac{160}{30} = z$$

$$\frac{4}{3} = x \qquad \frac{7}{3} = y \qquad \frac{16}{3} = z$$

Now add the three variables together: $x + y + z = \frac{4}{3} + \frac{7}{3} + \frac{16}{3} = \frac{27}{3} = 9$.

21. **D.** The easiest way to solve this problem is rewrite each of the values in decimal form and then organize the values from greatest to least.

Original Values	−5.15	$-\frac{26}{5}$	$-5\frac{1}{2}$	−5
Decimal Form	−5.15	−5.20	−5.50	−5.00

Remember to put $-\frac{26}{5}$ in decimal form. You must divide −26 by 5 to get −5.2 (the same as −5.20) in decimal form. When you rewrite $-5\frac{1}{2}$ in decimal form, you get −5.5 (the same as −5.50). When you rewrite −5 in decimal form, you get −5.0 (the same as −5.00).

The number line below will help you visualize the values. The farther to the right a number falls on the number line, the greater its value. Since the order requested is from greatest to least, look for the number value farthest to the right first and then list the numbers as you go to the left.

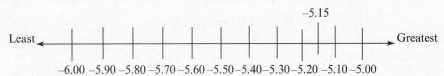

22. **C.** Solve the original equation for A.

$$4A + 20 = B$$

$4A = B - 20$ Subtract 20 from each side of the equation.

$A = \frac{B}{4} - \frac{20}{4}$ Divide each side of the equation by 4.

$A = \frac{B}{4} - 5$

$A + 12 = \frac{B}{4} - 5 + 12$ Add 12 to each side of the equation.

$A + 12 = \frac{B}{4} + 7$

23. **C.** Choices A, B, and E are incorrect. In order to be correct, they need to read "Divide b into a, move the decimal point two places to the right, and add a percent sign." Choice D is also incorrect; in order to be correct, it needs to read "Solve the proportion $\frac{a}{b} = \frac{x}{100}$ and add a percent sign to the value of x." Multiplying a number by 100 and adding a percent sign will not change its value but will express it as a percentage.

24. D. Probability compares favorable outcomes to total outcomes. To find total outcomes, you need to see how many natural numbers there are from 21 to 50. The most common error made is to simply subtract 21 from 50 to get 29. When you do this, you are forgetting to count the number 21. There are 30 natural numbers from 21 to 50.

Next, you need to list how many of the numbers from 21 to 50 are prime numbers. The prime numbers from 21 to 50 are 23, 29, 31, 37, 41, 43, and 47. So, there are 7 prime numbers. Therefore, the probability is $\frac{7}{30}$.

25. C. Six equal spaces are marked from 0 to 1, which makes each space represent a length of $\frac{1}{6}$. This puts C at $\frac{4}{6}$ and D at $\frac{5}{6}$. One method to determine which of the expressions has a value between $\frac{4}{6}$ and $\frac{5}{6}$ is to use decimal approximations: $\frac{4}{6} \approx 0.6667$ and $\frac{5}{6} \approx 0.8333$. Choice A, $\frac{1}{3} \times \frac{1}{5}$, has the value $\frac{1}{15} \approx 0.0667$, which is not between the C and D values. Choice B, $\frac{2}{3} - \frac{1}{5}$, has the value $\frac{7}{15} \approx 0.4667$, which also is not between the C and D values. Choice C, $\frac{1}{3} + \frac{2}{5}$, has the value $\frac{11}{15} \approx 0.7333$, which *is* between the C and D values.

Choice D, $\frac{1}{3} \div \frac{2}{5}$, has the value $\frac{5}{6}$, which is the D value, but is not *between* the C and D values.

Choice E, $\frac{2}{5} \div \frac{1}{3}$, has the value $\frac{6}{5}$, which is not between the C and D values.

26. A. First, find the quantity of hydrogen peroxide and purified water in the remaining mixture of the first solution.

$$\frac{1}{3} \text{ of } 210 = 70 \text{ ml of hydrogen peroxide}$$

$$\frac{2}{3} \text{ of } 210 = 140 \text{ ml of purified water}$$

Therefore, to obtain an equal mixture, $\frac{1}{2}$ and $\frac{1}{2}$,

$$70 + x = 140$$
$$x = 140 - 70$$
$$x = 70$$

Add 70 ml of hydrogen peroxide to the 210 ml leftover solution of hydrogen peroxide and purified water to obtain an equal mixture, choice A.

27. D. Use the following steps to solve this proportion problem. First, convert 3 hours and 30 minutes into minutes, or 210 minutes. Then use x to replace the unknown value.

$$\frac{\text{percentage}}{100} = \frac{\text{``is'' (number of minutes)}}{\text{``of '' (what number) } x}$$

$$\frac{70}{100} = \frac{210 \text{ minutes}}{x}$$

$$70x = 21{,}000$$

$$x = 300 \text{ minutes, or 5 hours}$$

28. C. The question requires a "shorter" distance to school. Therefore, choice E can be eliminated because 942 feet is greater than Jeremy's original walking distance of 800 feet.

To find the length of the diagonal walk, use the Pythagorean theorem. In any right triangle, the sum of the squares of the two legs is equal to the square of the hypotenuse.

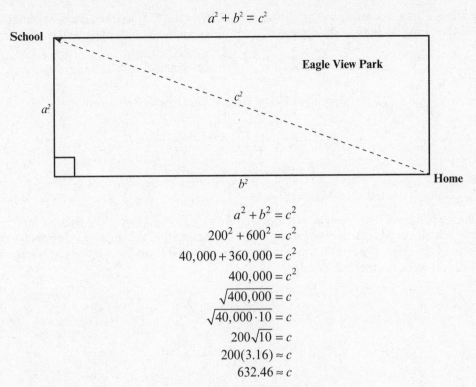

$$a^2 + b^2 = c^2$$
$$200^2 + 600^2 = c^2$$
$$40,000 + 360,000 = c^2$$
$$400,000 = c^2$$
$$\sqrt{400,000} = c$$
$$\sqrt{40,000 \cdot 10} = c$$
$$200\sqrt{10} = c$$
$$200(3.16) \approx c$$
$$632.46 \approx c$$

Therefore, the answer rounded to the nearest foot is choice C, 632 feet.

29. **B.** The top of the pyramid has 1 sugar cube. The second layer has 2 sugar cubes per side to form a square, or 4 sugar cubes. The layer below that forms a square with 3 sugar cubes per side, so it contains 9 sugar cubes. Keep adding these square numbers together until the total is 55: $1 + 4 + 9 + 16 + 25 = 55$. Hence, 5 layers of sugar cubes make up the pyramid.

30. **A.** Notice that all the choices have the variable x on the left side of the equation and the constants on the right. To answer this question, you must go through the solving process and stop when you recognize the answer.

$7x + 3(x + 5) = 2x - 7$	Distributive property.
$7x + 3x + 15 = 2x - 7$	Combine like terms.
$10x + 15 = 2x - 7$	Subtract $2x$ from each side of the equation.
$8x + 15 = -7$	Subtract 15 from each side of the equation.
$8x = -22$	

31. **E.** With segment DE parallel to segment BC, $\triangle ABC$ is similar to $\triangle ADE$. This makes corresponding sides (sides in the same relative position) proportional. Hence, $\dfrac{AD}{AB} = \dfrac{DE}{BC}$. $AD = 2$, $AB = 10$ ($AB = AD + DB$), and $DE = 6$.

Now substitute these values into the proportion and solve.

$\dfrac{2}{10} = \dfrac{6}{BC}$	Cross multiply to clear proportion.
$2BC = 60$	Divide both sides by 2.
$BC = 30$	

32. **A.** Since triangle ABC is obtuse, one of its angles is more than 90°. Since the sum of the angles of any triangle is 180° and one angle is already given as 45°, the remaining angle must be less than 45°.

(more than 90) + 45 + (remaining angle) = 180

(more than 135) + (remaining angle) = 180

(180 − more than 135 leaves less than 45)

remaining angle < 45°

The only answer choice less than 45° is choice A, 35°.

33. **C.** To find the perimeter of a triangle, add together the lengths of its sides. The triangle given is a right triangle, which means you can use the Pythagorean theorem to find the missing side because the other two sides are given. The legs of a right triangle refer to the sides that form the right angle; hence, the missing side is the hypotenuse, or the longest side.

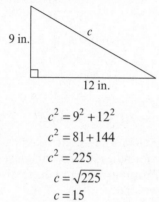

$$c^2 = 9^2 + 12^2$$
$$c^2 = 81 + 144$$
$$c^2 = 225$$
$$c = \sqrt{225}$$
$$c = 15$$

Remember, the question asked for the perimeter of the triangle, not how long the hypotenuse is. The perimeter is 9 + 12 + 15 = 36.

34. **B.** This problem tests your knowledge of the relationship between workers, time worked, and production by the workers. This problem assumes that workers work at a *constant rate,* and that the total production can be doubled by either doubling the number of workers OR doubling the length of time the workers work.

Draw a simple table to help you visualize this relationship.

# of Dozen Machines	# of Days Worked	# of Dozen Screws Produced	
$1\frac{1}{2}$	$1\frac{1}{2}$	$1\frac{1}{2}$	Starting values.
3	$1\frac{1}{2}$	3	Doubling the # of dozen machines doubles the production in the same # of days worked.
6	$1\frac{1}{2}$	6	Doubling the # of dozen machines again to represent 6 machines doubles the production in the same # of days worked.
6	3	12	Doubling the # of days worked to 3 days then doubles the # of screws produced with the same # of dozen machines.

The values in the table were easy to compute because simple doubling allowed us to reach the desired values. The same would be true if the ratios were not 2 to 1. Note that 12 dozen machines working $1\frac{1}{2}$ days or $1\frac{1}{2}$ dozen machines working 12 days would have also produced 12 dozen screws.

35. **C.** First, use proportions to find the actual distance to be traveled.

$$\frac{\text{map (cm)}}{\text{actual (miles)}}$$

$$\frac{1}{25} = \frac{15}{x} \qquad \text{Cross multiply to clear the proportion.}$$
$$x = 375$$

The distance traveled is 375 miles.

To find the amount of time it will take to travel this distance at 35 miles per hour, use the formula (rate) × (time) = (distance).

$$(35 \text{ mi/hr}) \times (t \text{ hr}) = 375 \text{ miles} \qquad \text{Divide each side of the equation by 35 mi/hr to solve for } t.$$
$$t \approx 10.7 \text{ hours}$$

The resulting time is estimated between 10 and 11 hours.

36. **A.** Since $\triangle ABC$ is congruent to $\triangle DEF$, segment AC has the same length as segment DF. Point A is located at $(-7, -5)$ and point C is located at $(-4, -1)$. To get from point A to point C, move 3 units to the right and 4 units up. Then to get from point D to point F, do the same thing. Point D is located at $(1, 6)$. Moving 3 units to the right and 4 units up brings you to $(4, 10)$.

37. **D.** Use the Venn diagram with three overlapping ovals to help visualize the information; then transfer the numbers onto a piece of paper. Then construct a table to summarize the information given. Let x represent the number of teachers registered in Workshop A only, let y represent the number of teachers registered in Workshop B only, and let z represent the number of teachers registered in Workshop C only. To answer the question, find the value of z.

Remember that <u>each</u> workshop has an enrollment of 30 teachers. Make sure you carefully read the question.

Workshop A	Workshop B	Workshop C
$x + 2 + 12 + 5 = 30$ $x = 11$	$y + 5 + 12 + 4 = 30$ $y = 9$	$z + 2 + 12 + 4 = 30$ $z = 12$

There are 12 teachers registered in Workshop C.

38. $\frac{7}{9}$ Probability is the comparison of the number of favorable outcomes in an event versus the total number of outcomes possible in the event.

$$\text{Probability} = \frac{\text{\# favorable}}{\text{\#total}}$$

The following table shows a setup for viewing all the possibilities. The top row contains the possibilities for one die, and the far left column contains the possibilities for the other die.

Product	1	2	3	4	5	6
1	✓	✓	✓	✓	✓	✓
2	✓	✓	✓	✓	✓	✓
3	✓	✓	✓	✓	✓	✓
4	✓	✓	✓	✓		
5	✓	✓	✓			
6	✓	✓	✓			

Notice there are 36 total spaces within the table, indicating a total of 36 possible outcomes. In this table, check marks are placed where the product of the numbers on the two dice is less than 20. Recall that *product* is the answer to multiplication. The locations for 4×5 and 5×4 are blank because 20 is *not* less than 20. There are 28 favorable outcomes.

Therefore, the probability is $\dfrac{28}{36} = \dfrac{7}{9}$.

39. D. One approach is to look for a pattern using the differences between the consecutive numbers.

From 1 to 4, there is a difference of 3.

From 4 to 9, there is difference of 5.

From 9 to 16, there is a difference of 7.

From 16 to 25, there is a difference of 9.

Based on this pattern, the next difference should be 11 and then 13 after that.

$$25 + 11 = 36, \text{ and } 36 + 13 = 49$$

Another approach is to recognize the numbers as being special numbers.

$1 = 1^2, 4 = 2^2, 9 = 3^2, 16 = 4^2, 25 = 5^2$, so the next two numbers should be 6^2 and 7^2, or 36 and 49.

40. D. This problem can be easily solved using proportions.

$$\frac{\text{kilograms}}{\text{pounds}} : \frac{1}{2.2} = \frac{x}{220} \qquad \text{Clear the proportion by cross multiplying.}$$
$$2.2x = 220 \qquad \text{Divide each side of the equation by 2.2.}$$
$$x = 100$$

41. C, D, and E. The triangle inequality theorem states that the sum of any two sides of a triangle must be greater than the third side. Since the given triangle has two sides with lengths of 7 and 15, the length of the third side, x, must be

$$15 - 7 < x < 15 + 7$$
$$8 < x < 22$$

Hence, 15, 16, and 21 are possible values of x.

42. C. The area A of a rectangle with base b and height h is

$$A = bh$$
$$= (100 \text{ feet})(180 \text{ feet})$$
$$= 18,000 \text{ square feet}$$

Since there are 9 square feet in 1 square yard (3 feet × 3 feet), the number of square yards of carpet needed is $18,000 \div 9 = 2,000$.

43. B. The median of a set of 15 different numbers is the middle (8th) number when the numbers have been written in order from smallest to largest or from largest to smallest. Decreasing the smallest number only would have no effect on the middle number of the set and the median would be unchanged. Each of the other answer choices would change the median.

44. D. The fastest method to solve this problem is to add all of the quizzes at 70% and then add all of the quizzes at 80%.

Score	Frequency (f)	Total Points
70	8	560
80	7	560
Total	15	1,120

The average is determined by dividing the total points by the number of quizzes,

$$1{,}120 \div 15 = 74\frac{2}{3}, \text{ or } 74.67\%$$

45. D. There are 6 perfect squares between 10 and 91: 16, 25, 36, 49, 64, and 81. Since there are 80 integers between 10 and 91, there are $80 - 6 = 74$ integers that are not perfect squares.

46. 300 Let x = the number of \$4 plants and $2x$ = the number of \$3 plants.

Since \$1,000 worth of plants were purchased,

$$4x + 3(2x) = 1{,}000$$
$$4x + 6x = 1{,}000$$
$$10x = 1{,}000$$
$$\frac{10x}{10} = \frac{1{,}000}{10}$$
$$x = 100 = \text{the number of \$4 plants.}$$
$$2x = 200 = \text{the number of \$3 plants.}$$

Hence, the total number of plants purchased was $100 + 200 = 300$ plants.

47. C. Since there are a total of 160 voters polled ($84 + 65 + 11 = 160$) with 84 voters favoring candidate x, the fraction of those polled who favored candidate x is

$$\frac{84}{160} = \frac{21}{40}$$

48. E. Since each of the 5 exterior colors can be paired with each of the 3 interior colors, there are $5 \cdot 3 = 15$ possible color combinations.

49. B. The percent of people in Baltimore earning less than \$10,000 per year is approximately 13.8%. The percent of people earning more than \$200,000 per year is approximately 2.5%. Therefore, the difference in earnings by percent is $13.8\% - 2.5\% = 11.3\%$. Choice B, 11%, is the closest approximation to 11.3%.

50. **A and B.** Test each of the answer choices:

Choice A: If $a = -3$, $a^2 - 3a = (-3)^2 - 3(-3) = 9 + 9 = 18 > 10$. -3 CANNOT be a value of a.

Choice B: If $a = -2$, $a^2 - 3a = (-2)^2 - 3(-2) = 4 + 6 = 10$. -2 CANNOT be a value of a.

Choice C: If $a = -1$, $a^2 - 3a = (-1)^2 - 3(-1) = 1 + 3 = 4 < 10$. -1 can be a value of a.

Choice D: If $a = 3$, $a^2 - 3a = (3)^2 - 3(3) = 9 - 9 = 0 < 10$. 3 can be a value of a.

Choice E: If $a = 4$, $a^2 - 3a = (4)^2 - 3(4) = 16 - 12 = 4 < 10$. 4 can be a value of a.

Therefore, only choices A and B cannot be values of a.

51. **D.** There are two methods you can use to solve this problem.

Method 1: Using arithmetic and logic. First convert 6 hours to minutes.

$$6 \text{ hours} \times 60 = 360 \text{ minutes}$$

Now find how long it takes to install one hinge.

$$15 \text{ dozen hinges equals } 15 \times 12 = 180 \text{ hinges}$$

$$360 \text{ minutes} \div 180 \text{ hinges} = 2 \text{ minutes to install one hinge}$$

Now, go back to the word problem, "How many minutes will it take to replace 36 hinges?"

$$36 \text{ hinges} \times 2 \text{ minutes each} = 72 \text{ minutes to install 36 hinges}$$

Method 2: Using algebra. Since 15 dozen $= 15 \cdot 12 = 180$ hinges,

$$\frac{6 \text{ hours}}{180 \text{ hinges}} = \frac{x \text{ hours}}{36 \text{ hinges}}$$
$$180 \cdot x = 6 \cdot 36$$
$$180 \cdot x = 216$$
$$\frac{180x}{180} = \frac{216}{180}$$
$$x = \frac{6}{5} \text{ hours}$$

The number of minutes is $\dfrac{6}{5} \cdot 60 = \dfrac{360}{5} = 72$ minutes.

52. **C.** To find the surface area of the right cylinder, picture the circular top and bottom removed and the shell rolled out to form a rectangle.

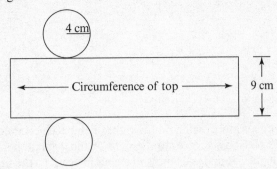

Add together the areas of the two circles and the area of the rectangular shell. The area of a circle is found by using the formula $A = \pi r^2$. The radius of each circle is 4 cm; therefore, the area of each circle is $(4)^2\pi$ or 16π cm^2. The rectangular shell has a length the same as the circumference of the top of the cylinder. The formula for the circumference of a circle is $C = \pi d$, where d is the diameter of the circle. Since the circle has a radius of 4 cm, its diameter is 8 cm. The rectangle has an area of $8\pi \times 9 = 72\pi$ cm^2. The total surface area is $2(16\pi) + 72\pi = 32\pi + 72\pi = 104\pi$ cm^2.

To find the volume of a right cylinder, use the formula $V = $ (area of base) $\times$ (height). The area of the base of the cylinder is 16π and the height of this cylinder is 9 cm. The volume of this cylinder is, therefore, $(16\pi$ cm$^2)(9$ cm$) = 144\pi$ cm^3.

The volume of the cylinder is greater than the surface area by 40π, choice C:

$$144\pi - 104\pi = 40\pi$$

53. **C.** The club has 25 married men and 15 single men as members, so there are 40 males total. The total number of members in the club is 120. The probability of randomly selecting a male is $\dfrac{40}{120}$, which reduces to $\dfrac{1}{3}$.

54. **B and E.** To find the solution, express each equation in the form $y = mx + b$, where m is the slope of the line:

Choice A: If $4x + 3y = 20$, then $y = \dfrac{-4}{3}x + \dfrac{20}{3}$ and $m = \dfrac{-4}{3}$.

Choice B: If $3x + 4y = 20$, then $y = \dfrac{-3}{4}x + 5$ and $m = \dfrac{-3}{4}$.

Choice C: If $4x - 3y = 20$, then $y = \dfrac{4}{3}x - \dfrac{20}{3}$ and $m = \dfrac{4}{3}$.

Choice D: If $3x - 4y = 20$, then $y = \dfrac{3}{4}x - 5$ and $m = \dfrac{3}{4}$.

Choice E: If $9x + 12y = 20$, then $y = \dfrac{-9}{12}x + \dfrac{20}{12} = \dfrac{-3}{4}x + \dfrac{5}{3}$ and $m = \dfrac{-3}{4}$.

Choices B and E have the same slope, $\dfrac{-3}{4}$.

55. E.

$4 = 2^2, 4^4 = (2^2)^4 = 2^8$

$8 = 2^3, 8^3 = (2^3)^3 = 2^9$

$16 = 2^4, 16^2 = (2^4)^2 = 2^8$

Therefore, $4^4 \cdot 8^3 \cdot 16^2 = 2^8 \cdot 2^9 \cdot 2^8 = 2^{25}$.

56. **E.** The tenth place is the number immediately to the right of the decimal point. To round off to the nearest tenth, check the hundredths place (two places to the right of the decimal point). If the number in the hundredths place is a 5 or higher, round the tenths place number up to the next number. For instance, 0.36 would round to 0.4. If the hundredths place number is a 4 or lower, simply drop any places after the tenths place. For instance, 0.74356 would round to 0.7. Thus, 4,316.136 rounded to the nearest tenth is 4,316.1, choice E.

Reading Test

TIME: 85 Minutes

56 Questions

Directions: A question or number of questions follows each of the statements or passages in this section. Using only the *stated* or *implied* information given in the statement or passage, answer the question or questions by choosing the *best* answer from among the choices given. You are not expected to have any previous knowledge of the topics in the passages or statements.

Remember: Answer choices in this study guide have lettered choices A, B, C, D, and E for clarity, but answer choice letters will *not* appear on the actual exam. On the actual computer version of the exam, you will be required to click on ovals, click on squares, or click on a sentence to highlight your answer in the passage.

Questions 1 and 2 refer to the following passage.

In order for an individual to judge whether two or more speech sounds are alike or different, the sounds must be kept in memory and retrieved for comparison. This process also comes into
(5) play when determining spatial elements of sounds, particularly when making more difficult judgments, such as determining the location of a muffled, ringing cell phone or whether a car horn is coming from a radio advertisement or a nearby
(10) vehicle.

1. The passage supports which of the following conclusions?

A. Most speech sounds are more different than they are alike.

B. Visual discrimination is easier than auditory discrimination.

C. A number of individuals cannot discriminate between different sounds.

D. People with good memories are also good listeners.

E. A person cannot compare two sounds at the moment they occur.

2. Which of the following illustrates an example of the *difficult judgments* as referenced in lines 6–7 of the passage?

A. Instinctively deciding to swerve when hearing a honking car horn

B. Detecting a faint cell phone vibration in one's pocket

C. Locating an out-of-view basketball teammate calling for a pass

D. Identifying the species of bird making a particular birdcall

E. Differentiating two similar voices on a conference call

GO ON TO THE NEXT PAGE

Questions 3–5 refer to the following passage.

Anthropologists and molecular biologists are working on a project to find forgotten human migration routes by searching for genetic footprints. They have run into some
(5) problems because many indigenous groups—for example, in the Americas and Australia—are reluctant to submit DNA samples. The reasons are varied. One is fear that pharmaceutical companies might exploit useful
(10) details in the genetic makeup of these groups, profit largely from it, and pay them nothing. Another reason unrelated to financial issues is that information about the migration routes of their ancestors might contradict a group's own
(15) cultural traditions about its origins. For example, Native Americans who believe they have always occupied certain lands don't want to be told that it is likely their ancestors arrived from Siberia 13,000 years ago. The desire for
(20) genetic privacy among some of these native peoples is understandable, considering a history of oppression and mistreatment.

3. It can be inferred from the passage that

A.   some indigenous groups do not believe in the validity of genetics.

B.   reluctance to submit DNA samples may be due to past injustices.

C.   indigenous people who won't submit DNA samples may prevent discovery of lifesaving pharmaceuticals.

D.   in spite of overwhelming evidence, Native Americans do not accept Siberia as their country of origin.

E.   the researchers probably have ulterior motives in their tracking of migrations.

4. In the context of the passage, many indigenous groups

A.   refuse to be part of the modern world.

B.   are uneducated.

C.   do not respect scientific inquiry.

D.   want to preserve cultural traditions about their origins.

E.   would be willing to submit DNA if they were paid for it.

5. Which of the following exemplifies a concern of the indigenous groups discussed in the passage?

Select **all** that apply.

A.   The DNA makeup of a Native American inspires a new drug, from which he or she only receives a small percentage of the profits.

B.   Migration information shows that the oral history of an Australian tribe is incorrect.

C.   A research group introduces a rural indigenous group to a virus to which they have no antibodies.

Questions 6–8 refer to the following passage.

Sales of hybrid electric bicycles have been increasing rapidly in European markets in recent years, with some countries reporting that as many as 50 percent of new bicycle purchases
(5) are electric. Particularly in compact urban areas, workers and students find that electric bicycles provide a practical compromise between the frustration of fighting road and rail traffic and the discomfort of arriving at work or
(10) class dripping in sweat from a strenuous bike ride. The American market has been slower to catch on, but early indicators show strong potential for sales growth. Proponents of electric bicycles point to anticipated rises in
(15) both fuel prices and population densities as evidence that sales should continue to increase over the coming decade.

6. Which of the following sentences could most logically be placed at the end of the passage after … *increase over the coming decade* (lines 16–17) to weaken the point in the last sentence?

A.   However, many electric bicycles are sold in cool climates.

B.   However, European fads often catch on in the United States.

C.   However, only a small portion of bicycles sold in some European markets are electronic.

D.   However, studies have shown that most electric bicycles are not very fuel-efficient.

E.   However, Americans are notoriously reluctant to use public transit.

GO ON TO THE NEXT PAGE

7. The author's primary purpose in the passage is to

   A. introduce the reader to the concept of electric bicycles.

   B. identify several potential roadblocks to the future growth of electric bicycles.

   C. describe the current and future market for electric bicycles.

   D. give a history of the electric bicycle's rise to prominence.

   E. convince the reader to consider the purchase of an electric bicycle.

8. Select the sentence in the passage that describes the niche in the transportation market filled by electric bicycles.

Questions 9–15 refer to the following passage.

Michael Shermer, author of the book *How We Believe,* uses the word "patternicity" to describe people's tendency to find meaningful patterns in what they see, or think they see, in
(5) nature. Our brains, Shermer says, are "pattern recognition machines." Sometimes the patterns or connections we see are real. When they are, we learn things about our environment that are useful in survival. As Shermer says, we are the
(10) descendants of "those most successful at finding patterns."

But, according to Shermer, our brains don't always distinguish between true and false patterns. We did not, as Shermer says, evolve a
(15) "Baloney Detection Network." Therefore, we need science with its "self-correcting mechanisms of replication and peer review" to help us separate false patterns from real ones.

If Shermer is correct, why didn't we, through
(20) natural selection, develop a "Baloney Detection Network"? Harvard University biologist Kevin R. Foster and University of Helsinki biologist Hanna Kokko tested Shermer's theory. Through evolutionary modeling and a series of complex
(25) formulas, Foster and Kokko concluded that "the inability of individuals, human or otherwise, to assign causal probabilities to all sets of events that occur around them will often force them to lump causal associations with non-causal
(30) ones.... Natural selection will favor strategies that make incorrect causal associations in order to establish those associations that are essential for survival and reproduction." For example,

predators avoid nonpoisonous snakes that mimic
(35) poisonous species in areas where the poisonous species is common. If they didn't employ this "false patterning," they would be in danger from the snakes that are actually poisonous. Natural selection, therefore, has perhaps rewarded
(40) patternicity, even when the patterns are false.

9. According to the passage, *patternicity* (line 2) can best be described as

   A. the tendency to see connections and patterns in nature.

   B. a uniquely human trait that causes the mind to make erroneous connections.

   C. the mind's ability to separate false patterns from real ones.

   D. a series of causal probabilities that are subject to interpretation.

   E. the willingness to create false meanings for connected events.

10. Shermer uses the term *Baloney Detection Network* (line 15) to describe which of the following?

   A. The function of science in detecting false patterning

   B. A natural ability to separate false patterns from real ones

   C. The replication of experimental results

   D. Nonscientific methodologies employed by scientists

   E. A characteristic of humankind developed through natural selection

11. According to Foster and Kokko's experimentation,

   A. false causal associations are a result of the failure of the "Baloney Detection Network."

   B. natural selection has eliminated the tendency of the human brain to make false connections.

   C. the ability to see both false and true causal relationships can lead to survival.

   D. natural selection favors predators that can discriminate between poisonous and nonpoisonous snakes.

   E. instinct is the key factor in a predator's ability to sense danger.

GO ON TO THE NEXT PAGE

12. According to the passage, Foster and Kokko's conclusions assume that

    A. what Shermer calls patternicity is actually instinct.

    B. nonpoisonous snakes can purposely mimic poisonous ones.

    C. nonhuman species share the tendency to recognize patterns with humans.

    D. patternicity is a negative phenomenon in humans.

    E. Shermer's referring to the brain as a "pattern recognition machine" is misleading.

13. According to the passage, which of the following presents an example of an incorrect but beneficial causal association?

Select **all** that apply.

    A. A solider reacting to a harmless sound that resembles a gunshot by ducking

    B. Having a phobia of water due to a childhood trauma

    C. Instinctively rolling one's car windows up upon hearing thunder

14. Select the sentence in the passage that best answers the question raised by the author in lines 19–21, reproduced below.

If Shermer is correct, why didn't we, through natural selection, develop a "Baloney Detection Network"?

15. Which of the following best describes the logical organization of the passage?

    A. Discuss the work of Michael Shermer; provide a critique of his work; provide supporting evidence for the critique.

    B. Define "patternicity"; give a background of the concept; discuss its implications on current scientific process.

    C. Define a theory; poke holes in the theory; discuss an alternate theory.

    D. Describe a concept; raise a question about the concept; answer the question.

    E. Define "patternicity"; present results of a related study; state a conclusion.

Questions 16–18 refer to the following passage.

If we must have evaluation, at least do it without grades. Grades are not good indicators of intellectual ability; we must eliminate them. Then we will have students who are motivated by (5) factors such as interest, factors more important than a letter on a transcript. And the abolition of grades will encourage us to concentrate less on evaluation and more on instruction.

16. According to the passage, the author would most likely agree that

    A. wherever grades exist, instruction is poor.

    B. there are better indicators of intellectual ability than grades.

    C. graded students are not good students.

    D. intellectual ability can be measured only in a scholastic situation.

    E. grades are the only remaining hindrance to effective education.

17. Based on the passage, readers would conclude that the author feels that students would ideally be more motivated by

    A. the prospect of a high grade point average.

    B. interest in the subject matter of their course.

    C. the grading criteria established by their instructors.

    D. a prepared and engaging instructor.

    E. the practicality of academic disciplines.

18. Which of the following best describes the intended audience for the passage?

    A. Politicians

    B. Parents

    C. Students

    D. Teachers

    E. Civic leaders

GO ON TO THE NEXT PAGE

Questions 19–21 refer to the following passage.

According to a recent Harris Poll of 2,600 respondents, 72 percent of Americans believe their actions have a significant effect on the environment. However, 25 percent of that subsection of (5) respondents also admit that they haven't taken any steps to reduce their environmental footprint. What the poll shows is that enthusiasm for "living green" is growing, but at the same time many respondents are uncertain of what steps to take in their daily lives.

19. It can be inferred from the passage that the author believes that

   A. the sampling in the polls was too small to be of any significance.

   B. people are unwilling to change their habits or their lifestyles.

   C. the failure to "live green" is based on a lack of information.

   D. the media doesn't cover environmental problems sufficiently.

   E. many people answered the poll questions dishonestly.

20. In the context of the passage, which of the following best describes the author's attitude about the data produced by the Harris Poll?

   A. Optimistic

   B. Elated

   C. Confused

   D. Frustrated

   E. Skeptical

21. Which of the following, if true, would cast the most doubt on the author's conclusion on the state of "living green" in the final sentence?

   A. The 25 percent statistic referenced in the passage was actually just 25 percent of the entire poll sample.

   B. Twenty-two percent of the respondents who believed their actions affected the environment also indicated that they did not care.

   C. Previous polls have shown that up to 50 percent of Americans have failed to take steps to reduce their environmental footprint.

   D. Younger generations are more likely to be environmentally aware than are older generations.

   E. A new initiative to educate Americans on how to reduce their environmental impact is about to be unveiled.

Questions 22–24 refer to the following passage.

Although the 1906 games in Athens are written into the record books as Olympic games, some purists argue that the 1906 games in Athens shouldn't really be considered Olympic games. (5) An Olympiad occurs once every four years, and the correct interval was not followed. The correct interval would be the St. Louis games (1904) followed by the London games (1908). The recognition of the 1906 games in Athens as (10) Olympic games is important for Americans in particular because the 1906 games were the first time the United States had a real Olympic team: thirty-five athletes, financed by nationwide donations. The participating athletes were (15) selected by an American Olympic committee, headed by its honorary chairman President Theodore Roosevelt, who had always enthusiastically supported all athletics.

22. The primary purpose of the passage is to

   A. explain why the 1906 games in Athens are not officially considered Olympic games.

   B. show the importance of Theodore Roosevelt to the development of an American team.

   C. describe the selection process for Olympic athletes.

   D. document the first time the United States had a real Olympic team.

   E. criticize those who don't accept the 1906 contest as true Olympic games.

23. As used in the first sentence (line 3), the term *purists* most nearly means

   A. Olympic historians.

   B. people of limited imagination.

   C. people who adhere strictly to a definition.

   D. people who are not corrupted by popular opinion.

   E. uninformed amateurs.

GO ON TO THE NEXT PAGE

24. According to the passage, which of the following conclusions can be drawn about the committee in charge of organizing the 1906 Olympics?

  A. They did not believe that the passing of an Olympiad was necessary for a new Olympic games.

  B. They had a particular appreciation for Athens' Olympic history.

  C. They were chaired by President Theodore Roosevelt.

  D. They funded the entire Olympics with donations.

  E. They lacked respect for standard Olympic traditions and customs.

Questions 25 and 26 refer to the following passage.

In many of Vincent van Gogh's best-known paintings, it is the vibrant strokes of yellow that catch the viewer's eye and linger in the mind. However, in some of the artist's signature works,
(5) such as *Starry Night* and his series of sunflower paintings, the formerly brilliant yellow hues are fading, changing to an unattractive muddy-looking brown. An international team of European scientists is now struggling to find the
(10) cause and, even more important, to ascertain if the process can be reversed. They at least hope to mitigate the damage.

25. Which of the following is an unstated assumption in this passage?

  A. Vincent van Gogh utilized an unusual shade of yellow in his paintings.

  B. The effect of the yellow hue van Gogh used is to attract the eye and to make the paintings more memorable.

  C. A number of paintings by Vincent van Gogh, such as *Starry Night* and the sunflower series, are quite well known.

  D. These paintings by Vincent van Gogh are treasured by many people and, thus, their restoration is considered to be very important.

  E. An international team of European scientists struggled for years before they finally discovered the cause of the damage.

26. The author suggests that which of the following is true about van Gogh's *Starry Night*?

Select **all** that apply.

  A. It was painted with streaks of vibrant yellow.

  B. It is van Gogh's most famous work of art.

  C. It has been ruined beyond the point of repair.

Questions 27 and 28 refer to the following passage.

The recycling of electronic waste (or "e-waste") is becoming an increasingly complicated issue. Only parts of electronics that contain reusable metals like copper are recycled; the rest of the
(5) waste is "outsourced" to third-world countries, including Ghana, where it is burned in scrap yards. Burning often releases chemicals such as lead and mercury into the air, which results in severe health implications for anyone who inhales
(10) the chemical vapors.

27. According to the passage, what conclusion can be drawn about the recycling of e-waste?

  A. The health of Ghanaians has suffered significantly as a result of recycling outsourcing.

  B. E-waste is never actually recycled, only burned.

  C. If a part of an electronic device does not contain a reusable metal, the device is not recycled.

  D. Immediate legislation is needed to reform the recycling of e-waste.

  E. Electronics should not be recycled under the current system.

28. The author finds fault with which of the following parts of the current e-waste recycling process?

  A. Inefficient recycling of reusable metals

  B. Long shipments to scrap yards that use significant fossil fuels

  C. Outsourcing of domestic jobs to overseas markets

  D. Burning of the non-reusable metals

  E. Precarious socioeconomic climate in Ghana

GO ON TO THE NEXT PAGE

Questions 29–34 are based on the following passage.

Some "Kermode" black bears have white fur—but why? This phenomenon ("Kermodism") is triggered by a recessive mutation at the MC1R gene, meaning both parents must carry the gene,
(5) even if the parents themselves do not have white fur.

One theory for the source of the trait was the "glacial bear" hypothesis: that Kermodism represented a remnant adaptation from the last
(10) great ice age. At that time, most of modern-day British Columbia was still icebound, and a white coat may have offered camouflage. But the glacial bear theory raised a question: Why didn't the white fur trait die out when the glaciers
(15) receded?

Researchers have recently proven that the white coat of these "spirit bears" gives them an advantage when fishing. Although white and black bears tend to have the same success after
(20) dark, scientists Dan and Reimchen Klinka noticed that white-furred bears caught almost 10% more fish during the daytime. "The salmon are less concerned about a white object as seen from below the surface," Reimchen speculates.
(25) That may answer part of the question about why the white-fur trait continues to flourish today. If salmon are a coastal bear's primary fat and protein source, a successful female can feast on salmon to store more fat for winter, potentially
(30) increasing the number of cubs she can produce.

29. Which of the following titles best summarizes the contents of the passage as a whole?

A. "A Study in Contrast: White Bears, Kermode Bears, and Spirit Bears"

B. "Feeding and Hunting Habits of Spirit Bears"

C. "Why Do Black Bears Produce White Offspring?"

D. "Black Bears Before and After the Great Ice Age"

E. "An Overview of Recessive Mutation Traits in Spirit Bears"

30. According to the passage, the author would agree with which of the following statements?

Select **all** that apply.

A. A white bear could be born to a black mother.

B. When fishing at night, black bears are more successful than white bears.

C. The glacial bear hypothesis is inadequate to explain the current prevalence of white bears.

31. In the context of the passage, the purpose of the second paragraph is to

A. expand on a secondary theme of the passage introduced earlier.

B. provide statistics that support claims made earlier in the passage.

C. propose a potential solution to the passage's main question, then discredit it.

D. acknowledge that the mystery of black bears having white fur may never be adequately solved.

E. present the most currently accepted solution to the passage's main question.

32. Which of the following outlines for a detective novel most logically follows the structure of the passage?

A. A crime with an unknown motive occurs; one detective proposes a motive that is ultimately found to be inadequate; in the second half of the book, another detective produces a motive that better fits the facts of the case.

B. Two detectives each attempt to reconstruct a robbery by assuming two different points of entry to the crime scene; the plot thickens when they discover a third point of entry, which proves to be correct.

C. An heiress disappears and foul play is assumed; a private detective is hired to question several possible assailants; in a surprise ending, the heiress is found to have staged her own disappearance.

D. A bank robbery occurs, but only a small amount of money appears to have been stolen; it turns out the robbery was staged to camouflage embezzlement by a bank manager.

E. A detective interviews two suspects who both appear guilty; ultimately, both suspects turn out to be equally culpable accomplices.

GO ON TO THE NEXT PAGE

33. According to the author, the *"glacial bear" hypothesis* (line 8) is unconvincing because it explains the

    A. behavior of white bears but not black bears.

    B. reason spirit bears are white, but not how they survived the ice age.

    C. original emergence of white bears but not their continued survival.

    D. advantage that white bears have in daytime fishing but not in reproduction.

    E. method by which some black bears are born white, but not the reason why.

34. Select the sentence in the passage that describes the most direct, current benefit of a black bear having white fur.

Questions 35–41 refer to the following two paired passages.

Passage 1

       Mexican muralists have been cognizant of Mexico's pre-Columbian past, with Diego Rivera at the forefront of those who champion it and José Clemente Orozco equally forceful in
(5) denouncing it. Rivera presented the past as an ideal world, while David Alfaro Siqueiros invoked a successful fight against the oppressor. To Orozco, however, this pre-Columbian world was inhabited by vengeful, inhospitable gods.
(10)   At any rate, whatever the attitudes toward their pre-Columbian past, negative or positive, all used a European pictorial expression and fresco technique. The content is Mexican, the expression is Mexican, but the language is European.

Passage 2

(15)   The Mexican painter who epitomized the tendency toward romanticized nationalist history was Diego Rivera. To revitalize Mexico's poor Indian class, he created a mural to present not only its idealized ancient tradition but also its power to
(20) reconstruct the present and control the future.
      This nationalism and "indigenism" was present in the work of both Siqueiros and Orozco, but served a different purpose. Siqueiros focused on the natives' brave struggle against seemingly
(25) overwhelming forces. On the surface, Orozco disdained the use of romanticized nationalism, but nevertheless, his treatment of the positive aspects of the human condition often presented pre-Columbian figures in grand, heroic terms.

35. Which one of the following best expresses the relationship between the subject of Passages 1 and 2?

    A. The reaction to colonialism by twentieth-century Mexican muralists

    B. The techniques dominating the work of Mexican muralists

    C. Pre-Columbian gods and goddesses in the works of the muralists

    D. The differences among the three main Mexican muralists

    E. Pre-Columbian influence on three Mexican muralists

36. Which of the following can be inferred from information presented in Passage 1 and Passage 2?

    A. Diego Rivera most successfully captured pre-Columbian history in his murals.

    B. The three major muralists rejected European painting techniques.

    C. Of the three major muralists, Orozco's attitude toward the pre-Columbian past was the most ambivalent.

    D. Siqueiros primarily produced murals depicting life during the period of colonialism.

    E. Only Rivera used his art for political purposes.

37. Which one of the following statements illustrates a contrast in the relationship between Passage 1 and Passage 2?

    A. Passage 1 mentions the technique used by the muralists, whereas Passage 2 does not.

    B. Passage 2 praises the work of Rivera, Orozco, and Siqueiros, whereas Passage 1 is neutral toward Siqueiros.

    C. Passage 1 places the works of the muralists in historical context, whereas Passage 2 places them in a current sociopolitical context.

    D. Passage 2 describes the public's reaction to the works of the muralists, whereas Passage 1 does not.

    E. Passage 1 identifies Rivera as the most important of the Mexican muralists, whereas Passage 2 makes no judgment.

GO ON TO THE NEXT PAGE

38. According to Passage 1 or Passage 2, which of the following is attributed to Orozco?

Select **all** that apply.

- A. A tendency to use caricature in his works
- B. Portrayal of the gods as unfriendly
- C. A romanticized picture of the indigenous population

39. Which of the following best describes Passage 1 and Passage 2 discussions of Rivera?

- A. Passage 1 paints him as naïve; Passage 2 portrays him as sympathetic.
- B. Both passages imply that he was the most important of the muralists discussed.
- C. Passage 1 discusses his place in history; Passage 2 details his background.
- D. Both describe themes in his art; Passage 2 expands on his motives.
- E. Passage 1 presents a more intimate discussion than does Passage 2.

40. According to Passage 2, Diego Rivera's primary political intention in his mural of Mexican history was to

- A. denounce overly romanticized nationalism.
- B. depict the heroic battles of the revolution.
- C. energize the Indian population and direct it to the future.
- D. create an artistic language for modern Mexico.
- E. preserve pre-Columbian symbolism and mythology.

41. Which of the following is mentioned or implied as characterizing the Mexican muralists by Passage 1 or Passage 2?

Select **all** that apply.

- A. The use of Mexican subject matter
- B. Disdain for European art
- C. Recognition of the indigenous population

Questions 42 and 43 refer to the following passage.

While Chinese history is not the oldest in the world, Chinese civilization has remained recognizably the same in the essentials, making it the oldest homogeneous major culture in the
(5) world. The Chinese people, their language, and the essence of their culture, in spite of innovative and sometimes violent changes, have maintained certain constant characteristics. The country is so large, and the regional differences so great,
(10) that in the course of its history China might have broken up into separate nations, as Europe did after the fall of the Roman Empire, but it didn't. The reason may be that it was ruled by a very powerful and stable bureaucracy.

42. The primary purpose of the passage is the author's concern with

- A. differences between China and Europe after the fall of the Roman Empire.
- B. the relative insignificance of China's regional differences.
- C. the stability of Chinese culture and civilization.
- D. the effects of internal conflict on Chinese civilization.
- E. the effect of China's size on its culture.

43. According to the passage, China may have remained intact as a country because

- A. the Chinese people believed in the same religion.
- B. a powerful bureaucracy ruled the country.
- C. the Chinese people spoke the same language.
- D. the country was isolated from outside influences.
- E. violence and change were not part of the national character.

GO ON TO THE NEXT PAGE

Questions 44–48 refer to the following passage about The Adventures of Huckleberry Finn *by Mark Twain, 1884.*

Some tried to spoil the centennial celebration of one of America's greatest novels, *The Adventures of Huckleberry Finn,* by claiming that it and author Mark Twain were racist.

(5)   Most readers over the years have viewed this masterpiece as anything but offensive to blacks. The misunderstanding of some may lie in Twain's unmatched use of irony and the crude vernacular of river folk to tell the now-famous story.

(10)   Any doubts about Mr. Twain's views on slavery should have been dispelled by an even later work about an eccentric but clever lawyer, *Pudd'nhead Wilson* (1894) or even one particular letter from Mr. Twain himself.

(15)   Written the same year as *Finn* (1884), the letter details Twain's offer to pay the expenses of one of the first black students at Yale Law School. "I do not believe I would very cheerfully help a white student who would ask a benevolence of a stranger, but I do (20) not feel so about the other color," Twain wrote. "We have ground the manhood out of them and the shame is ours, not theirs; and we should pay for it."

On this 100th anniversary of his death, Twain might find ironic delight in the timing of the (25) publication of a letter vindicating his commitment to racial progress.

44. It can be concluded that the author wrote the passage

A.   to promote the sale of *The Adventures of Huckleberry Finn.*
B.   100 years after Mark Twain's death.
C.   to exonerate those who claim Twain's writing was racist.
D.   to tell a lesser-known story from Twain's personal life.
E.   as a condemnation of racism.

45. According to the passage, Mark Twain offered to pay the expenses of a Yale Law School student (lines 15–17) because the student

A.   was an exemplary student who deserved the opportunity.
B.   had the courage to ask him for help.
C.   was rightfully owed the assistance of whites.
D.   was poor and couldn't afford the tuition.
E.   was also a severe critic of slavery.

46. As used in the second paragraph (line 8), the word *irony* appears to have

A.   confused some readers about Twain's intentions.
B.   made the language of the river folk difficult to understand.
C.   convinced most readers that Twain's work was actually racist.
D.   provided detractors with valid reason to condemn *Pudd'nhead Wilson.*
E.   appeased Twain's critics about the author's feelings regarding slavery.

47. The term *centennial celebration* (line 1) is used to mean

A.   an annual party held in Mark Twain's honor.
B.   an anniversary of Twain's *Pudd'nhead Wilson.*
C.   the 100th anniversary of Mark Twain's birth.
D.   the 100th publication of *The Adventures of Huckleberry Finn.*
E.   the 100th anniversary of the publication of *The Adventures of Huckleberry Finn.*

48. In the context of the passage, Pudd'nhead Wilson was

A.   a Yale law student Twain befriended and financially assisted.
B.   in receipt of a letter written by Twain.
C.   a character in one of Twain's works that critics believed to be racist.
D.   the runaway slave in *The Adventures of Huckleberry Finn.*
E.   a clever but somewhat bizarre fictional character.

GO ON TO THE NEXT PAGE

Questions 49–51 refer to the following chart.

Percentage of Students Involved in Extracurricular Activities

	Music/Drama	Newspaper/Yearbook	Sports	Miscellaneous
Sophomore Girls	53%	22%	13%	12%
Sophomore Boys	62%	23%	10%	5%
Junior Girls	42%	25%	13%	20%
Junior Boys	58%	20%	10%	12%
Senior Girls	51%	26%	14%	9%
Senior Boys	63%	20%	10%	7%

49. What conclusion about the percentage of students involved in extracurricular activities in the chart above can logically be derived?

Select **all** that apply.

A. A greater percentage of senior girls are involved in sports than are sophomore girls.

B. A smaller percentage of junior girls are involved in the newspaper/yearbook than are senior girls.

C. A greater percentage of sophomore girls are involved in music/drama than are senior girls.

50. According to the chart above, which of the following identifies the third-highest percentage of participation in any group?

A. Sophomore boys involved in music/drama

B. Sophomore boys involved in miscellaneous

C. Junior boys involved in music/drama

D. Senior girls involved in newspaper/ yearbook

E. Senior boys involved in music/drama

51. The data presented in the chart above supports the development of which of the following?

A. An initiative to encourage more girls to play sports

B. Extra credit for male participation in music and drama

C. A program that encourages students not to drop sports as they age

D. Incentivizing involvement of upperclassman boys with newspaper/ yearbook

E. More broadly appealing programs in the fields of music and drama

Question 52 refers to the following statement.

Graduate students who expect to specialize in The Teaching of Writing must take English 600; either English 500 (Advanced Composition) or English 504 (Writing of Criticism); at least three literature courses concentrating on the same single century or movement; English 740 (Teaching of Writing); English 741 (Classical Rhetoric); and English 742 (Modern Rhetorical Theory).

52. According to the statement, which of the following schedules does NOT satisfy the requirements for The Teaching of Writing?

A. English 740–742, Advanced Composition, twentieth-century drama, twentieth-century poetry, twentieth-century novels, English 600

B. English 740–742, eighteenth-century poetry, eighteenth-century prose fiction, eighteenth-century drama, English 504, English 600

C. English 600, Victorian poetry, Victorian prose fiction, Victorian novels, English 500, English 740–742

D. English 600, English 500, seventeenth-century poetry, seventeenth-century drama, nineteenth-century Victorian novels, English 740–742

E. English 740, Classical Rhetoric, Modern Rhetorical Theory, English 500, English 600, Victorian poetry, Victorian prose fiction, Victorian novels

GO ON TO THE NEXT PAGE

Questions 53 and 54 refer to the following passage.

Respiration and breathing are sometimes used synonymously, but it is necessary to understand the distinction between them. All living cells respire, whereas breathing is a function of many (5) multicellular animals. Respiration is a chemical process within the cells, whereas breathing is a renewal of air or water on a surface through which an exchange of oxygen and carbon dioxide can take place. Respiration is a process of (10) releasing energy from food, whereas breathing is a method of providing oxygen for absorption and of removing carbon dioxide after respiration is complete.

53. In the context of the passage, *respiration* is a process within cells that

    A. provides oxygen.
    B. removes carbon dioxide.
    C. absorbs oxygen.
    D. provides carbon dioxide.
    E. releases energy.

54. According to the passage, it can be inferred that

    A. respiration is more important than breathing.
    B. not all multicellular animals breathe.
    C. respiration takes place on the surface, whereas breathing is cellular.
    D. without breathing, respiration could not take place.
    E. breathing and respiration are different types of chemical reactions in the cells.

Questions 55 and 56 refer to the following passage.

Parallax is a range-finding technique used to measure the distance to some nearby stars from the annual angular displacement of a nearby star against the background of more distant, relatively (5) fixed stars. Parallax can be experienced by noting the apparent position of a vertical pencil in front of your face with only your right eye, then your left eye; the pencil shifts across the background.

55. In order to make this passage clearer to a general audience, the author could do which of the following?

    A. Concede that parallax is not the only range-finding technique used by astronomers.
    B. Define "annual angular displacement" in nontechnical terms.
    C. Cite references from *Scientific American*.
    D. Explain that stars are never even "relatively" fixed.
    E. Eliminate the demonstration using a pencil.

56. The exercise in the second sentence suggests which of the following?

    A. Most people have never really considered the position of a pencil.
    B. The perceived position of any object varies according to the point from which it is observed.
    C. Parallax is also a technique used by nonscientists.
    D. One eye is always a more reliable estimator of distance than the other.
    E. A pencil is similar to a star in certain ways.

IF YOU FINISH BEFORE TIME IS CALLED, CHECK YOUR WORK ON THIS SECTION ONLY. DO NOT WORK ON ANY OTHER SECTION IN THE TEST.

Writing Test: Selected Response

TIME: 40 Minutes
40 Questions

General Directions: For each question, indicate the best answer using the directions given.

Directions for Questions 1–20: Each of the following questions contains five underlined portions (four with possible errors and one with no error). The parts not underlined in the sentence are correct and cannot be changed. Read the sentence and identify whether any of the first four underlined parts of the sentence contain an error in grammar, diction, punctuation, or capitalization. If the sentence contains no mistake, select choice E, <u>No error</u>. *No sentence has more than one error.*

1. John Steinbeck's novels <u>are memorable</u> not
   A
   only for their characters and plots <u>but also for</u>
   B
   <u>their settings</u>, which are <u>generally</u> in the Salinas
   B   C
   area, <u>and which</u> Steinbeck makes come alive
   D
   for the reader. <u>No error</u>
   E

2. Some child psychologists <u>believe that</u> children
   A
   can be so <u>affected</u> by violence in movies that
   B
   <u>they</u> may resist going to bed without a parent
   C
   checking underneath it and staying with <u>him</u>
   D
   <u>until he falls</u> asleep. <u>No error</u>
   D   E

3. The soccer team members were <u>laying</u> on the
   A
   grass instead of <u>beginning</u> practice, and the
   B
   coach, <u>who</u> seldom lost his temper, <u>began</u>
   C   D
   yelling at them. <u>No error</u>
   E

4. People <u>who</u> write <u>letters frequently recount</u> the
   A   B
   <u>same</u> experience to <u>different</u> people. <u>No error</u>
   C   D   E

5. Huong and <u>yourself</u> will attend the conference
   A
   <u>on behalf</u> of the entire company <u>and report</u>
   B   C
   the latest software technological advances to <u>us</u>
   D
   next week. <u>No error</u>
   E

6. To <u>help</u> students understand and use the
   A
   concepts of <u>science</u>, science educators <u>place</u>
   B   C
   much emphasis on observation, discovery, and
   <u>the inquiry method</u>. <u>No error</u>
   D   E

7. The <u>scope</u> of the community-redevelopment
   A
   project in Detroit <u>has been</u> enlarged and <u>will</u>
   B   C
   require a minimum of twenty-three new
   <u>workers, more or less</u>. <u>No error</u>
   D   E

8. <u>Graduate students who</u> write <u>formal</u> term
   A   B
   papers, <u>even the most hardworking,</u> sometimes
   C
   have difficulty <u>with</u> placement and order of
   D
   footnotes. <u>No error</u>
   E

9. *Avatar* <u>received</u> an Oscar, <u>a coveted award,</u>
   A   B
   <u>for its</u> extraordinary achievement in
   C
   <u>visual affects</u> and cinematography. <u>No error</u>
   D   E

10. Rachel <u>Carson, a great American</u> writer and
    A
    marine biologist, produced a series of books
    <u>that tells</u> what people are doing to the delicate
    B
    balance of the earth's <u>life forms</u> on the land
    C
    <u>and in and near</u> the sea. <u>No error</u>
    D   E

GO ON TO THE NEXT PAGE

11. The organizers of the benefit that <u>was to be</u>
                                         A
    <u>held</u> in September <u>have asked</u> for a delay
     A   B
    because the artists <u>who</u> they <u>had scheduled</u> to
                          C   D
    appear will be unavailable. <u>No error</u>
                                     E

12. Heathcliff and Cathy, the <u>protagonists</u> of
                                A
    Wuthering Heights, are characters who have

    captivated readers since the novel <u>was written,</u>
                                          B
    and they have <u>inspired</u> both movies and
                     C
    romantic novels, <u>using</u> them as models.
                        D
    <u>No error</u>
       E

13. An episode of the television series <u>was</u> to be
                                          A
    filmed when either the director or assistant

    director <u>were</u> able <u>to get</u> a permit from the
              B   C
    town <u>council</u>. <u>No error</u>
            D   E

14. The dog didn't come when Lewis called

    <u>it; however,</u> several people <u>who</u> lived in the
         A   B
    neighborhood said they <u>had seen</u> <u>him</u> running
                              C   D
    after the children on their way to school.

    <u>No error</u>
       E

15. The effect of the <u>libraries</u> campaign to
                         A
    encourage <u>children's</u> reading <u>has been</u>
                 B   C
    overwhelmingly successful, according to the

    <u>fact-finding team</u>. <u>No error</u>
           D   E

16. We must think <u>long and hard</u> about the design
                      A
    and <u>constructing</u> of a new youth center
           B
    <u>because</u> the citizens are objecting to
       C
    <u>our spending</u> more money. <u>No error</u>
          D   E

17. <u>Traditionally</u>, close cooperation <u>among</u> all the
       A   B
    university clubs <u>have led</u> to the most successful
                        C
    campaigns <u>against</u> vandalism on campus.
                 D
    <u>No error</u>
       E

18. Although orange blossoms are killed by <u>frost;</u>
                                              A
    cherry blossoms <u>will develop</u> only if <u>their</u> buds
                       B   C
    <u>have been</u> adequately chilled. <u>No error</u>
       D   E

19. Economic factors had an <u>effect</u> on art <u>when</u>
                               A   B
    artists no longer had wealthy patrons to

    <u>subsidize</u> their work, but <u>they have</u> to sell their
       C   D
    paintings themselves. <u>No error</u>
                              E

20. Political pressure is growing <u>to achieve</u> energy
                                     A
    independence from <u>overseas</u> suppliers and
                         B
    <u>to use</u> sources such as natural gas <u>to create</u>
       C   D
    electricity. <u>No error</u>
                    E

GO ON TO THE NEXT PAGE

Directions for Questions 21–30: In each question below, part of the sentence or the entire sentence is boldfaced. The first of these answer choices, choice A, repeats the boldfaced portion of the original sentence, while the next four choices offer alternative answers. For each sentence, consider the requirements of standard written English. Focus on grammar, word choice, sentence construction, and punctuation. If an answer choice changes the meaning of the original sentence, do not select it. Your answer should be a correct, concise, and effective expression, not awkward or ambiguous.

21. Reading in any language can be viewed as a developmental task much the same as learning to walk, to cross the street independently, to care for one's possessions, or **accepting responsibility for one's own decisions**.

    A. accepting responsibility for one's own decisions
    B. accepting one's own decisions responsibly
    C. to accept responsibility for one's own decisions
    D. accepting responsibility and making one's own decisions
    E. to make one's own decisions

22. Sea forests of giant kelp, which fringe only one coastline in the Northern Hemisphere, **is native to shores** throughout the Southern Hemisphere.

    A. is native to shores
    B. is native to most shores
    C. are native only in shores
    D. are native
    E. are native to shores

23. The social worker, the physician on call, and, most important, both parents of the patient **has agreed upon the same course of treatment that the nurse was in suggestion of three days ago**.

    A. has agreed upon the same course of treatment that the nurse was in suggestion of three days ago
    B. have agreed upon the same course of treatment that the nurse suggested three days ago
    C. is in agreement as to the same course of treatment that the nurse had suggested three days ago
    D. are agreeing upon the same course of treatment suggested by the nurse three days ago
    E. agree upon the same course of treatment being suggested three days ago by the nurse

24. Like so many characters in Russian fiction, *Crime and Punishment* **exhibits** a behavior so foreign to the American temperament that many readers find the story rather incredible.

    A. *Crime and Punishment* exhibits
    B. those in *Crime and Punishment* exhibit
    C. those in *Crime and Punishment* exhibits
    D. often exhibiting
    E. characterized by

25. *Don Quixote* provides a cross section of Spanish life and **portrays the feelings of many Spaniards** at the end of the chivalric age.

    A. portrays the feelings of many Spaniards
    B. portrayal of the feelings of many Spaniards
    C. feelings portrayed by Spaniards
    D. feelings
    E. Spanish feelings

26. To a large degree, **poetry, along with all the other arts, is** a form of imitation.

    A. poetry, along with all the other arts, is
    B. poetry along with all the other arts is
    C. poetry, along with all the other arts, are
    D. poetry, and other arts, is
    E. poetry and art are

GO ON TO THE NEXT PAGE

27. Perhaps too eager to learn from "The Lost Decade," **debt is piling up at an unsustainable rate in Japan.**

    A. Perhaps too eager to learn from "The Lost Decade," debt is piling up at an unsustainable rate in Japan.

    B. Perhaps too eager to learn from "The Lost Decade," Japan is piling up debt at an unsustainable rate.

    C. Perhaps to eager to learn from "The Lost Decade," Japan is continually piling up debt at an unsustainable rate.

    D. Due to the "The Lost Decade," Japan is currently piling up debt at an unsustainable rate.

    E. Perhaps too eager to learn from "The Lost Decade," Japan piled up debt at an unsustainable rate.

28. The hypoglossal canal, which carries the nerve complex required for speech, is as large in the skulls of Neanderthals **as modern humans which may indicate** an ability to speak.

    A. as modern humans which may indicate

    B. as modern humans, which may indicate

    C. as modern humans, and this may indicate

    D. as in modern humans that may indicate

    E. as in modern humans; this may indicate

29. **Between the twelve board members, there was** a high level of tension.

    A. Between the twelve board members, there was

    B. Between the twelve board members, there were

    C. Among the twelve board members, there was

    D. Among the twelve board members, there were

    E. Among the board members was

30. Twice a year, the city of Cleveland is invaded by swarms of small flies called midges; however, **much of these flies die out over a week**.

    A. much of these flies die out over a week

    B. much of these flies die out over the span of a week

    C. the majority of these flies die out over a week

    D. many of these flies die out within a week

    E. many of these flies die out over a week

GO ON TO THE NEXT PAGE

Directions for Questions 31–36: The following passage represents an early draft of an essay. Some portions of the essay will require editing and revising. Read the essay carefully and answer the questions that follow. Questions may address the whole essay or selected items from paragraphs. Select the answer that will most effectively express the intended meaning. The correct answer follows the development, organization, word choice, style, and tone of standard written English. If the indicated portion of the original sentence is the most effective, no changes will be required.

---

(1) Since its beginning, America was basically a rural society, with most people living on farms or in villages. **(2)** They made their living off the land or from small businesses. **(3)** In the nineteenth century, however, the economy underwent major changes, and these changes were often disruptive due to the fact that they disturbed people. **(4)** The Industrial Revolution brought factories and mass production, which meant that many people had to move to larger towns and cities in order to support themselves. **(5)** In addition to creating a large working class of people who had to endure low wages, long hours, and sometimes dangerous conditions, an upper class of wealthy individuals who owned the new factories and businesses were created. **(6)** For example, men like John D. Rockefeller and Andrew Carnegie, who became major figures. **(7)** In 1894, Henry Demarest Lloyd wrote a vicious attack on John D. Rockefeller and Standard Oil Company. **(8)** For the working class, the slower pace and simpler pleasures of the countryside vanished. **(9)** In the 1890s and early 1900s, vocal critics worried that individual democracy was in danger. **(10)** Some of them lashed out in articles and books at the new industrialists for introducing corruption and exploitation into the American economy. **(11)** Theodore Roosevelt coined the term "muckrakers" to describe many of the writers who he believed were "wallowing in the mud" and exaggerating their stories.

31. In context, which of the following is the most effective way to revise Sentence 3 (reproduced below)?

In the nineteenth century, however, the economy underwent major changes, and these changes were often disruptive due to the fact that they disturbed people.

A. The economy underwent major changes during the nineteenth century, however, and these changes were often disruptive.

B. With the advent of the nineteenth century, however, the economy underwent major changes, and these changes were oftentimes disruptive and disturbing to people.

C. Disruptions which disturbed people occurred during the nineteenth century, however, because the economy underwent major changes.

D. In the nineteenth century, however, the economy underwent major changes, which caused disruption and made people disturbed.

E. The major changes that occurred in the nineteenth century with the economy, however, not only disrupted people but also disturbed them.

GO ON TO THE NEXT PAGE

32. In context, which of the following is the best version of Sentence 5 (reproduced below)?

In addition to creating a large working class of people who had to endure low wages, long hours, and sometimes dangerous conditions, an upper class of wealthy individuals who owned the new factories and businesses were created.

A. A large working class of people who had to endure low wages, long hours, and sometimes dangerous conditions was created by the Industrial Revolution; as well as a new upper class of wealthy individuals, many of whom owned the new factories and businesses.

B. In addition to creating a large working class of people who had to endure low wages, long hours, and sometimes dangerous conditions, the Industrial Revolution created a new upper class of wealthy factory and business owners.

C. The Industrial Revolution created a large working class of people who had to endure low wages, long hours, and sometimes dangerous conditions, and also gave rise to a new upper class of wealthy individuals who owned the factories and businesses.

D. Both a large working class of people who had to endure low wages, long hours, and sometimes dangerous conditions and a wealthy upper class made up of individuals who owned factories and businesses was created by the Industrial Revolution.

E. In addition to creating a large working class of people who had to work for low wages, long hours, and sometimes dangerous conditions, an upper class of wealthy individuals who owned factories and businesses came into being at the time of the Industrial Revolution.

33. In context, which is the best version of the underlined portion of Sentence 6 (reproduced below)?

For example, men like John D. Rockefeller and Andrew Carnegie, who became major figures.

A. Carnegie became
B. Carnegie, both of whom became
C. Carnegie, both of who became
D. Carnegie, and they both became
E. Carnegie, who will become

34. In context, where is the best place to insert Sentence 7 (reproduced below)?

In 1894, Henry Demarest Lloyd wrote a vicious attack of John D. Rockefeller and Standard Oil Company.

A. Between Sentences 5 and 6
B. After Sentence 11
C. Between Sentences 10 and 11
D. Between Sentences 8 and 9
E. Between Sentences 4 and 5

35. In context, where is the best place to insert Sentence 8 (reproduced below)?

For the working class, the slower pace and simpler pleasures of the countryside vanished.

A. Where it is now
B. After Sentence 2
C. After Sentence 6
D. After Sentence 4
E. After Sentence 10

36. Which sentence, if added immediately after Sentence 11, would make the most suitable conclusion to the final paragraph?

A. The term "muckraker" is used today to describe social reformers, showing the profound effect that Theodore Roosevelt had on the American people.

B. Thus, the Industrial Revolution affected many people in America.

C. The average citizen at the time of the Industrial Revolution wanted nothing more than to return to the simpler, rural existence that had been left behind.

D. The changes in America society were beneficial to its diverse citizenry, as both workers and owners thrived during the nineteenth and twentieth centuries.

E. Whether the "muckraker" stories were exaggerated or not, the changes in society triggered by the Industrial Revolution created a widening gap between the industrialists and factory owners and the people who worked for them.

GO ON TO THE NEXT PAGE

Directions for Questions 37–40: For each of the questions below, answer by selecting the correct response.

37. Which of the following is the LEAST reliable source for a college-level scientific research paper?

    A. Academic electronic database (i.e., EBSCOhost)

    B. Scholarly academic digital journal published this year

    C. Scholarly academic journal published in 1970

    D. Scholarly academic journal published in 2000

    E. Academic class lecture notes from this school year

Question 38 refers to the following table.

	References
1	Cotton, Kathleen. Principals and Student Achievement: What the Research Says. Alexandria, VA. Association for Supervision and Curriculum Development, 2004. Print.
2	Geno, J. A. (2014). Using Tests to Improve Student Achievement. Techniques: Connecting Education & Careers, 89(2), 50-53.
3	Karpinski, A. C., & D'Agostino, J. V. (2013). The role of formative assessment in student achievement. In J. Hattie, E. M. Anderman (Eds.), International guide to student achievement (pp. 202–204). New York, NY, US: Routledge/Taylor & Francis Group.
4	Lawrence, A. S. Arul, and A. Vimala. "Self-Concept and Achievement Motivation of High School Students." Online Submission (June 1, 2016): ERIC, EBSCOhost (accessed February 18, 2016).

38. The table above represents a list of four references from a research paper on "student achievement." Which of the following identifies the sequence of the four citation types from the list of references?

    A. Online journal, book collection, book, academic journal

    B. Academic journal, book, book collection, online journal

    C. Academic journal, book collection, book, online journal

    D. Book, academic journal, book collection, online journal

    E. Book collection, online journal, academic journal, book

39. Which of the following best describes a primary source for researching "leaders of national civil rights movement campaigns"?

    A. The film *Selma,* about the civil rights leader Reverend Martin Luther King, Jr.

    B. An academic journal article entitled, "Leadership in the Gay and Lesbian Movement"

    C. The speech given by Mexican-American civil rights leader Cesar Chavez after ending his 36-day "Fast for Life"

    D. A thesis paper written about the "The Civil Rights Act of 1964"

    E. A report on "Civil Rights and Immigration," published by the United States Commission on Civil Rights

40. Which of the following most accurately identifies the proper method to document a quotation in a research paper?

    A. A parenthetical in-text paraphrasing or summarizing of an author's words, image, or information taken from a scholarly article, journal, or book

    B. A parenthetical in-text documentation incorporating an author's ideas and concepts taken from a scholarly article, journal, or book

    C. A parenthetical in-text documentation incorporating an author's direct words or information taken from a scholarly article, journal, or book

    D. A parenthetical in-text documentation incorporating an author's theoretical views taken from a scholarly article, journal, or book

    E. None of the above

IF YOU FINISH BEFORE TIME IS CALLED, CHECK YOUR WORK ON THIS SECTION ONLY. DO NOT WORK ON ANY OTHER SECTION IN THE TEST.

STOP

Writing Test: Essay

Essay 1: Argumentative Essay

TIME: 30 Minutes

1 Essay

Directions: You will have 30 minutes to plan and write an argumentative essay on the topic specified. You will probably find it best to spend time considering the topic and organizing your thoughts before you begin writing. Do not write on a topic other than the one specified. The essay should be based on your readings, experiences, or observations. You must write on the specified topic. An essay on another topic will not be accepted.

The essay is intended to give you an opportunity to demonstrate your writing skills. Be sure to express your ideas clearly and effectively. The quality of your writing is much more important than the quantity, but to cover the topic adequately, you will likely want to write more than one paragraph. Be specific and provide relevant examples that are related to the topic.

Read the opinion stated below:

According to the Wildlife and Nature Conservancy Group, "There is so much untapped potential for increased recycling and conservation efforts. It's time for public institutions to step up again because the status quo is not good enough."

Assignment: Discuss the extent to which you agree or disagree with this opinion. Support your views with specific reasons and examples from your own experiences, observations, or readings.

IF YOU FINISH BEFORE TIME IS CALLED, CHECK YOUR WORK ON THIS SECTION ONLY. DO NOT WORK ON ANY OTHER SECTION IN THE TEST.

Essay 2: Informative/Explanatory Essay

TIME: 30 Minutes

1 Essay

Directions: You will have 30 minutes to read two different passages and then plan and write an informative/explanatory essay using information from BOTH sources provided. Take time organizing your ideas before you discuss the most important concerns regarding the specified issue. Explain the reasons why they are important. You must write on the specified topic. An essay on another topic will not be accepted.

The essay is intended to give you an opportunity to demonstrate your writing skills. Be sure to express your ideas clearly and effectively. The quality of your writing is much more important than the quantity, but to cover the topic adequately, you will likely want to write more than one paragraph. Be specific and provide relevant examples that are related to the topic.

Assignment:

Both of the following passages address children and play. In particular, both discuss the importance of make-believe play in the classroom. Read the two passages carefully and then write an essay in which you identify the most important concerns regarding the issue and explain why they are important. Your essay must draw on information from BOTH of the sources. In addition, you may draw upon your own experiences, observations, and readings.

When paraphrasing or quoting from the sources, cite each source by referring to the author's last name, the title of the source, or any other clear identifier.

Source 1:

Adapted from: Ciciora, Phil. *All Work and No Play Makes for a Troubling Trend in Early Education*. Urbana: University of Illinois at Urbana-Champaign, 2009. 1–2. Web. 7 Oct. 2015.

Parents and educators who favor traditional classroom-style learning over free, unstructured playtime in preschool and kindergarten may actually be stunting a child's development instead of enhancing it. Anne Haas Dyson, a professor who studies childhood learning and literacy development at the University of Illinois, College of Education, says playtime for children is a "fundamental avenue" for learning, and attempts by parents and educators to create gifted children by bombarding them with information is well intentioned but ultimately counterproductive.

"That approach doesn't appreciate the role of play and imagination in a child's intellectual development," Dyson said. "Play is where children discover ideas, experiences, and concepts and think about them and their consequences. This is where literacy and learning really begins." What Dyson calls the "banning of the imagination" in schools may be influenced by what some critics have called the "Baby Genius Edutainment Complex," a cottage industry of mind-enrichment products developed specifically for infants and toddlers and marketed to anxious parents eager to give their children's cognitive abilities an early boost. "I see this 'Einstein in the crib' trend as a societal reduction of children to the means for fulfilling parents' desires for intellectual distinction," Dyson said. "Children learn the way we all learn: through engagement and through construction. They have to make sense of the world, and that's what play or any other symbolic activity does for children."

While Dyson does see some value in teaching the ABCs to children in pre-kindergarten, she thinks that trying to accelerate learning actually works against a child's development. Kindergarten and preschool, she

GO ON TO THE NEXT PAGE

said, should be a place for children to experience play as intellectual inquiry, before they get taken over by the tyranny of high-stakes testing. "I'm certainly not opposed to literacy in the early grades," Dyson said, "but the idea that we can eliminate play from the curriculum doesn't make sense. Kids don't respond well to sitting still in their desks and listening at that age. They need stimulation." Dyson doesn't believe there should be any sort of compromise in the amount of learning by rote and play that children experience, especially in preschool and kindergarten. "We have to intellectually engage kids," she said. "We have to give them a sense of their own agency, their own capacity, and an ability to ask questions and solve problems. So we have to give them more open-ended activities that allow them the space they need to make sense of things."

Source 2:

Adapted from: Leong, Deborah, and Elena Bodrova. "Assessing and Scaffolding: Make-Believe Play." *National Association for the Education of Young Children.* Washington, DC: NAEYC Publications. 2012. 26–27. Print.

It is the third week that Ms. Sotto's preschool classroom has been turned into an airport. The literacy center is a ticket counter, with a travel agency complete with child-made passports, tickets, and travel brochures. In the block area, the children have constructed an X-ray scanner from cardboard boxes. A smaller box functions as the screening device for carry-on luggage. An airplane cockpit is made out of cardboard with child-drawn instruments, an upside-down egg carton for a keyboard, and a paper plate for a steering wheel.

What is happening in Ms. Sotto's classroom is an example of what most early childhood educators mean when they talk about make-believe play—a fantasy world created by children where their imagination soars, their language expands, and their social skills develop. Unfortunately, play observed in many early childhood classrooms rarely reaches this level; often children act out a series of simple and stereotypical scripts with little interaction with their peers. Research provides increasing evidence of the positive effects that well-developed play has on various areas of child development, such as social skills, emerging mathematical abilities, early literacy concept mastery, and self-regulation (see Singer, Golinkoff & Hirsh-Pasek, 2006). It is also becoming increasingly clear that without adult support, the play of many children is destined to never reach this fully developed status.

Mature make-believe play is an important and unique context, providing learning opportunities not afforded by other classroom activities. It should not be considered something extra to be cut to accommodate more time for academic skills, nor should it be used to add "entertainment value" for boring and decontextualized drills. Instead, play should be preserved and nurtured as one of the "uniquely 'preschool'" (in the words of Vygotsky's colleague and student Alexander Zaporozhets) activities that provide the most beneficial context for children's development.

IF YOU FINISH BEFORE TIME IS CALLED, CHECK YOUR WORK ON THIS SECTION ONLY. DO NOT WORK ON ANY OTHER SECTION IN THE TEST.

Mathematics Test

TIME: 85 Minutes

56 Questions

Directions: Select the best answer of the five choices given. Answer choices have several different formats. Unless otherwise directed, indicate a single answer choice.

Remember: Answer choices in this study guide have lettered choices A, B, C, D, and E for clarity, but answer choice letters will not appear on the actual exam. On the actual computer version of the exam, you will be required to click on ovals, click on squares, or fill in your answer.

1. After a 40% discount, the price of a pair of shoes was $25.50. What was the price of the shoes before the discount?

   A. $35.70
   B. $40.80
   C. $42.50
   D. $102.00
   E. $153.00

2. Sean knows that a geometric figure is a rectangle and that it has sides of 18 and 22.

   In the context of math reasoning, which of the following steps should Sean take to calculate the area of a square that has the same *perimeter* as the rectangle discussed above?

   A. Add 18 and 22, double this sum, divide by 4, then multiply by 2.
   B. Add 18 and 22, double this sum, divide by 4, then multiply by 4.
   C. Add 18 and 22, double this sum, divide by 4, then square the quotient.
   D. Add 18 and 22, double this sum, then multiply by 4.
   E. Add twice 18 to twice 22, divide by 2, then square the quotient.

Question 3 refers to the figure below.

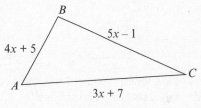

(Not drawn to scale)

3. Triangle *ABC* is isosceles. Which of the following could be the perimeter of $\triangle ABC$?

   Select **all** that apply.

   A. 35
   B. 47
   C. 59
   D. 83
   E. 89

4. Which of the following is the smallest?

   A. $\dfrac{3}{5}$

   B. $\dfrac{4}{9}$

   C. $\dfrac{7}{13}$

   D. $\dfrac{23}{44}$

   E. $\dfrac{2}{3}$

GO ON TO THE NEXT PAGE

Use the following formula to answer question 5.

The relationship between voltage, amperes, and wattage is expressed in the following equation:

$$\text{volts} \times \text{amps} = \text{watts per hour}$$

5. If your electric vehicle has a 0% charge and you would like to charge the vehicle to 100% capacity, how long will it take a standard 12-amp, 120-volt electrical outlet to charge your electric vehicle that has a battery capacity of 16,000 watts?

   Write your answer to the nearest whole number in the box below.

6. On average, a taxi travels 40 miles per hour while taking passengers from one location to another. The fare is $7.50 for each passenger and 6 cents for each quarter of a mile traveled. How much will the fare be for three passengers over a 1 hour and 45 minute time period?

   A. Less than $30
   B. At least $30, but less than $35
   C. At least $35, but less than $40
   D. At least $40
   E. At least $40, but less than $50

7. 210,000 equals

   A. $(2 \times 10^4) + (1 \times 10^3)$
   B. $(2 \times 10^5) + (1 \times 10^4)$
   C. $(2 \times 10^6) + (1 \times 10^5)$
   D. $(2 \times 10^7) + (1 \times 10^6)$
   E. $(2 \times 10^8) + (1 \times 10^7)$

Question 8 refers to the following table.

Ft. Collins, Colorado Homes Sold in May

Age of Home (years)	Number of Homes Sold
1–2	1,200
3–4	1,570
5–6	1,630
7–8	1,440
9–10	1,720

8. According to the table above, how many more houses from 5 to 10 years old were sold than those from 4 to 8 years old?

   A. 2,455
   B. 1,570
   C. 150
   D. 130
   E. The number cannot be determined from the information given.

9. The product of two numbers is greater than 0 and equals one of the numbers. Which of the following must be one of the numbers?

   A. –1
   B. 0
   C. 1
   D. A prime number
   E. A reciprocal

10. If the length of a rectangle is doubled and its width is decreased by 25%, how many times greater is the area of the new rectangle than the area of the original rectangle?

   A. 1.5
   B. 2
   C. 2.5
   D. 3
   E. 3.5

GO ON TO THE NEXT PAGE

Question 11 refers to the following graph.

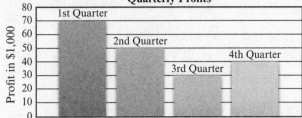

EcoSystems Technology Company Quarterly Profits

11. The bar graph above shows the average quarterly profits for EcoSystems Technology Company. According to the graph, what is the approximate percent change in profits from the 3rd quarter to the 4th quarter?

   A. 20%
   B. 33%
   C. 43%
   D. 50%
   E. 75%

Question 12 refers to the following pictogram.

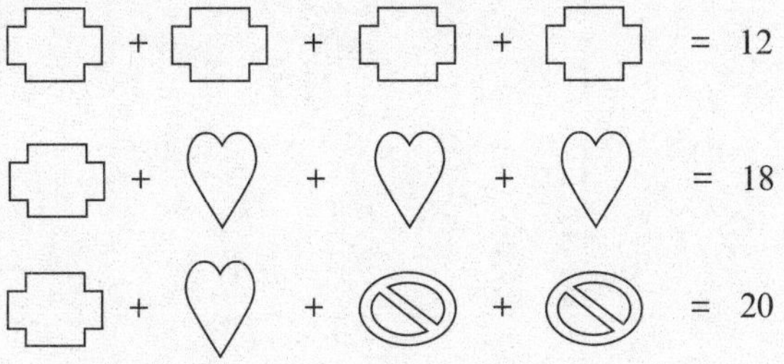

12. In the picture above, what is the value of the  ⊘ symbol?

   Write your answer in the box below.

13. If the pattern established in the first five fractions in the following list continues, what is the next fraction in the list?

$$\frac{2}{3}, \frac{3}{5}, \frac{5}{9}, \frac{8}{15}, \frac{12}{23}, \boxed{}$$

   Write the answer as a fraction in the two boxes below.

14. A fair die is rolled three times. What is the probability that all three rolls resulted in different numbers?

   A. 0.50
   B. 0.56
   C. 0.58
   D. 0.60
   E. 0.61

15. How many pounds of nuts worth $2.10 per pound must be mixed with nuts worth $1.30 per pound to yield 8 pounds of nuts worth $1.80 per pound?

   A. 3
   B. $3\frac{3}{5}$
   C. $4\frac{5}{8}$
   D. 5
   E. $5\frac{3}{8}$

16. David's age is 4 years greater than four times Alex's age. Alex's age is 2 years less than half of Tony's age. If Tony is y years old, what is David's age in terms of y?

   A. $y + 6$
   B. $2y + 6$
   C. $4y + 2$
   D. $4y - 2$
   E. $2y - 4$

GO ON TO THE NEXT PAGE

17. Teachers will be assigned special camp duty one day of the week during a 7-day camping trip. If all the days of the week (Monday through Sunday) are tossed into a cap and each teacher chooses one day of the week, what is the probability that the first teacher will randomly select a weekday (Monday through Friday)?

A. $\dfrac{1}{7}$

B. $\dfrac{2}{7}$

C. $\dfrac{1}{5}$

D. $\dfrac{5}{7}$

E. $\dfrac{5}{2}$

Question 18 refers to the following number line.

$$Q \qquad +7 \qquad +9$$

18. On the number line above, what is the point 15 units to the left of point Q?

A. 10
B. 5
C. 0
D. –9
E. –10

19. If the product of two numbers is five more than the sum of the two numbers, which of the following equations could represent the relationship?

A. $XY + 5 = X + Y$
B. $5XY = X + Y$
C. $XY = X + Y + 5$
D. $\dfrac{X}{Y} = 5 + X + Y$
E. $X(Y) + 5 = X + Y + 5$

20. The average of six numbers is 8. If three additional numbers are combined with these six numbers, the average of the nine numbers increases to 11. What is the average of the three additional numbers?

Write your answer in the box below.

21. It is estimated that at a classroom party each student will drink $\dfrac{1}{5}$ of a gallon of lemonade. How many gallons of lemonade should be brought to the classroom if 28 students are expected to attend?

A. 3
B. Between 3 and 4
C. 5
D. Between 5 and 6
E. More than 6

Question 22 refers to the following diagram.

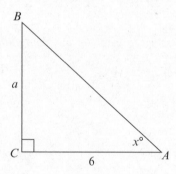

22. In right triangle ABC above, if $30° \le x° \le 60°$, which of the following could be the value of a?

Select **all** that apply.

A. 4
B. 5
C. 6
D. 7
E. 8

23. Marcella spent $100 for a cell phone and accessories. If the accessories cost $20 more than the cell phone, how much did she pay for the accessories?

A. $20
B. $30
C. $40
D. $50
E. $60

GO ON TO THE NEXT PAGE

24. What is the sum of the positive integer divisors that are greater than 1, that 96 and 80 have in common?

Write your answer in the box below.

25. Which of the following is equal to $\frac{1}{5}$ of 0.02 percent?

A.   0.4
B.   0.04
C.   0.004
D.   0.0004
E.   0.00004

Question 26 refers to the following table.

Data Value	Frequency
3	4
4	1
5	2
8	3

26. Which of the following expresses the mean and the median for the values in the frequency table above?

A.   Mean: 4, median: 4
B.   Mean: 4, median: 5
C.   Mean: 5, median: $4\frac{1}{2}$
D.   Mean: $5\frac{1}{2}$, median: $4\frac{1}{2}$
E.   Mean: 5, median: 5

27. If 10 kilometers equal 6.2 miles, then how many miles are in 45 kilometers?

A.   4.5
B.   7.25
C.   27.9
D.   29.7
E.   62

28. Last year, Robin spent between 15% and 20% of her $40,400 salary on lodging. This year she estimates she will spend between 20% and 25% of her $45,000 salary on lodging.

Which of the following could be the percent change in the amount Robin spends on lodging from last year to this year?

Select **all** that apply.

A.   0%
B.   35%
C.   45%
D.   85%
E.   90%

Question 29 refers to the following diagram.

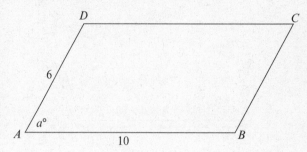

29. Given parallelogram $ABCD$ above, if $45° < a < 90°$, which of the following could be the area of the parallelogram?

Select **all** that apply.

A.   35
B.   40
C.   45
D.   50
E.   55

GO ON TO THE NEXT PAGE

30. Gavin bought 200 decks of cards for $2.20 per deck. He plans to sell these decks at a swap meet and make a profit of 15% to 25% per deck. If he sells all 200 decks, all at the same price, which of the following could be the total sales revenue?

Select **all** that apply.

A. $500
B. $520
C. $540
D. $560
E. $580

Question 31 refers to the following pictograph.

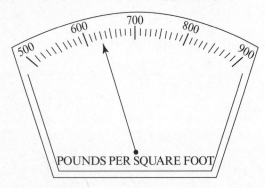

31. What are the pounds per square foot in the pressure gauge pictured above?

A. 600.3
B. 603
C. 630
D. 730
E. 770

32. Twelve people are discussing three popular movies—a drama, a comedy, and an action movie. Three of the people viewed all three movies. Four viewed exactly two of the movies. Eight of the people viewed a drama. Six of the people viewed a comedy. Seven of the people viewed an action movie. How many of the twelve people did not view any of the three movies?

A. 0
B. 1
C. 2
D. 3
E. 4

Question 33 refers to the following.

Academic School Supply Co. Birmingham, Alabama		
Invoice No. 5232		
Bill to: Burbank Middle School		
Quantity	**Description**	**Total**
60	Integrated Science Textbooks– Grade 6	$840
30	Science Lab Equipment	$460
30	Formaldehyde Test Kits	$320
10	Integrated Science Textbooks– Grade 6 Teacher's Manuals	$120
TOTAL DUE		$2,220

33. Academic School Supply Company (ASSC) sent the above invoice to Burbank Middle School. Although the invoice included the cost of science lab workbooks, ASSC forgot to list them on the invoice.

How much did the science lab workbooks cost Burbank Middle School?

A. $480
B. $500
C. $520
D. $560
E. $620

GO ON TO THE NEXT PAGE

Question 34 refers to the following chart.

**Providence High School
State Testing Score Averages**

	Math	Verbal
Year 1	520	540
Year 2	515	532
Year 3	518	528
Year 4	510	525
Year 5	507	510

34. According to the chart above, what is the mean (average) of the verbal state testing scores for the 5-year period?

A. 512
B. 514
C. 521
D. 527
E. 528

35. Brandon purchased a pair of slacks, a dress shirt, a tie, and a sports coat. The shirt and slacks each cost three times what the tie cost. The sports coat cost twice what the shirt cost. If Brandon paid a total of $156 for all four items, what was the price of the pair of slacks?

A. $12
B. $36
C. $48
D. $78
E. $84

Question 36 refers to the following diagram.

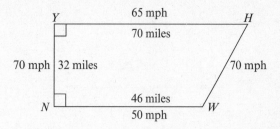

36. A car trip route from Newark (N) to New Haven (H) can go through either New York (Y) or White Plains (W). Using the distances and average speeds on the diagram above, approximately how many minutes would be saved by taking the quicker route?

A. $2\frac{1}{2}$ minutes
B. 5 minutes
C. $7\frac{1}{2}$ minutes
D. 10 minutes
E. $12\frac{1}{2}$ minutes

GO ON TO THE NEXT PAGE

Question 37 refers to the following graph.

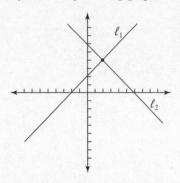

37. In the graph above, what is the solution of the equations of the two lines ℓ_1 and ℓ_2?

A. $x = 4$, $y = 2$

B. $x = 0$, $y = 2$

C. $x = 2$, $y = 0$

D. $x = 2$, $y = 4$

E. The solution cannot be determined from the information given.

Question 38 refers to the figures below.

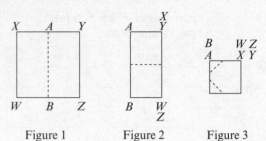

Figure 1   Figure 2   Figure 3

38. In Figure 1 above, a square piece of paper is folded along dotted line AB so that X is on top of Y and W is on top of Z (Figure 2). The paper is then folded again so that B is on top of A and WZ is on top of XY (Figure 3). Two small corners are cut out of the folded paper as shown in Figure 3. If the paper is unfolded, which of the following could be the result?

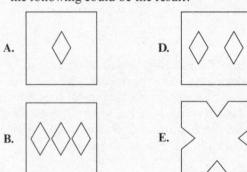

GO ON TO THE NEXT PAGE

39. If socks cost $2.98 for a package of two pairs, how much change will Hunter receive from a twenty-dollar bill if he purchases twelve pairs of socks?

    A. $2.02
    B. $2.12
    C. $2.18
    D. $2.22
    E. $3.02

40. Which of the following is equal to the equation $2x + 4 = 3x + 3$?

Select **all** that apply.

    A. $4 = x + 3$
    B. $-x + 4 = 3$
    C. $2x + 1 = 3x$
    D. $x = -1$
    E. $2x = 3x - 1$

41. What is 30% of $\dfrac{25}{18}$?

    A. $\dfrac{5}{108}$
    B. $\dfrac{5}{12}$
    C. $\dfrac{25}{54}$
    D. $\dfrac{25}{6}$
    E. $\dfrac{125}{3}$

42. If $\dfrac{3}{x} = 6$, then $x - 1 =$

    A. 1
    B. $\dfrac{1}{2}$
    C. $-\dfrac{1}{2}$
    D. $-\dfrac{2}{3}$
    E. $-1\dfrac{1}{2}$

43. Maya budgeted for her cruise vacation. She planned to spend 10% of her budget for air travel, 60% for the cruise fare, 20% for onboard expenses, and 10% on gifts. When she returned home, she found that she had spent 20% more than the budgeted amount on air travel, 10% less than the budgeted amount on the cruise fare, 20% more than the budgeted amount on onboard expenses, and 20% less than the budgeted amount on gifts. Her overall actual cruise vacation expenses amounted to what percent of her budgeted amount?

    A. 97%
    B. 98%
    C. 99%
    D. 100%
    E. 101%

Question 44 refers to the figure below.

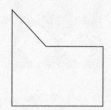

44. Which of the following figures represents the best method for splitting up and computing the area of the figure above?

    A.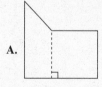
    D.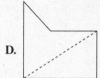

    B.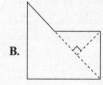
    E.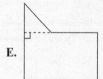

    C.

GO ON TO THE NEXT PAGE

45. If $10m - 50 + 20p = 0$, what is the value of $m + 2p$?

    A.   2
    B.   5
    C.   10
    D.   20
    E.   500

46. Round off 0.14739 to the nearest thousandth.

    A.   0.1473
    B.   0.1474
    C.   0.147
    D.   0.148
    E.   0.15

Question 47 refers to the following diagram.

47. The large square above consists of squares and isosceles right triangles. If the large square has a side of 4 centimeters, then the area of the shaded portion in square centimeters is

    A.   2
    B.   4
    C.   6
    D.   8
    E.   12

48. Juan approximated 35×45 as 40×50, but the answer was much too high. To get a better approximation, he should multiply

    A. 50×50
    B. 45×50
    C. 30×50
    D. 30×40
    E. 20×30

Question 49 refers to the following information.

> Statement 1: The price of car *A* if it costs six times the price of car *B*
>
> Statement 2: The difference in temperature between two cities
>
> Statement 3: The number of yards in 39 feet

49. Which of the above statements can be solved by division?

    A.   Statement 1 only
    B.   Statement 2 only
    C.   Statement 3 only
    D.   Statements 1 and 2
    E.   Statements 1 and 3

Question 50 refers to the following bar graph.

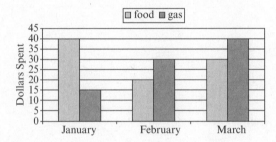

50. Based on the graph above, what is the percent change in the amount spent on food from February to March?

Write your answer in the box below, rounded to the nearest whole percent.

GO ON TO THE NEXT PAGE

51. Given the following data set, which of the following numeric values lies between the mean and the median?

{2, 2, 3, 3, 3, 4, 6, 7, 7, 7, 7, 8, 10, 12, 12}

Select **all** that apply.

A.   6.2
B.   6.6
C.   6.8
D.   7.0
E.   7.2

Question 52 refers to the following chart.

Hourly Snowfall Rate

Temperature in Degrees	Average Snowfall in Inches
−10	2
−15	2.5
−20	3
−25	3.5
−30	4

52. The chart above shows the temperature and snowfall during one day in Moose Jaw, Saskatchewan. Which of the following is true about the data published in the chart?

A.   As the temperature increased, the amount of snowfall increased.
B.   As the temperature decreased, the amount of snowfall decreased.
C.   As the temperature increased, the amount of snowfall remained the same.
D.   As the temperature decreased, the amount of snowfall increased.
E.   As the temperature decreased, the amount of snowfall remained the same.

53. A parallelogram has two sides of dimensions 9 and 7. What would be the side of a square with the same perimeter?

A.   32
B.   18
C.   14
D.   8
E.   4

54. If Blake can type 20 pages in 4 hours, how many hours will it take him to type 50 pages?

A.   5
B.   6
C.   8
D.   9
E.   10

Question 55 refers to the following graph.

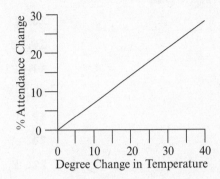

55. According to the graph above, if the temperature falls 30°, what percentage will school attendance drop?

A.   10
B.   20
C.   30
D.   40
E.   50

56. Maria needs to compute 30% of a total restaurant bill of $50. Which of the following math operations will help her calculate the correct answer?

Select **all** that apply.

A. 0.30×50
B. 0.50×30
C. $\dfrac{3}{10} \times 50$
D. $50 \div \dfrac{10}{3}$
E. $50 \div \dfrac{3}{10}$

IF YOU FINISH BEFORE TIME IS CALLED, CHECK YOUR WORK ON THIS SECTION ONLY. DO NOT WORK ON ANY OTHER SECTION IN THE TEST.

STOP

Scoring the Practice Test

The following section will assist you in scoring and analyzing your practice test results. Use the answer key below to score your results, then carefully review the analysis chart to identify your strengths and weaknesses. Finally, read through the answer explanations starting on page 328 to clarify the solutions to the problems.

Answer Key

Reading Test

1. E
2. C
3. B
4. D
5. B
6. D
7. C
8. *Particularly in compact urban areas, workers and students find that electric bicycles provide a practical compromise between the frustration of fighting road and rail traffic and the discomfort of arriving at work or class dripping in sweat from a strenuous bike ride.*
9. A
10. B
11. C
12. C
13. A and C
14. *Natural selection will favor strategies that make incorrect causal associations in order to establish those associations that are essential for survival and reproduction.*

15. D
16. B
17. B
18. D
19. C
20. A
21. B
22. D
23. C
24. A
25. D
26. A
27. C
28. D
29. C
30. A and C
31. C
32. A
33. C
34. *"The salmon are less concerned about a white object as seen from below the surface," Reimchen speculates.*

35. E
36. C
37. A
38. B
39. D
40. C
41. A and C
42. C
43. B
44. B
45. C
46. A
47. E
48. E
49. A, B, and C
50. C
51. D
52. D
53. E
54. B
55. B
56. B

Writing Test: Selected Response

1. E	11. C	21. C	31. A
2. D	12. D	22. E	32. B
3. A	13. B	23. B	33. A
4. B	14. D	24. B	34. C
5. A	15. A	25. D	35. D
6. E	16. B	26. A	36. E
7. D	17. C	27. B	37. C
8. C	18. A	28. E	38. D
9. D	19. D	29. C	39. C
10. E	20. E	30. D	40. C

Mathematics Test

1. C	15. D	30. B and C	44. E
2. C	16. E	31. C	45. B
3. A, C, and D	17. D	32. B	46. C
4. B	18. E	33. A	47. D
5. 11	19. C	34. D	48. C
6. C	20. 17	35. B	49. C
7. B	21. D	36. A	50. 50%
8. E	22. A, B, C, D, and E	37. D	51. B and C
9. C	23. E	38. C	52. D
10. A	24. 30	39. B	53. D
11. B	25. E	40. A, B, C, and E	54. E
12. 6	26. C	41. B	55. B
13. $\frac{17}{33}$	27. C	42. C	56. A, B, C, and D
14. B	28. A, B, C, and D	43. B	
	29. C, D, and E		

Charting and Analyzing Your Test Results

The first step in analyzing your test results is to chart your answers. Use the following analysis sheet to identify your strengths and areas of improvement. Complete the process of evaluating your results and analyzing problems in each area. Re-evaluate your results as you look for trends in the types of errors (repeated errors), and look for low scores in the results of *specific* subject areas. This re-examination and analysis is a tremendous asset to help you maximize your best possible score. The answers and explanations following this analysis sheet will provide you with clarification to help you solve these types of problems in the future.

Practice Test 2 Analysis Sheet					
			Number Incorrect		
Test	**Total Possible**	**Number Correct**	**(A) Simple Mistake**	**(B) Misread Problem**	**(C) Unfamiliar Concept**
Reading Test	56				
Writing Test: Selected Response	40				
Mathematics Test	56				
Total Possible Explanations for Incorrect Answers: Columns A, B, and C					
Total Number of Answers Correct and Incorrect	152	Add the total number of correct answers here: _____	Add columns A, B, and C _____ Total number incorrect answers		

Answers and Explanations

Reading Test

1. **E.** The passage states that sounds must be recalled from memory; therefore, it follows that there must be some delay between when the sound occurs and when the comparison happens (choice E). There is no discussion of the magnitude of difference between sounds (choice A) or visual discrimination (choice B), and choice C is not suggested. Choice D is incorrect because while the passage implies that a reasonably good memory is necessary for speech discrimination, it does not imply that having a good memory alone equates to being a good listener.

2. **C.** The *difficult judgments* referred to in the passage are those used when *determining spatial elements of sounds;* for example, locating a basketball teammate based on his or her shout (choice C). Choice A misinterprets the car horn example given in the passage. Choice B incorrectly presents an example that relates to touch rather than hearing. Choices D and E are incorrect because they contain no spatial elements.

3. **B.** The last sentence of the passage suggests that reluctance to submit DNA samples may be due to past injustices (choice B). Choice D may seem a possible inference, but the passage doesn't indicate that the evidence is *overwhelming*. Also, nothing in the passage suggests choices A or C, which may or may not be true. The author does not indicate that the researchers have *ulterior motives* (choice E).

4. **D.** According to the passage, information about migration routes might contradict a group's own legends and traditions about its origins (choice D). Choices A, B, and C are overly negative assumptions and interpretations of the indigenous groups' hesitance to submit DNA samples, and choice E makes an unsubstantiated leap in logic.

5. **B.** Choice B presents an example of the concern discussed in the passage that *information about the migration routes of [a group's] ancestors might contradict [their] own cultural traditions about its origins.* Choice A is incorrect because the Native American in the example *does* receive a share of the profits, albeit a small percentage; the concern discussed in the passage is that companies would *pay them nothing.* Choice C is incorrect because viruses are never discussed.

    D. Since all five choices begin with *However,* we know that the answer must provide a counterargument to the idea that electric bicycle sales should continue to increase due to the *anticipated rises in … fuel prices and population.* Choice D undermines this argument by implying that a rise in fuel prices would not necessarily result in increased sales of electric bicycles. Choice A is incorrect because it merely states a minor geographic exception based on the premise that avoiding sweating is the main point of the purchase. Choices B and E support, rather than weaken, the idea that sales will increase by implying that American demand for electric bicycles may soon increase, and choice C is irrelevant to the author's argument.

7. **C.** The passage is concerned with the current market for electric bicycles, along with their prospect for future growth and sales (choice C). Choice A incorrectly characterizes the passage as an overview of the actual vehicle, rather than its market prospects. Choice B is incorrect because no such potential roadblocks are discussed, while choice D incorrectly focuses on the past. Choice E incorrectly suggests that the author is trying to sell something to the reader.

8. The following sentence from the passage (lines 5–11) describes the niche between vehicles and trains and traditional bicycles: *Particularly in compact urban areas, workers and students find that electric bicycles provide a practical compromise between the frustration of fighting road and rail traffic and the discomfort of arriving at work or class dripping in sweat from a strenuous bike ride.*

9. **A.** Patternicity can best be described as the tendency to see connections and patterns in nature (choice A). Choice B describes *patternicity* as *uniquely human,* but the passage refers to experiments showing that other animals also seem to have the trait. The passage also makes it clear that patternicity doesn't distinguish false from real patterns, choice C. Choice D is irrelevant to the passage, and although patternicity can involve false meanings, it isn't limited to them, choice E.

10. **B.** Shermer refers to a *Baloney Detection Network* that would allow people to separate false patterns from real ones (choice B). Unfortunately, Shermer says, humans did not develop such a network, so choice E is incorrect. Choices A, C, and D are also incorrect.

11. **C.** The results of the experiments indicated that predators avoided nonpoisonous snakes that mimicked poisonous ones and that this example of patternicity led to the predators' survival (choice C). Nothing suggests that instinct is the key factor, choice E. The experiments are unrelated to Shermer's Baloney Detection Network (choice A). Choices B and D contradict the point made by the experiments.

12. **C.** The experiments dealt with nonhuman predators, which indicates that Foster and Kokko assumed that nonhuman species also find patterns in nature (choice C). Choice A is not indicated, and the word *purposely* in choice B rules it out as the correct answer. Shermer makes a point in the passage that the ability to recognize patterns is a positive trait in humans and helps us understand our environment, although sometimes what we see as a pattern is false; this eliminates choice D. Choice E is irrelevant to the experiments and not supported by any evidence in the passage.

13. **A and C.** Choice A is correct, as it is beneficial for soldiers to be on alert for gunshots, even if it results in the occasional "false positive." Choice C is also correct, as while thunder itself does not cause the inside of one's car to get wet, it *is* associated with rain, which does. The phobia in choice B appears to confer no benefit upon its holder, so choice B is incorrect.

14. The author asks why we have not developed a so-called "Baloney Detection Network," a question that is later answered by the findings of Foster and Kokko's study. The correct selection reads *Natural selection will favor strategies that make incorrect causal associations in order to establish those associations that are essential for survival and reproduction.* (lines 30–33), thus explaining why no "Baloney Detection Network" is needed or even beneficial.

15. **D.** As described in choice D, the passage describes a concept ("patternicity"); raises a question about the concept (why the tendency for false causal associations?); and then answers the question (because the

associations are still beneficial). Choice A is incorrect for its implication that Shermer's work is being criticized. Choice B is incorrect because it ignores the substantial third paragraph. Choice C is incorrect because only one potential "hole" is poked in the theory, and no alternate theory is discussed. Choice E is incorrect because it omits the significant discussion of the potential flaw in the theory in the second and third paragraphs.

16. **B.** The author presents the argument for abolishing grades with the reasoning that *grades are not good indicators of intellectual ability;* to accept this argument, the author must presume that there are viable, superior alternatives (choice B). Choices A and C are overextensions of the argument's implications, while choice D is irrelevant to the argument. Choice E is incorrect because the author does not present grades as the *only* current issue in education.

17. **B.** The author argues that abolition of grades would increase student interest in subject matter (choice B), and uses this argument in support of the abolition of grades. The author then explicitly states that motivational factors such as subject matter are *more important than a letter on a transcript,* thus emphasizing its value. Choices A and C are incorrect because the author does not argue that grade point average is a motivator or that grading criteria should be *more* important. Choices D and E are not mentioned in the passage.

18. **D.** The words *we will have students* indicate that the author is a teacher or principal talking to other teachers; the use of *us* in the third sentence (when discussing evaluation and instruction) solidifies this notion. It would not make sense for politicians (choice A), parents (choice B), students (choice C), or civic leaders (choice E) to *concentrate* on *evaluation* or *instruction.*

19. **C.** In the last sentence, the passage states that respondents to the poll are *uncertain* of what steps to take, even though they support *living green,* which suggests that a lack of information is the problem (choice C). Choice D is the second-best answer, but it is a reach, as the passage does not single out the media as being at fault. The other choices are not implied.

20. **A.** By giving the nonacting respondents the benefit of the doubt and assuming that their lack of action is due to a lack of information—an easily remediable issue—despite their good intentions, the author takes on an optimistic tone (choice A). Elated, choice B, is overly positive, and nothing in the passage suggests any negativity or confusion in the author's tone, as put forth by choices C, D, and E.

21. **B.** Choice B contradicts the author's conclusion by implying that it is disinterest, rather than lack of information, that causes some people not to reduce their impact on the environment. If true, choice A would actually support the author's conclusion, as would choice D. Choice C does not necessarily contradict the author's conclusion, as it allows for a lack of action. Choice E is irrelevant.

22. **D.** The second sentence makes the main point of the passage: that 1906 was the first time the United States fielded a real Olympic team (choice D). Choices A, B, and C are secondary points; choice A is only discussed in the first sentence to provide an introduction, and choices B and C are only briefly mentioned in the last sentence as interesting asides. There is no criticism in the passage as suggested by choice E.

23. **C.** From the context, it is clear that *purists* refers to those who insist that because an Olympiad is four years, the 1906 games in Athens cannot be considered Olympic games; in other words, people who strictly adhere to the definition of *Olympiad* (choice C). Choices A, B, D, and E do not make sense in the context of the sentence.

24. **A.** The 1906 Olympics occurred despite the lack of an Olympiad (four years) having passed since the 1904 games. Therefore, those who put on the 1906 games must not have believed that the passing of a four-year period was necessary (choice A). Choices B and E provide unsubstantiated speculation about their motives, while choices C and D confuse the Olympic organizers with the American Olympic committee.

25. **D.** This is a hidden idea question because it asks one to understand an assumption, rather than finding explicitly stated material; one has to read between the lines to choose the correct answer. The passage makes the point that top European scientists are trying to preserve these paintings, and so it follows logically that their restoration is considered important (for if not, why go to the effort?). Thus, choice D is an accurate assumption behind this passage. Most of the other choices simply parrot facts from the passage; for example, choice A, he *utilized an unusual shade of yellow;* choice B, *the yellow hue … is to attract the eye;* and choice C, the *paintings … are quite well-known* are all explicitly stated and thus are not assumptions. Choice E contradicts the facts in the passage in its assertion that the scientists have finally discovered the cause, when in fact, the passage states otherwise.

26. A. The author uses *Starry Night* as an example of one of van Gogh's works that contained *formerly-brilliant yellow hues,* so choice A is correct. Choice B is incorrect because the passage merely references *Starry Night* as being included in van Gogh's signature works (rather than being his single most famous), and choice C is incorrect because the passage expresses hope for a reversal of its deterioration.

27. C. The passage reads *only parts of electronics containing reusable metals like copper are recycled;* therefore, choice C is correct. Choice A is incorrect because the passage never states that any Ghanaians have actually inhaled the chemical vapors (nor does it state that harmful vapors are *always* released by the burning of e-waste), only that it would be harmful if they did. Choice B is incorrect because the passage claims that only devices with nonreusable metals are burned, not all metals. Choice D is not a safe conclusion to draw from the information given, or one for which the author advocates. Choice E is incorrect because it is possible that the recycling of e-waste is better than any alternate options, despite the flaws of the system; plus, no issues are raised with the actual recycling of products with reusable metals.

28. D. The author notes that the burning often releases chemicals such as lead and mercury into the air, which results in severe health implications for anyone who inhales the chemical vapors. Choices A, B, C, and E are never suggested as issues by the author.

29. C. The main idea of the passage is to explore Kermodism, which is the production of white offspring (spirit bears) by black bears. Thus, choice C is the correct answer. Choice A is incorrect because white bears, Kermode bears, and spirit bears are all different names for the same animal, so there is no contrast among them. Rule out choice B; while the feeding and hunting habits of black bears and white bears are explored, this study tries to address the large question of why Kermodism exists. Similarly, choice D is incorrect because the article mentions the ice age theory as one possible answer to Kermodism, but then dismisses it and seeks an alternate explanation. Finally, eliminate choice E because Kermodism is the only recessive mutation trait that the article explores.

30. A and C. Choice A is correct because lines 1–6 state that white bears are commonly born to black parents, and choice C is correct because lines 12–15 point out that the glacial bear hypothesis fails to explain why white bears have continued to survive since the ice age ended. Lines 18–20 state that black bears and white bears tend to have the same success when fishing at night, so choice B is incorrect.

31. C. In the second paragraph, the author introduces the glacial bear hypothesis as a possible theory to explain the existence of white bears, but then shoots it down because it fails to explain why white bears continue to flourish in the absence of constant snow and ice. Thus, the correct answer is choice C. Eliminate choice A because the glacial bear theory is not really a secondary theme and, in any case, no reference is made to it earlier. Choice B is incorrect because the second paragraph includes no statistics. Choice D is incorrect because the third paragraph does not claim that the question of why black bears produce white offspring is unanswerable. Choice E incorrectly describes the third paragraph.

32. A. The passage centers on the mystery of why black bears produce white offspring. It proposes the glacial bear theory as a possible explanation, but then finds that this explanation fails to explain the white bear's continued existence. Finally, the Klinkas propose the theory that white bears have an advantage in daytime fishing, which answers the objections that the glacial bear theory raises. This overall arc is most similar to a detective story with one motive ultimately displacing another, so the correct answer is choice A. Choice B is incorrect because the passage offers two explanations, not three. Choice C is incorrect because it implies willful duplicity that is not present in the passage. Eliminate choice D because, again, duplicity is implied. Choice E is incorrect because the passage concludes with one explanation being preferable, rather than both being equally valid.

33. C. The glacial bear hypothesis is unfounded because it explains how white bears may have emerged during the ice age, but it fails to account for how they have continued to survive since then. Thus, the correct answer is choice C. Choice A is incorrect because the glacial bear hypothesis relates directly to white bears and isn't intended to explain the existence of black bears. Choice B is incorrect because ice age survival is irrelevant to the premise. Eliminate choice D because the hypothesis doesn't focus on fishing or reproduction. Choice E can be ruled out because the hypothesis does not explain the method by which bears are born white.

34. *"The salmon are less concerned about a white object as seen from below the surface,"* Reimchen speculates. (lines 22–24) is correct.

35. E. Both passages show how the pre-Columbian past affected Mexico's most prominent muralists (choice E). It could be argued that choices A, B, C, and D present secondary relationships, but are too narrow and briefly discussed to clarify the overall relationship between both passages.

36. C. According to Passage 1, Orozco denounced the pre-Columbian past, but according to Passage 2, he *often presented pre-Columbian figures in grand, heroic terms.* These conflicting perspectives suggest ambivalence (choice C). Although Passage 2 states that Rivera *epitomized* the creation of a romanticized version of ancient Mexico, it does not imply that he "most successfully" captured history in his murals, as suggested by choice A. Choice B is contradicted by Passage 1, and the passages do not discuss the subject matter of the majority of Siqueiros's work, as in choice D. Lastly, while Passage 2 implies that Rivera did use his art for political purposes, it does not imply that the other muralists did not also do so (choice E).

37. A. Passage 1, in the last paragraph, states that the muralists' pictorial language and fresco technique fit into the European tradition, but Passage 2 makes no reference to techniques. Therefore, choice A is correct. Choice B inaccurately characterizes Passage 1 as praising the muralists when it simply presents facts. Choice C inaccurately places the discussion within context of the current socioeconomic climate. Choice D is incorrect because no public reaction is described. Choice E is incorrect because Rivera is not identified as the most important Mexican muralist by Passage 1.

38. B. Passage 1 notes that Orozco envisioned the pre-Columbian world as *inhabited by vengeful, inhospitable gods* (line 9). Choice A is not mentioned. Choice C is incorrect, as Orozco *disdained the use of romanticized nationalism* (lines 25–26).

39. D. Both describe the championing and romanticizing of Mexico's pre-Columbian history, but Passage 2 also provides some insight into the motivation for his murals (choice D). Passage 1 does not paint him as naïve, choice A; neither passage implies that he was the most important muralist, choice B; Passage 2 does not describe his background, choice C; and if anything, Passage 2 provides a more intimate discussion, choice E.

40. C. See lines 17–20. Diego Rivera's primary political intention was to energize the Indian population and direct it toward the future (choice C). Choice A confuses Rivera with Orozco. Although choices B, D, and E may have been of interest to Rivera, the passage makes it clear that revitalizing the Indian population was the purpose of his mural.

41. A and C. Both passages reference or imply the use of Mexican subject matter, choice A, and Passage 2 discusses Rivera's recognition of the *poor Indian class* (choice C). However, neither passage indicates that the muralists disdained European art, as suggested by choice B; in fact, Passage 1 states that the muralists used traditional European techniques.

42. C. It is the stability of the Chinese civilization (choice C) that is emphasized in the passage. Choice A is a secondary point, and choices D and E, though mentioned, are not main points. The regional differences, choice B, are not described as *relatively insignificant,* even though they have not significantly destabilized China's civilization.

43. B. The last sentence suggests that the powerful bureaucracy may have been responsible for the country's stability (choice B). The other choices may or may not be true, but they are not given as the possible cause of China's stability.

44. B. The passage reads *On this 100th anniversary of his death, Twain...*, making choice B correct. The author does not attempt to sell any books (choice A), and choice C contradicts the author's purpose. Choice D references only a supporting point of the passage, while choice E misrepresents the passage's focus.

45. C. As the passage quotes Twain, *"We have ground the manhood out of them and the shame is ours, not theirs; and we should pay for it."* Choices A, D, and E are never mentioned in the passage, and Twain specifically mentioned that he would not have helped just any student who had asked, choice B.

46. A. The irony and vernacular in *The Adventures of Huckleberry Finn* may have confused some readers and led to a *misunderstanding* of Twain's feelings about slavery and issues of race. Choice B is never discussed, and choice C incorrectly suggests that *most* readers interpreted the work as racist. Choice D references the wrong book, while choice E presents the opposite of what actually happened.

47. E. Later in the sentence, the author confirms that the term refers to the 100th anniversary of *The Adventures of Huckleberry Finn*. Choice A incorrectly characterizes the party as annual, while choice B attributes the anniversary to the wrong book. Choice C is incorrect because the passage was published on the 100th anniversary of Twain's *death*. Choice D is not suggested.

48. E. According to the passage, Pudd'nhead Wilson was an *eccentric but clever lawyer* in one of his novels. Choices A and B represent real people, and choices C and D confuse the character with the slave in *The Adventures of Huckleberry Finn*.

49. A, B, and C. 14% of senior girls are involved in sports, compared with 13% of sophomore girls, choice A; 25% of junior girls are involved in the newspaper/yearbook, compared with 26% of senior girls, choice B; 53% of sophomore girls are involved in music/drama, compared with 51% of senior girls, choice C.

50. C. 63% of senior boys are involved in music/drama, the highest of any group/activity combination (choice E); 62% of sophomore boys are involved in music/drama, second-highest (choice A); and 58% of junior boys are involved in music/drama, the third-highest of any group/activity combination, making choice C the correct answer. Choice B (5%) and choice D (26%) represent percentages that are too small.

51. D. Junior and senior boys are significantly less involved with the newspaper/yearbook than are girls in each respective year, despite being more involved than their female counterparts as sophomores. Therefore, the data supports incentivizing involvement of upperclassman boys with newspaper/yearbook (choice D). More girls already play sports than boys in each grade, choice A; more boys than girls participate in music/drama in each year, choice B; involvement in sports is consistent or slightly increases from year to year in each group, choice C; and music/drama already represent the strongest program area in terms of involvement, by far, choice E.

52. D. Choice D does not satisfy the requirements set forth in the passage because it includes only two literature courses from the same century or movement. All of the other choices include three literature courses from the same century or movement, along with English 600, either English 500 or English 504, and English 740–742.

53. E. The last sentence of the passage defines respiration as *releasing energy from food* (choice E). Choices A, B, C, and D all present functions that the passages attribute to breathing rather than respiration.

54. B. The second sentence states that breathing is a function of many multicellular animals. From this it can be inferred that not all multicellular animals breathe. The passage doesn't imply that either respiration or breathing is more important than the other. Choices A, C, D, and E are simply incorrect according to the information provided in the passage.

55. B. Clarifying the confusing term *annual angular displacement* would help make the passage easier for a general, nonscientific audience to understand. Choices A and D suggest changes that would make the passage more complex, if anything, and choice C would address concerns about legitimacy, rather than clarity. Choice E suggests eliminating the only portion of the passage that attempts to portray the concept in layman's terms.

56. B. The position of the pencil seemingly shifts according to which eye is seeing it—that is, according to the point from which it is observed (choice B). Choices A and E incorrectly focus on the identity of the object used in the example, while choice C is not implied by a simple demonstration. Choice D is never suggested.

Writing Test: Selected Response

1. E. This sentence contains no error. The construction of *not only for … but also for* is parallel; *generally* is correctly used, choice C, and *and which,* choice D, correctly introduces the dependent clause that follows.

2. D. The antecedent of the pronouns is *children,* which requires plural pronouns; *him* in choice D should be *they*. Choice B (*affected*) is the correct verb here. *Effected* and *affected* are frequently confused.

3. A. *Lie* and *lay* are frequently confused. Here, the word should be *lying* because the verb does not take an object. *Laying* is used when the verb does take an object. For example, "The team members were laying their books on the grass." Choice C (*who*) is correct in the sentence; it is the subject of *lost*. Choices B (*beginning*) and choice D (*began*) are the correct verb tenses. Remember to look at other words in the sentence to establish a time scheme so that verb tenses (present, past, and future) are logical and consistent.

4. **B.** Because of the placement of the word *frequently* in this sentence, it is unclear whether the people *wrote letters* frequently or *recount* frequently. To solve the problem, the word *frequently* could be placed preceding the word *write*. Using a comma between *letters* and *frequently* or between *frequently* and *recount* would be inappropriate because it would set off the subject from its verb.

5. **A.** *You* is the correct pronoun in this sentence instead of *yourself*. *Yourself* is the reflexive form of the pronoun and is correct only in such structures as *You, yourself, must be there* (subject repeated for emphasis) and *You hurt yourself* (subject repeated as object).

6. **E.** This sentence contains no error. *The inquiry method,* choice D, is parallel to *observation* and *discovery* (all nouns). Adding the article *the* and the adjective *inquiry* to the noun does not change the fact that it is parallel.

7. **D.** *More or less* contradicts the idea of *minimum* and should be eliminated for the sake of clarity.

8. **C.** The placement of *even the most hardworking* makes it seem that the phrase refers to *term papers* rather than to *graduate students* (which it correctly modifies). The problem may be solved by moving the phrase to the beginning of the sentence. There should be no comma between *students* and *who,* choice A, because *who write formal term papers* is restrictive (not all students are discussed here). *Have difficulty with,* choice D, is the correct idiom.

9. **D.** *Visual affects* should be *visual effects. Affect* is a verb, meaning to act upon or influence. *Effect* is a noun, meaning a distinct impression (as in this example) or a verb meaning to bring about.

10. **E.** The present tense is always used when referring to *a series of books;* therefore, *tells* is correct. As *tells* refers to *a series* (singular) not to *books* (plural), the singular form of the verb is correct.

11. **C.** The pronoun *whom,* not *who,* is correct here. It is the object, not the subject, of *they had scheduled to appear. Who* is used for subjects and *whom* is used for objects. For example: "The man *who* spoke" and "the man *whom* we saw."

12. **D.** *Using* should be *which use. Was written,* choice B, is the correct tense of the verb, and choice A, *protagonists,* is the correct word choice.

13. **B.** The construction *either ... or* in this sentence should be followed by a singular verb (*was*) because the subject closest to the verb is singular. The same rule applies to *neither ... nor.*

14. **D.** In the first clause of the sentence, the pronoun *it* is used to refer to the dog; in the second clause, *him* is used. Pronouns should be consistent within a sentence. The use of the semicolon before *however* is correct. A period or a semicolon is required to prevent a comma splice or run-on sentence.

15. **A.** *Libraries* should be either *libraries'* (the plural possessive) or *library's* (the singular possessive), depending on the intent of the writer. *Children's,* choice B, is the correct formation of an irregular plural possessive (*woman's/women's—man's/men's—mouse's/mice's*) where the root word changes to form the plural. *Fact-finding* correctly hyphenates two words used as a single adjective *preceding* a noun (*She was a well-known author* but *The author was well known*).

16. **B.** *Constructing* is not parallel with *design. Construction,* a noun, is the correct word. Choice D is correct; with *spending* (a gerund, which is a participle used as a noun), and the possessive pronoun is appropriate (*our,* not *us*).

17. **C.** *Have led* should be singular (*has led*) because the subject of the verb is singular (*cooperation*). *Clubs* is not the subject. Also, when more than two things are referred to, *among,* choice B, rather than *between* is correct.

18. **A.** The problem in this sentence is that by placing a semicolon after *frost,* a fragment is created (choice A). The opening clause of the sentence is not independent, so the semicolon should be a comma.

19. **D.** The correct tense of the verb here is *had. They* should also be eliminated. The noun *effect* is correct, and *subsidize* is used and spelled correctly.

20. **E.** This sentence contains no error. The infinitive forms of the verbs in the sentence are correct; they give the sentence parallel structure.

21. **C.** The original sentence lacks parallel structure. Choices B and D do not change *accepting* to the parallel verb form *to accept.* Choice E changes the meaning of the sentence. Choice C is correct and parallel to the three other verb phrases *to walk, to cross the street independently,* and *to care for one's possessions.*

22. **E.** The singular verb *is* needs to be plural to agree with *sea forests.* Choice B is singular. Although *are* is used in choices C and D, C is idiomatically wrong, and D does not make sense. Choice E corrects the verb error and structurally fits with the rest of the original sentence.

23. **B.** The subject of this sentence includes four people—*the social worker, the physician,* and *both parents*—so it requires a plural verb instead of *has.* Additionally, *in suggestion of* as an adjective to describe *the nurse* is awkward and ungrammatical. Choices A and C are incorrect because the subject of the sentence is plural, but the verbs *has* and *is* are singular. Choice D is incorrect because the progressive tense verb *are agreeing* is awkward and the passive construction *suggested by* is a weak word choice. *Being suggested,* choice E, is an incorrect verb tense in reference to an event that occurred *three days ago.* The plural verb *have,* choice B, is in agreement with the subject; the verb *suggested* is correctly in the past tense and active voice.

24. **B.** Characters cannot be compared to the novel *Crime and Punishment.* Choice B inserts *those,* which correctly words the comparison. Choices D and E create an incomplete sentence and leave out necessary information. *Exhibits* in choice C is singular and incorrect.

25. **D.** Choices A and B are not parallel and contain the redundant phrase *of many Spaniards.* Choices C and E are also redundant because they include the words *Spaniards* and *Spanish.* Choice D is parallel and concise.

26. **A.** In the original sentence, *along with all the other arts* is correctly set off by commas, and *is* is the correct verb form to agree with *poetry,* a singular subject. Choice E changes the meaning of the original sentence.

27. **B.** Choice B is the only grammatically correct choice that does not change the meaning. Choice A contains a dangling modifier, as the phrase beginning *Perhaps too eager ...* mistakenly modifies *debt* rather than *Japan.* Choice C incorrectly uses *to* rather than *too* and arbitrarily adds the adverb *continually;* choice D changes the meaning of the sentence by adding *currently;* and choice E changes the meaning by putting Japan's actions in the past tense.

28. **E.** The original sentence contains a parallelism error; the phrase *as large in* [Neanderthals] requires the parallel *as in* [modern humans], which limits the correct answer choices to D or E. Choice D, however, contains an error in its nonrestrictive use of the pronoun *that,* such that its reference is unclear (its antecedent is *humans*), and the sentence no longer makes sense. Choice E creates a separate, independent clause and correctly separates the two clauses with a semicolon, followed by the more specific pronoun *this,* thus providing a clear, grammatically correct choice.

29. **C.** The original sentence contains a diction error; *between* should be used only to refer to two objects. As there are twelve board members, *among* should be used. Thus, choice B is incorrect. Choices C, D, and E correct this diction error, but choice D introduces a verb agreement error (using the plural *were* to refer to the singular *level of tension*), and choice E omits key information (the fact that there are twelve board members). Thus, choice C is correct.

30. **D.** The original bolded phrase contains two errors. First, *much* should be used only to refer to uncountable terms (e.g., *knowledge, respect*), while *many* should be used for quantifiable items such as *flies.* Second, *die out over a week* is idiomatically incorrect; the correct phrasing is *die out within a week.* Choice D fixes both of these errors. Choice B does not fix the *much/many* error and unnecessarily adds words (*the span of*), while choices C and E do not fix the idiomatic error.

31. **A.** As it is, the sentence is wordy. To say that the changes were disruptive because they disturbed people is redundant; the word *disruptive* indicates that the changes disturbed people. *Due to the fact* is also wordy. The version in choice A eliminates the redundancy and is concise. The other choices do not address the redundancy problem.

32. **B.** This sentence shows an agreement problem between subject and verb (*class was created,* not *class were created*). Choice C, although it does use the active voice for both subjects, is awkward. The active voice (*created*) in choice B is more effective and concise than *gave rise to* in choice C. Choice D has a subject/verb agreement problem and also uses the passive voice of the verb. Choice E has a dangling participle.

33. **A.** Choice A is the only choice that corrects the sentence fragment by removing *who*. Choice D removes *who*, but its structure still makes it a fragment.

34. **C.** This sentence is an example of the statement made in Sentence 10; therefore, its best placement would be between Sentences 10 and 11.

35. **D.** Sentence 4 states that people had to move to larger towns and cities, which indicates that for them the simpler pleasures of the countryside vanished; therefore, the best placement is after Sentence 4. Choice B is incorrect; the effect of the Industrial Revolution has not yet been stated. Choices A, C, and E are not good locations for Sentence 8. Sentence 8 deals with the working class, while those locations deal with the industrialists and factory owners.

36. **E.** Although none of these sentences may be ideal as a conclusion, choice E provides a link to the previous sentence as well as addresses the content of the passage as a whole and, therefore, is the best choice. Choice B is flat and mechanical. Choice C is not connected to the previous sentence, and choice A focuses on Roosevelt, not the subject of the passage. Choice D is simply inaccurate in terms of the rest of the paragraph.

37. **C.** Evaluating the origin and credibility of your sources can be challenging. One of the best sources is an article from a scholarly (peer-reviewed) academic journal, but citing outdated information, as in choice C, can diminish the validity of your research paper. Choices A, B, and D are the most reliable sources. These sources include current information written by qualified and recognized authors in their respective academic fields. Choice E, class lecture notes, are frequently cited in research papers.

Note: The most unreliable sources have anonymous or unrecognized authors. Always evaluate the credibility of your sources and be wary of information circulated in chat rooms, on discussion boards, on bulletin boards, and in newspaper reports that appear biased or inaccurate.

38. **D.** Reference 1 uses the correct format for a book. Reference 2 uses the format for an academic journal. Reference 3 is a citation from a book anthology, reference, or collection. Reference 4 is an online academic journal. Online sources always indicate where the information was retrieved from and the date on which it was accessed.

39. **C.** Choice C is a primary source because it is an actual speech that was presented by the civil rights leader, Cesar Chavez. A primary source is a document that was written, expressed, or spoken during the time under study. Primary sources are *original* sources that offer an "inside view" of the particular event or person being studied and are often written by someone who witnessed or experienced the event directly. For example, the book, *Anne Frank: The Diary of a Young Girl,* is a primary source, because it is a personal diary written by a girl who experienced the Holocaust.

Internet search key words that identify primary sources are interviews, letters, diaries, early works, correspondence, manuscripts, sources, speeches, and personal documents. Choices A, B, and D are secondary sources. Although these choices may be historically accurate, they are "secondhand" accounts told by a third party. Secondary sources are often published in literary criticisms, newspaper commentaries, reports, magazine articles, encyclopedias, and textbooks. Choice E is incorrect because it is a report on "civil rights and immigration," not on "leaders of national civil rights."

40. **C.** Choice C is the only answer that illustrates the correct use of in-text documentation of quotations. If you reference a direct quote from an author, always use quotation marks around the author's words, followed by parenthetical, in-text documentation. Choices A, B, and D refer to paraphrased versions of the author's original work, not direct quotations. When paraphrasing or summarizing an author's ideas, concepts, or theoretical views (choices A, B, and D), parenthetical documentation must be inserted to avoid plagiarism. However, if you paraphrase and restate an author's direct quote, you can exclude the quotation marks.

Writing Test: Essay

Essay 1: Argumentative Essay

A high-scoring strong student response is provided below to help you evaluate your essay. The commentary at the end of this section will further help you identify your areas of improvement.

Read the opinion stated below:

According to the Wildlife and Nature Conservancy Group, "There is so much untapped potential for increased recycling and conservation efforts. It's time for public institutions to step up again because the status quo is not good enough."

Assignment: Discuss the extent to which you agree or disagree with this opinion. Support your views with specific reasons and examples from your own experiences, observations, or readings.

High-Scoring Strong Response

The Wildlife and Nature Conservancy Group's assertion that public institutions should "step up again because the status quo is not good enough" is a statement that should be taken to heart by those with the ability to implement change. Public institutions have the ability to initiate programs, both mandatory and voluntary, that can increase awareness and encourage the individual to take action. While it is the individual who should ultimately care for their environment and take personal responsibility, it is incumbent upon federal, state, and local governments to provide added incentives and institute new laws that will not only encourage, but require citizens to participate in conservation and recycling efforts.

In many states, recycling is highly encouraged, but in others it is largely ignored. For example, in California most public utilities provide recycling containers for their customers. In addition, the CRV (California Redemption Value) is mandated throughout the state. The CRV is a charge added to plastic and aluminum products, which can then be redeemed when the container is recycled. This method of both mandating a charge upon purchase, and providing an incentive for recycling, has brought real change in both thought and behavior throughout the state. However, many other states and local municipalities are not voluntarily instituting programs to promote recycling. In those states, it may be necessary to implement mandates at the federal level.

Although some people who have the power to institute change don't agree, I believe conservation should be mandatory. For example, the state of California has been in a serious drought since 2011. As a result, the Governor issued a state of emergency requiring water agencies throughout the state to cut water usage by 25%. While this measure may be considered extreme, voluntary water rationing did not provide the needed results to insure an adequate water supply throughout the state. In addition, many counties throughout the state of California have created legislation that bans the use of plastic bags due to the fact that plastic bags are a non-renewable resource, are harmful to animals, and add to the landfill problem. On the other hand, the state of Arizona recently passed legislation that actually prohibits local counties from enacting plastic bag bans. This lack of awareness, and overall ignorance, exacerbates the challenge of stepping up conservation efforts.

Governments can also provide incentives, such as tax credits and rebates, for voluntary conservation. The Southern California Water District offered its customers turf removal rebates to replace grass with drought-tolerant landscaping. While this was a popular way to promote water conservation, the program funds were exhausted quickly. Since most tax credits and incentives have limitations in funding, they end all too quickly. Legislators should recognize the need to innovate and provide continued funding for conservation programs.

Public institutions have the power and the responsibility to "step up" their efforts to promote recycling and conservation efforts. By taking a proactive approach, and searching for innovative ways to encourage these efforts, the "powers that be" have the potential to change the way the public thinks and, hopefully, how they take action in conservation and recycling. While public institutions can "set the tone" and implement policy, it is, ultimately, up to each individual to shift their own thinking and habits. Through a collaborative effort between the individual and public institutions, we can provide a sustainable world for our generation and generations to come.

Commentary

The author's strong response clearly states the thesis that public institutions should take the lead in promoting recycling and conservation. The essay is well organized and logical in sequence. Each paragraph is carefully constructed, and the introductory sentences relate directly to the supporting sentences in the corresponding paragraphs. In addition, a variety of pertinent examples and details are used to strengthen the writer's opinion and viewpoint. The essay follows the conventions of standard written English with minimal errors in grammar, usage, and sentence structure. In addition, the writer uses the concluding paragraph to reinforce the thesis. The author provides relevant examples, states a clear position, and uses a logical and well-organized structure to communicate the point of view that public institutions should "step up" their efforts in promoting recycling and conservation.

Essay 2: Informative/Explanatory Essay

Assignment:

Both of the following passages address children and play. In particular, both discuss the importance of make-believe play in the classroom. Read the two passages carefully and then write an essay in which you identify the most important concerns regarding the issue and explain why they are important. Your essay must draw on information from BOTH of the sources. In addition, you may draw upon your own experiences, observations, and readings.

When paraphrasing or quoting from the sources, cite each source by referring to the author's last name, the title of the source, or any other clear identifier.

High-Scoring Strong Response

Make-believe play is an important component of preschool education that provides children with a variety of benefits, and a time that must not be lost in the pursuit of additional classroom learning. Parents and educators who encourage elaborate forms of collaborative, make-believe play provide their preschoolers with maximum opportunity to grow and develop.

Ciciora (2009), the author of Source 1, notes that adults tend to have good intentions when they minimize playtime for preschoolers and "bombard them with information," but that this "banning of the imagination" actually does children a disservice. As Dyson puts it, play is "where literacy and learning really begins." The authors of Source 2, Leong and Bodrova (2012), echo this warning, noting that playtime should not be thought of as a gimmick or an optional activity, but as one that provides the "most beneficial context" for a child's development. The biggest takeaway from the two passages is one in which the two authors are in agreement: play is a crucial element of preschool and should be treated as such.

However, according to Source 2, merely allowing time for unstructured play is insufficient. Source 2 takes Source 1's argument a step further, claiming that the greatest benefits of play come from the creation of intricate, interactive worlds of make-believe, and that "without adult support, the play of many children is destined to never reach this fully developed status." This lesson resonates with my own preschool experience; although I was a reserved child who tended to play independently when left to my own devices, I always felt most engaged and creative when encouraged to collaborate with others.

The authors of Sources 1 and 2 both make compelling arguments against the sacrifice of playtime in favor of traditional classroom education of preschoolers. However, as put forth by Source 2, it is also necessary for adults to take on a proactive role in the encouragement and development of such make-believe play. Through the facilitation of complex, dynamic make-believe play, parents and educators can provide children with the best possible environment in which to learn and develop.

Commentary

This "informative/explanatory" essay critically analyzes both perspectives on the issue of children and play. It provides explicit supporting evidence to explain each author's viewpoint. The logical organization of the essay is well developed and follows the four-paragraph model to compare and contrast relevant perspectives of each source. Specific citations are used from both sources to offer details and reasons for each author's line of reasoning. The essay follows the conventions of standard written English with minimal errors in grammar, usage, and sentence structure. The concluding paragraph sums up the supporting connections between both sources. The key is that the writer does a good job of extracting information from both sources while making clear connections between the two sources related to the issue of children and play.

Mathematics Test

1. **C.** Let x represent the price of the pair of shoes before the 40% discount. That is, 100% of x was the original price. Then $100\%x - 40\%x = \$25.50$, or $60\%x = \$25.50$.

   Now divide $25.50 by the decimal name of 60%, 0.60, to find x: $\$25.50 \div 0.60 = \$42.50$, choice C.

2. **C.** Since the figure is a rectangle, its opposite sides are equal. To find its perimeter, first add the two touching sides, 18 and 22, and then double the sum (or double each of the sides and add the results).

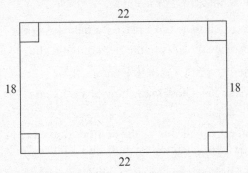

   Now, to determine the side of a square with the same perimeter, simply divide the perimeter by 4, since the side of a square is $\dfrac{1}{4}$ its perimeter. Finally, to find the area of the square, multiply its side times itself (square it). Choice C correctly outlines these steps.

3. **A, C, and D.**

$$\text{The perimeter of } \triangle ABC = \quad AB \quad + \quad BC \quad + \quad AC$$
$$= (4x+5)+(5x-1)+(3x+7)$$
$$= 12x+11$$

$$\text{If } AB = BC, \text{ then } 4x+5 = 5x-1$$
$$6 = x$$

   If $x = 6$, then the perimeter of $\triangle ABC = 12(6) + 11 = 83$, choice D.

$$\text{If } AB = AC, \text{ then } 4x+5 = 3x+7$$
$$x = 2$$

   If $x = 2$, then the perimeter of $\triangle ABC = 12(2) + 11 = 35$, choice A.

$$\text{If } AC = BC, \text{ then } 3x+7 = 5x-1$$
$$8 = 2x$$
$$4 = x$$

   If $x = 4$, then the perimeter of $\triangle ABC = 12(4) + 11 = 59$, choice C.

   Therefore, choices A, C, and D are all possible perimeters for $\triangle ABC$.

4. B. Note that all choices except B are larger than $\frac{1}{2}$. Choice B, $\frac{4}{9}$, is smaller than $\frac{1}{2}$ and is therefore the smallest among the answer choices.

5. 11 Use the formula provided to plug in the numeric information from the word problem.

$$12 \text{ amps} \times 120 \text{ volts} = 1{,}440 \text{ watts per hour}$$

$$16{,}000 \text{ total watts} \div 1{,}440 \text{ watts per hour} \approx 11.11 \text{ hours}$$

Rounded to the nearest whole number, the answer is 11.

6. C. The three passengers will be charged $7.50 each for a total of $22.50. One hour and 45 minutes is $1\frac{3}{4}$ hours. Traveling at an average rate of 40 miles per hour for $1\frac{3}{4}$ hours, the taxi will have traveled $40\left(1\frac{3}{4}\right) = 70$ miles. At 6 cents for each quarter of a mile, the charge would be 24 cents a mile. At 24 cents per mile, the cost for traveling 70 miles is ($0.24)(70) = $16.80. The total cost is then $22.50 + $16.80 = $39.30, choice C.

7. B. 210,000 is equivalent to $(2 \times 10^5) + (1 \times 10^4)$. A fast way of figuring this is to count the number of places to the right of each digit that is not zero. For instance,

     $\underline{2}10{,}000$ Note that there are 5 places to the right of the 2, thus 2×10^5.

     $2\underline{1}0{,}000$ There are 4 places to the right of the 1, thus 1×10^4.

So 210,000 may also be written $(2 \times 10^5) + (1 \times 10^4)$, choice B.

8. E. Since the chart does not distinguish how many houses are 3 years old or 4 years old, the number cannot be determined, choice E.

9. C. If the product of two numbers equals one of the numbers, then $(x)(y) = x$. If this product is more than 0, neither of the numbers may be zero. Therefore, y must be 1, choice C: $(x)(1) = x$.

10. A. This problem can be solved using simple number replacements or using an algebraic approach.

Method 1: Suppose the original length was 6 and the original width was 4. The original area would be 24. The new length is 12 (double the 6) and the new width is 3 (25% of 4 is 1 and 4 decreased by 1 is 3). The new area is 36 (12 × 3). Then 36 is 1.5 times more than 24, choice A.

Method 2: If you let l be the original length and w be the original width, then lw is the original area. The new length will be $2l$ and the new width will be $0.75w$, making the new area become $(2l)(0.75w) = 1.5lw$. That is, the new area is 1.5 times the original area.

11. B. In the 3rd quarter, the profit was $30,000. In the 4th quarter, the profit was $40,000.

$$\text{Percent change} = \frac{\text{amount of change}}{\text{original amount}} \times 100\%$$
$$= \frac{10{,}000}{30{,}000} \times 100\%$$
$$\approx .33\overline{3} \times 100\%$$
$$\approx 33\%$$

12. 6

= Cross symbol

= Heart symbol

= E-symbol

The problem requires that you translate symbols into numbers. Begin by calculating the value of one cross symbol. Because four of these cross symbols have a value of 12, one of them has a value of 3. The second line now is translated into 3 + three heart symbols = 18. Thus, three heart symbols have a value 15, or one heart symbol has a value of 5.

The third line is now translated into 3 + 5 + two E-symbols = 20. Two E-symbols, therefore, have a value of 12, and each E-symbol has a value of 6.

13. $\dfrac{17}{33}$ Look for patterns in numerators and denominators. In this case, the numerator increases, first by 1, then by 2, then by 3, and then by 4. If this pattern continues, the next numerator would increase by 5, making it 17. The denominators increase as well, first by 2, then by 4, then by 6, and then by 8. If this pattern continues, the next denominator would increase by 10, making it 33. Therefore, the next fraction in this list would be $\dfrac{17}{33}$.

14. **B.** A die has six sides. If it is rolled three times, there are (6)(6)(6) = 216 possible outcomes. Some of these result in all three rolls containing different numbers, and some rolls include duplicate numbers. The probability of rolling different numbers on all three rolls is the quotient between favorable outcomes divided by the total number of outcomes. The first roll can be any of the six sides, since it will not match anything. The second roll is limited to five choices, since one has already been selected by the previous roll. The third roll is limited to four choices, since the first two rolls have selected two of the choices.

Therefore, the probability of all three rolls resulting in different numbers is $\dfrac{(6)(5)(4)}{(6)(6)(6)} = \dfrac{120}{216} \approx 0.56$, choice B.

15. **D.** There are two methods to solve this problem: (1) arithmetic logic and (2) algebra computation.

Method 1: Determine the ratio of the differences between the balance point (average) of $1.80 and both endpoints ($2.10 and $1.30). The differences are $0.30 and $0.50. Their ratio is 3 to 5. Divide the 8 pounds into two numbers that are in that same ratio. Clearly, that is 3 pounds and 5 pounds. Since the balance point (average) of $1.80 is closer to the $2.10, the larger weight must be assigned there, thus the 5-pound weight is assigned to the $2.10 nuts, choice D.

Method 2: Let x be what we are looking for; that is, the number of pounds of the $2.10 nuts. Set up an equation and solve for x.

$$(x)(2.10) + (8-x)(1.30) = (8)(1.80)$$
$$2.10x + (8)(1.30) - 1.30x = (8)(1.80)$$
$$2.1x + 10.4 - 1.3x = 14.4$$
$$0.8x = 4$$
$$x = \dfrac{4}{0.8}$$
$$x = 5$$

16. **E.** If Tony's age is y, then Alex's age is $\dfrac{y}{2} - 2$.

If Alex's age is $\dfrac{y}{2} - 2$, then David's age is $(4)\left(\dfrac{y}{2} - 2\right) + 4 = 2y - 8 + 4 = 2y - 4$, choice E.

17. **D.** Using the probability formula, probability $= \dfrac{\text{number of "lucky" chances}}{\text{total number of chances}}$, the chance of choosing a weekday is $\dfrac{5 \text{ weekdays}}{7 \text{ total days}}$, or $\dfrac{5}{7}$, choice D.

18. **E.** Note that since there is a mark between +7 and +9, that mark equals +8. Thus, each mark equals 1. Counting back, point Q is at +5.

Therefore, 15 units to the left of +5 would be +5 −15 = −10, choice E.

19. C. The *product of two numbers* indicates the numbers must be multiplied together. Their *sum* means "add." Therefore, choice C is correct:

$$\underbrace{\text{the product of two numbers}}_{(X)(Y)} \underbrace{\text{equals}}_{=} \underbrace{\text{five more than their sum}}_{X+Y+5}$$

20. 17 If the average of six numbers is 8, their total must be $6 \times 8 = 48$. After the three additional numbers are combined, the total must be $9 \times 11 = 99$. This is an increase of $99 - 48 = 51$. Therefore, the sum of the three additional numbers is 51. Thus, their average is $\frac{51}{3} = 17$. So, the correct answer is 17.

21. D. If each student drinks $\frac{1}{5}$ of a gallon of lemonade, 1 gallon is consumed by 5 students. Since 28 students are in attendance, $\frac{28}{5} = 5\frac{3}{5}$, which is a number between 5 and 6, choice D.

22. A, B, C, D, and E. Calculate the value of a for the two extremes of the range of $x°$.

If $x = 30°$, then using the 30-60-90 ratio relationship $\left(1:2:\sqrt{3}\right)$, the length of side AB is $2a$, and the length of side AC is $a\sqrt{3}$. Since side AC is given as length 6, we have $a\sqrt{3} = 6$, or $a = \frac{6}{\sqrt{3}} = \frac{6\sqrt{3}}{3} = 2\sqrt{3}$. Similarly, if $x = 60°$, using the 30-60-90 ratio relationship $\left(1:2:\sqrt{3}\right)$, the length of side AB is $2 \times 6 = 12$, and the length of side BC is $6\sqrt{3}$. Therefore, $a = 6\sqrt{3}$. These are the two extremes for the value of a. The relationship can be written as $2\sqrt{3} \leq a \leq 6\sqrt{3}$.

What remains to be done is to determine between what pairs of consecutive integers these values are located. If we square $2\sqrt{3}$, we get 12. The square root of 12 is between 3 and 4. If we square $6\sqrt{3}$, we get 108. The square root of 108 is between 10 and 11. Also, remember that you have the use of a calculator. Therefore, possible values of a are 4, 5, 6, 7, and 8—choices A, B, C, D, and E. (*Note:* 9 and 10 are also possible values, but they aren't among the choices given.)

23. E. Be sure you answer the question. The question is to find the cost of the accessories, not the cost of the cell phone. This problem can be worked algebraically or by trial and error.

Method 1: To do the problem algebraically, start by either representing the cost of the cell phone or the cost of the accessories. Suppose x = the cost of the cell phone, and then $x + 20$ = the cost of the accessories, since the accessories cost \$20 more than the cell phone. The combined cost is \$100, so

$$x + x + 20 = 100$$
$$2x + 20 = 100$$
$$2x = 80$$
$$x = 40$$

But the "x" is the cost of the cell phone, and the question asks for the cost of the accessories. Because the accessories cost \$20 more than the phone, the answer is \$60, choice E. Suppose x = the cost of the accessories, and then $x - 20$ = the cost of the cell phone. Then the equation would have been

$$x + x - 20 = 100$$
$$2x - 20 = 100$$
$$2x = 120$$
$$x = 60$$

Since the "x" here represents the cost of the accessories, you have the desired answer.

Method 2: The answer can also be found by trial and error. Remember, the answer choices represent the cost of the accessories.

cost of accessories + cost of cell phone = 100 (recall that the accessories are $20 more than the cell phone)

Choice A: 20 + 0 = 100   NO

Choice B: 30 + 10 = 100   NO

Choice C: 40 + 20 = 100   NO

Choice D: 50 + 30 = 100   NO

Choice E: 60 + 40 = 100   YES

24. **30** One approach is to list the divisors for each number:

$$96: \underline{2}, 3, \underline{4}, 6, \underline{8}, 12, \underline{16}, 24, 32, 48, 96$$
$$80: \underline{2}, \underline{4}, 5, \underline{8}, 10, \underline{16}, 20, 40, 80$$

The common divisors are 2, 4, 8, and 16. Their sum is 30.

Another approach would be to factor each number to determine the common factors:

$$96 = \underline{2} \times \underline{2} \times \underline{2} \times \underline{2} \times 2 \times 3$$
$$80 = \underline{2} \times \underline{2} \times \underline{2} \times \underline{2} \times 5$$

The common factors are 2, 2, 2, and 2. Therefore, the common divisors must be 2, 4, 8, and 16. This also gives the sum of 30.

25. **E.** Simplifying this problem first means changing $\frac{1}{5}$ to 0.2. Next, change 0.02 percent to 0.0002 (that is, $0.02 \times 0.01 = 0.0002$).

Now that you have simplified the problem, multiply 0.2×0.0002, which gives 0.00004, choice E. Notice that simplifying can make a problem much easier to solve.

26. **C.** The mean of a set of data is found by finding the sum of all the data values and dividing by how many data values there are. Using the frequency table, we find the sum of the data as follows:

$$(3)(4) + (4)(1) + (5)(2) + (8)(3) = 12 + 4 + 10 + 24 = 50$$

Since there are 10 data values, the mean $= \frac{50}{10} = 5$.

The median of a set of data is the middle value when the values are listed from least to greatest. From the frequency column, we see that there are 10 data values ($4 + 1 + 2 + 3 = 10$). The median is then the average (arithmetic mean) between the 5th and 6th scores. From the table we see that the first four scores are 3, the 5th score is 4, and the 6th score is 5. The median then is found by finding the sum of 4 and 5 and dividing it by 2. The median $= \frac{4+5}{2} = \frac{9}{2} = 4\frac{1}{2}$.

Since the mean is 5, and the median is $4\frac{1}{2}$, choice C is the correct answer.

27. **C.** One way to solve this problem is to set up a proportion: 10 kilometers is to 6.2 miles as 45 kilometers is to how many miles? This proportion is expressed in mathematical terms as

$$\frac{10 \text{ kilometers}}{6.2 \text{ miles}} = \frac{45 \text{ kilometers}}{x \text{ miles}}$$

Cross multiplying yields

$$10x = 6.2 \times 45$$
$$10x = 279$$

Dividing both sides by 10 yields

$$\frac{10x}{10} = \frac{279}{10}$$
$$x = 27.9$$

There are 27.9 miles in 45 kilometers, choice C.

Another method is to realize that 45 kilometers is exactly $4\frac{1}{2}$ times 10 kilometers.

Therefore, the number of miles in 45 kilometers must be $4\frac{1}{2}$ times the number of miles in 10 kilometers, or $4\frac{1}{2}$ times 6.2. Thus, 4.5 × 6.2 = 27.9.

28. A, B, C, and D. First determine the four lodging amounts in question:

$$15\% \text{ of } 40,400 = 0.15 \times 40,400 = 6,060$$
$$20\% \text{ of } 40,400 = 0.20 \times 40,400 = 8,080$$
$$20\% \text{ of } 45,000 = 0.20 \times 45,000 = 9,000$$
$$25\% \text{ of } 45,000 = 0.25 \times 45,000 = 11,250$$

Since the two ranges overlap, the minimum change would be $0.00 or 0%. To determine the maximum change, consider the two extremes:

$$8,080 \rightarrow 9,000$$

$$\% \text{ change} = \frac{\text{change}}{\text{starting value}} = \frac{920}{8,080} \approx 0.114 = 11.4\%$$

$$6,060 \rightarrow 11,250$$

$$\% \text{ change} = \frac{\text{change}}{\text{starting value}} = \frac{5,190}{6,060} \approx 0.856 \approx 85.6\%$$

Therefore, the percent change could range from 0% thru 85.6%, choices A through D.

29. C, D, and E. If $a = 90°$, then the height would be 6, since the parallelogram would be a rectangle. But, $a < 90°$, so the height is almost 6. Therefore, the area would be just under 60.

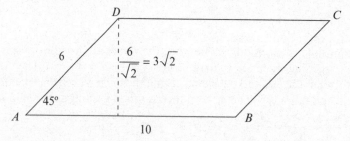

If $a = 45°$, then the height would be $3\sqrt{2}$. (Recall that in the 45-45-90 right triangle, the relationship is $1:1:\sqrt{2}$ and if the hypotenuse is 6, the height would be $\frac{6}{\sqrt{2}} = 3\sqrt{2}$.) But, $a > 45°$, so the height is a little more than $3\sqrt{2}$. Therefore, the area would be a little more than $10 \times 3\sqrt{2} = 30\sqrt{2}$. We can determine between which two given choices $30\sqrt{2}$ lies by squaring it along with the answer choices. Squaring $30\sqrt{2}$ gives 1,800. Since squaring 40 gives 1,600 and squaring 45 gives 2,025, $30\sqrt{2}$ must be greater than 40 and less than 45.

Using a calculator, $30\sqrt{2} \approx 42.4$. Therefore, 45, 50, and 55 (choices C, D, and E) are all possible areas of parallelogram $ABCD$.

30. **B and C.** If all 200 decks were sold at a price yielding a 15% profit, the price per deck would be (1.15)($2.20) = $2.53. Total revenue would be (200)($2.53) = $506. If he sold each deck at a price yielding a 25% profit, the price per deck would be (1.25)($2.20) = $2.75. Total revenue would be (200)($2.75) = $550. Only choices B and C, $520 and $540, yield a revenue between $506 and $550.

31. **C.** The gauge indicator is between 600 and 700, which eliminates choices D and E, each of which is over 700. The space between 600 and 700 is divided into 10 equal sections. Since the total between 600 and 700 is 100 pounds per square foot, each of these 10 sections equals 10 lbs. per square foot. The indicator is exactly three sections beyond 600, so 600 + 3(10) = 630 lbs. per sq. foot, choice C.

32. **B.** This problem can be solved using a Venn diagram. Draw three intersecting circles representing the three movies.

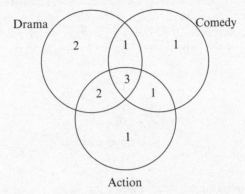

Since three people saw all three movies, place a 3 in the intersection of all three circles. Then, because four people saw exactly two movies, but we don't know which two, distribute the four friends into the three parts of the diagram that are inside exactly two of the circles. It does not matter how you distribute them. In this case, we put a 2 in one of these regions and two 1's in the other two. (You could put 3 in one region 1 in another and zero in the third.) Now fill in the remaining regions of the diagram.

Since eight people saw a drama, we put a 2 in the region in the drama circle that is not inside either of the other two. This gives a total of 8 in the drama circle. Repeat for the comedy circle and the action circle. Adding all the numbers inside at least one of the circles gives a total of 11. This means that one person did not see any of the three movies, choice B.

33. **A.** The four listed items total $1,740. Therefore, by subtracting from the listed total of $2,220, we can see that the missing item must have cost $480: $2,220 – $1,740 = $480, choice A.

34. **D.** The total of the five verbal state test scores is 2,635. Dividing that total by 5 (the number of scores) gives 527 as the average, choice D.

35. **B.** If we call the price of the tie x, then the price of the shirt is $3x$, the price of the slacks is $3x$, and the price of the coat is twice the shirt, or $6x$. Totaling the x's, we get $13x$. Since the total spent was $156, $13x = $156. Dividing both sides by 13 shows

$$\frac{13x}{13} = \frac{\$156}{13}$$
$$x = \$12$$

Therefore, the price of the pair of slacks, $3x$, is 3($12) = $36, choice B.

36. **A.** The first thing you notice is that the distance from W to H is missing and must be calculated. Looking just at the distances, we have the following.

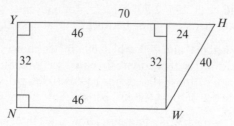

Draw a perpendicular line from W to side $\overline{YH}$. This divides the original trapezoid into a rectangle and a right triangle. The upper side of the triangle has a length of 24 miles since $70 - 46 = 24$. The left side of the triangle is the same as the width of the rectangle, or 32 miles. Therefore, we have a right triangle with legs of 24 and 32, and we need to find the length of the hypotenuse. You could use the Pythagorean theorem directly:

$$a^2 + b^2 = c^2$$
$$24^2 + 32^2 = c^2$$
$$576 + 1{,}024 = c^2$$
$$1{,}600 = c^2$$
$$40 = c$$

The value of 40 miles can be determined more quickly if you remember the Pythagorean triple of 3, 4, 5. (Other common Pythagorean triples are 5, 12, 13 and 8, 15, 17.) These form ratios of right triangles. Since $24 = 3 \times 8$ and $32 = 4 \times 8$, the third side must be 5×8, or 40 miles.

Now calculate the time required for each route and subtract:

Route through Y: $\dfrac{\text{miles}}{\text{miles per hour}} = \dfrac{32}{70} + \dfrac{70}{65} \approx 0.457 + 1.077 \approx 1.534 \text{ hours} \approx 92.0 \text{ minutes}$

Route through W: $\dfrac{\text{miles}}{\text{miles per hour}} = \dfrac{46}{50} + \dfrac{40}{70} \approx 0.920 + 0.571 \approx 1.491 \text{ hours} \approx 89.5 \text{ minutes}$

The difference is approximately $2\frac{1}{2}$ minutes, choice A.

37. **D.** The solution of two lines can be determined by the coordinates of the point at which the lines intersect.

Lines ℓ_1 and ℓ_2 intersect at $(2, 4)$. Therefore, $x = 2$ and $y = 4$, choice D.

38. **C.** Figure 3 shows that cuts are made through the original corners at A and B. This means that only choices C and E could be correct. Look at Figure 3 again and notice that the other cut was made at the original center, choice C.

39. **B.** To purchase twelve pairs of socks, Hunter must buy six packages. At $2.98 per package, he spends $17.88. His change from a twenty-dollar bill will be $20.00 - $17.88 = $2.12, choice B.

40. **A, B, C, and E.** To solve the equation $2x + 4 = 3x + 3$, first subtract $2x$ from each side.

$$2x + 4 - 2x = 3x + 3 - 2x$$
$$4 = x + 3$$

Now, subtract 3 from both sides.

$$4 - 3 = x + 3 - 3$$
$$1 = x$$

By plugging in the above value of x (that is, 1) for each of the answer choices, we find that 1 satisfies all the equations, except choice D.

41. **B.** $\dfrac{\text{percent}}{100} = \dfrac{\text{is number}}{\text{of number}}$

Cross multiplying

$$\frac{30}{100} = \frac{x}{\frac{25}{18}}$$

$$100x = \frac{\overset{5}{\cancel{30}}}{1} \times \frac{25}{\cancel{18}_3}$$

$$100x = \frac{125}{3}$$

$$x = \frac{\overset{5}{\cancel{125}}}{3} \times \frac{1}{\cancel{100}_4}$$

$$x = \frac{5}{12}$$

The correct answer is choice B, $\dfrac{5}{12}$.

42. **C.** Because $\dfrac{3}{x} = \dfrac{6}{1}$, cross multiplying gives

$$6 \cdot x = 3$$
$$x = \frac{1}{2}$$

Therefore, $x - 1 = \left(\dfrac{1}{2}\right) - 1 = -\dfrac{1}{2}$, choice C.

43. **B.** Maya budgeted 10% for air travel. She spent 20% more, or another 2%, bringing the amount for air travel to 12%. She budgeted 60% for the cruise fare. She spent 10% less than this amount, or 6%, bringing the amount for cruise fare down to 54%. She budgeted 20% for onboard expenses. She spent 20% more than budgeted, or another 4%, bringing the amount for onboard expenses to 24%. She budgeted 10% for gifts. She spent 20% less than budgeted, or 2%, bringing the amount she spent on gifts to 8%. Adding the actual percentages gives 12% + 54% + 24% + 8% = 98%. She spent approximately 98% of her budgeted amount on her cruise vacation, choice B.

44. **E.** The best way to compute the area of the figure is to divide it into as few parts as possible, making each part a simple shape whose area is easily calculated (for instance, a triangle, rectangle, or square). Choice E divides the shape into a rectangle and a triangle.

45. **B.** This problem requires an algebraic solution. First add 50 to each side of the equation:

$$10m - 50 + 20p = 0$$
$$10m + 20p = 50$$

You want to find $m + 2p$, so divide the left side of the equation by 10. However, to keep the equation balanced, you must do the same to the right side as well:

$$\frac{10m + 20p}{10} = \frac{50}{10}$$
$$m + 2p = 5$$

The answer is choice B, 5.

46. **C.** Rounding 0.14739 to the nearest thousandth means first looking at the digit one place to the right of the thousandths place: 0.147<u>3</u>9. Since that digit is 4 or less, simply drop it. (There is no need to replace with zeros because they are not needed to the right of a decimal point.) Therefore, the answer is 0.147, choice C.

47. D. Since the large square has a side of 4 centimeters, its area must be 16. By careful grouping of areas, you will see that there are four unshaded smaller squares and four shaded smaller squares (match the shaded parts to form four squares). Therefore, half of the area is shaded, or 8 square centimeters, choice D.

48. C. Note that only choice C raises one of the numbers by 5 while it lowers the other number by 5. Choice C will give the best approximation of the five choices.

49. C. Only Statement 3 can be solved by using division ($39 \div 3$). Statement 1 is determined by using multiplication ($6 \times B$). Statement 2 is determined by using subtraction (note the word *difference*).

50. 50% Use this formula when solving percent change problems.

$$\text{percent change} = \frac{\text{amount of change}}{\text{starting amount}} \times 100\%$$

Amount spent for food in February was 20, and in March it was 30.

The percent change becomes $\dfrac{30 - 20}{20} \times 100\% = \dfrac{10}{20} \times 100\% = 50\%$.

51. B and C. The median of a set of numbers is the middle number when the numbers in the data set are ranked in order. In this case, since there are 15 numbers in the data set, the eighth number, 7, is the median. The mean is the arithmetic average of the numbers in the data set.

$$\text{mean} = \frac{\text{sum}}{\text{quantity}} = \frac{93}{15} = 6.2$$

The correct answers must lie "between" (not including) the median and mean. Only choices B and C are between 6.2 and 7.0.

52. D. Note that, for example, as the temperature decreased from –10° to –15°, the average amount of snowfall per hour increased from 2 to 2.5 inches. (Watch out for the minus sign, which means the temperature drops when it goes from –20° to –25°.) This relationship exists throughout the chart. Therefore, choice D is correct.

53. D. Remember that a parallelogram has equal opposite sides. Therefore, its sides are 9, 7, 9, and 7. Its perimeter, then, is 32. If a square has the same perimeter, one of its sides must be one-fourth of its perimeter (since the four sides of a square are equal). One-fourth of 32 is 8, choice D.

54. E. There are several quick methods of solving this problem. A proportion can be set up.

$$\frac{20 \text{ pages}}{4 \text{ hours}} = \frac{50 \text{ pages}}{x \text{ hours}}$$

Cross multiplying will give $20x = 200$, or $x = 10$, choice E. This is done by dividing each side of the equation by 20. Or determining Blake's hourly rate (20 pages ÷ 4 hours = 5 pages per hour) tells us he will need 10 hours to type 50 pages.

55. B. Note that on the graph a 30° drop in temperature on the line correlates with a 20% drop in attendance.

56. A, B, C, and D. Note that 30% of $50 may be expressed as 0.30×50 or $\dfrac{3}{10} \times 50$. Whichever way it is expressed, it will still total 15. The only answer choice that does not total 15 is choice E, which totals $166\dfrac{2}{3}$.